THE
READER'S DIGEST ILLUSTRATED

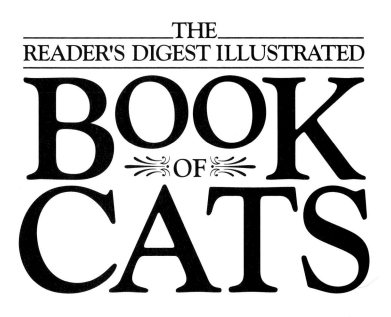

BOOK
OF
CATS

Reader's Digest

Published by The Reader's Digest Association (Canada) Ltd.

MONTREAL • NEW YORK • LONDON • SYDNEY • CAPE TOWN

The Reader's Digest Illustrated Book of Cats

Reader's Digest

Editor: Alice Philomena Rutherford
Art Supervisor: John McGuffie
Senior Editors: Andrew Byers, Sandy Shepherd
Research Editor: Wadad Bashour
Copy Preparation: Joseph Marchetti
Designers: Cécile Germain, Andrée Payette
Co-ordinator: Susan Wong
Production Manager: Holger Lorenzen
Editorial Assistant: Elizabeth Eastman

St. Remy Press

President: Pierre Léveillé
Publisher: Ken Winchester
Managing Editor: Carolyn Jackson
Senior Art Director: Diane Denoncourt
Contributing Editor: Mike McGarry
Translators: Jill Corner, C. Roy Keys, Judith Terry
Designer: Irene Huang
Research Editor: Heather Mills
Administrator: Natalie Watanabe
Production Manager: Michelle Turbide
Systems Coordinator: Jean-Luc Roy

Consultants:

Dr. P. K. Basrur, professor of veterinary medical genetics, University of Guelph, Guelph, Ont.
• **Leslie Bowers,** executive secretary, The International Cat Association • **R. G. Browne,**
Ph.D., University of Massachusetts, Amherst, Mass., nutritional consultant to the Canadian
Veterinary Medical Association • **John Burch,** all-breeds judge • **Dr. Charlotte Cushman,**
Chaton Santé Clinique vétérinaire, Montreal, Que. • **Dr. Deborah Edwards,** All Cats
Hospital, Largo, Fla. • **Dr. Michael Fox,** veterinarian, animal behaviourist and author of *The
Healing Touch* and *Love Is a Happy Cat* • **Richard Gebhardt,** author of *The Complete Cat
Book* • **Yvonne Patrick,** all-breeds judge • **Dr. James Richards,** Cornell Feline Health Center,
Cornell University, Ithaca, N.Y. • **Gloria Stephens,** feline geneticist, all-breeds judge and
author of *The Legacy of the Cat*

CAVEAT

The Reader's Digest Illustrated Book of Cats is not designed to supplant professional
diagnosis and treatment of feline disorders: if your cat is ill, take it to a veterinarian.
Furthermore, veterinary practices may vary among countries, so information here may
sometimes conflict with recommendations of other experts.
In such cases, follow your veterinarian's advice.

Canadian Cataloguing in Publication Data
Main entry under title:
    The Reader's Digest illustrated book of cats

Includes index.
ISBN 0-88850-198-6

    1. Cats. 2. Cat breeds. I. Reader's Digest Association (Canada)

SF442.R42 1992   636.8   C92-090249-9

The credits and acknowledgements that appear on page 256 are hereby made a part of this copyright page.

Based on the book first published in France as *Guide des chats*
Copyright © 1992, Sélection du Reader's Digest, S.A.

92 93 94 95 96 / 5 4 3 2 1

Introduction

The cat is the only animal that leads a solitary existence in the wild to have become domesticated. It is now the most popular household pet in many countries, and has increased in numbers that run to the millions across the world.

Perhaps it chose to become domesticated, just as it chooses to do as it pleases today. This strength of personality is one of the reasons for its popularity. The others are immediately evident. Its small size, meticulous cleanliness and independence make it the perfect household pet. A cat is also beautiful to look at—its movements are neat and fluid and its posture is elegant. Its companionship is tactile as well as audible, often in the most charming way. The sensuous rubbing of its fur against you, the sinuous winding of its tail around your legs, and its rumbling purr of pleasure when you stroke it are irresistible. And who cannot feel the warm affection of the gaze of a cat, with its eyes half-closed. It is not surprising that cats have gained recent status as therapists—they have been found to lower blood pressure in the sick and improve the well-being of the old, the feeble, and the emotionally disturbed.

In our appreciation of cats we have created many new breeds, most for show. Today, most cat registry associations recognize between 40 and 50 breeds as eligible for championship contests. This book represents the standards for 44 breeds of cat. They were selected from cat registries in Australia, Britain, Canada, New Zealand, South Africa, and the United States, and from the various associations that link cat fanciers around the world. But cat associations also recognize the beauty of non-pedigree cats and encourage their owners to show them in classes such as Household Pet or Other Variety.

Apart from telling you how to show your cat, this book covers all aspects of living with it—feeding, care, health, breeding, and behaviour. Here is something for every cat-lover, whether you are a breeder of fancy cats or the devoted owner of a domestic puss.

—The Editors

Table of Contents

YOUR CAT'S PHYSIOLOGY

THE CAT AND ITS OWNER

UNDERSTANDING CATS

THE CAT THROUGH HISTORY

Feline ancestry

Fossilized remains of Miacis, one of the forest-dwelling Miacids, early ancestors of the carnivorous animals.

Despite what cat lovers might like to believe, the cat has not been around for ever. In fact, over millions of years, it was preceded by scores of species. For close to one million of those years, the dinosaurs ruled the world by dint of their sheer size. They became extinct some 65 million years ago, when some as yet unexplained cataclysm wiped them out. Mammals, of which the cat is one, had to wait for their disappearance to thrive.

The disaster that killed the dinosaurs also claimed other families. Between 65 and 60 million years ago, all marine and flying reptiles disappeared, as did most land animals of any size—say 22 pounds (10 kg) or more. The only ones to survive this upheaval were small creatures, mostly primitive long-nosed insect-eating mammals. During the Palaeocene epoch, which marked the dawn of the Cainozoic era (from some 65 million years ago to recent times: see chart, pages 12-13), these insectivores developed rapidly in many directions. The primates, a distinctive forest group, appeared quite early, giving rise to lemurs, monkeys, apes and, eventually, man. The ungulates or hoofed animals evolved, and these in turn led to horses, cattle, elephants, rhinoceroses, raccoons, and aardvarks. Rabbits, hares, and rodents appeared, as did seals, bats, whales, and sabre-toothed cats.

The polecat, an important member of the mustelid family, distant relatives of the cat.

Forerunner to today's cat

To find the forerunner to today's cat we must return to the species explosion that occurred following the dinosaurs' disappearance. In this 'era of new life,' as the Cainozoic era is called, mammals split into plant-eaters and flesh-eaters. Among the latter were the claw-footed, short-legged (and short-lived) fish-eating Creodonts, once mistakenly thought to be feline ancestors.

About the time the Creodonts began dying off (some 60 million years ago), the insect-eating Miacids were emerging. These short-legged, long-bodied, weasel- to wolf-size forest dwellers are generally regarded as ancestors to the felids (cats, lynxes, and cheetahs), as well as to other carnivorous land mammals: canids (wolves, foxes, and dogs), hyaenids (hyenas), mustelids (weasels, minks, badgers and skunks), procyonids (raccoons), ursinids (bears), and viverrids (civets and mon-

The raccoon, a North American member of the procyonids.

gooses), all of which feed chiefly on the flesh and blood of other vertebrates.

That the Miacids were better hunters than the Creodonts may have been a factor in the latter's extinction. The Miacids may have been more intelligent—they had larger brains than the Creodonts—but sharper teeth may also have played a role. Although the Miacids had only 40 teeth compared to the Creodonts' 44, four of these were carnassial, ideal for holding and shearing flesh.

Of course one identifying characteristic of all carnivores is their carnassial or shearing teeth—large sharp molars or premolars in the upper and lower jaws that cut food with a scissoring action. Through early carnivores' teeth, and sometimes through traces of tooth enamel, it has been possible to retrace some of these animals' history. (Tooth enamel survives for aeons in the ground, where soft tissue and sometimes even bones decompose.)

From the mid-Eocene through early Oligocene epochs (50 to 40 million years ago), carnivores developed and diversified rapidly and extensively, perhaps responding to changes in climate, plant life, and prey. The diversification followed two distinct paths, producing the Carnivora superfamilies *Aeluroidea* (or *Feloidea*), which evolved into felids, hyaenids, and viverrids, and the *Arctoidea* (or *Canoidea*), which contains the other carnivorous families.

Eusmilus was a primitive felid of the late Oligocene epoch. We do not know whether it was a hunter or, like the modern hyena, subsisted on carrion.

Fossils from that time include a lynx-sized animal known as *Dinictis*, which is generally regarded as an important evolution in feline development. It had longer legs and tail than the Creodonts or Miacids, and cat-like teeth for stabbing prey. Around the time it appeared, feline evolution took off in two directions. One branch produced the now extinct *Nimravidae* or paleofelids, large sabre-toothed cats that flourished in the Oligocene epoch (some 34 to 23 million years ago). Smaller teeth characterized the second group, which diverged into several subspecies in the late Miocene epoch (some 15 million years ago) and continued developing through to the Pliocene epoch (1 million years ago), evolving into *Felidae* (the neofelids), today's family of cats.

The *Nimravidae* existed for some 30 million years. One striking example of *Nimravidae* was *Eusmilus*, a sabre-toothed tiger, somewhere between a lynx and a puma in size, but with claws that were not completely retractable. Its upper jaw had two remarkable canine teeth: slightly flattened like sabre blades, they were edged like saws. This creature's claws were not as efficient as those of today's felines. Because it walked not on its toes like today's cat, but on its pads, it could not run very fast.

Was *Eusmilus,* then, simply a clumsy carrion-eater, and its sabre teeth just butcher's meat hooks for scavenging dead flesh, as some have suggested? Or, as others are equally convinced, was *Eusmilus* a predator? Whatever their survival techniques, these sabre-toothed tigers spread out across Africa, Asia, Europe, and North America. Their huge size, limited intelligence, and cumbersome teeth are believed to have led to their extinction 5 million years after they first appeared.

Another paleofelid, *Nimravus*, developed about the same time as *Eusmilus*, but it flourished for 10 million years. As big as a jaguar and sometimes the size of

THE FOSSA

To get an idea of what the ancestors of cats looked like, consider the incredible fossa *Cryptoprocta ferox* of Madagascar. Originally thought to belong to the cat family, zoologists eventually classed it as primitive viverrid, a member of the same family as genets, civet cats, and mongooses. The fossa looks like a small puma with a long tail, walks partly on its pads, and has completely retractable claws. Like a cat, it has vertical pupils. It weighs about 22 pounds (10 kg), making it Madagascar's largest native carnivore, and it hunts lemurs and birds in the trees by night.

The remains of a similar creature have been found in rocks that were formed some 10 to 20 million years ago. These fossils are thought to be one of the cat's early ancestors.

Most likely the fossa survived in Madagascar, protected by the ocean from competition with more highly evolved carnivores. But how did it get there in the first place? According to one theory, when a large African river, which disappeared some 5 million years ago, overflowed into the straits of Madagascar, it carried with it rafts of whole trees pulled up from its banks, virtual Noah's Arks supporting a lot of animals. It is possible that several of these rafts and the animals aboard reached the shores of Madagascar. This could explain why all the island's mammals belong to species that live in trees and represent versions of species long extinct everywhere else. Later, other mammals were introduced to the island of Madagascar by man.

a lion, *Nimravus* roamed Europe and North America. It had unusually long canine teeth and long slender legs, with four-toed back paws similar to a cat's that would have enabled it to run and hunt efficiently.

While the larger paleofelids, the *Nimravidae*, dominated the scene during the Oligocene epoch (see chart, pages 12-13), some of the smaller neofelids developed a similar form and structure. The neofelid *Proailurus*, for example, not only preceded *Nimravus* but survived it by centuries.

True ancestor

Another small neofelid, *Pseudoailurus*, appeared in Europe and North America during the Miocene epoch (about 23 million years ago). This direct ancestor of today's cats had a flattish skull, acute hearing through two chambers in the middle ear, and walked almost flat-footed. It and the earlier *Proailurus* were very similar to the present-day fossa, a 'living fossil,' native to Madagascar (see box at left).

An odd sort of regression appeared in the first descendants of *Pseudoailurus*: they were sabre-toothed felines much like the ancient Paleofelids, which had already died out. This phenomenon, called convergence, happens when groups of animals more or less distant from each other on the zoological scale are exposed to the same food sources and environmental conditions. The dolphin and the shark, for example, both gradually acquired a very similar streamlined shape, an adaptation dictated by their everyday problems of living in and moving through an aquatic environment and by their quest for similar food.

These sabre-toothed neofelids appeared 12 million years ago in the Miocene epoch (see chart, pages 12-13). By the Pliocene epoch (3 million years ago), this family had evolved into two slightly built species, *Homotherium* and *Machairodus*, and the heavier *Megantereon* and *Smilodon*. *Smilodon* (see facing page) would survive until 2 million years ago, dying out in the Holocene, or Recent epoch, relatively close to our own time.

The lighter of the neofelid sabre-tooths had serrated blade-like teeth while their heavier cousins had longer, curving, conical fangs, that were obviously suited for piercing, not cutting. The lighter cats probably cut the throats or disembowelled the soft underbellies of their victims, while heavier cats like *Smilodon* stabbed.

These larger cats, though formidable, had problems: their deadly teeth were fragile because they were long and exposed. They were useless for tearing apart prey and were so long—up to 6 inches (13 cm)—that when the mouth was wide open to deliver a fatal blow, the animal could dislocate its neck.

Fossil links on the feline trail

Of all the sabre-toothed beasts, the neofelid *Smilodon* is the one we know most about. The remains of many of them have been found reasonably well preserved in the La Brea tar pits in West Hollywood, California. The tar pits are pools of viscous asphalt formed by seepage from petroleum deposits. They were natural death traps for animals—camels, condors, coyotes, mammoths, and mastodons—that came to drink from pools of water atop the asphalt, but became bogged in the tar. The *Smilodons*, coming to feed off what appeared to be sitting prey, then became trapped in the tar themselves.

Their remains suggest that *Smilodon,* with its stocky legs, short tail and sharp claws, appeared more suited to ambushing game than to chasing it. About the size of a tiger, it had very few teeth: just two premolars and one molar on either side of each jaw—ideal for crushing bones. The lower jaw, which could drop open vertically, did not have the same bony projection on the chin that had supported the tips of *Eusmilus's* canines when its mouth was closed.

As with *Eusmilus* (see page 9), there are several theories about *Smilodon's* eating habits. Some scientists think that *Smilodon* stabbed its victims and then sucked their blood. Others believe that it ate only rotting meat, which seems likely because even modern-day predators find it hard to tear open the tough skin of an elephant or rhino carcass. The sharp canines might have been useful in this respect, but this conjecture is based on the small number of other teeth *Smilodon* had. This would seem to indicate that the animal would only be able to chew meat that was already decomposing.

It seems certain that *Smilodon's* muscular neck gave it extraordinary strength for lowering its head and embedding its canine teeth. Those who believe *Smilodon* to have been a predator claim, however, to have found corroborating evidence to bolster their case: one of its canine teeth embedded in the skull of a kind of jackal.

Primitive man did not appear on the evolutionary scale until the Pleistocene epoch some 1 to 2 million years ago, and modern man did not arrive until the Holocene, or Recent, epoch 10,000 years ago. By then many of the massive prehistoric animals had disappeared. The coming of the Ice Age was partly responsible for this extinction of giant relatives of many animals alive today. But another important factor in the disappearance was the hunting activities of the original big game hunter, early man. And so, by the time that man was using fire, the paleofelid sabre-toothed cats had died out, yielding place to the final version of the neofelid *Felidae*.

For the most part, these *Felidae* were cats of the kind we know today: panthers, lynxes, leopards, and so on. These animals had a number of recognizable physical characteristics: powerfully muscled jaws, teeth designed for cutting rather than grinding, bones and muscles adapted to running and, in most cases, retractable claws.

The domesticated cat appeared first in the Middle East more than 3500 years ago, though there is some evidence—a jawbone discovered on Cyprus in 1983—that such cats existed in 6000 B.C.

At first, man and cat must have competed as predators. Then, after domesticating horses for transportation, cattle and swine for food, and dogs and leopards for hunting, man began a cautious relationship with the equally cautious, but always independent, somewhat solitary, and ever-delightful domestic cat.

Smilodon: the last example of sabre-toothed tigers. Early man may well have encountered one. Above: artist's reconstruction and skull.

The cat's

*PALAEOCENE
From 65 million
years ago

*EOCENE
From 53 million
years ago

*OLIGOCEN
From 34 millio
years ago

The Miacids appeared early in the Cainozoic era, the age of
advanced mammals, birds, and molluscs, which followed
the extinction of the dinosaurs and other ruling reptiles.
Insect-eating, forest-dwelling creatures, they are ancestors
to felids (cheetahs and small and roaring cats) and other
carnivorous land mammals such as canids (wolves, foxes,
and dogs), hyaenids (hyenas), mustelids (weasels, minks,
badgers, and skunks), procyonids (raccoons), ursinids
(bears), and viverrids (civets and mongooses). Only the
evolution of the felid families is shown here.

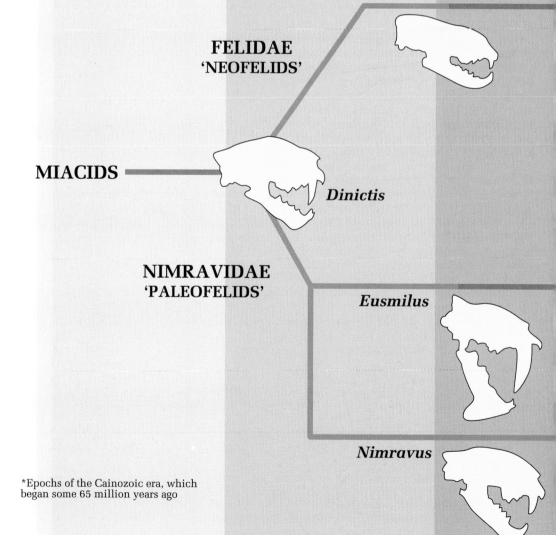

Proailurus

FELIDAE
'NEOFELIDS'

MIACIDS

Dinictis

NIMRAVIDAE
'PALEOFELIDS'

Eusmilus

Nimravus

*Epochs of the Cainozoic era, which
began some 65 million years ago

12

family tree

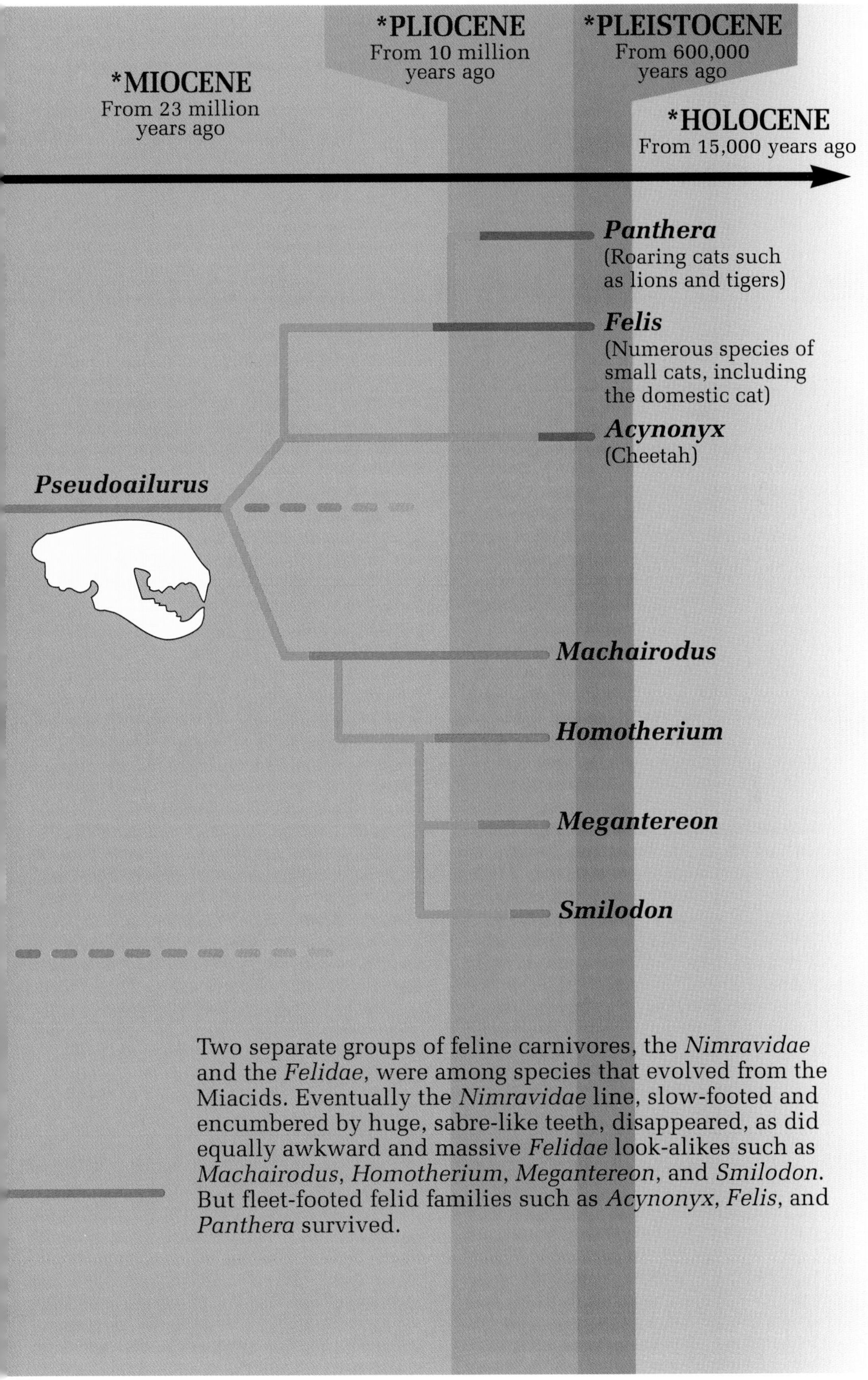

*MIOCENE
From 23 million
years ago

*PLIOCENE
From 10 million
years ago

*PLEISTOCENE
From 600,000
years ago

*HOLOCENE
From 15,000 years ago

Panthera
(Roaring cats such
as lions and tigers)

Felis
(Numerous species of
small cats, including
the domestic cat)

Acynonyx
(Cheetah)

Pseudoailurus

Machairodus

Homotherium

Megantereon

Smilodon

Two separate groups of feline carnivores, the *Nimravidae*
and the *Felidae*, were among species that evolved from the
Miacids. Eventually the *Nimravidae* line, slow-footed and
encumbered by huge, sabre-like teeth, disappeared, as did
equally awkward and massive *Felidae* look-alikes such as
Machairodus, *Homotherium*, *Megantereon*, and *Smilodon*.
But fleet-footed felid families such as *Acynonyx*, *Felis*, and
Panthera survived.

The cat's kith and kin

The tiger and lion, both roaring cats, are the largest of the big cats.

Cats, a very uniform animal group, are sometimes classified into big and small species, distinguished by a surprising but fundamental difference: the big cats' roar. This awe-inspiring sound is actually due to the absence of a section of hyoid bone on each side of the big cat's throat. Normally this bone is made up of two symmetrical chains of bones attaching the base of the tongue to the skull. The joints linking these little bones control movements connected with swallowing and the production of vocal sounds.

In the big cats (lions, tigers, leopards or panthers, and jaguars), one of these bones is replaced on each side by a pliable sheath of cartilage that allows greater movement of the larynx, and thus the roar. Cats with ordinary hyoid bones can only mew or caterwaul.

Taxonomists, specialists in scientific classification of animals, classify the cat family in different ways. Three genera are used here: *Panthera* for the Big Cats, *Acynonyx* for the cheetah, and *Felis* for all other feline species. Naturalists have had a hard time classifying some species because many avoid man. This is one reason why classifications vary.

All species of *Felis* are solitary, generally nocturnal, and frequently arboreal. They are predominantly meat-eaters, although the Asian flat-headed cat relies heavily on fruit and the fishing cat, also found in the Far East, is so partial to fish that it catches them in its claws (see page 19). All cats have well-developed sight and very sharp hearing, which allow them to make successful hunting forays at dawn and dusk. They have a strong sense of smell, which is used more for detecting and communicating with other animals than for hunting.

A single cat usually has several lairs in its territory, one of which is used by the female to give birth. The male and female will live together only during the mating season, and few males actually take any part in rearing the young. The litter may number from one to six cubs depending on the species. All feline offspring are born blind but covered in fur.

Cheetah: swift and gentle

A streamlined shape, unretractable claws, small head, and two black markings running like tears from the inside corners of the eyes to the outer corners of the mouth distinguish the cheetah from every other big cat. It used to be common across the Middle East and India, and throughout the less densely forested areas of Africa. Today not only has its African habitat shrunk considerably (the main populations are now in Namibia and Zimbabwe in southern Africa), but also it has become rare in the Middle East, and has disappeared from India.

A diurnal rather than nocturnal cat that hunts hares, gazelles, and low-flying birds, the cheetah is the fastest runner of all land-based animals. It has been known to reach top speeds of more than 65 miles an hour (100 km/h) in 550-yard (500-m) sprints. A gentle creature, the cheetah has always been easily tamed.

Egyptian Pharaohs were the first to do this, and from 1500 B.C. onwards cheetahs and dogs were their hunting animals. Greek geographer and historian Strabo, who died in A.D. 23, described how the people of India captured cheetahs found in great numbers in the bamboo forests along the Ganges, trained them to hunt, and tamed them so well that they wandered freely through palaces and gardens.

When the native Indian species died out, maharajas imported cheetahs from Africa, mostly Kenya, and continued the hunt until the early 20th century. Cheetah hunting was somewhat like falconry or coursing hares with greyhounds. The cheetah was taken by cart to the hunting area, blindfolded, and restrained by a body harness. Once the quarry was in sight, the blindfold was removed and the cheetah freed. On a good day, the cheetah could down its prey in less than a minute. It would then wait for the master to arrive and complete the kill. Other times, if the chase were too long, the cheetah collapsed, exhausted from its high-speed efforts.

During the Middle Ages this form of hunting was all the rage throughout eastern Europe and Asia, but was practised only intermittently in the Western World. Cheetahs were trained to ride on the horse's crupper behind the rider, as can be seen in the reproduction below of a detail from *The Journey of the Magi*, a mural by Benozzo Gozzoli, who died in the late 1400s. The fresco was commissioned by Piero de Medici of the Italian family of bankers and merchants. The Medicis ruled Florence, and later Tuscany, for all but 21 years between 1434 and 1737. The cheetah was a Medici family symbol.

Russian princes, British royals, and numerous French kings have hunted with cheetahs. Austrian Emperor Leopold I used cheetahs on deer hunts in the Vienna woods. Indeed many blame the huge cheetah stables of various royal houses for the eventual decline of this superb cat.

The leopard (or panther), a magnificent and dangerous big cat, is widespread in the equatorial regions of Africa and Asia.

Cheetahs of Italy's merchant princes. The cheetah, a phenomenal short-distance runner, was first tamed and used for coursing hares in Ancient Egypt. The great lords of the Italian Renaissance were among scores of rulers who owned hunting cheetahs. Here, a nobleman has a cheetah riding pillion on a saddle cloth, while another rider has dismounted and is preparing to loose his cheetah.

The colocolo hunts guinea pigs.

Small cats of the Americas

Various ecological niches produce different kinds of creatures. Neither Antarctica nor even Australia with its particularly rich fauna has native cat species. Yet native species of small cats are abundant in South America. Descriptions of some of these cats, a few of them also found in North America, follow. (See also Lynxes, page 20).

Puma

This cat, which ranges from Canada to southern South America, is known by many names: cougar, mountain lion, painter, panther, catamountain. Spanish colonists in Argentina called it the American lion, and Portuguese in Brazil knew it as the red jaguar. The biggest of the genus *Felis*, it is comparable in size to the lion or leopard. It can weigh up to 220 pounds (100 kg) and flourishes in habitats as diverse as conifer forests and swamps. Because pumas prey on domestic animals, they have been hunted mercilessly since Europeans settled in the Americas. It is now the most endangered of the cats. The puma has a yellow-brown coat, lighter on the underbody. Like the jaguar, the large American feline, it plays a major role in the mythology of most pre-Columbian civilizations, which have left highly stylized images of these animals.

Colocolo or pampas cat

This cat is also called *gato pajero* (straw cat), because of its straw-coloured fur. The colocolo is the size of a domestic cat and has a long-haired striped coat that varies from yellowish white to a greyish brown. It lives mostly on the pampas, but has been found in the rain forests and even in mountainous regions. The colocolo lives mostly on the ground and preys on ground-nesting birds, small mammals, especially guinea pigs, and sometimes domestic fowl. When excited, the hairs on its back become erect, giving it a most formidable appearance. Found from Ecuador south to northern Chile and Argentina, it is said to be aggressive, and difficult to tame.

THE CATS OF LATIN AMERICA

They are divided into five sub-groups:

- *Felis concolor*: the puma
- *Felis colocolo*: the colocolo or pampas cat
- *Felis leopardus*, with five species:
  - *Felis pardalis*: the ocelot
  - *Felis wiedi*: the margay
  - *Felis tigrinus*: the tiger cat
  - *Felis geoffroyi*: Geoffroy's cat
  - *Felis guigna*: the kodkod
- *Felis jacobita*: the mountain cat
- *Felis yagouaroundi:* the jaguarundi

The jaguar, largest of American cats, played a major role in Aztec mythology.

Felis leopardus (ocelot, margay, tiger cat, Geoffroy's cat, and kodkod)

•The ocelot, once the most widely distributed feline in Central and South America, has been hunted almost to extinction for its handsome tawny coat, marked with jaguar-like, black-ringed brown spots. Its present range is from the southern United States to northern Argentina. An accomplished climber, it not only hunts in trees, but naps among the branches in the daytime. Rarely more than 18 inches (45 cm) high at the withers, the ocelot weighs 24 to 33 pounds (11-15 kg). Ocelots mark their territory with droppings, appear to live in couples, but hunt separately.

•The margay, also known as the Long-tailed Spotted Cat, looks like a miniature ocelot, has huge eyes, and excellent night vision. A tree-dweller, it moves easily among the branches, spiralling upwards and hanging by its back legs. Its acrobatic prowess is largely due to the specialized structure of its rear paws, which have wide toes that can grip a surface readily. An endangered species, it is now extinct in most of its range: Panama to Paraguay.

•The tiger cat, also known as the Oncilla or Little Spotted Cat, is sometimes mistaken for the margay. It too is a tree-dweller, but a less skilled climber. This endangered species is now rare in its range: Costa Rica south to Argentina.

•Geoffroy's cat comes in various colours, but is often a spotted grey. It climbs well and, like all members of the subgenus *Leopardus*, is a fine swimmer. It ranges from Bolivia and Brazil south through Argentina.

•The kodkod is a very small grey-brown spotted tree-dweller weighing from 4½ to 6½ pounds (2-3 kg). Found in parts of Argentina but mostly in central Chile, it is reputed to raid henhouses.

The ocelot, an arboreal cat of the Americas, has paid dearly for having a coat that became very fashionable.

Mountain cat

This animal is also called the Andean Highland Cat. In Chile and Argentina, it inhabits arid zones of the Andes Mountains up to 16,000 feet (5000 m) above sea level. It can tolerate the bitter night cold of such high altitudes thanks to its very thick silver-grey fur, which is spotted and striped in brown or orange. Now very rare, it has been a protected species since 1978.

The Andean or mountain cat, an extremely rare feline.

Jaguarundi

This cat looks somewhat like an otter or a weasel: in fact its German name is *Weisel Katze* (Weasel Cat). Found from Texas southward through Central America to Paraguay and northern Argentina, the jaguarundi's favourite habitat is the rain forest or dense undergrowth. Despite being an agile climber, it prefers to live on the ground. Since its fur is not valuable, hunters leave it alone. A short-legged animal with a long supple body, its smooth coat varies in colour from one cat to the next. Kittens from a single litter may be grey, almost black, or reddish-brown. The Indians say this cat had been tamed and used for rodent control long before the Spanish reached South America. Present-day jaguarundis still eat rodents as well as rabbits, birds, frogs, fish, and poultry. They are most active in the morning and the evening.

The jaguarundi.

Cats of the Far East

Cats must be able to blend in with their surroundings, to escape the hunter and to track their prey. In jungles, stripes hide the tiger well; in deserts, the lion's sandy colouring is good camouflage when the pride sets out on a hunt; in light-dappled forests, the spotted coats of the cheetah and the leopard are all but invisible, as is the black leopard hunting by night. Big cat coats are especially distinctive in the East.

Felis pardofelis (marbled cat, bay cat of Borneo)

- The rare marbled cat used to inhabit the eastern Himalayas, Burma, Indo-China, and Malaysia. It weighs between 4½ and 11 pounds (2-5 kg), and has a yellowish coat with irregular spots ringed in black and a similarly marked long bushy tail. It generally lives on forested slopes but is found in low country in Borneo. This cat is now protected in India and Thailand.
- The bay cat, also called the Bornean red cat, has a bright chestnut-brown coat, and is limited to a few areas of Borneo. Some cats with bluish fur have also been seen there. They too are found in rocky forested areas, but only a few have been spotted in recent years.

Felis prionailurus (leopard cat, Iriomote cat, rusty-spotted cat, fishing cat, flat-headed cat)

- The leopard cat, a protected species, has an extremely broad range. It extends from Manchuria to India and includes all southeast Asia together with Borneo, Java, and Sumatra. In areas as far apart as these, the leopard cat varies considerably in size and colouring. In tropical regions it weighs about 11 pounds (5 kg) and is brown with black markings, while further north in Manchuria it can reach 33 pounds (15 kg) and be a silvery grey with pale ring-like markings. Because it needs a lot of water, this cat is not found in dry or desert regions. An accomplished swimmer and climber, it lives in scrubland and forests.

Like many wild species, the marbled cat has suffered from encroachment on its habitat.

The fishing cat is the only feline that lives almost exclusively on fish and other freshwater creatures.

The leopard cat was formerly widespread in southeast Asia, but is now so rare that it is a protected species.

• The Iriomote cat was discovered by scientists in 1967 on a Japanese-owned island (Iriomote) off Taiwan. Naturalists initially classified it as a separate subgenus of the leopard cat, but now believe it to be an insular form of that animal. By night, it hunts small rodents, small water animals such as crabs, and water birds, each cat keeping to a 1-mile² (2.5-km²) territory. As the island's agricultural development has encroached on the forests that are this cat's normal habitat, only a few dozen specimens are left.

• The rusty-spotted cat, found in southern Sri Lanka and southern India, is also believed to be a variation of the leopard cat. It is smaller, and more vividly coloured, than the leopard cat.

• The fishing cat or tarai is found in Sri Lanka, India, China, and as far south as Myanmar. It is semiaquatic and seen in mangrove swamps and fishing from rocks on riverbeds, scooping up fish with its front paws. Some people have seen it dive into water and grab fish in its jaws. It also eats shellfish, snakes, and small mammals. Quite a big cat, it can weigh up to 30 pounds (14 kg). Its long body, grey with dark regular markings, resembles that of the civet cat.

• The flat-headed cat, also known as the marten cat, is found in India, from Sri Lanka to southern China, and in Sumatra, Java, and Bali. Its most striking feature is its long, flat head. Its longish soft fur is a dark reddish brown tipped with white, which gives it a silvery shimmer.

The golden cat.

**OTHER SUBGENERA OF
AFRICA AND ASIA**

- *Profelis*, the golden cats
  - *Felis temmincki*, Temminck's golden cat
  - *Felis aurata*, the African golden cat
- *Otocolobus*
  - *Felis manul*, the manul cat or Pallas's cat
- *Lynx*, with three subgenera
  - *Felis lynx*, the Northern lynx
  - *Felis pardina*, the parded lynx or Southern European lynx
  - *Felis rufus*, the bobcat, bay lynx, red cat, or American wildcat
- *Caracal*
  - *Felis caracal*, the caracal
- *Leptailurus*
  - *Felis serval*, the serval

Many bizarre beliefs surround the lynx.

Other cats of Africa and Asia

Most big cats are solitary animals, a trait found also in today's domestic cat. Lions, which live in family prides ruled by one leader, are an exception. Other male and female big cats cohabit only for mating. The tiger is not only a loner, but can be a dangerous one at that. It was nicknamed 'man-eater' many years ago for good reason. Records from the mid-1800s show that at that time tigers ate 400 human victims a year in the Singapore area alone.

The following cats are neither as large as lions nor probably as fierce as tigers, except perhaps when cornered, but they do live in a wide range of habitats in Africa and Asia.

Golden cats

As their names indicate, the African and Asian golden cats are usually a dark auburn colour but sometimes their fur is slate grey. A darker band of colour runs along the golden's back from head to tail. The underbelly is lighter, with round dark markings, and the tail is ringed and sometimes white at the tip. Medium-sized animals, they can weigh from 13 to 35 pounds (6-16 kg).

• The African golden cat lives in equatorial jungles of Senegal, Kenya, and northern Angola. Although it can climb quite well, it tends to live on the ground, making its lairs under rocks or in holes dug by other animals. In some of its habitats, local tribes credit the cat with magical powers and trap it to use its whiskers in poisonous potions, and its fur in ceremonial robes. Other tribes believe possession of a golden's tail will guarantee success in the elephant hunt.

• The Asian golden cat, often called Temminck's golden cat in honour of the Dutch naturalist who described the African golden cat, makes its home from Nepal to south China, and Sumatra.

• Temminck's cats often hunt in pairs, and the male plays a part in rearing the offspring, which is unusual for the genus *Felis*. It roams the forested Himalayan foothills hunting birds, lizards, and small deer. Like its African relative, it has a fondness for rocky terrain. It is now a protected species.

Lynxes

The northern lynx, distinguished by its pricked-up, tufted ears, small head, rear paws higher than the forepaws, and short tail ranges from Europe to Siberia, is widespread in Canada and the northern United States, but is not found in Africa. Lynxes ordinarily dwell in coniferous forests, but they have been seen on rocky outcrops in Mongolia's Altai Mountains and above the tree line in Tibet. They sleep by day, often in caves or hollow trees, but are very active at night, often travelling long distances in search of prey. Expert stalkers, they can creep close to their prey, then bound for the kill. But they also hunt by lying in ambush, waiting quietly for hours on a limb over a trail.

Seldom seen, the lynx's wariness gave rise to strange beliefs in the Middle Ages. It was said the lynx could see through the thickest walls, that its urine crystallized into precious stones, and that it was a gigantic cat. In reality, it is rather a small animal, weighing about 65 pounds (30 kg). Hunters say a wounded lynx is particularly dangerous animal.

The Canada lynx (*Felis lynx canadensis*) is found throughout Canada and the northern United States. It has spectacular fur, pale with dark spots, and black tips to its ears and the tip of its tail. It feeds mainly on snowshoe hares.

Pallas's cat

Also called the manul cat (from its scientific name *Felis manul*), Pallas's cat lives in the rocky deserts and steppes stretching across central Asia from the Caspian Sea to western China. This small, short-legged animal weighs between 9 and 11 pounds (4-5 kg). It is remarkable mainly for its fur, a uniform light brown colour with black markings on the head and some stripes running across the hindquarters and tail. The fur is very long on the lower part of the body, an aid to survival in the snow and bitter winter cold of its native habitat. Because of the long fur, this cat was once incorrectly considered to be a branch of the Angoras.

The manul or Pallas's cat. Because of its thick fur, it was once wrongly thought to be an ancestor of the Persian cat.

Pallas's cat has small round ears set back on the sides of the skull, and wide bushy whiskers that make its head look broad and flat. It eats mainly rodents and other small animals.

Caracal

This cat, a lynx that has adapted to the heat and humidity of the tropics, has a short-haired, fawn-coloured coat with rust-coloured spots, and weighs between 17½ and 40 pounds (8-18 kg). It is found everywhere in Africa except in dense jungles, in the Middle East, and in western India on territory once native to the cheetah. Like the cheetah, it has been domesticated by Indian hunters and has been used for running down hares. However, it is not so gentle a creature as the cheetah; while some caracals have been tamed, others remain incorrigibly ferocious.

The caracal.

Serval

The serval is found throughout Africa, except for the great rain forests, and it ranges from South Africa up to the northern coastal hills of the Sahel. It looks and

The serval.

moves like a long-legged cat, stands about 20 inches (50 cm) high at the withers, and weighs about 30 pounds (14 kg). It is a pale fawn with black spots and stripes, and a tail ringed in black. Like the leopard, it often has a darker coat in wet regions; some servals are almost black. Servals have a high-pitched cry, but they can also purr. Though a wily and solitary animal, and a henhouse thief, the serval is easily tamed. It can jump 10 feet (3 m) to down a bird.

Other feline family members

Jungle cat

The jungle cat is misnamed, although nobody seems to be quite sure why. Its habitats are many—dense woods, open country, reedy areas near rivers and lakes—but it cannot be found in tropical jungles. Commonly found in the deltas of the Nile and Volga rivers, and in low-lying swampy regions in the Near East, in Turkestan, India, China, and Indo-China, it is sometimes more appropriately named the Reed Cat, Swamp Cat, and Marsh Cat.

A large cat that can weigh up to 35 pounds (16 kg), the jungle cat has a short tail reaching only to the hocks. It has tufts on its ears, though they are not as noticeable as those of the lynx. This greyish-brown cat—depending on the habitat, it may be coloured differently—has

> ### THE SUBGENUS FELIS
>
> - *Felis chaus*, the jungle cat
> - *Felis margarita*, the sand cat or Margueritte's cat
> - *Felis nigripes*, the black-footed cat
> - *Felis silvestris*
>   - *Felis silvestris*, the European wildcat
>   - *Felis lybica*, the Caffre cat or African wildcat
>   - *Felis ornata*, the Indian desert cat
> - *Felis bieti*, the Chinese desert cat
> - *Felis catus*, the domestic cat

The sand cat is perfectly adapted to its existence as a desert predator.

ring markings on its tail. Mainly active at twilight, it feeds on frogs, reptiles, and small mammals such as hares. It lives in the abandoned lairs of badgers and porcupines, sometimes even in old buildings. Although they are excellent climbers, jumpers, runners, and swimmers, jungle cats tend to move slowly and cautiously.

Sand cat or Margueritte's cat

The size of a domestic cat, the sand cat, also known as Margueritte's cat (*Felis margarita*), is short-legged and sandy-coloured, with a head that seems bigger than it is because of large ears set on the sides. The placement of the ears and their oversized resonating chambers, or tympanic bullae, are an adaptation for desert life: in vast empty spaces with little wildlife, acute hearing is a great advantage to animals that hunt by night. The sand cat has adapted to desert life in other ways too. It can apparently go without drinking at all, finding enough liquid in its prey—jerboas and other rodents, reptiles, birds, and locusts.

Its pads are covered with thick fur, and it was once believed that this thick fur was to protect the cat's paws from burning desert sands. It is now known, however, that the sand cat spends much of the hot day prudently underground, rarely emerging before nightfall. The hairy pads are more likely the desert version of snowshoes: they enable the cat to walk on sand without sinking.

Found only in the Sahara and Arabian deserts, the sand cat is a rare species whose survival has been threatened as traffickers sought it for its fur, for study, and for sale as a household pet. As always, capturing wild animals for pets not only leaves them open to inappropriate care, but endangers the species as a whole. The sand cat has been an endangered species since the late 1970s.

Black-footed cat

This smallest of the wild felines is even smaller than the domestic cat. It weighs at the most 5½ pounds (2.5 kg). Well adapted to desert life, it has furry pads for easy movement on sand and huge tympanic bullae that give it excellent hearing. For its size, it has an extraordinarily strong voice: this tiny cat can roar as loudly as any tiger—although with the pitch an octave higher, the effect is less awesome. The roar is a signal enabling male and female of this exceptionally solitary species to find each other during the mating season. It has to be loud enough to attract a mate which, by its solitary nature, lives some distance away. And there is little time to spare. The female's heat is said to last 5 to 10 hours.

Immediately after copulation, male and female go their separate ways, a way of life that persists in captivity where the black-footed cat demonstrates strong antisocial tendencies. This is most likely its survival mechanism at work. The paucity of desert fauna in its natural habitat limits how many predators can survive in one spot.

The black-footed cat is found in the Namib, the Kalahari, and the Great Karroo deserts of Namibia, Botswana, and South Africa respectively.

Felis silvestris,
the European wildcat.

Wildcat

The wildcat lives on birds, mice, and other small mammals, seeking out insects such as grasshoppers as needed. (Contrary to folklore, wildcats are incapable of attacking a hare, much less a deer.) It leads a solitary life on a territory of some 25 acres (50 ha). In spring, the female produces a single litter of two or three kittens.

No one disputes the close kinship between the wildcat and the domestic cat. What is uncertain is which subspecies of wildcat is the ancestor of the domestic species. Like all widely distributed species, wildcats vary considerably in appearance and habits; they are so different that they have never been classified, even though more than 20 subspecies have been identified. However, these subspecies can be placed in three groups:

— the wildcat of Asia Minor, the Caucasus and Europe, including the Mediterranean islands;

— the African wildcat or gloved cat;

— the Indian desert cat, the Asian link between the first two species.

• The European wildcat is a third bigger than the domestic cat, and weighs up to 17½ pounds (8 kg). But a large percentage of this is muscle weight, as opposed to the fat weight of the less active domestic cat. The European wildcat's coat is a yellowish grey, with markings more pronounced on the feet and on the ringed tail than on the rest of the body. The throat is almost white. This wildcat has long thick fur, and a bushy tail that looks the same thickness along its whole length, unlike the more usual tapering tail of the domestic cat.

The European wildcat dislikes snow, which hinders its progress and deprives it of mice. It lives in forests or rocky terrain, sometimes even open country, and hunts at dusk or during the night. In daytime it rests in thick bush, often seeking shelter in the hollow of a dead tree or under a rock, though it also likes to sun itself.

Systematically hunted and almost wiped out in 19th-century Europe for preying on game and domestic animals, the European wildcat got a break during two world wars. When the hunt ceased, populations in Scotland, Germany, eastern France, and the Pyrenees recovered. Meantime, the wildcats have clearly on occasion mated with domestic cats. Naturalists say that present-day specimens are noticeably different from the original stock.

An accomplished hunter, the wildcat attacks only relatively small game.

• The African wildcat, also known as the gloved cat or Caffre cat, is smaller and more elegant than the European wildcat. It has a narrow head, big ears, a long tapering tail, and lives on African savannahs, not in jungles or deserts.

• The Indian desert cat, found throughout Asia as far east as China and central India, keeps to dry regions and avoids snow and cold. Its thick soft fur, resembling that of the domestic cat, is a pale yellow or sand colour with spots, and it has a long tapering tail.

• Biet's cat, or the Chinese desert cat, is very similar to the Indian desert cat. This cat is found only in southern Mongolia and central China.

• Many naturalists consider the domestic cat to be a variation of the African wildcat (the gloved or Caffre cat), changed by domestication. The domestic cat has undergone minor genetic changes since it was more

The wildcat of the European forests is not the ancestor of our domestic cat, although it is a close relative. It is larger in size, and its solitary nature makes it impossible to domesticate. Even kittens taken from the wild when very young cannot be tamed.

or less isolated from its wild relatives and subjected to breeding programmes by man. This directed breeding has brought out previously unknown fur colourings and textures.

As shipboard companion to those sailing the high seas, the domestic cat spread all over the world with the explorers and colonizers. A female Siamese that spent 16 years aboard a British cargo ship is credited with being the most travelled cat on record. In many areas, especially on the American continents, the wildcat (*Felis silvestris*) was previously unknown. The domestic cat might easily have reverted to its wild state once it was set free to explore its comparatively wild surroundings of the New World. But this did not happen. The cat remained domesticated, relying on man's protection in the New World as it had in the Old.

Sadly that protection has not always been given. At times, the cat has been persecuted and ritually tortured. Even in relatively good times, it often had to fend for itself. Man tended to care for horses, goats, and cattle, but to leave cats to hunt down their own rodent nourishment.

Whenever wars and accidents separated cats from their caretakers, the cats did what their primitive ancestors did and what homeless cats do today. They gather together in a kind of loose co-operative on rooftop or fenced-off area, forget their domesticated manners, and revert to the wild. Secluded in groups, they sit peacefully, each night, grooming each other, making vocal exchanges, and moving from group to group much like people at a cocktail party. Before sunup, the gathering breaks up and they all drift away to their daytime hideouts. It seems these feral cats are very close indeed to their wildcat cousins, even if their habitat is a gutted urban building rather than the bush or jungle.

INGRAINED INSTINCT

'We really didn't need a domestic cat until the Egyptians invented the silo and began storing their crops,' writes Roger A. Caras in *A Cat Is Watching*. 'When the mice found out, they put out the word and engaged in one long picnic. The better mousetrap had to be adapted from wild stock. That was barely two thousand years before the dawn of Christianity. When we speak of wild species and their behavioural evolution, we speak of hundreds of thousands of years and sometimes millions. Dogs and bears, for instance, had a common ancestor in Miacids 60 million years ago.

'It just doesn't seem likely that we have been the cause of much in the way of instinctive changes or additions in the short time there has been anything like domestic cats. They probably had all the instincts they needed from the outset to handle us. There is another factor: the matter of training. Dogs for instance have been with us for almost six times as long as cats, and have been trained as cats never have been trained. Cats in general have always had as their chief assignment our aesthetic satisfaction. The cat's one economic value has been the result of an instinct, hunting small animals like mice and rats.

'But I believe cats have an instinctive knowledge of man taken directly from their instinctive knowledge of all other life forms. They are, however, conditioned by us from birth. And they do have another strong influence—a parent. All the mammals identified as Carnivora spend long periods with one parent, as do primates and whales.

'Guinea pigs, on the other hand, are off almost immediately after birth. But then, what can a guinea pig teach anyone?'

Ancient Egypt:
the cat's first home

A wall painting from the tomb of Nakht, in the Valley of the Kings near Luxor, shows a cat waiting to retrieve waterfowl from the riverside marshes of the Nile. The ancient Egyptian hunters used throwing-sticks to kill the birds. The tomb dates from the period of the New Kingdom (1560-1080 B.C.)

The domestication of the cat is a relatively recent event. Some evidence suggests that small wild feline species may have been tamed in different parts of the world only about 8000 years ago. By comparison, the dog was domesticated as early as 50,000 years ago.

The remains of a cat excavated at Jericho (now Eriha, Jordan) date from 6700 B.C. At Harappa (Pakistan), once the centre of the Indus Valley civilization, archaeologists have discovered other cat remains roughly 4000 years old. The remains probably belong to the Asiatic desert cat (*Felis sylvestris ornata*), also known as the Asiatic steppe wildcat, which still exists in Afghanistan, Iran, and Pakistan. There is no evidence to suggest the cats were domesticated. However, some scientists believe the Asiatic wildcat may be an ancestor of today's cat. They point out that the skulls of the wildcat and the modern domestic cat are about the same size.

Gods and tombs

The overwhelming body of evidence points to ancient Egypt as the place where the cat was first domesticated. The ancestor of the ancient Egyptian cat is known to be the African wildcat (*Felis sylvestris lybica*), also called the 'gloved' or Caffre cat. It probably entered early farming villages along the Nile to hunt river rats infesting granaries. Farmers, recognizing a useful ally, took the first step towards domestication by trying to keep the cat near their homes. But the process was to take thousands of years.

The cat first found a niche in the ancient Egyptian imagination. As early as 3500 B.C., the Book of the Dead refers to the 'great cat at the pool of the Persea in Heliopolis.' In this religious work, the cat seems to be a symbol for the sun god Osiris or Re who overcomes a serpent—Set or Apophis—who is the ruler of darkness. The image of the cat slicing off the head of snake-like Apophis—representing the victory of good in the battle with evil—recurs in other Egyptian works of art, including two papyrus manuscripts, now in the British Museum in London.

Evidence of the cat as a part of daily Egyptian life appears in wallpaintings in tombs built during the

A satirical illustration of cats and mice, from a papyrus manuscript prepared by Egyptian scribes about 100 B.C.

A wall painting from the tomb of Nebamun, built about 1400 B.C., depicts a cat holding two fallen birds by its paws and another in its mouth. The painting is now in the British Museum.

New Kingdom (1560-1080 B.C.). The paintings show an animal resembling today's domestic cat in size and appearance. For example, an image of a cat crouched under a table eating a fish appears in the tomb of the scribe Nakht, found in the Valley of the Kings near present-day Luxor, Egypt. Another painting from the time of New Kingdom, now in the collection of the British Museum, shows a man, known as Nebamun, hunting waterfowl and using a cat apparently trained as a retriever.

Birth of the cat goddess

Traditionally, the Egyptians revered certain animals—the bull, lion, baboon, ibis, and dog—for admired or feared qualities. Eventually they began to think of the sacred animals as deities with human traits. One such deity was named Bastet, originally depicted as a lion-headed woman.

According to legend, Bastet was the daughter or the wife-sister of Re, the sun god of Lower Egypt. She fled in anger from Re to Upper Egypt, where she disguised herself as a lion. The sun god sent for her to fight his enemies. At the beginning of her journey down the Nile, Bastet drowned her rage by bathing at Philae, where she assumed the shape of a cat. As Bastet sailed down the Nile, she was acclaimed by people on the banks, before making a triumphant entry into a city in the Nile delta known as Bubastis (now Tell Basta, near the modern city of Zagazig).

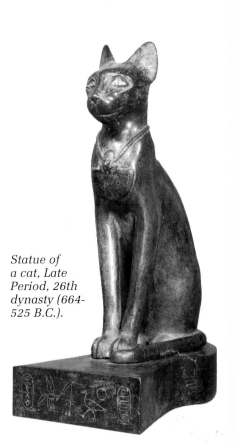

Statue of a cat, Late Period, 26th dynasty (664-525 B.C.).

A sanctuary for sacred cats

A great stone temple in Bastet's honour was built at Bubastis between 2050 and 1800 B.C. According to Herodotus, the Greek 'father of history,' who visited Bubastis in the 5th century B.C., the city was situated on a high mound of earth dredged up during the creation of the canal system in the Nile delta. However, the walled temple was situated—at ground level—in a small valley at the centre of the city. It was almost surrounded by a moat, except for a causeway linking the city market to the temple. The sanctuary that contained the image of the goddess was at the heart of the temple complex. Within the temple, the priests watched over the sacred cats. They searched for signs of Bastet's wishes and warnings, and interpreted the vagaries of feline behaviour for the devout who came to revere the goddess.

Lion into cat

At first, Bastet was depicted as a lion-headed goddess, who symbolized light, heat, and solar energy. But when she assumed the role of a cat, she became a symbol of the night and of the moon. Egyptians believed she controlled fertility, cured illness, and guarded the dead. She was considered a gentle, benevolent guardian of home, family, and love, but she—like many other ancient deities—was sometimes cruel and wrathful.

Bastet was also revered as the Corn Spirit that protected crops and ensured rich harvest. She acquired this role when she bathed at Philae during her journey down the Nile to Bubastis. Philae was the site of the main temple to Isis, who symbolized the fertile land of Egypt. The image of Bastet as the Corn Spirit appears on an ancient Egyptian wall painting (see page 30), now at the Louvre Museum in Paris. According to the ancient Egyptians, a farmer who dreamt of a large cat was sure to enjoy a rich harvest.

The priests in charge of the cult of Bastet may have transformed the goddess—symbolically—from a lion to a cat. (They probably found the lion too ferocious and cumbersome to handle, preferring the cat that was easy to manage.) After the transformation, Bastet was shown as a cat-headed woman. Her right hand held a sistrum—a metal rattle for beating out rhythm—and the left hand, a semicircular pendant on which was inscribed a lion's head. She also carried an aegis, or ceremonial basket, in the crook of her left arm.

Bastet had other names: Ubastes and Pasht, which may be the source of the endearment 'puss.' Bubastis meant 'the house of Bast'—yet another one of her names. Further up the Nile, near Beni Hassan, she was adored by another cult, whose members referred to her as Pekhet.

Flutes and sistrums

Initially, Bastet was merely a local deity. About 950 B.C., when Bubastis became the capital of Egypt, the cat goddess assumed greater significance. For the next six centuries, she was revered as one of the greatest

Mummy of a cat. The face was covered with a painted mask, and the embalmed body swathed in colourful wrappings.

deities of the land. When the Greek historian Herodotus came in Egypt in the 5th century B.C., her cult was nearing its zenith. Bastet's festival at Bubastis was one of the most popular religious events of the year.

In the second book of his *Histories,* Herodotus says 700,000 pilgrims (excluding children) thronged to the celebration at Bubastis from every part of Egypt. Following Bastet's legendary journey, men and women sailed in barges down the Nile. Many of the men played flutes, while some of the women beat out wild rhythms with sistrums. Everyone else sang and clapped in rhythm. Along the way, the barges stopped near riverside communities. Some pilgrims started to dance, while others bantered with the local people on the bank. The barges followed the canals to the temple at Bubastis. At the ensuing celebration, there were sacrifices, feasting, drinking, revelry, promiscuity, and licentiousness. Herodotus viewed the spectacle with a certain amount of distaste.

Tattoos, blood, and ashes

Rituals enlisting the protection of the cat pervaded Egyptian life. Parents dedicated their newborns to Bastet, hanging a pendant inscribed with her image around their necks. In adolescence, the cat's silhouette was tattooed on the arms to attract the goddess's gifts. At special ceremonies, a few drops of blood from a sacred cat might be injected to ward off sickness and evil spirits.

When a child fell seriously ill, the family shaved their heads and sold the hair for gold or silver, which was used to buy fish offerings for sacred cats. The family gathered at the temple to study the cat for signs of their child's recovery.

For Egyptians, Herodotus reports, there was no loss more painful than the death of a cat. At fires, people showed more concern for saving cats than putting out the blaze. (Herodotus also mentions that Egyptian cats had a strange propensity for running into fires.) If a cat died in a house fire, its inhabitants covered themselves with ashes and ran about the streets, beating their breasts and tearing their clothes to shreds.

Bastet, the cat goddess, holds a sistrum (a metal rattle) in her right hand, and a pendant showing the head of a lion, in her left hand. The aegis, or ceremonial basket, is in the crook of her left arm.

MUMMIFIED CATS

In 1890, archaeologists discovered more than 300,000 cat mummies buried in an underground sanctuary at Ben Hassan. The site had once been a temple dedicated to the cat goddess Bastet. Built about 1400 B.C. the temple was situated at the top of a cliff; and the sanctuary, at its base. The mummified cats had been placed in small cases. Beside the cases were mummified mice—food for the cat's long journey to the afterworld. Sadly, the significance of the discovery escaped the archaeologists. As a result, all the mummies—weighing 24 tons—were sent to England, where they were ground up and used as fertilizer.

In recent years, researchers at the British Museum in London X rayed unopened cat mummies. They discovered that the necks of many of the cats had been broken. This suggested that the cats may have been strangled to death. In some cases, the creatures died before they were 4 months old. Researchers speculate that these cats may have been bred as sacrificial offerings. The mummies date from the Ptolomaic period (330 to 30 B.C.). The practice of animal sacrifice was completely abhorrent to the Egyptians before this time.

Researchers have also unwrapped the bandages and shrouds covering the cats and discovered the vestiges of striped and spotted fur on the desiccated bodies. The colour of the fur is light ginger or reddish yellow. In some cases, researchers have found cat mummies contain only parts of the animal—paws, hindquarters, and bodies without legs. They believe embalmers may have divided cats to meet the demand of the devotees of Bastet for mummies.

The responsibility and care of the domestic cat passed from father to son. At a cat's death, every member of the family shaved off their eyebrows in mourning. (However, they shaved the whole of their heads and bodies when a dog died.) The dead cat was embalmed and swathed in rich-coloured wrappings before it was packed in straw and placed into a wooden case. The face was covered with a mask, on which the nose, the eyes, ears, and whiskers were painted. Embalmed mice were included for the voyage to the hereafter and were tucked in the sarcophagus beside the cat. The wealthier the family, the more lavish the arrangements for the cat's funeral, though even the most humble household went into mourning.

An Egyptian wall painting, now in the Louvre in Paris, shows the cat goddess Bastet in her symbolic role as the Corn Spirit, helping harvesters.

A shield of cats

The killing of cats (and other sacred animals) was an unthinkable offence, punishable by death. Because cows and fish were also considered sacred, the ancient Egyptians remained resolutely vegetarian throughout most of their history.

According to legend, the prohibition against killing cats led to a major military defeat. In 522 B.C., Cambyses II, the king of Persia (present-day Iran), invaded Egypt, attacking the strategically important city of Pelusium in the Nile delta. To overcome Egyptian resistance, Cambyses's soldiers marched into battle with cats affixed to their shields. The Egyptians, appalled at the possibility of killing or even wounding the animals, threw down their arms, leaving Pelusium to the Persians.

Five centuries later, a cat complicated Egypt's uneasy relations with Rome. According to the Greek historian Diodorus Siculus, a Roman visiting Egypt killed a cat and, even though the incident was said to be accidental, the outraged public demanded his execution. Although the Egyptian king—Ptolemy XII, father of Cleopatra—was unwilling to antagonize the Romans, he could not stay the offender's execution.

Cat, falcon, and baboon inscribed on an Eygptian pottery fragment known as an ostracon.

Egypt eventually fell to Rome in 30 B.C., when Cleopatra—the last monarch of Egypt's Ptolemaic dynasty—committed suicide. Despite Roman domination, the ancient Egyptian religious cults lingered on for more than 400 years. At the end of the 4th century A.D., Emperor Theodosius the Great, who ruled from 379 to 395 A.D., abolished pagan practices, and established Christianity throughout the Roman Empire. But the glory days of the Egyptian cat—and its cult—had already ended.

The cat in Greece and Rome

Ancient Egyptians guarded their cats closely, prohibited their export from Egypt, and bought back any that had been illegally exported or smuggled out of the country. Eventually, however, the cat became established in Europe, but with considerably less status than what it had enjoyed in Egypt. The Greeks were too rational, and the Romans too practical to elevate a cat to the status of a deity

The route by which the Egyptian cat reached Europe is uncertain. From 2000 B.C. onwards, Phoenicia (present-day Syria and Lebanon) was trading briskly with Egypt. Its ships may have carried the cat—and its cult—back to home ports. Remains of animal sacrifices—including cats—have been found at the ancient Phoenician city of Byblos. Phoenician traders probably used Egyptian cats as rat-catchers on their ships and sold the creatures as 'exotic' but useful novelties in Crete, Greece, and Italy.

According to one legend, the Greeks rather than the Phoenicians brought the cat to Europe. Greek traders, eager to acquire cats for their home market, offered to buy some from the Egyptians. When the Egyptians refused to consider a god the object of a commercial transaction, the Greeks stole six pairs and sailed back to Greece. After the first litters were born, the breeders carried the cats to Italy and Gaul (modern France). The cat's natural prolificity ensured survival and gradual dispersal throughout Europe.

Throughout the ancient Mediterranean, semidomesticated weasels and skunks, and small snakes, were used to catch mice. (The mongoose was also popular for this purpose.) The Greeks may have planned to replace these smelly beasts with clean, refined cats. If so, their plan failed. They soon came to care for cats as companions and put little value on their mouse-catching skills.

During the 6th century B.C., Aesop, the Greek author of moral fables, used cats to satirize some of the worst human characteristics—dishonesty and deceit.

For these young Greeks, who have just discovered the dog-cat antipathy, the cat is still a novelty, an exotic animal from Egypt. This illustration appears on a Greek funerary stele in the National Archaeological Museum, Athens.

A domestic cat and ornamental birds depicted on a Roman mosaic, now in the British Museum, London.

In this detail from a Greek vase, two women watch as a cat leaps up in an attempt to seize a bird.

Herodotus (485-430 B.C.) described the Egyptian cult of the cat—a curiosity from the Greek perspective—in the second of his *Histories.* There are also references to cats in two literary works of the 4th century B.C.— Aristophanes' comedy *Archanians* and Callimachus's *History of the Animals.* Two centuries later, the poet Theocritus, who lived in Alexandria, then a Greek city, praised cats in the *Dialogue of the Syracusans.*

The cat plays an important role in Greek and Roman myth. Apollo, the sun god, created the lion; his sister, Artemis, the cat. Artemis personifies the moon. This was the beginning of the legend that the moon gave birth to the cat. The Greeks identified Artemis with the Egyptian cat goddess Bastet. Later the Romans connected Bastet-Artemis with their goddess Diana.

From the 5th century B.C. onwards, there is increasing evidence in Greek art that the cat has become a domesticated animal. A Greek funerary stele from this period, now in the National Archaelogical Museum at Athens, shows a confrontation between a cat and a dog, which are held on leashes by two youths.

During the first century B.C., the Roman statesman and orator Cicero was the first to write about the Egyptian cat. By the following century, the cat was still relatively rare in Rome and the rest of Italy. But in the ruins at Pompeii, which was destroyed in the eruption of the volcano Vesuvius in 79 A.D., the surviving mosaics show images of cats, including one of a spotted feline killing a chicken. A woman trapped in the Vesuvian lava was found clutching the remains of a cat. Pliny the Elder, who observed the terrible eruption, wrote about the Egyptian cat in his *Natural History,* one of the great works of Latin literature. Pliny noted the stealth with which a cat hunted birds and mice.

Romans saw the cat as a symbol of liberty. Although the cat was domesticated, it was not easily restrained. Therefore, it was seen as representing Roman independence. Its image decorated the flags of the legionnaires who served in far-flung reaches of the Empire. The goddess of liberty—Libertas—was usually shown with a cat lying at her feet.

At the beginning of the 4th century A.D., when the Roman Empire entered its long decline, eastern religions were introduced into Italy. One of these religions was that relic of ancient Egypt—the cult of the cat goddess Bastet. At Portici, near Naples, a painting shows a woman devotee—with a sistrum—worshipping a cat. In the same century, Palladius published *De re rustica,* an agricultural treatise that recommended cats as a means of getting rid of moles in gardens.

By the end of the Roman Empire, the cat was part of the everyday life of the capital and its environs. But, in the distant provinces, it was a rarity—a pet of Roman officials or local aristocrats.

Names of the cat

In ancient Egypt, the cat's first home, the animal was called mau, presumably because of its miaow.

The Greek historian Herodotus, who lived in the 5th century B.C., translated cat by the Greek word *ailourus,* which means 'the waving ones'—a reference to the cat's tail. Today, cat lovers and haters are *ailourphiles* and *ailourphobes.* Another Greek word—*gale*—is sometimes translated as cat or 'weasel.' The word appears in the writings of Homer, Aristophanes, Theocritus, and other classical Greek authors.

The earliest Roman term for cat—*Felis*—was also used to describe martens and weasels. The first specific use of *Felis* for the domesticated cat appears in the first century B.C. in the writings of the Roman orator Cicero.

The Latin term *cattus* or *catus,* source of our English word, appears in a 4th-century agricultural treatise by the Roman Palladius. This word identifies the cat in many European languages: *chat* (French); *katze* (German); *gato* (Spanish); *katta* (Swedish); and *kat* (Dutch and Danish). Originally it may have come from the Byzantine Greek *katos,* which has roots in the Arabic *qatt,* the Syrian *qatì,* and the African *kadis.* The Berbers of Morocco use another variant of the African word—*kadiska.*

Mediaeval documents, religious or judicial in content and invariably written in Latin, use the terms *musio, muriceps,* or *murilegus,* meaning 'mouse-catcher,' rather than *cattus,* when referring to the cat.

Gallo-Roman stele, found at Alise-Sainte-Reine in the Côte-d'Or region of France, shows a young boy holding cat.

The cruel Middle Ages

The cat's long and comfortable existence with man—at least in Western Europe—received a major setback with the fall of Rome. The city was little more than an impoverished backwater when the barbarians seized control in 476 A.D. Cats shared a harsh and precarious life with their masters in the last outposts of Roman glory, the decaying communities and the isolated country estates of Italy and France. Even in the Roman world, the cat had been a rarity. Usually it was the pet of an aristocratic family. During the Dark Ages—roughly the period from the 6th to the 10th century—cats survived, but numbers were few relative to other animals. Excavations in northern France at the village of Brébières—founded during this period—reveal two cats to every six dogs.

The cat and the law

In parts of the post-Roman world, the cat disappears altogether from the archaeological record during the Dark Ages. But, in Britain, it was a familiar creature, highly valued as a mouser. The laws of the Welsh king Howel the Good, who died in 950, list the price of kittens: a penny, from birth until its eyes open; two pence, when it first kills; four pence, after four kills.

The Howel's laws also required sellers to ensure that ears, eyes, claws, and teeth were in perfect condition. If a tom was a poor mouser, or a female, an inadequate mother, a third of the initial price had to be refunded. Stealing or killing a cat carried a fine of one ewe with her lamb, or enough wheat to cover a cat, which was hung by its tail with its jaw touching the ground.

The cat was also known in Germany, Scandinavia, and Ireland and other regions that had escaped Roman rule. In Norse mythology, the cat—probably the wildcat and the lynx—is associated with the goddess of fertility and wealth, Freyja, who introduced the arts of magic to the gods. She is usually shown riding in a chariot drawn by two cats. Even today, the cat holds a privileged place in Scandinavian homes.

In Ireland, a cat-headed god was worshipped as early as the first century A.D. According to folklore, Saint Ciaran killed a King of Cats, known as Iruscan.

In the First Phase of Cruelty, *the 18th-century English artist Hogarth showed that cruelty towards cats was as common in his time as it had been during the Middle Ages.*

A 17th-century engraving taken from the Recueil des plus illustres proverbes.

During the Dark Ages, the monasteries opened their doors to cats, who protected the grain supplies against mice. Saint Patrick, the 5th-century patron saint of Ireland, reared cats. Thereafter, the Irish monks became active breeders of cats. One of the great achievements of the Irish monks was the creation of magnificent illuminated—that is, illustrated—manuscripts, which the copyists sometimes embellished with the images of their cats. One of the copyists, whose companion was a beloved cat, left behind a poem, which compares their tasks:

I and Pangur Ban my cat
'Tis a like task we are at;
Hunting mice is his delight
Hunting words I sit all night...

When the monks adopted cats as companions, they followed the example of Pope Gregory the Great (c. 540-604), who organized the early Church. At the end of his life, Gregory retired from the papacy to a monastery, where his only worldly possession was a cat. A mediaeval theologian, John the Deacon, reported Gregory 'liked stroking his cat better than anything else.' In the late Middle Ages, anchoresses—women who lived secluded religious lives—were permitted to have a cat as their sole companion.

Many saints of the early Christian church, such as Saint Martha, who lived during the 1st century A.D., had cats as companions. In some instances, the cat was a symbol of a saint's virtues or concerns—just as it had been for pagan deities such as Bastet and Freyja. According to legend, Saint Agatha, the second-century saint, appeared as an angry cat to scold women who worked on her saint's day. Even today, she is known as Santo Gato—Saint Cat—in the Pyrenees Mountains of northern Spain. The 7th-century Saint Gertrude of Nivelles is the patroness of gardeners, widows, travellers—and cats. The 11th-century Saint Ives, the patron of lawyers, is depicted with a cat, the symbol of justice.

Mediaeval cats

Until the 10th century—the beginning of the Middle Ages—the cat enjoyed the protection of the Church. The image of the cat appeared in the carvings and other architectural features of mediaeval churches and as a decorative element on church furniture.

Outside the monasteries, the cat was admired as an aggressive mouser by the owners of barns, granaries, and warehouses. Nevertheless, its value was less than that of other domestic animals—cows, pigs, sheep, and horses—which supplied food, leather, wool, and driving power for ploughing and other agrarian tasks. Even the dog earned greater esteem because of its hunting prowess.

In northern Europe, where the winters were colder and harsher than they are today, the soft, warm, and inexpensive fur of the cat was used to line and decorate garments. (Lawyers often had their gowns trimmed with cat fur.) In times of famine, the flesh of the cat was sometimes added to the soups and stews of hungry farming folk.

Mediaeval attitudes

In mounting its persecutions, the Church played on widespread superstitions about the cat. Common folk associated it with the predatory wildcat and lynx, and believed sorcerers could change themselves into cats. Moreover, they saw the cat as a plaything of the old nobility, whose paganism was discredited and condemned as evil.

The cat's behaviour fed these fears. The animal submitted to no one; it showed affection spontaneously and without invitation; and, just as suddenly and unpredictably, it lost interest and went on its way. Its freedom and lack of fidelity were troubling to people who lived within the closely knit and rigidly organized society of the Middle Ages.

Cats. depicted in a 16th-century engraving, after M. G. Brugense.

Cats and crusades

During the 11th and 12th centuries, the Crusaders, returning to western Europe from their conquests in the Middle East, brought back the black rat in the holds of their ships. The cat was called upon to battle the new scourge, which had a voracious appetite for cereals and fruit. For two centuries, the cat fought the black rat, renewed the admiration of its supporters, and earned itself a period of respite from persecution.

In the early 13th century, the Church launched a crusade against the Albigenses and the Waldenses, two powerful heretical sects in southeastern France. One of the accusations brought against the sects was participating in religious rites involving cats.

The Albingensian crusade, which lasted from 1208 to 1229, laid waste the region and its flourishing culture. In 1233, Pope Gregory IX declared the sects had worshipped the devil in the form of a black cat. Another of his acts also established the Inquisition, which, for more than seven centuries, ruthlessly pursued those accused of being in league with the devil.

The devil in the shape of a cat

In the early Middle Ages, the devil was represented with a human form. Saint Bernard, in the 12th century, associated it with night and the powers of darkness. Gradually, the devil assumed different animal shapes—dog, goat, monkey, toad, or wolf. But its most enduring form was the black cat.

The cat was depicted as scraggy and hairy, with cloven hoofs, claws, horns in his forehead and, sometimes, with cat's ears. According to Gregory IX, the devil's followers ritually kissed the black cat's genitals or rump before embarking on indescribably lascivious orgies.

In the mid-13th century, the Church hurled the accusations of cat-devil worship at the renewed cult of the goddess Freyja in the German Rhineland. At the beginning of the 14th century, the same charge was brought against the Knights Templars—a rich military order of the Crusades. In both instances, the Church emerged victorious and, in the case of the Knights Templars, wealthier.

From 1347 to 1350, the Black Death—also known as the bubonic plague—swept Europe. After a century of fanatical decimation, there were too few cats to kill the rats infested with the disease-carrying bubonic fleas. As a result, more than a quarter of Europe's population died.

Fire festivals

During the Middle Ages, the Church encouraged the revival of pre-Christian fertility and purification rites. One of the rites was the fire festival—at the beginning of Lent and on St. John's Eve in June—where the public burning of cats occurred.

In Paris, the St. John's Eve fire was held at the Place de Grève. A basket, barrel, or sack, full of a dozen or so live cats was suspended from a pole or tree trunk above a huge pile of kindling. After the fire, the Parisians gathered the ash and charred wood as tokens of good luck. In 1648, Louis XIV, wearing a crown of roses, set the fire ablaze, danced, and later banqueted. But the event was the last of its kind in Paris. It was abolished by the king, who may have found its mediaeval brutality distasteful. Fire festivals outside Paris, however, remained popular events throughout rural France. They were prohibited in 1796 during the period of the French Revolution known as the Directory.

A 16th-century illustration depicts a cat in the company of witches.

Cats and witches

Towards the end of the 15th century, Pope Innocent VIII stepped up the war on heresy with a condemnation of witchcraft. The document unleashed three centuries of persecution, in which 300,000 to 1 million people went to their deaths due to suspected association with the devil. Witches were usually outcasts or misfits, whose eccentric behaviour was seen as demonic possession. In many cases, the witch's only companion was a cat—or 'familiar'—which onlookers took to be the devil's representative. It was also widely believed a witch could take a cat's shape. At witchcraft trials, cats sat beside their masters in the dock. Both were tortured for 'confessions' and burnt alive. In these troubled times, even a passing fondness for a cat was enough evidence to persecute.

The tribulations of the cat were complicated by the Reformation, which split Europe into warring factions. In England, during the reign of Mary Tudor (1553-1558), who was also known as 'Bloody Mary,' cats were burnt as a sign of Protestant heresy. Her successor, the Protestant Elizabeth I (1558-1603), matched her predecessor's cruelties by burning a cat-filled effigy of the pope as a highlight of her coronation procession. According to accounts of the event, live cats caged in a wicker frame 'squalled in a hideous manner as soon as they felt the fire.' The screeching was 'the language of the devil within the Holy Father.'

In later centuries, cat massacres lost all magical and religious significance, and acquired secular overtones. During the 1730s, a crowd of impoverished, unemployed youths in Paris rampaged through the streets and broke into the houses of the wealthy, where they seized pampered pet cats and slaughtered them.

A mediaeval mouser carved in the choir stall at the Cathedral of Saint-Pierre, Poitiers, France.

A Cat Washing Itself.
*From a 13th-century
album by Villard de
Honnecourt.*

The prophet's cat

The fear and hatred of the cat in Europe was unknown in Africa and Asia. The cat may have crossed from Egypt to the Arabian Peninsula, where it became a revered animal among desert tribes. In the early 7th century, the prophet Muhammad founded Islam and united the tribes into a world-conquering force.

In the Koran, the cat is described as a pure animal, whereas the dog is said to be impure. Because the cat possessed the *baraka,* or blessing, it was always cherished by Muhammad's followers. A 13th-century sultan of Egypt willed a small garden for the homeless and needy cats of Cairo. Legacies and charitable donations provided funds to buy meat and offal for the cats.

Even Muhammad had a favourite cat called *Muezza.* According to legend, the creature once fell asleep on the sleeve of his master's *gellaba* or robe. When time came for Muhammad to go to prayer, he cut off the sleeve rather than disturb the cat's sleep.

Islamic folklore credits the cat's origins to the work of the biblical Noah, who feared the Ark might be overrun by mice. To solve the problem, he passed his hand over the lion's head three times. The lion sneezed forth a cat that kept the mice in check.

In India, the earliest mention of cats dates from 200 B.C. Fables about cats appear in the Indian epics, the *Rayamana* and *Mahabharata,* which date from 500 B.C., but they may be interpolations from a later date. The Indians have a feline deity—Sastht—whose attributes are similar to Bastet, the cat goddess revered by the ancient Egyptians.

Oriental cats

Some experts claim the cat reached China as early as 2000 B.C., but this is doubtful. The cat may have been shipped by caravan along the great trading route—known as the Silk Road—which, from Roman times, linked the Mediterranean with the Orient. Once the cat reached China, it was appreciated as a mouser, and became the symbol of good fortune, peace and beauty.

According to Chinese folklore, the cat's ability to see in the dark is a sign of its power to keep evil spirits at bay. Chinese dwellings are often adorned with images of cats. Small lamps with slit-like apertures—resembling cat's eyes—are lit at dusk to ward off evil night spirits.

In the Far East, Buddhists admire the cat's meditative powers. Yet the cat is not mentioned in Buddhism's original sacred

In this 13th-century psalm book illustration, dog and cat share the hearthside.

texts. According to legend, the cat's description was excluded because the creature fell asleep during the Buddha's funeral.

According to Gaston Phébus (1331-1391), 'cats are hunted infrequently and only by chance.' This illumination, of wild cats, is from an early 15th-century edition of Phébus's book on hunting.

Cats at court

Legend says cats first reached Japan in 999 A.D. On arrival, they became pampered guests at the imperial court in Kyoto. The Japanese treated cats as beloved companions—to be fondled and nourished like lap-dogs—rather than like hunters. (To combat the swelling numbers of mice, the Japanese decorated dwellings with sculpted and painted images of fierce-looking felines.) As a result, the Japanese cat lost its mouse-catching skills. Only in the 17th century, after centuries of spoilt existence, were cats again permitted to hunt freely.

In Japanese folklore, the cat is usually described as a benevolent animal. But the Japanese, like the Europeans, also thought some cats had sinister, magic powers. For example, they believed long-tailed cats assumed human shapes and cast spells on innocent people. In one Japanese tale, a demon cat sucks the blood of a beautiful maiden and assumes her shape in order to deceive her suitor, who is a prince. Eventually, the demon cat is hunted down and slain by the prince. The maiden is released from the magic spell, and restored to her human shape and her suitor.

Cat lore and legend

During the Middle Ages, cats were often used in fertility rites that dated from pre-Christian times. In parts of Europe, they were buried in furrows of newly ploughed fields to improve yields. Sometimes a cat was buried in a field to clear weeds, or at the foot of a tree to ensure growth. The cat was a protective presence while crops ripened. Parents warned children against going into cultivated fields 'because the cat sits there.'

At harvests, the reapers cut off the paws of the cat with the last swathe of the scythe. (In earlier times, people may have used wildcats, bears, foxes, or dogs.) In some parts of Europe, the cat was cooked and eaten to ensure future fertility.

In France, cats were burnt in bonfires on the first Sunday of Lent and, again, on St. John's Eve in late June. As the fires blazed, local people leaped over the flames or forced domestic animals through the smoke.

CATS IN ENTERTAINMENT

Concert of amateurs. A 19th-century lithograph.

Throughout history, the cat has rarely appeared on stage or in the circus. A relatively small creature, the cat can never thrill audiences as the mighty lion can. Moreover, the cat is as difficult to train as the lion, although obviously less dangerous. A cat can be taught tricks, but it may be unwilling to repeat them on demand in public.

The cat's lack of commitment and its unexpected displays of temperament have always been drawbacks to its career. An entertainer offered to put on a show with his acrobatic cat for the French king Henry IV (1553-1610). Despite its ability to perform a thousand tricks, the cat was banished from the stage for fear it might attack the monarch.

According to legend, monkeys have been used to conduct cat concerts. A remarkable attempt to tap feline vocal talents was the cat pipe organ created by the citizens of Brussels for a procession honouring Charles V (1500-1558), who held the titles of King of Spain and Holy Roman Emperor. The pipes of the organ were replaced by narrow boxes, in which cats were hidden. The tails, sticking through holes in the boxes, were tied by strings to a keyboard. When a performing bear pressed the keys, the strings pulled the cats' tails. The cat organ was played in London and Paris. The last appearance of this musical curiosity was in 1796.

Cats have been more successful in film, where a carefully coaxed performance once captured on celluloid need not be repeated. In 1951, *Rhubarb,* a comedy about a ginger alley cat that inherits a fortune, won the first Patsy (Picture Animal Top Star Award Film) for its eponymous feline hero.

The Audrey Hepburn classic, *Breakfast at Tiffany's* (1962), based on Truman Capote's novel, and Paul Mazursky's *Harry and Tonto* (1985), which starred Art Carney, are memorable cat movies. Cats have also figured in horror films, such as Val Lewton's *Cat People* (1942). The Japanese *I Am a Cat* film tells a story from a cat's perspective. Film animators have captured the comic and rambunctious side of the felines in *Felix the Cat* and *Tom and Jerry* cartoons.

There followed torchlight parades through fields, gardens, and meadows. Shaking the sparks from the torches on cultivated ground was thought to improve crops. The Lenten fires were believed to ensure the growth of spring crops, and the fires of St. John's, to protect crops against storms and droughts. The fire ceremonies—and the burning of the cats—continued until the end of the 18th century.

Early farmers said the cat was fat or lean when they described the size of the harvest. The cat was used to predict future harvests. It was a tradition to throw a cat off the top of a church. If the cat landed on its feet, there was hope for a good harvest. In 1938 and again after World War II, the tradition was revived (with a stuffed velvet cat replacing the live animal) at *Kattefest* (Cat Fair) in Ypres, Belgium. The fair, held annually in May, features a parade with floats dedicated to Bastet, Freyja, and other cats of lore and legend.

Guardian spirits

From earliest times, the cat was seen as a benevolent guardian spirit. For example, the ancient Egyptians believed the cat goddess Bastet protected them from contagious diseases. It was the custom to inject offspring with a few drops of blood from a sacred cat.

In the Middle Ages, some folk thought of the cat as the protector of their house. The custom of immuring the animal in walls or burying them alive in the foundations was an early kind of house insurance. After the Italian poet Petrarch (1304-1374) embalmed his dead cat 'in the Egyptian manner,' he had it buried above the doorway to prevent evil spirits from threatening his house.

The traditional way to keep a new cat at home was to rub its paws in butter and to sharpen its claws on the outside of the chimney. It was bad luck to let an adult cat be carried away from the house or carried into a house. (The cat should be allowed to walk into a house by itself.) Three-coloured cats were said to protect houses from fire.

Other traditions that have persisted for centuries: if a black cat visits, good luck may follow; if it stays, bad luck. In England, it is said that a black cat in a house can save a sailor from danger at sea. In Germany, France, and parts of the United States, black cats are seen as followers of the devil and, therefore, bad luck. In some parts of France, people still think a black cat with a small white tuft will bring good luck.

A legendary figure is the magic cat that brings good luck in return for a share of his master's wealth. In Germany and eastern Europe, a kindly household sprite or goblin was said to appear in the form of a black cat. The story of Puss in Boots—the tale of a poor boy who becomes rich with the aid of a cat—is a well-known example of the notion. In Italy, cats received first portions of every meal in the expectation of good fortune. In parts of France, the magic cat is called a *matagot*. In Brittany, someone who suddenly acquired riches had found 'the silver cat.'

It was said that cats had the power to foresee death. If a cat jumped on to a sick person's bed, death was imminent. However, some swore the sick person would die if the cat jumped off the bed. In Belgium and

OVERCOMING FEAR

It's hard for cat lovers to understand that there are people who are terrified of cats. The fear may begin during childhood when a cuddly kitten suddenly scratches or bites. After the incident, all cats may be seen as threatening.

The fear may also be caused by an anxious parent who shouts in panic when a cat jumps on a new baby. The parent may be afraid the cat will smother the baby, although it is unlikely that the animal would sit for long on a squealing, squirming infant. If the episode recurs, the parent may communicate a sense of panic about the cat to the child.

Cats are often drawn to individuals who suffer from cat phobia. In the presence of a cat, the individual may become paralysed with terror. The cat may misread the stillness as an invitation to jump on a welcoming and comfortable lap.

Desmond Morris, author of *Catlore* (1988), offers a step-by-step procedure for victims of cat phobia. The first step is to show the individual cat photos and cat-like objects such as toy cats. The second step is to place the victim in a room with a cat. Initially, the cat is in a wicker cage at the opposite side of the room. Gradually, the animal is moved nearer and nearer, until the victim can comfortably pick it up. According to Morris, the procedure works within a few months.

Count Georges de Buffon (1707-1788). The great naturalist did not like cats, but the caricaturist has mischievously inserted one at lower right.

France, families tied a small black ribbon around their cat's neck when someone died at home. When a dying cat senses its own death, it may leave the house. This was considered a bad omen for the house or someone in the family, because the protective power of the cat was gone.

The cat was a symbol of sacred and profane love. In Belgium, a girl who cherished a cat was sure to marry. But it was a bad omen if the cat sat by the doorstep before the wedding as it was thought to be reproaching the young bride for neglect.

If a girl was uncertain about marrying her suitor, she might 'leave it to the cat.' Three hairs from a white cat's tail were placed in a folded piece of paper, which was placed under the girl's doorstep. Next morning the paper was unfolded carefully. If the hairs were found to cross each other, the girl should accept her suitor's offer. If not, she should reject him. When a young bride refused a suitor, she was said 'to have given him the cat.'

In Scandinavia, if the sun shone on a bride at her wedding, she was seen 'to have fed the cat well'—that is, she was a good housekeeper. Someone who wished to harm the newlyweds might mistreat a cat during the wedding ceremony. In the Balkans, it was customary to bring the newlyweds a cradle with a cat to ensure fine offspring.

A second marriage was often treated with suspicion or derision. In Egypt and parts of Europe, a cat might be hung outside the door as a sign of neighbourly disapproval. Burning the cat—the guardian of the marriage—was said to destroy its protective power. A cat was the symbol of illicit love. An adulteress was put into a sack of terrified cats that clawed her to death.

From head to tail

The superstitious believed a cat's head belonged to the devil, and the rest of the body to God. According to legend, when God created the cat, the devil said: 'Make the cat if you like, but its head shall be mine.'

A cat's head was thought to be the seat of magical powers, sometimes good, sometimes evil. When eaten warm, it made a person invisible. Although it was often used in health-giving remedies, it could also cause madness.

Cat Concert. Engraving after Pieter Brueghel (1564-1638).

Cat Concert or Charivari:
*Moritz von Schwind
(1804-1871).*

In a fable by the French writer Countess d'Aulnoy (1650-1705), a wicked fairy transforms a princess into a white cat. The prince cuts off the cat's head and tail, and throws them into a fire. His act breaks the spell, and the princess regains her human shape.

The cat's tail was thought to be dangerous because it moved even while its owner slept, suggesting the presence of an evil force. Stepping on the tail was considered unlucky. For example, if a bride-to-be stepped on the tail, she might have to delay her wedding for a year. On the other hand, if a cat's tail was cut off, it can be used as an antidote for poisons and as protection against snakes. Also, it could prevent an animal from becoming a witch. Clipping the cat's ears was said to stop the animal from attending a witches' sabbath; clipping the tail improved the cat's domesticity.

Fiction and fact

The Greeks were the first to describe cats in literature. Aesop, who may have lived in the 6th century B.C., used cats in his fables. But Aesop's cats usually embody some of the worst human traits—craftiness and dishonesty. This unflattering image also appeared in the works of other writers.

An objective view might have been expected from a man of science. But this was not the case with the French naturalist Buffon (1707-1788), whose *Histoire naturelle* was one of the most widely read 18th-century works. According to him, the cat is a 'fawning and adaptable knave' with 'a deceitful character, a perverse nature that grows worse with age and which education only disguises.' But another French scientist, Louis Pasteur (1822-1895), eventually reversed the harsh judgments of Buffon and others by praising the cleanliness of cats.

THE LAW VERSUS CAT

In 1949, a bill that would confine cats to their owner's property was tabled in the Illinois State legislature. But Governor Adlai Stevenson, who was in office from 1948 to 1952, vetoed the proposed law with this speech:

'I cannot agree that it should be the declared public policy of Illinois that a cat visiting a neighbour's yard or crossing the highway is a public nuisance. It is the nature of cats to do a certain amount of unescorted roaming. Many live with their owners in apartments or other restricted premises, and I doubt if we want to make their every brief foray an opportunity for a brief game hunt by zealous citizens—with traps or otherwise.

'I am afraid this bill could only create discord, recriminations, and enmity. Also consider the owner's dilemma: To escort a cat abroad on a leash is against the nature of the cat, and to permit it to venture forth for exercise unattended into a night of new dangers is against the nature of the owner.

'Moreover, cats perform useful services, particularly in rural areas, in combatting rodents—work they necessarily perform alone and without regard for property lines.

'We are interested in protecting certain varieties of bird. That cats destroy some birds, I well know, but I believe this legislation would further but little the worthy cause to which its proponents give such unselfish support. The problem of cat versus bird is as old as time. If we attempt to resolve it by legislation, who knows but we may be called upon to take sides as well in the age-old problem of dog versus cat, bird versus bird, or even bird versus worm.'

Cat lovers

Throughout European history, the cat has had many enemies. Famous cat haters include Napoleon, and such dictators as Mussolini and Hitler. Queen Elizabeth I of England disliked them, and Henry III of France was terrified of them. Some early cat haters included scientists, such as the 16th-century French surgeon Ambroise Paré, who described cats in a chapter on poisons in a 1583 medical treatise.

During the 17th century, there was a renewed appreciation of the cat's intelligence and serenity, particularly among the powerful, wealthy, and educated. The French cardinal and statesman Richelieu (1585-1641) was fond of the kittens that kept him company during his long hours at his desk. At his death, he asked his guards to care for the kittens but, in keeping with the widespread anti-cat prejudice of the period, they burnt them instead.

Cats as heirs

The 17th-century rehabilitation of the cat had its comic side. Wellborn ladies decked cats with jewels and bequeathed them their worldly goods, much to the despair of human heirs. In 1678, Madame Dupuis, a celebrated French harpist, left the greater part of her fortune to her cats. Her will obliged the other heirs, a sister and a niece, to ensure the cats were properly cared

44

The Ball of Wool: *Jean-Baptiste Greuze (1725-1805). In the 18th century, cats often appeared as companions in portraits.*

for. She stipulated that, if the relatives died before the cats, 30 sous a week should be spent on the cats 'in order that they may live well.' But the relatives contested the will, which the courts overturned. What happened to the cats is not recorded.

Cats and writers

In general, writers, painters, and musicians have been the cat's best allies. Writers maintained a fondness for the cat, even when it was an object of witch-hunts, burnings, and other cruelties. The 14th-century Italian poet Petrarch publicly declared his love of cats. The remains of his beloved cat are still preserved at a Padua museum honouring the poet.

Another Italian poet, Torquanto Tasso (1544-1595), wrote a sonnet to a cat. The 16th-century French essayist Montaigne was intrigued by the cat's independence. He asked: 'When I play with my cat, who knows if I am not a pastime to her more than she to me?' The Spanish dramatist Lope de Vega (1562-1635) composed *Gattomachia* (Battle among cats), in which he praised cats and ridiculed people. In act III of *Romeo and Juliet*, Shakespeare celebrates the longevity of cats with this exchange:

Tybalt: *What wouldst thou have of me?*
Mercutio: *Good king of cats, nothing but one of your nine lives.*

Hodge and Jeoffrey

During the 1800s, various English literary figures wrote about the cat. Dr. Samuel Johnson's *Dictionary* (1755) offers the following definition: 'a domestic animal that catches mice, commonly reckoned by naturalists the lowest order of the leonine species.' Despite the objectivity of the entry, Dr. Johnson showed great affection for his own cats. His biographer, James Boswell (who was a cat hater), records how Johnson fed oysters to one cat called Hodge. When the cat jumped up on his chest, Dr. Johnson said: 'I have had cats whom I liked

Boy with His Cat: *John Hoppner (1758-1810).*

better than this,' then, as if perceiving Hodge to be out of countenance, adding, 'but he is a very fine cat, a very fine cat indeed.'

Other 18th-century English poets who celebrated the cat include John Gay, William Cowper, and Thomas Gray, who wrote an *Ode on the Death of a Favourite Cat Drowned in a Tub of Gold Fishes*. Christopher Smart is still remembered for 'Consider my cat Jeoffrey,' a passage from his strange poem *Jubilate Agno*. Smart was briefly an inmate in an asylum, where his only companion was a cat. A popular phrase dating from this period—'not enough room to swing a cat'—first appeared in Tobias Smollett's 1771 novel, *The Expedition of Humphrey Clinker*.

Woman with a Cat:
Edouard Manet,
(1832-1883).

Some Victorian cats

The English and American writers of the 19th century were among the cat's warmest admirers and staunchest defenders. They included William Wordsworth, Robert Southey, Joanna Baillie, John Keats, Alfred Tennyson, Algernon Swinburne, Matthew Arnold, Thomas Hardy, Mark Twain, and Henry James. Rudyard Kipling added *The Cat Who Walked by Himself* to the world of cat lore. The early Victorian playwright and antiquary James Robinson Planché (1796-1880) is remembered for a single line: 'It would have made a cat laugh.'

Edward Lear (1812-1888), the artist and writer of nonsense verse, created the Runible Cat and the famous Pussy-Cat that went off with the Owl in the beautiful pea-green boat. Lewis Carroll (1832-1898), who wrote *Alice in Wonderland* and *Through the Looking Glass,* invented the Cheshire Cat, who 'vanished quite slowly, beginning with the end of the tail, and ending with the grin, which remained some time after the rest of it had gone.'

The Victorian novelist Charles Dickens (1812-1870) was not that fond of cats. However, the household cat, Williamina, gave birth to kittens and carried them into his study, showing the instinctive attraction for writers common to cats. Dickens asked his daughter to remove cat and kittens. But Williamina returned with them, and again Dickens ordered them removed. A determined Williamina returned a third time, depositing her kittens at Dickens' feet and beseeched 'him with such an imploring glance that he could resist no longer.' The kittens stayed and an erstwhile enemy of the cat was vanquished.

Colette (1873-1954)
by M. Vertès.

Admirers past and present

Under the spell of the Romantic movement, which swept the arts and literature in the first half of the 1800s, writers considered themselves outcasts of society, marginal and solitary. Some saw the cat as a symbol of their own social status. The German E.T.W. Hoffmann wrote in the first person as his favourite cat Murr. Another writer of this period fascinated by the cat's mystery was Edgar Allen Poe, who endowed the creature with eerie power in his tale, *The Black Cat*.

The cat also had numerous French admirers. The French poet Charles Baudelaire (1821-1867) wrote:

'Both ardent lovers and austere scholars, when once they come to the years of discretion, love cats, so strong and gentle, the pride of the household, who like them are sensitive to the cold, and sedentary.' The French poet Theophile Gautier (1811-1872), who lived in a house full of cats, said: 'God has created the cat to give man the pleasure of caressing the tiger.' Gautier described their habits in *La Nature chez elle et la Ménagerie intime* (Innate nature and the intimate menagerie). Virtually every major French novelist of the 19th century had an attachment to a cat. George Sand (1804-1876) drank from the same cup as her cat; Victor Hugo (1802-1885) built a chair in the shape of a throne for a cat. Alexandre Dumas *fils* (1824-1895), who had his own small zoo, was described as the 'defense lawyer of cats around the world.'

In the 20th century, writers from W. B. Yeats to T. S. Eliot have added to the treasury of fiction and poetry about cats. Hector Munro, otherwise known as 'Saki' (1870-1916), told the tale of the talking cat *Tobermory.* Don Marquis (1878-1937) is best known for his creations 'mehitabel the cat' and her typewriting friend 'archy the cockroach.'

Ernest Hemingway (1899-1961) was an ailurophile, who crossed imported Cuban cats with American varieties, believing that he was creating a new breed. His house in Key West, Florida, now a museum, still swarms with cats.

Other modern writers who certainly can be counted as cat lovers include Raymond Chandler, Olivia Manning, Compton Mackenzie, Walter de la Mare, and the Czech playwright and novelist Karl Capek. Truman Capote made Cat a character in his book, *Breakfast at Tiffany's* (1959).

Two 20th-century French writers had high praise for cats. Jean Cocteau commented: 'I love cats, because I love my home, and after a while they become its visible soul.' However, the last word on cats undoubtedly belongs to the French novelist Colette (1873-1954). She said: 'Our perfect companions never have fewer than four feet.' Cats appear in many of her stories, which take pride of place on the bookshelves of cat lovers. There is a pair of Siamese cats in her libretto for Maurice Ravel's pantomime-opera-ballet, *L'Enfant et les sortilèges* (The child and the magic spells) (1925). She herself played the part of a cat—*La Chatte amoureuse*—on the stage in 1912. When her beloved cat—'La Chatte dernière'—died in 1939, she refused to replace it out of respect to its memory.

Cats and artists

In ancient Egypt, anonymous craftsmen created cat amulets and charms, and sculpted feline heads representing the cat goddess Bastet. The Greeks and Rome bequeathed statues, mosaics, and frescos with images

The White Cat: *Pierre Bonnard (1867-1947).*

The novelist Colette, famous for her stories about cats, played a feline role, La Chatte amoureuse, *on stage in 1912.*

The French playwright, artist, and filmmaker Jean Cocteau (1889-1963), shown with his Siamese cats.

The cat and advertising...

Cat at a Window: *Hiroshige (1797-1858). This short-tailed cat sits contemplating a view of the Japanese city of Edo (now Tokyo).*

of cats. In the Middle Ages, builders adorned cathedrals with carvings of cats.

From the Renaissance onwards, the image of the cat occurs with greater frequency in European painting. The Italian genius Leonardo da Vinci (1452-1519) painted the *Virgin of the Cat*. Other Renaissance and late-16th-century Italian and Flemish masters who depict the cat on their canvases include: Domenichino, Pinturicchio, Tintoretto, Titian, and Veronese. The cat figures in the work of the Flemish master Rubens (1577-1640) and the fantasies of the Dutch Hieronymus Bosch and the Brueghel family.

The cat is a regular feature of 17th-century paintings of Dutch domestic life. In the following century, the animals often appear as pets in portraits of children. Two delightful portraits of this kind are *La Pelote de laine* (The ball of wool) by the French artist Jean-Baptiste Greuze and *Boy with His Cat* by the Englishman John Hoppner (see page 45). Other important 18th-century Italian and French artists who included cats in their paintings are Giovanni Tiepolo, Jean-Baptiste Chardin, François Desportes, Jean Fragonard, and Jean-Baptiste Oudry. Jean-Antoine Watteau (1684-1721) left behind sketches of cats (see page 44) and the painting *The Sick Cat*.

The 19th-century French painter Edouard Manet included a black cat in his 1863 painting, *Olympia*, now in the Louvre, Paris. Manet also prepared cat illustrations for Champfleury's *Les Chats*, the first major book about cats, which was published in 1870. The impressionists Renoir, Bonnard, and the American-born Mary Cassatt depicted cats in domestic scenes.

Funny felines

At the turn of the century, the French graphic artist Alexandre Steinlen (1859-1923) featured cats on his posters advertising tea and coffee. Steinlen also published *Images sans paroles*, an illustrated collection showing a cat raiding a fish bowl, playing with a ball of wool, and other comic episodes. Steilen loved cats, and his home became known as 'Cat's Corner.'

In the 20th century, the cat has inspired quite a few popular cartoons. George Herriman introduced *Krazy Kat* (and his brick-slinging chum Ignatz Mouse) in 1913. The latest in comic cats is Jim Davis's Garfield.

Cat lovers appreciate the animal for its character and independence.

Musical cats

During the 18th century, the cat was rhapsodized in *Fuga del Gatta* by Italian Domenico Scarlatti. In the 1800s, another Italian, Rossini, wrote *Duetto Buffo due Gatti*, a musical depiction of two cats miaowing in tuneful ecstasy. The 19th-century Russian Tchaikovsky included music for the figures of Puss in Boots and the White Cat in the ballet *The Sleeping Beauty*.

The best-known modern musical tribute is Andrew Lloyd Webber's 1981 show, *Cats*, whose lyrics are based on *An Old Possum's Book of Practical Cats*. This collection of poems about colourful cat characters, such as Rum Tum Tugger and the Old Gumbie Cat, was originally written by Anglo-American poet T. S. Eliot (1888-1965) for the amusement of children.

Cat's progress

Throughout history, the cat has been both venerated and persecuted. In ancient Egypt, the mightiest pharaoh and the humblest farmer deified the cat; in the mediaeval world, the Church persecuted the cat as being a demon or a creature associated with the devil and witchcraft. Cats were sometimes valued only as mousers or as guardians who bestowed protection and good fortune. But even in the darkest days, a few individuals, such as the Italian poet Petrarch, cherished the cat as a companion. During the 17th century, cats found their niche in the family household. The paintings of Dutch interiors from this period depict the cat creating a bit of domestic havoc, filching food from the kitchen table and so on.

In the next century, the cat assumed its role as a beloved pet—a role it still plays in our lives. The 18th-century portraitists often show children with cats, a notable example being William Hogarth's portrait of the Graham children, which is found in the Tate Gallery, London. But Hogarth also depicted the vicious attacks on street strays in his etching *The First Phase of Cruelty* (see page 34). Country cats of these times fared little better. Many were barely fed in the belief that hunger made them better mousers. They suffered from mange—a skin disease caused by a parasitic mite—and other diseases eradicated only in the 19th century.

The cat's progress was significantly furthered by two important Victorian developments: an improvement in the treatment of domestic animals, and an enthusiasm for exhibiting and breeding cats.

Show cats

The first cat show was organized by the Victorian artist and author Harrison Weir, in London, England, on July 13, 1871. The setting for Weir's cat show was the Crystal Palace, the great glass hall originally built to house the Great Exhibition of 1851 and re-erected in 1853 in the south London suburb of Sydenham.

Weir's show attracted about 160 cats for display or competition. Its success sparked a fashion for showing pedigree cats. Two years later shows were held at Alexandra Palace in north London, and another was staged at Birmingham. In 1875, 325 entrants appeared at Crystal Palace, and more than 550 entrants were shown at a show in Scotland's capital, Edinburgh. These early shows exhibited mainly short-haired specimens, but imported breeds were introduced in the 1880s. Two Siamese cats—a gift from the King of Siam (present-day Thailand) to Owen Gould, the British consul general in Bangkok—were exhibited in 1885.

During the late 1880s, the enthusiasm for breeding and exhibiting cats began to spread abroad. The British breeders exported their finest specimens, which formed the basis of foreign breeds. The breed standards established by Harrison Weir were widely adopted. France, Belgium, and Holland became the first European countries to organize cat shows. The first American show was staged at Madison Gardens in New York in 1895.

Modern status

Today countless organizations encourage an interest in the cat, although they often disagree about breed standards. Cat shows around the world continue to attract large, eager crowds of fans. There are now more than 50 recognized breeds, and numbers are growing. Some new breeds—such as the exotic Sphynx—get a lot of publicity, but receive guarded recognition. But the biggest news is that the cat has surpassed the dog as the world's favourite pet.

MORRIS THE TV CAT

Morris the cat is a television star in the United States who has become known throughout the world. His good looks—big, orange-striped and macho—caught the attention of advertisers looking for a cat to represent a brand name cat food.

Once called the feline Burt Reynolds by TIME magazine, Morris has appeared as a a personality in his own right on prime-time television, when he hosted 'A Salute to America's Pets' with Bob Hope and Lily Tomlin.

With proper supervision, a dog and a cat can forget their ancestral aversion, and happily share a home.

YOUR CAT'S ANATOMY

Anatomical features

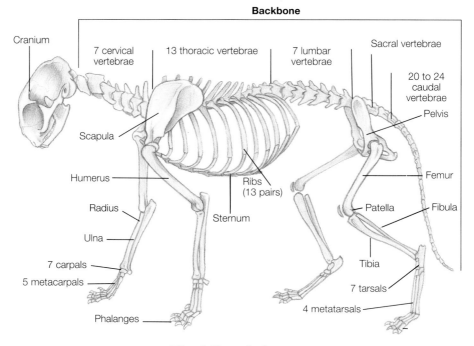

Backbone

Cranium

7 cervical vertebrae

13 thoracic vertebrae

7 lumbar vertebrae

Sacral vertebrae

20 to 24 caudal vertebrae

Pelvis

Scapula

Humerus

Radius

Ulna

7 carpals

5 metacarpals

Phalanges

Ribs (13 pairs)

Sternum

Femur

Patella

Fibula

Tibia

7 tarsals

4 metatarsals

The feline skeleton

A knowledge of the cat's anatomy helps us understand how its body functions and how its system can get out of balance when it is ill. The cat, a carnivore, has a skeleton of approximately 240 bones, bound by a powerful network of muscles. Together these form a small, very lithe mammal.

The head

Most of the cat's sense organs and nerve centres are inside its head. The cat has a short, broad face for the size of its skull. Its very wide, forward-facing eyes give it binocular (three-dimensional) vision. The bony structures forming the cat's cheeks, the zygomatic arches, project far to the side of the skull to accommodate the powerful jaw muscles. These enable the cat to grab and tear off bites of its meaty prey. These muscles are anchored on either side of the skull, and extend down to the lower jaws, or mandibles. The large masseter muscles attached to the zygomatic arches raise the lower jaw and, together with the temporal muscles, allow the cat to close its teeth tightly on its food.

At the opening to the broad, front-facing nasal cavities, cartilage gives the nostrils their shape. The cavities are almost completely filled with cone-shaped nasal turbinates, each consisting of a very thin, curled layer of bone. Before it enters the trachea and lungs, air is heated and moist-ened by a mucus membrane, rich in blood vessels, that covers the labyrinthian folds of the turbinates. When a cat develops an upper respiratory infection, swelling of the mucus membrane or accumulations of mucus and pus can easily block the tiny openings of the nasal turbinates, forcing the cat to breathe through its mouth. Air-filled spaces—the sinuses—in the bony walls of the cat's face are connected to the nasal cavities.

In the wild, the cat's survival certainly owes a lot to its sense of smell, but the domestic cat's olfactory sense is also highly developed. Even cats who have no need to hunt for food use their noses to check

Cross-section of the head

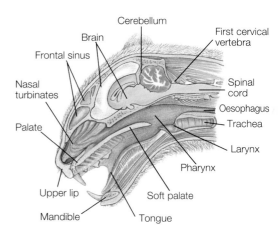

Cerebellum

Brain

First cervical vertebra

Frontal sinus

Nasal turbinates

Spinal cord

Oesophagus

Trachea

Palate

Larynx

Pharynx

Upper lip

Soft palate

Mandible

Tongue

out food sources, to sniff for traces of other cats, and generally keep tabs on their domains. And even a whiff of catnip (*Nepeta cataria*) may transport a feline to

Bones of the head

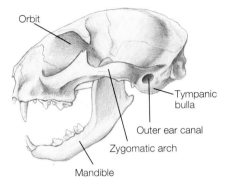

Orbit

Tympanic bulla

Outer ear canal

Zygomatic arch

Mandible

seventh heaven, as this plant's scent excites most cats.

A cat's mouth opens very wide. The mucus membranes of the cheeks, lips, and palate often show natural patches of dark colour. These may look especially strange if black. However, they are normal.

Five or six lateral ridges cross the palate. The thin, mobile tongue is covered not only with taste buds, but also with hard, cone-shaped papillae that point backwards and are rough to the touch. The tongue's texture is ideal for grasping food and especially for grooming; when a cat neglects its grooming for a few days, its coat will appear dull and dirty. Located in folds of tissue at the back of the throat, near the base of the tongue, are the tonsils. They are composed of lymphoid tissue and they swell and become reddish if inflamed. The role of the tonsils, as in humans, is to help resist disease.

The tongue is suspended beneath the back of the skull by two parallel chains of bone, much like the seat on a swing. You can feel this extended structure, called the hyoid apparatus, by putting your hands on either side of the cat's throat.

The cat's teeth are especially suited to handling the carnivorous diet typical of all predatory mammals. The long, pointed canines are especially effective for biting. These are flanked by sets of much smaller incisors and first molars. Another carnivorous adaptation is that the third molars on both the lower and upper jaw— called the carnassial teeth—are sharpened like scissor blades; these teeth are used to slice and cut—rather than to grind— chunks of meat.

Kittens are born without teeth. Deciduous or milk teeth, 26 in all, begin to appear when the kitten is two or three weeks old. Fourteen teeth (six incisors, two canines, and six premolars) occur in the upper jaw; 12 (six incisors, two canines, and four molars) in the lower.

These are replaced by adult teeth when the kitten is between three and seven months, thus providing a temporary clue to a cat's age. Though tartar builds up during the cat's lifetime and its teeth become worn, both are unreliable indicators of a cat's age because the state of a cat's teeth will often depend on its diet.

The first adult teeth begin to protrude from the upper jaw at about three months, starting with the inner incisors, then the outer incisors, and finally, when the kitten is five or six months old, the canines. The kitten's milk teeth, which are much smaller, finer, and more pointed, may stay alongside the adult teeth for a while, but if they are allowed to remain, they will cause eating problems. For this reason, they should be removed.

Tooth development in adults: left teeth seen from the outside

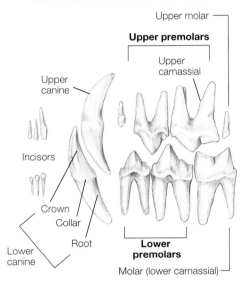

Upper molar

Upper premolars

Upper carnassial

Upper canine

Incisors

Crown

Collar

Root

Lower canine

Lower premolars

Molar (lower carnassial)

The adult's full set of teeth numbers 30. There are six incisors, two canines, six premolars, and two molars in the upper jaw and six incisors, two canines, four premolars, and two molars in the lower. By the time the animal is seven months of age, all the teeth should be fully developed and the kitten should be eating like a fully developed cat. Basically, the cat's teeth are designed to tear and bite at its food rather than to chew it. However, the carnassial teeth do chop the food into digestible chunks. Accordingly, a cat will usually tear off a piece of meat and swallow it whole, leaving it to the strong digestive juices of its stomach to transform the food into energy.

53

Eyes

A cat's vision is its most important sense, followed closely by its hearing. Its eyes, adapted over the years for night vision, can detect the faintest glow. Cats have a wide angle of vision, up to 285 degrees. With some 130 degrees of their visual field binocular vision (compared to 120 degrees for humans), they can judge distance more accurately than people can.

The eye's front surface is a wide aperture—the transparent cornea—that lets in lots of light. The rest of the eye is a nearly spherical fibrous shell called the sclera. Its visible front is the 'white' of the eye, a thick, solid wall which is the eye's outer casing. An opening in the back of the eye leads to the optic nerve.

space between the iris and the cornea. Eye pressure is maintained as this fluid is secreted and drained.

Behind the iris is the one-half-inch (12.7 millimetre) diameter crystalline lens which occupies more than a tenth of the eye's volume. Cats' eyes are wide and quite large compared to those of other mammals. The crystalline lens is held in place on its outer edge by muscles that can contract to vary its curve, ensuring that a focused image is projected onto the retina. After passing through the cornea, the front chamber, the pupil, and the crystalline lens, the light travels through another transparent filling, the gel-like vitreous humour, and forms an inverted image on the retina.

The retina is attached to the surface of the choroid. This light-sensitive coating

Cross-section of the eye

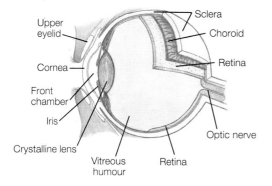

is an extension of the optic nerve, which transmits nerve impulses. Two kinds of cells, rods and cones, convert light into nerve impulses that are then carried into the brain. The cat's retinas have a lot of rods, which means it has superior night vision. Humans, on the other hand, have more cones, giving them better daylight vision. The cones in human eyes also distinguish colour, but researchers are uncertain as to whether cats can see colour.

Behind the cat's rod-rich retina is a mirror-like layer of highly reflective cells that collects light from dim sources. It is this layer, called the tapetum lucidum, that makes cats' eyes glow when light shines on them—when they are caught in a car's headlights, for example, or in photographs taken with a flash.

As with other animals, the back of the cat's eye can be examined for vision impairment by dilating the pupil with special eye drops—something which should be done only by a veterinarian.

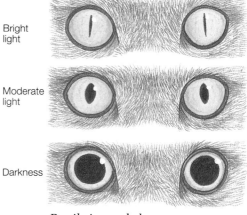

Pupil size and shape vary according to lighting

Behind the transparent cornea is the iris, which opens and closes the pupil to adjust the amount of light reaching the retina. In darkness, the cat's pupil can dilate fully, forming a circle. In moderate lighting, the pupil flattens to an upright oval shape, while in direct sunlight or harsh lighting it contracts to a vertical slit. This slit protects the highly sensitive retina, though the cat can still see perfectly well. The iris is blue when the cat is young, and though it can remain blue in some adult cats, it almost always changes to yellow or orange. Sometimes one eye will remain blue—a condition called heterochromia iridis, or wall-eye—but this will in no way affect the cat's vision. However, white cats with blue eyes are frequently deaf because of a connection between the dominant white gene and a defect in the inner ear.

The iris is just the visible portion of the choroid, a layer of tissue containing many blood vessels. The choroid membrane covers the internal surface of the sclera. A clear liquid called the aqueous humour fills the eye's front chamber, the hollow

Like most vertebrates, the cat has three eyelids. The third, called the nictitating membrane, is a sheet of pale white tissue that lies at the inner corner of the eye. This third eyelid is a good indication of feline health: if you can see it, the cat is not well. The inner surface of the eyelids and the visible part of the sclera are covered with a membrane that is kept moist by tears and cleaned by the opening and closing of the eyelids. Tears exit through two tiny holes, the lachrymal puncta, at the inner corner of the eye, and flow down a channel, the lachrymal canal, or tear duct, to moisten the nostrils. (The nostrils are also moistened by nasal secretions.)

Kittens' eyes are shut at birth; the lids open after about two weeks.

Ears

Cats' ears have three sections: the external, the middle, and the inner ear.

The external ear consists of the pinna and the outer section of the canal that leads to the eardrum. The pinna, a triangular flap of cartilage and skin, stands erect

Cross-section of the ear

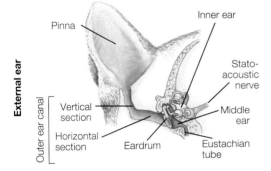

except in a few breeds in which the ears fold over. Perhaps today's best example of this is the Scottish Fold; a similar Chinese breed has become extinct. In some cats, such as the American Curl breed, the ears curl backwards. Cats' highly manoeuvrable ears are attached to the scutiform cartilage, a cartilaginous disc that is controlled by a set of muscles at its base. These enable the cat to swivel its ears to locate a source of sound quickly, or to pin back its ears to express worry or fear.

The outer ear canal consists of cartilage folded into what looks like a pipe with a bend in the middle. The vertical, visible section leads down to a horizontal section, at the end of which is the eardrum. The outer section of this ear canal is covered with a hairless skin that is rich in

sebaceous glands, which sometimes produce thick wax.

The middle ear is a complicated cavity inside the skull. It contains a chain of tiny bones—the hammer, the anvil and the stirrup—that transmits and amplifies vibrations from the eardrum to the inner ear. The middle ear is linked to the throat by way of the eustachian tube.

The inner ear contains the cochlea, a spiral tube where sound vibrations are transformed into nerve impulses, a cavity known as the vestibule, and three semicircular canals that gauge the position of the head in relation to gravity. These canals give the cat its incredible sense of balance. Auditory impulses from the cochlea and sensations of movement and gravity from the semicircular canals are transmitted to the brain by the vestibulocochlear nerve, sometimes called the stato-acoustic nerve. This name reflects both roles it plays in the cat's daily life: hearing and balance.

The cat has excellent hearing when young and can hear sounds in the ultrasonic range that humans cannot hear. But many cats begin to lose their sharp sense of hearing from the age of five.

Neck and torso

The backbone, or spine, is composed of many individual, cylindrical bones called vertebrae. A solid but highly flexible stem, this backbone is the skeleton's central axis and extends from the skull at one end of the cat to the tip of the tail. Running the length of the backbone is the spinal canal, which is occupied by the spinal cord.

Seven cervical vertebrae form the neck; they are connected to 13 thoracic vertebrae each supporting a pair of ribs which, together with the breastbone, make up the rib cage. Owing to their length, the seven lumbar vertebrae between the rib cage and the pelvis make the backbone especially flexible. Three fused vertebrae which form the sacrum, the last bone of the spine, are firmly anchored to the three pelvic bones—the ilium, the ischium and the pubis—to create the rigid cup of the pelvis.

Behind the sacrum are 20 to 24 tail bones, called caudal vertebrae. These give the cat's long tail the flexibility necessary to act as a counterbalance. This becomes important when the animal is climbing a tree or walking along the top of a fence. In some breeds, these caudal vertebrae have atrophied, resulting in a kinked tail, as in some Siamese breeds. One breed, the Manx, has no tail at all yet still manages to maintain a good sense of balance.

The ligaments that run the length of the spine connecting the vertebrae are relatively small and leave considerable room for muscle. This makes the backbone flexible, allowing the cat to stretch its back and propel itself forward in a series of leaps and bounds. The cat is a sprinter, and a domestic cat in good shape can run at 30 miles (48 kilometres) an hour.

Inside the rib cage, or thorax, which extends to the diaphragm in the rear, are the two lungs, the heart and the large blood vessels, as well as part of the oesophagus, the tube that carries food from the throat to the stomach. Air enters the lungs through the trachea, commonly called the

Thoracic and abdominal organs
(front leg, torso wall and diaphragm removed)

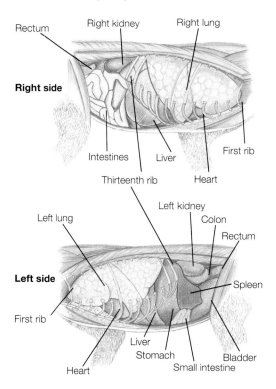

windpipe. Above the heart, this separates into two large bronchial tubes that enter the lungs, subdividing repeatedly until they become tiny air sacs called alveoli. This is where oxygenation of the blood takes place—and at a much higher rate of exchange than in humans. The cat's heart beats 110 to 140 times a minute, which is about twice as fast as a human heart. When a cat is excited, the heart rate can increase to 240 beats per minute.

Each lung is enclosed in a kind of double-walled membrane, called the pleura, whose inner wall is joined to the lungs and whose outer wall lines the thorax. A small quantity of liquid in the space between these two thin sheets allows the surfaces of the lungs to slide against the

thoracic wall as the cat breathes. Too much of this liquid can compress the lungs.

The egg-shaped heart lies almost on top of the breastbone, its point facing the rear. Just in front of the heart, in the space between the right and left pleural sacs between the lungs, is the thymus. If a cat gets thymic lymphosarcoma, an increasingly common cancer in young cats infected with feline leukemia virus, the lymph nodes enlarge considerably.

The abdominal cavity is bounded by the abdominal muscles, the sublumbar muscles and the diaphragm, with the pelvic cavity behind.

At the front of the abdominal cavity and just below the diaphragm are the liver, the stomach, the pancreas and the spleen. In the sublumbar region near the backbone, but not tightly attached to the body wall, are the kidneys, the adrenal glands and, in the female cat, the ovaries. The bladder is close to the entrance to the pelvis. The abdominal region also contains the intestines, and, in the female cat, houses the uterus as well.

Most of the abdomen's internal organs are enclosed in the peritoneum, a double-walled membrane resembling the pleural sacs. One side of the membrane fits closely around the organs and their blood vessels; the other is attached to the abdomen wall. Inflammation of the peritoneum causes fluid buildup and a dangerous condition called peritonitis.

The digestive tract includes all the organs that perform digestion, and these are not concentrated solely in the stomach. Digestion starts in the mouth with the salivary glands and continues into the pharynx, or throat, which leads through the oesophagus to the stomach. A cat's stomach can hold about 12 fluid ounces (350 millilitres).

The digestive juices in the stomach break down the food which moves slowly through to the intestines—the small intestine, 3 to 5 feet (1 to 1.5 metres) long and consisting of the duodenum, the jejunum, and the ileum, and the large intestine, 8 to 16 inches (20 to 40 centimetres) long and comprising the cecum, the colon, and the rectum. The duodenum receives secretions from two very important auxiliary organs: bile from the liver and digestive enzymes from the pancreas. The liver and the pancreas also serve as endocrine glands, secreting substances into the blood that are crucial for regulating the cat's blood sugar levels.

The digestive process is completed in the small intestine, where much of the liquid is removed. The remaining semi-solid waste travels into the large intestine and is then expelled through the anus.

Two anal sacs are located on either side of the anus. Researchers think the liquid discharged from these sacs by healthy cats serves to mark out a cat's territory, but there is as yet no scientific proof of this. Occasionally these sacs become blocked, causing discomfort to the cat.

The urinary tract contains organs concerned with the formation and excretion of urine. The urine itself is produced by the

Female urogenital apparatus, front view

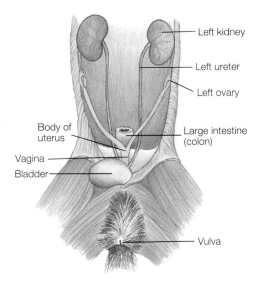

kidneys, a pair of yellowish, bean-shaped organs, each weighing approximately 3/4 ounce (20 grams). Their main function is to filter waste products from the blood and eliminate them with any excess water in the body. The urine travels down the ureters to the bladder, where it remains until forced out through the urethra during urination. In the female, this canal leads to the base of the vulva, while in the male it extends into the penis.

The genital apparatus includes the reproductive organs. Its anatomy, similar in both sexes when the embryo is first forming, becomes male or female shortly before birth. During the first five or six weeks, the male's testicles are not visible. As a result, it is quite easy to confuse male and female kittens.

The gonads are glands that produce sex hormones as well as ova in the female and spermatozoa in the male. These unite during fertilization. The female gonads, or ovaries, are two almond-shaped bulbs about 1/3 inch (8 millimetres) long located directly behind the kidneys. In the male, the gonads are the two testicles, which are carried in a pouch, the scrotum, in the perineal region under the anus. These appear in the same location as the

ovaries in the embryo, and then migrate through the abdomen and its muscle wall to their final position in the scrotum.

In some cases, the testicles may fail to descend, remaining instead inside the abdomen, a condition called cryptorchidism. When this happens, they cannot produce sperm but continue to generate the male hormone, testosterone. Castration, in these cases, requires removal of the testicles that are inside the abdomen.

In the female, the genital tract begins with the fallopian tubes that are attached to the ovaries from which they collect ova. This is where fertilization, the union of the sperm and the ovum, occurs after mating. Each tube leads to a Y-shaped uterus, a 2- to 3-inch (5- to 8-centimetre) long, 1/8-inch (3-millimetre) diameter canal that expands considerably during gestation to

Male urogenital apparatus, left side view

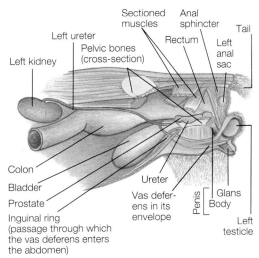

accommodate the foetuses. A cylindrical cervix links the uterus and vagina. The female's external genitalia—the vulva, consisting of two skin folds called labia, and a small erect clitoris—guard the cervix.

Puberty most often occurs in the female cat when she is about nine months old, though she may have her first heat as early as four months of age. The cat's usual gestation period is about 65 days, and kittens born before the 57th day are very unlikely to survive. At the other extreme, though, live kittens have been born after the 72nd day.

In the male, spermatozoa from the testicles move up a duct called the vas deferens, which enters the abdomen where it connects to the urethra. The prostate gland, which produces part of the fluid found in semen, is located here. In cats, the prostate is small and does not entirely surround the urethra. This might explain why these animals rarely have prostate problems, a common affliction of aging human males. A more likely reason is that most male cats are neutered when quite young.

The penis, the male organ of copulation, is towards the rear, and contains two erectile tissues reinforced with a penile bone almost 1 inch (2.5 centimetres) long. During erection, these fill with blood so that coitus can take place and the sperm can be deposited in the female's genital tract. The head of the penis, the glans, bristles with hooked spines, or papillae, that disappear after castration. A fold of skin called the foreskin covers the glans.

The female usually has four pairs of teats, two on the chest and two on the abdomen; these are occasionally supplemented by a fifth pair located in the fold of the groin. Males also have teats.

Limbs

Except for a few specific adaptations, the cat's front legs have the same bone structure as human legs.

The collar-bone is reduced to a bony vestige that lies concealed within the muscles, though it is visible in frontal X-rays of the shoulder. As in most quadruped mammals, the front leg is not rigidly attached to the torso. The thorax is suspended between the front legs by serrated muscles, which makes for good shock absorption when a cat lands from a jump.

The paw consists of a number of bones, tendons, and ligaments that together help give the cat its superb agility. The wrist, or carpus, of each front paw has seven bones—five metacarpals in the palm and a pollex, or dew-claw, with two bones. Each of the four toes consists of three bones called the first, second, and third phalanxes. The paw's highly developed muscles allow the toes to spread, while the radius is hinged on the ulna inside the front leg so that the palm can rotate as it does in humans. Just watch a cat play with a mouse or climb a tree and you will see how it uses its front legs. Each hind paw has a tarsus with seven bones, including five metatarsals; and four toes, each with three phalanxes.

The cat walks on the tips of its toes, using only the four digits of each front paw, since the short dew-claw, or thumb, does not reach the ground. The underside of the paw has skin pads of elastic fibre and fatty tissue.

These are hairless, but are covered with a tough outer skin, which may be pigmented. These pads have a lot of nerve

Front right paw, bottom view

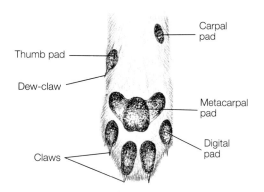

- Carpal pad
- Thumb pad
- Dew-claw
- Metacarpal pad
- Digital pad
- Claws

endings and are highly sensitive to pressure. They also contain eccrine sweat glands so that when a cat gets agitated, its paws, like a nervous human's hands, become sweaty. If the cat walks on a clean surface, the pads will leave visible wet spots in their path.

Each front paw has seven pads, five with digits, one larger, heart-shaped metacarpal (palm) pad, and one carpal pad located higher up the foreleg. Each digit is tipped by a claw, a curved hollow spike extending from the final (third) phalanx and held in place by a section of skin which produces the claw, and is called the germinal epithelium. As the claw grows, it produces overlapping and flat-

The claw-sheathing mechanism

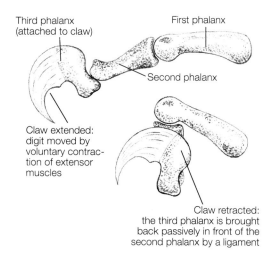

Third phalanx (attached to claw)

First phalanx

Second phalanx

Claw extended: digit moved by voluntary contraction of extensor muscles

Claw retracted: the third phalanx is brought back passively in front of the second phalanx by a ligament

tened cones that curve downwards to a sharp point. These are regularly shed through wear or when the cat sharpens its claws on something rough. The outer part of the claw falls off like a scale, leaving a new claw with its sharp point. Unlike the tough, thick nails of the dog, the cat's claws do not get worn down by scraping the ground when it walks because they are completely retractable.

A flexible ligament connects the upper surfaces of the second and third phalanxes of each digit, allowing the third one to tilt upwards and retract in front of the second one, where it is hidden in a deep sheath of skin. The claws are extended only when the cat pulls on digit-connecting muscles. Since this is a voluntary contraction, the cat can extend or sheathe its claws at will.

The back legs are firmly attached to the pelvis by a ball and socket joint at the top of the femur and extend like springs when the cat leaps or runs. The back legs have fewer claws—four, because there is no dew-claw—and only five pads. The function of the claws in the back legs is limited to supporting the cat during climbing. Compared to the sharper claws in the front legs, they are less retractable, duller and much shorter.

Skin

As every cat owner knows, the cat's skin is pliable and in some places hangs very loosely from the body. Interestingly, the skin is exceedingly thin, but even so, it is made up of many elements: the hair, whiskers, sweat and sebaceous glands, and anal sacs. Like the skin itself, the hair and whiskers contain microscopic granules of melanin, a brownish-black pigment. Variations in colour come from the amount of melanin present in skin and hair. Generally speaking, the more melanin, the darker the cat: the less melanin, the lighter it will be. (The fur takes on the colour of the the skin.)

Cat skin in cross-section

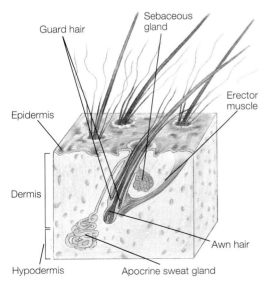

Guard hair
Sebaceous gland
Epidermis
Erector muscle
Dermis
Hypodermis
Apocrine sweat gland
Awn hair

However, light and temperature influence the degree to which melanin is activated. If a cat is genetically disposed to be white, for example, its coat will contain light-reflecting elements that interfere with full activation. Accordingly, the cat may be lighter than the concentration of melanin would suggest. This is why a Siamese who spends time outdoors may have a substantially lighter colour than one who remains in the house.

Cat hairs are produced in tiny cutaneous cavities called hair follicles, which receive secretions from the sebaceous and apocrine sweat glands. Tiny muscles are attached to the base of some hairs, and these erector muscles can bristle and puff up the fur when a cat is scared, preparing for a fight or wants to intimidate an adversary. The cat has three kinds of hair: down hair, the soft, crinkled hair that forms the undercoat; guard hair, the topcoat, which is the longest; and awn hair, which is not as long as guard hair, but is denser depending on where it is on the cat.

Fur colour

Fur may be classified as solid or self-coloured, shade, smoke, tabby, pointed, or multicoloured. A coat is solid when hair from root to tip is one basic colour—mostly black, blue, chestnut, chocolate, cinnamon, cream, ebony, fawn, lavender, lilac, red, or white.

Shade and smoke indicate a white undercoat with tinting occurring somewhere along the shaft. (If only the tip of the shaft is tinted, it is called shade; very pronounced tipping is described as smoke.)

Tabby coats, characterized by the striped markings inherited from the cat's wild ancestors, are determined by two sets of genes: the tabby gene is responsible for the pattern of vertical stripes, longitudinal bands, spots, or ticked coats such as those in the Abyssinian breed; the agouti gene determines the underlying pattern, in effect the colour between the stripes.

Pointeds have a pale body colour with darker hair on what are called the points—the nose, ears, paws, and tail. Siamese, Himalayan, Balinese, and Birman are among the pointed breeds. The dark colouring at the points is linked to warm temperatures, which activate melanin in the skin. At high temperatures, the hair is only lightly coloured, while at low temperatures it takes on a darker hue. Kittens have a paler coat at birth and then darken slightly as they mature. Similarly, cats kept in warmly heated homes or living in tropical zones remain paler than pointeds that spend a substantial period of their time outdoors. After shearing, in preparation for surgery for example, the body hair grows in darker, but will not take very long to lighten.

A typical multicolour coat is tortoiseshell, which can appear with or without the addition of white. When it appears with white, it is called calico. Basic tortoiseshell is a patchwork of black and orange, sometimes mottled, with areas coloured anywhere from chocolate to cinnamon, blue and lilac. The tortoiseshell pattern is found in females and also, though rarely, in males carrying two X chromosomes. When white is present, for genetic reasons, the three colours tend to occur in larger patches scattered randomly over the whole body.

The blue Maltese dilution is a recessive characteristic which dilutes black to blue as in the Chartreux breed, orange to cream, and the seal point of the Siamese to a blue point. In black-haired cats, melanin is distributed uniformly along the hair. In a cat with blue dilution, melanin grains are clumped irregularly. The large variety of colourings in cat breeds today is due to the interchange of characteristics between three original groups: the European, the Persian, and the Oriental. Some cat associations now recognize 148 coat varieties in the Persian breed alone.

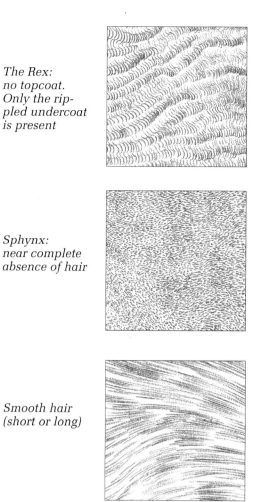

The Rex:
no topcoat.
Only the rippled undercoat
is present

Sphynx:
near complete
absence of hair

Smooth hair
(short or long)

Fur texture

Coats may be soft and silky or thick and coarse, depending on the fur type—short-haired, long-haired, curly, or wire-haired. There are hairless varieties, too, but even these cats have fur on their faces, ears, paws, and tails.

Short-hair is genetically dominant in cats, long-hair being a recessive trait. In short-hair cats, the longer guard hairs measure almost 2 inches (about 5 centimetres), while the coat of a good show Persian can be 5 inches (12.5 centimetres) long.

The so-called hairless Sphynx is not really hairless, but has a short, extremely fine, almost suede-like coat. Curly hair occurs in two major breeds: the Devon Rex and the Cornish Rex. Wire-hair breeds are characterized by rough coats that are irregularly frizzy or barbed.

The cat's fur protects it from excessive heat and cold. When it is hot, the cat is able to raise its fur away from its body to allow the circulation of some cooler air.

Cat whiskers, or vibrissae, are stiff and very long. The nerve endings at the roots of the cat's moustache and eyebrows make these whiskers very sensitive organs, much like antennae. Cats use their whiskers to sense the location of prey or of obstacles in the dusk. Cats also may use their whiskers like a distant-early-warning system to tell them if there is danger nearby. A cat on the lookout will swivel its ears, use its wide-eyed vision, and push its whiskers forward, ready to spring into action—or to head back into a safe place if it senses too much danger. Small whiskers are also found on the cat's front legs behind the carpus, or wrist.

The sebaceous glands produce an oil, called sebum, that forms a film on the skin to keep it from dehydrating. When spread on the fur by grooming, the sebum makes the hairs supple and brilliant. The sebaceous glands are concentrated under the chin, between the toes, where the skin meets the mucus membrane, and under the tail.

Cats have two different kinds of sweat glands. They differ according to how they secrete and where they are. Apocrine glands are found in the same locations as sebaceous glands; eccrine glands are found only on the paw pads. These glands are fairly insignificant because sweat plays no role in cooling the feline body, as it does in the case of horses and humans.

ALBUM
OF CATS

Preface to
the Album of Cats

What does an Egyptian Mau look like? What colour will my Persian's kittens be? Is there such a thing as a Red Point Burmese? Where does the hairless cat come from? Why is the Siamese's nose so long and the Persian's so short? What is a cobby cat? These are some of the questions we will attempt to answer in this section.

The Album of Cats opens with a Catalogue of Breeds, introduced by a three-page pictorial table of contents. For fast, easy reference, this catalogue of 44 breeds has been arranged alphabetically. (Note, however, that the Cymric and the Nebelung are shown with the Manx and the Russian Blue respectively.) The page, or spread, on each featured cat outlines the origins and history of that particular breed, describes the breed conformation and ideal coat, has a chart showing how championship points are allocated, tips on what lessens a cat's competitiveness at shows, and information on the genetic makeup and cross-breeding possibilities. Characteristics are based on standards of The International Cat Association (TICA). Accompanying each featured cat are an illustration of an ideal specimen and six small squares that identify countries where the breed is registered and/or recognized by at least one cat association. Countries are identified by the following abbreviations: AUS. for Australia, CAN. for Canada, N.Z. for New Zealand, S.AF. for South Africa, U.K. for the United Kingdom, and U.S.A. for the United States of America.

Five pages of what are sometimes termed exotic breeds follow the alphabetized, main section of the catalogue. Though accepted by some registries, these are cats that have not yet gained widespread recognition.

Sections on genetics and colours provide detailed information on the standards and characteristics for all parts of the body, on colours, on outcrossing, and on genetic anomalies. The album ends with a glossary that defines the technical terms used regularly by cat lovers, breeders, judges, and veterinarians.

Before consulting the catalogue, note that cats are classified according to three categories of coat:
• the Shorthairs, the largest group, which includes Siamese, British and American Shorthairs, and Exotic Shorthairs;
• the Semi-longhairs, with soft, silky fur, such as the Angora, Maine Coon, Balinese, and Norwegian;
• the Longhairs, actually the many different colours of a single breed—the magnificent Persian.

Within each coat category, there are a number of sub-categories related to build: cobby (sturdy and rounded) and semi-cobby, foreign (tubular) and semi-foreign. There are also sub-categories for the orientals and for the large, powerful cats such as the Maine Coon and the Ragdoll. All these categories and colours will become familiar as you read about the wide range of breeds. Some of them are unusual, some surprising, but all are fascinating.

Abyssinian, p. 66

American Bobtail, p. 68

American Shorthair, p. 72

American Wirehair, p. 74

American Curl, p. 70

Balinese, p. 75

Bengal, p. 77

Birman, p. 79

Bombay, p. 81

British Shorthair, p. 82

Burmese, p. 84

Burmilla, p. 137

California Spangled, p. 86

Chartreux, p. 88

Cornish Rex, p. 90

Cymric, p. 107

Devon Rex, p. 92

Egyptian Mau, p. 94

Exotic Shorthair, p. 96

German Rex, p. 138

Havana Brown, p. 98

Himalayan, p. 99

Household pet, p. 100

Japanese Bobtail, p. 101

Japanese Bobtail Longhair, p. 102

Korat, p. 103

Maine Coon, p. 104

Manx, p. 106

Nebelung, p. 120

Norwegian, p. 108

Ocicat, p. 110

Oriental Longhair, p. 111

Oriental Shorthair, p. 112

Black Persian, p. 115

Cameo Persian, p. 115

Brown Tabby Persian, p. 116

Calico Persian, p. 114

Chinchilla Persian, p. 117

Golden Persian, p. 116

Red Persian, p. 115

Smoke Persian, p. 115

Tortoiseshell Persian, p. 116

Ragdoll, p. 118

Scottish Fold, p. 121

Scottish Fold Longhair, p. 122

Russian Blue, p. 119

Siamese, p. 123

Singapura, p. 126

Snowshoe, p. 128

Somali, p. 129

Sphynx, p. 130

Tonkinese, p. 133

Turkish Angora, p. 135

Turkish Van, p. 136

Abyssinian

The Abyssinian comes first in this catalogue because of the alphabet, but its position is well merited. An imposing appearance, striking carriage, and lively intelligence have earned the Abyssinian a foremost place in the feline hierarchy. Its rich, warm colours and long, agile body make this beautiful cat an obvious cousin to the cougar and the puma.

By temperament though, the Abyssinian is gentle and friendly. It is also lively and athletic, and therefore less suited to apartment living than other breeds. According to some owners, it has one unusual trait—it loves to play in water.

AUS.	CAN.	N.Z.	S.AF.	U.K.	U.S.A.
●	●	●	●	●	●

The Abyssinian is active, curious, and as well balanced physically as it is psychologically. This exceptionally energetic animal requires plenty of space if it is to develop as it should.

Ancestor of them all?

Documents and mummified animal remains from ancient Egypt have convinced many people that the Abyssinian is the ancestor of the domestic cat. Whether this is true or not, the characteristics of the breed have changed scarcely at all since it was first recognized in Britain in 1882. Initially, its basic colouring was similar to that of a hare. Since then, breeders have developed many other colours, giving the Abyssinian a wide-ranging palette of subtle shades.

This medium-sized cat—the male is larger than the female—shows a fine but firm muscular development and athletic look. Its legs are long and it moves with grace and fluidity.

Characteristics

Head: Viewed from the front, a modified wedge with rounded contours. In profile, showing gently curved transition between brow, nose, and muzzle with no flat planes. Rise from the bridge of the nose to the forehead with no sharp break. Of ample length, in balance with the rest of the cat, and gently curved from the forehead over the skull into an arched neck. Muzzle gently contoured to conform with the head. Chin full and rounded, neither projecting nor receding. Allowance made for jowls in adult males. No snippiness, foxy appearance, or whisker pinch.

Ears: Large, alert, moderately pointed, broad, cupped at base, and arched forward as though listening. Hair on ears short, preferably tipped to match colour requirements. Thumbprint mark is desirable on the back of the ear.

Eyes: Almond-shaped, large, brilliant, and expressive, neither round nor oriental. Eyes accentuated by darker lids, encircled by a lighter area. Short, vertical pencil stroke above each eye. Curved pencil line at the side of each eye.

Body: Medium-long, lithe, and graceful, showing well-developed muscles without coarseness. Solid to the feel. Rounded rib cage without flat sides, back slightly arched. Proportion and general balance more important than size. Legs proportionately slim, long, and well muscled. Abyssinian stands well off the ground. Feet oval and compact when standing, giving the impression of being on tiptoe. Long, tapering tail.

Coat: Coat fine and resilient to the touch, with a lustrous sheen. Medium length, long enough to accommodate four of six alternating light and dark coloured bands. Coat longest at the spine, gradually shortening over the saddle, flank, legs, and head.

Colours
(four are recognized in show breeds):
• **Ruddy:** Orange-brown (burnt sienna), ticked with two or three bands of black or dark brown. Outer parts of the body have at least one band of ticking. Darker shadings along spine if fully ticked. Underside of body, chest, and inside of legs an even orange-brown without ticking, barring, necklaces, or belly marks. Colour varies from warm apricot to deeper burnt sienna. White or off-white on only the upper throat, lips, and around nostrils. Tail tipped with black, without rings or grey. *Paw pads:* Black or dark brown with black between toes and just beyond paws. *Eye colour:* Gold, copper, green, or hazel, the more richness and depth the better. *Nose leather:* Brick-tile red.

• **Sorrel (Cinnamon):** Warm sorrel red ticked with chocolate brown. *Paw pads:* Pink with chocolate brown between toes. *Eye colour:* Same as ruddy. *Nose leather:* Rosy pink.

• **Blue:** Warm, soft blue-grey ticked with deeper blue. Base hair and undersides of the body, chest, and inside of legs pale cream, spine darker. Tail tipped with deep blue. *Paw pads:* Blue-mauve with blue between toes. *Eye colour:* Same as ruddy. *Nose leather:* Dark pink.

• **Fawn:** Warm pinkish buff ticked with a deeper shade of pinkish buff. Base hair, underside of the body, chest, and inside of legs pale oatmeal. Spine darker. Tail tipped with deep pinkish buff. *Paw pads:* Pink-mauve with deep pinkish buff between toes. *Eye colour:* Same as ruddy. *Nose leather:* Pink-mauve.

Subject to penalty: *Colour*—Cold, grey, or sandy tone to coat colour in ruddies or sorrels, or grey hair next to skin with absence of correct undercoat colour. Broken necklaces, leg bars, mottling or speckling in unticked areas (underside of body, chest, and inside legs), tabby stripes or bars. Slick coat or excessive plushness. Wrong colour or patching in pads. *Ticking and pattern*—Unevenness, lack of desired markings on head and tail. *Condition*—Flabbiness, lack of coat lustre, eye colour, evidence of illness, emaciation, lack of good muscle tone.

Disqualifying fault: White locket, or white anywhere except around nostril, chin, and upper throat. Unbroken necklace. Reversed ticking—outermost tip of hair light instead of dark.

Basic genetic makeup of a homozygous ruddy Abyssinian:
AA BB CC DD LL $T^a T^a$ *(see pages 142-151)*

Mating authorized with other breeds:
Yes, with the Somali.

TICA Standards	Points
Head	30
Coat texture	10
Body	35
Colour and pattern	25

American Bobtail

If this animal were to bear a label, it would read 'Made by hand in the U.S.A.'

In the 1960s, an American family named Sanders was vacationing in an Arizona motel near an Indian reservation. There they spotted a wild-looking yet friendly male kitten with an unusually short, upraised tail. Since the animal appeared homeless, they adopted him, naming him Yodie. The new pet soon became friends with Mishi, the family Siamese, and the two animals mated before there was time to have Yodie neutered.

Some kittens from the resulting litter were black, the rest tabby; some had the short tail of their father, others the long one of their mother. A few kittens from the litter found homes with friends of the Sanders family, but others began to live on their own in the wild.

Standards proposed

Soon afterwards fate intervened in the shape of a cream point and white cat. It mated with one of Yodie and Mishi's offspring, and the result was a litter of white and colour points with quite short tails. A neighbour of the Sanders, Mindy Schultz, was charmed by these kittens and drew up a possible list of characteristics for the breed she called the American Bobtail. At the time–the 1970s–she described the breed as a colour point with a shortened and knotted or slightly curled upraised tail, showing white on the paws and breast, and a white blaze on the nose.

Originally the breed's fur was short, but crossing with Himalayans, which are colour-point

AUS.	CAN.	N.Z.	S.AF.	U.K.	U.S.A.
	●				●

The ideal American Bobtail should resemble a small lynx sporting its winter coat. It is a strong, stocky cat. Good-tempered, calm, gentle, and patient, it is a breed that adapts well to other animals. An excellent hunter, it can run extremely fast for short periods. It prefers keeping to the ground to scrambling up trees, and its most favoured spots are the soft cushions of its owners' living-room furniture.

Persians, eventually resulted in a very dense, semi-long coat. The animal was also crossed with other breeds, and some lines resulted in litters that had no tails at all— kittens similar to the variety known as the Manx. A Manx with no tail is called a Rumpy, while one that displays a tail measuring 1 to 4 inches (2.5 to 10 cm), like that of the Bobtail, is called a Stumpy. In fact, the Bobtail is the result of the same genetic mutation that had given rise to the Manx a century before; varying lengths of tail among this group are quite usual.

Characteristics

General description: A stocky, heavy, long-haired cat of medium size. Well fleshed and muscular without being overly fat. Short tail. Medium coat should be double, dense, and shaggy.

Head: Broad with strong jaws, without flat planes. Top of the head should be slightly rounded. Muzzle almost as long as it is wide, tapering slightly. There should be a slight muzzle break, with full cheeks. Chin full and strong, and well developed in males. In profile, the nose has a gentle dip between the eyes.

Ears: Medium-sized ears are wide at the base and set well down on the head in an alert position. Slightly rounded, with lynx tipping preferred, and with long hairs inside.

Eyes: Large, oval in shape and tipped slightly upward to the outside corner of the ears. Colour must conform to coat colour, but is considered only when all other points are equal.

Body: Stocky, rounded, and well muscled, and slightly longer than tall. Neck length medium, though it may appear shorter because of the ruff and the cat's strong muscles. Back should have a slight curve from the withers to the base of the tail. Chest broad and full, and the hips substantial. Muscles and bones should also feel strong and substantial. Body shape semi-cobby. Males are heavily built, with wide shoulders and a muscular appearance. Females are also muscular, but may be smaller. Hind legs may be slightly longer than the front legs. Feet are large and may have toe tufts. Tail long enough to be visible, but should not extend below the knee of the hind leg. The tail may be straight, knotted, or slightly curled, but it must have longer hair than rest of body.

Coat: Medium-length, double coat has a shaggy appearance. May be longer on the ruff, britches, and tail, although ruff itself may be slight. Texture must be non-matting and have the density of a double coat with a thick undercoat. Seasonal variations in coat are recognized.

Subject to penalty: Tail that is too long or too short. Coat that lies flat on the body. Too fine-boned or foreign type. Extremely short muzzle; nose break.

Disqualifying fault: If there is no tail at all, or if the tail is full length.

Basic genetic makeup of a homozygous seal point American Bobtail:
aa BB c^sc^s DD LL *(see pages 142-151)*

Mating authorized with other breeds:
Yes, while the standards remain open.

TICA Standards	Points
Head	25
Ears	5
Eyes	5
Body	25
Legs and feet	5
Tail	5
Colour/pattern	5
Coat	15
Condition and balance	10

American Curl

This animal's name makes its origins clear: American because it was first discovered in Lakewood, California, and Curl because of its attractively curled ears.

Set on the outer corners of the head, the ears curve back in a smooth arc away from the face, pointing towards the centre of the skull. The insides of the ears are full of tufts of fur that stick out like antennae. Firm cartilage makes the ears quite hard to the touch. This cat's unique ears are the result of a spontaneous mutation rather than genetic engineering—the product of a happy marriage between domestic cats.

Shorthair and longhair

The American Curl is a medium-sized cat, well proportioned, solid, and surprisingly heavy for its size. By the time it is fully mature, between 2 and 3 years of age, it weighs from 7 to 11 pounds (3 to 5 kg).

In the long-haired variety, the coat is moderately long and smooth, without an undercoat, and not at all woolly. The coat has a glossy shine and a silky texture that is very pleasing to the touch. The Shorthair American Curl has a thick, non-woolly coat, also very soft and silky.

As is the case for many new breeds, the conformation of the American Curl is still being devel-

AUS.	CAN.	N.Z.	S.AF.	U.K.	U.S.A.
	●				●

A NEW BREED WITH A SHORT HISTORY

In 1981, two stray kittens were found on the doorstep of a Mr. and Mrs. Joe Ruga. One of the kittens, a black female with unusual curled ears, decided to stay. The couple called her Shulamith. On December 12, 1981, she gave birth to four kittens, two of which displayed the same peculiar ears as their mother. A friend of the Rugas was keen to have this new breed recognized, and she entered Shulamith in a show in Palm Springs, California. Judges, breeders, and the general public all proved enthusiastic.

In 1985, the breed was officially registered by TICA under the name of the American Curl.

oped. Only after many meetings, much deliberation, and many votes by cat associations and breeders to recognize the breed and decide on its standards did the Curl earn its place in the well-bred cat world.

Breeders debate whether the Curl should be more cobby, that is more sturdy and rounded, or have a finer shape, whether it should be long-haired or short-haired, and so on. But, there is universal agreement about the ears. Three angles of inclination are permitted: in the first and least admired, the ear is hardly turned back at all; in the second, it is a little more curved; and in the third and most preferred curl, it forms a complete crescent.

Since the gene that transmits this curvature of the ear is dominant, the peculiarity need only be present in a single parent to be passed on. The cartilage of the ear does not start to curve or harden until the fourth day of life, and the curvature does not take its final form until the fourth month.

> The American Curl has both the look and the personality of a pixie: mischievous, intelligent, lively, funny, curious. It is also a bit of a thief, very affectionate towards its owners, something of a character, and well integrated both physically and mentally.

Characteristics

General description: The distinctive feature of the breed is its unique, attractively curled ears. Set on the corners of the head, they curve back in a smooth arc away from the face and point towards the back of the skull. The American Curl is a well-balanced, medium-sized cat, weighing 7 to 11 pounds (3 to 5 kg), and taking two to three years to reach maturity. Conformation is more important than size.

Head: In profile, a straight nose with a slight rise from the bottom of the eyes to the forehead, a gentle curve to the top of the skull, and a firm, even chin. The head is a modified wedge, more long than wide. Muzzle neither pointed nor square; gentle transition to muzzle break.

Ears: The degree of curl should be in a 90-degree arc or better, but not more than 180 degrees. Wide at the base, then curving back in a smooth arc and ending in rounded tips. Moderately large, erect, and set on corners of head facing outwards at a slight angle, curling back away from the face towards the back of the head. Inside hairs must be well extended; lynx tips desirable.

Eyes: Walnut-shaped, moderately large and set on a slight bias about one eye-width apart. Colour has no relation to coat colour, except blue eyes in the Pointed Division.

Body: Semi-foreign and 1 1/2 times longer than the cat's height at its shoulder. Body size and bone structure are intermediate—neither heavy

nor fine. Tail must be wide at the base, tapering, and equal to the body length. Legs and feet neither heavy nor fine, set straight when viewed from front or rear. Muscles must be firm and moderately developed in both strength and tone. Feet medium and round.

Coat: Texture must be silky, with a minimal undercoat. Hair semi-long and lying flat, with the tail coat full and plumed.

Subject to penalty: Ears low set, mismatched, or pinched; a vertical crimp or horizontal kink, or corrugated on inner surface. Any deep nose break, a heavy undercoat, ruffs, or coarse texture. Colour on buttons, lockets.

Disqualifying fault: An extreme curl in an adult, where the tip of the ear touches the back of the ear or the head. Any ear lacking firm cartilage from the base to at least one-third of its height; tail faults.

Basic genetic makeup of a homozygous blue long-haired American Curl:
aa BB CC dd ll *(see pages 142-151)*

Mating authorized with other breeds: No.

TICA Standards	Points
Head	15
Ears	30
Eyes	10
Body	30
Coat and colour	15

American Shorthair

This cat, a descendant of domestic cats brought to North America by European settlers, was originally simply called the Shorthair. As short-haired breeds increased on the continent, breeders decided a more specific name was required; and so this cat became the Domestic Shorthair. The first of the breed to be registered in a stud-book was a male Orange Tabby from Britain called Champion Belle of Bradford. Belle was born on June 1, 1900. The first to become a show champion was a white female with blue eyes, born in April 1948 and called Nor Month' Angelique.

Cat fanciers vacillated about the breed for several more years. The cats often competed in household pet categories of shows since championship classes frequently offered no rosettes or trophies for Domestic class winners. But some breeders persevered, continuing to show their animals at every opportunity. In 1966 they renamed the breed the American Shorthair.

A perfect balance

The breed's reputation then improved dramatically, thanks largely to a male Silver Tabby called Shawnee Trademark winning the 'Best Cat of the Year' award in 1965. Despite the resulting surge in popularity, breeders have respected the animal's unsophisticated charm and allowed the processes of natural selection relatively free rein, rather than weakening the strain by inbreeding. The American Shorthair remains a well-proportioned and strong cat, the fine hunter it was on its arrival in the New World.

The American Shorthair is medium to large in size. It has a firm, powerful body, the males showing a particularly well-developed chest and hindquarters. The head is broad, with cheeks espe-

AUS.	CAN.	N.Z.	S.AF.	U.K.	U.S.A.
●	●				●

A BRIEF HISTORY

The most likely ancestor of this breed is the British Shorthair. Whatever its precise heritage, the American Shorthair is a pioneer. The first cats to arrive on North American shores were the companions of Europeans, including the Pilgrims of *Mayflower* fame, who crossed the Atlantic Ocean to North America in 1620. There was no free ride for these seagoing felines. It was their job to catch the rats that lived among the supplies filling the ships' holds. Because these cats reached North America from different parts of Europe, once ashore they could reproduce without the dangers of inbreeding. After some development of its genetic potential by breeders, the American Shorthair was eventually established as the healthy, solid, and well-balanced animal we know today.

cially developed in males. The nose and face are medium short, the eyes and ears set wide apart, and the muzzle squarish but not foreshortened. No part of the cat should look out of balance with any other part. It must appear solidly built, and above all symmetrical—of a shape, in other words, that gives an impression of agility and strength.

A working cat

The American Shorthair is the working cat par excellence. It combines patience, stamina, and the qualities of a great hunter with total self-control. It is constantly aware of its own capacities and potential, and of its position in space.

Its long, powerful limbs make the American Shorthair something of an all-terrain animal, while its solid muzzle pushes forward just enough to make grasping its prey in its firm, solid jaws an easy business. Its fur adapts well to all kinds of weather, being dense enough to protect it from cold, rain, wind, and minor injuries, but short and fine enough not to get easily tangled or to catch in the undergrowth.

TICA Standards	Points
Head	15
Nose	5
Ears	5
Neck	5
Chin	5
Eye shape	5
Eye colour	5
Body	20
Tail	5
Legs and feet	10
Colour	10
Coat	10

Characteristics

Head: Broad and rounded; in profile must show a slight depression in the forehead where it meets the foreface. Rounded skull reaches down to square cheeks and chin. Cheeks well developed in males. Nose medium to short.

Ears: Rounded at the tips and wide-set. Must not be too large at the base nor unduly open. Hair in ears must be short.

Eyes: Rounded, medium to large in size, set wide, at slight angle. Colour conforms to coat.

Body: Medium to large body is well-rounded, and rectangular rather than slender. Well-knit and powerful with a broad chest, especially in males. Neck medium-short and in proportion to the body, neither too short and thick nor too long and thin. Legs have medium bone structure and sturdy musculature. Medium-sized feet are rounded. Tail is thick at the base and of medium size, tapers from a well-rounded rump to a rounded tip. Taper must be slight, neither blunt nor pointed, and carried almost level with the back.

Coat: Short and even-textured with a lustrous and natural protective appearance. Must be close-lying. Colour: Solids, 10 points; others, 5 points for pattern and 5 points for colour.

Colour: All traditional colours are recognized as well as all tabby patterns. Best-known is the classic silver tabby: a shiny silver coat with perfectly contrasting black stripes. Must also have a letter 'M' on the forehead, its outside lines descending from the outside of the eyes to the cheeks.

Subject to penalty: Eye colours that are not completely green in the silvers, or not gold in the browns. Long and pointed ears, or ears set too closely together. Neck too short and thick, or too long, slender, and snake-like. The tail must not be thin or whip-like, nor too short and thick, nor carried over the back in a squirrel-like fashion. Body must not be foreshortened and stocky, nor long and sleek. Coat must not be fine, thin or long, and must not have a fluffy texture. The hindquarters must not be weak. No part of the cat should look out of balance with any other part.

Disqualifying fault: White buttons or lockets in the Solid Division.

Basic genetic makeup of a homozygous silver classic tabby American Shorthair:
AA BB CC DD S^i S^i LL t^b t^b

Mating authorized with other breeds: No.

American Wirehair

The Wirehair is a spontaneous mutation of the American Shorthair, in which the original breed's soft fur has become rough, springy, or hooked, and almost prickly to the touch. The tip of the guard, or primary, hairs is bent.

The Wirehair appeared originally in 1966 in Verona, New York. The first male kitten to display this unusual rough fur was called Adam, and all members of the breed currently registered are descended from him. The Wirehair gene is recessive; only two Wirehairs or a Wirehair and a carrier of the gene can produce Wirehair kittens. This explains the extreme rarity of these cats.

AUS.	CAN.	N.Z.	S.AF.	U.K.	U.S.A.
	●				●

TICA Standards	Points
Coat	45
Head	25
Body	20
Colour and eye colours	10

Characteristics

General description: All three hair types–down, awn, and guard–are present, resulting in a full coat, which should be short to medium-short.

Head: In proportion with the body, with rounded bone structure on back, sides and front. Nose and face medium-short, neither protruding nor foreshortened, with the nose showing a gentle concave curve. High cheekbones and moderately developed muzzle and chin.

Eyes and ears: Eyes round, medium to large, slightly tilted, bright and clear. Ears medium-large, rounded at the tips, set moderately close, neither widely flared nor erect.

Body: Medium-sized, rectangular with slightly rounded angles, a level back, and moderate boning. Somewhat trim and compact, yet well muscled. Torso neither too sturdy nor snaky.

Shoulders and hips the same width. Neck neither short and thick nor long and slender. Legs sturdy, in proportion to body. Paws compact. Tail tapers from the well-rounded rump to a rounded tip that is neither blunt nor pointed.

Colour: Clarity of both coat and eye colours desirable; no particular combination is favoured.

Subject to penalty: Deep nose break; fluffy coat.

Disqualifying fault: Incorrect coat.

Basic genetic makeup of a homozygous male red self American Wirehair:
BB CC DD LL OO Wh Wh
(see pages 142-151)

Mating authorized with other breeds: No.

Balinese

Some people have compared the Siamese cat to a graceful, scantily clad ballerina. The Balinese resembles another exquisite dancer, one whose elegance is masked by delicate silk veils. The reference, of course, is to the exotic Balinese dancers of the South Pacific.

In the same way that the Somali is a long-haired Abyssinian and the Exotic a short-haired Persian, the Balinese cat is a long-haired Siamese. Along with other long-haired cats, the Balinese probably originated in cold countries because it has a fine and full double coat. This winter coat, though not as thick and woolly as a Persian's, has thick, soft undercoat hairs and, covering these, a layer of coarser and slightly longer guard hairs. In some show cats, these guard hairs have been measured at almost 5 inches (12 cm) long. The Balinese, overcoat and all, is a svelte and dainty breed with all the elegance of a fashion model.

A struggle to be recognized

In the past, Siamese litters occasionally included a kitten with longer-than-average fur, especially around the ruff and hindquarters. Some breeders considered these long-coated 'sports' worthless and gave them away as pets. Others, however, saw them as 'miracles of mutation.' In fact, Balinese are neither, but rather the product of two carriers of the long-hair gene, present among certain Siamese who have an Angora ancestor many generations back. During the 1940s, U.S. breeders strove hard to get the breed recog-

AUS.	CAN.	N.Z.	S.AF.	U.K.	U.S.A.
✳	●	●	●	●	●

✳ In Australia the Balinese may also be known as Oriental Longhair. Check with local associations.

The character of the Balinese is very similar to that of its Siamese cousin. It is active, curious, lively, friendly, expressive, and loyal. Above all, it loves company, whether feline, canine, or human. It tends to fix its magnificent eyes of Mediterranean blue boldly on one's face.

75

nized, but it was not until 1968 that the Balinese Club was finally formed.

The conformation was recognized by various cat associations in 1970. Many clubs only accept certain colours—the Seal, Blue, Chocolate, and Lilac Point. They maintain that other colours (Tortie and Red Tabby, for example) belong to the Javanese breed.

The standards for the Balinese are identical to those for the Siamese. Elegance is the essential feature, since the length of the Balinese fur tends to give a slightly heavy look. Moreover, the breed is descended from an earlier type of Siamese that was somewhat stockier than those admired today.

To produce a finer Balinese, the cats must be outcrossed with contemporary Siamese. The kittens from these unions, known as variants, are short-haired, although their coat is fluffier and finer than that of a pure Siamese. But when these offspring are interbred or mated with a Balinese, the long fur reappears in the new litter. Breeders often remain dissatisfied with this solution, however, for although the body produced is finer and the feather-like tail is present, the fur is often not as long as desirable in the ruff and the hind-leg areas.

Like the Siamese, the Balinese craves attention and enjoys human companionship, though it usually relates best to one person.

Characteristics

Head: A long and tapering wedge of medium size. No break in the muzzle, and the skull should be flat. Cheeks smooth. Nose long and straight with no dip or bulge. Chin of medium size and in line with tip of nose.

Ears: Pointed and wide at their base, strikingly large, and a continuation of the wedge of the head. Should be held alertly.

Eyes: Almond-shaped, of medium size and slanted towards the nose in harmony with the lines of the head and the ears.

Body: Long and svelte, of medium size, and firmly muscled. Neck long and slender. Tail thin and tapering. Long legs mostly hidden by the heavy coat; hind legs longer than forelegs. Fine bone structure in legs. Small, oval feet.

Coat: The Balinese is a Siamese cat with a longer coat. Texture should be soft and silky.

Colour: TICA recognizes 15 colour divisions, divided into three major categories: Traditional Colour, Pointed Colour, and Intermediate Colour. The Balinese falls into the Pointed category along with other members of the long-haired Siamese group.

Basic genetic makeup of a homozygous female chocolate tortoiseshell Balinese:
aa bb c^S c^S DΓ ll Oo *(see pages 142-151)*

Mating authorized with other breeds:
Yes, with Siamese and Orientals.

TICA Standards	Points
Head and ears	20
Eyes	5
Body and tail	20
Coat	20
Body colour	10
Point colour	15
Condition	10

Bengal

The Bengal is a hybrid, the result of crossing domestic cats with the Leopard Cat of Asia. It is one of the most recent breeds to be created, but its conforming standards have already been accepted and recognized.

This large and powerful cat possesses a long and very muscular body; males can weigh up to 22 pounds (10 kg), females slightly less. The Bengal's likeness to its wild counterpart is obviously an important breeding feature.

A long selection process

In recent years especially, cat fanciers have been extremely ingenious in developing new breeds. One of the biggest successes has been the Bengal. The name is derived from the scientific name of the Asian leopard, *Felis prionailurus bengalensis*, its progenitor. It was with the aim of retaining the beauty of the jungle cat in a domestic setting that the Bengal was developed by cross-breeding the Asian Leopard Cat with domestic breeds such as the American Shorthair. The first kittens were bred with another spotted cat, the Egyptian Mau.

This breeding process took some time. The first hybrids were created in 1963, but the Bengal we know today was created in the late 1970s by Jean Mills of Covina, California. She obtained eight female cats cross-bred from an Asian Leopard Cat and domestic shorthairs by a University of California researcher. She mated them with two very different male cats: a feral orange domestic cat with deep brown spots from a zoo in India, and a brown-spotted tabby shorthair from an animal shelter in Los Angeles, California. Some 10 years later there were 200 Bengals in the United States and the breed was recognized by TICA. Bengals became eligible for show competitions in 1991.

AUS.	CAN.	N.Z.	S.AF.	U.K.	U.S.A.
●	●			●	●

From its jungle ancestors the Bengal has inherited a rather independent nature. It is a fine hunter and loves to wade in water. It also likes to climb and needs considerable activity—and consequently plenty of space. When playing, the kittens feint and prowl just as if they were really hunting, and attack their toys like prey.

The Bengal is not as vocal as some other breeds, but its voice, although not harsh, is strangely reminiscent of a wild animal's call. Though the breed is easy to care for, requiring the same amount of attention as any other domestic cat, take care when choosing a kitten. Temperaments vary; study its character carefully so that the kitten integrates well into the family group. If care is taken, you can become the proud owner of a friendly, miniature leopard.

Characteristics

General description: The goal of the Bengal breeding programme is to replicate the appearance of the wild leopard cat while maintaining the loving, dependable temperament of the domestic cat. In competition, the Bengal must be unchallenging; any sign of challenge will disqualify. It may exhibit fear, seek to flee, or complain aloud, but it must not threaten to harm. Bengals are confident, alert, and friendly.

Head: Broad with rounded contours, longer than it is wide. Allowance made for jowls in adult males. Slightly small in proportion to the body, but not taken to extreme. In profile, face curves gently from forehead to bridge of nose, which extends above the eyes. Nose has a slight concave curve and must be large and wide with a slightly puffed nose leather. Muzzle full and broad, with large, prominent whisker pads and high, pronounced cheekbones.

Ears: Medium-small and short, with a wide base and rounded tips; set as much on the side as on the top of the head. Ears follow contour of face and point forward alertly. Light horizontal furnishings inside ears are acceptable, but lynx tipping undesirable.

Eyes: Oval; may be slightly almond-shaped. Large but not bugged. Set back into the face, on a slight bias towards base of the ears. Any colour is acceptable except blue or aquamarine.

Body: Long and substantial, neither oriental nor foreign. Not quite as large as the largest domestic breeds. Bones are robust, never delicate. Muscular body, legs and neck, especially in males. Medium-length legs are slightly longer in back than in front. Feet large and round. Thick tail tapered at the end, with a rounded tip.

Coat: Short to medium in length; kittens may have a slightly long coat. Thick, luxurious, and unusually soft to the touch.

Pattern: Spots should be random, or aligned horizontally. Rosettes formed by a circle of spots around a distinctly redder centre are preferable to single spotting. Contrast with ground colour must be extreme, with distinct pattern and sharp edges. Strong, bold chin strap and mascara markings are desirable. Blotchy horizontal shoulder streaks also desirable. The belly must be spotted.
• **Marbled pattern:** Markings must be unique, with as little bull's-eye similarity as possible. Pattern should be random, giving the impression of marble. Vertical-striped mackerel pattern undesirable. Preference given to cats with three or more shades: ground colour, markings, and dark outlining.

Colour: All variations of the brown spotted tabby are allowed; however yellow, buff, tan, golden, or orange ground colours are preferred. Spots may be black, brown, tan, or shades of chocolate or cinnamon. White ground colour on whisker pads, chin, chest, belly, and inner legs desirable. Smoky undercoat not a fault. Rims of eyes, lips, and nose should be outlined with black, and centre of nose brick red. Paw pads and tail tip must be black.
• **Seal lynx point:** Spots can vary in colour from dark seal brown to light brown, tan, or buff. Ground colour should be ivory to cream. There should be little difference between body colour and point colour. Tail tip must be seal brown and may be as dark as black. Eye colour blue.
• **Sepia or seal mink tabby:** Ground colour should be ivory, cream, or light tan with pattern clearly visible. Pattern may be various shades of sable brown to dark chocolate. Ivory cream spectacles encircling the eyes, and ivory cream whisker pads and chin are desirable, giving a wild appearance. Little or no difference between body colour and point colour. Paw pads dark brown, with rosy undertones allowed. Tail tip dark chocolate through sable brown to black. Eyes copper to blue-green.

Subject to penalty: Spots forming a mackerel tabby pattern. (Smoky undercoat permitted.)

Disqualifying fault: Tail tip not black. Belly not spotted. Rose-coloured paw pads. Aggressive behaviour that threatens to harm.

Basic genetic makeup of a homozygous brown spotted tabby Bengal:
AA BB CC DD LL t^s t^s *(see pages 142-151)*

Mating authorized with other breeds: No.

TICA Standards	Points
Head	10
Ears	10
Eyes	5
Neck	5
Body	10
Legs	5
Feet	5
Coat	10
Colour	10
Pattern	30

Birman

One of the most beautiful cat legends comes from Burma, now known as Myanmar. There, the local people built a temple and dedicated it to a beautiful golden goddess with sapphire eyes, Tsun-Kyan-Kse, who watched over the transmigration of souls. The temple was said to house 100 white cats. Mun-Ha, a most respected, white-haired priest, often meditated before the statue of the goddess with Sinh, one of the handsome white cats, always at his side.

One night Mun-Ha was attacked by bandits who raided the temple. As the priest lay dying, Sinh leaped on to his master's head and turned to face the goddess. His white fur immediately became as golden as the radiant light beaming from Tsun-Kyan-Kse, and his eyes became as blue as hers. The cat's legs, mask and tail turned a velvety earth-brown; only his feet, still touching the dead priest's snowy head, remained white, conjuring up the old man's pure spirit. Next morning it was discovered that all the other white cats had undergone the same transformation. From then on, the cats were regarded as sacred and were protected.

At the turn of this century, the same temple was attacked again and a number of priests were killed. Two foreigners, a Major Gordon Russell and Auguste Pavie, helped several priests and their sacred cats escape to Tibet. The two men were told about the legend and, when they

AUS.	CAN.	N.Z.	S.AF.	U.K.	U.S.A.
●	●	●	●	●	●

The Birman is a very faithful creature, devoted to its owner and very attached to all family members. Its silky coat and soft voice may give the impression that this is a docile animal. In reality it has a lively temperament and can become a real presence in the household. The Birman is well balanced both physically and psychologically, and its gaze gives it a gentle, calm, and dignified demeanour.

BIRMAN AND SIAMESE

Since these two breeds come from the same part of the world and are similarly shrouded in legend, it seems logical to assume that they are closely related. Today, however, the two breeds are quite different.

returned to France in 1919, they were given a pair of sacred cats by the priests they had saved. The male cat died on the journey, but the queen proved to be pregnant. Thanks to her, the breed survived, flourished, and was formally recognized in 1925.

The Birmans were further developed in France and it was there that the standard for the breed was established and accepted by the rest of the world. Birmans are still exported from France, where breeders have produced different colours.

Birmans became scarce during World War II, and did not reappear until 1955. At that time they began to be exported to England, other European countries, and North America. Birmans were officially recognized in Britain in 1966 and in North America the following year.

TICA Standards	Points
Head	30
Body	30
Coat	10
Colour	30

Characteristics

General description: The Sacred Cat of Burma is a long-haired pointed cat with white feet. Imposing in appearance, medium to large in size, with heavy boning in proportion to that size. Females smaller than males. Must be healthy, muscular, and in perfect balance. Coat, though long and silky, should not mat or tangle.

Head: From the front, must appear broad and round; in profile, slightly longer than wide. Forehead slopes back with a slight transverse flat spot just above the eye ridge, leading to a rounded top head. A definite stop between the forehead and the Roman nose, whose nostrils are set low. Medium-length muzzle has heavy jaws and well-developed chin, forming perpendicular line with upper lip. Cheeks full, with high, prominent cheekbones.

Ears: Almost as wide at the base as tail. Rounded tips, of medium size and placed moderately far apart. Inside furnishings should be heavy.

Eyes: Large blue eyes almost round and set wide apart. The deeper the blue the better.

Body: Sturdy and medium long; back should be level. Bone structure heavy, muscles firm and well built. Medium-long legs and tail in proportion to body. Feet large, round, and firm.

Coat: Semi-long to long, with a silky texture. Heavy ruff desirable, especially in males. Fur must be slightly curly on the stomach. Seasonal changes considered when judging the length of coat.

Pattern: Gloves and laces: Front paws have white gloves ending in an even line where toes meet paws; back paws have white gloves extending up the back of the legs ending halfway up the hock (laces). Matched gloves and laces desirable.

Colour:
Paw pads must be pink or pink spotted with point colour; solid pink preferred.
• **Seal point:** Body an even pale fawn to cream, warm in tone, with subtle shadings allowed on back and haunches, lightening to creamy white on stomach and chest. Points, except gloves and laces, deep seal brown; gloves and laces pure white. Nose leather deep seal brown.
• **Blue point:** Body an even platinum grey to bluish-white, subtle shadings allowed on back and haunches gradually shading to almost white on stomach and chest. Points, except gloves and laces, deep blue-grey. Gloves and laces are white.
• **Chocolate point:** Body an even ivory with no shading. Points, except gloves and laces, a warm milk chocolate. Gloves and laces pure white. Nose leather cinnamon pink.
• **Frost point:** Body an even milk white, cold in tone with no shading. Points, except gloves and laces, frost grey. Gloves and laces pure white.
• **Cinnamon point:** Body an even buff to ivory colour with no shading. Points, except gloves and laces, reddish cinnamon brown. Gloves and laces pure white. Nose leather burnt rose.
• **Fawn point:** Body a creamy off-white with no shading. Points, except gloves and laces, warm fawn or buff. Gloves and laces pure white. Nose leather pink.

Basic genetic makeup of a homozygous seal mackerel tabby Birman:
AA BB c^S c^S DD ll TT *(see pages 142-151)*

Mating authorized with other breeds: No.

Bombay

The Bombay is a miniature panther produced by outcrossing Burmese to Black American Shorthairs. The first of these outcrossings occurred in 1958, and the breed was recognized and admitted to championship shows by the cat clubs after 1976.

The primary characteristic of the breed is its glossy, jet-black coat—a fur so short, smooth, and close-lying that it resembles patent leather. The cat was named for the city of Bombay because it looks like a smaller version of the Indian black leopard. Unlike its wild cousin, however, the Bombay loves the company of humans.

AUS.	CAN.	N.Z.	S.AF.	U.K.	U.S.A.
●	●			●	●

Although it looks like a small black panther, the Bombay is a particularly affectionate and gentle cat. It has a healthy appetite and a soft voice. It is also confident, a good hunter, active, inquisitive, and patient.

Characteristics

General description: A patent-leather coated cat, medium-sized with substantial bone structure, good muscular development, and deceptively heavy. Large, round eyes, described as new copper-penny eyes, give the face a sweet, open expression.

Head: Pleasingly rounded and without flat planes. Considerable breadth between the eyes, blending gently into a broad, well-developed short muzzle. In profile, a moderate stop, and the forehead rounded, not domed. Chin firmly rounded, reflecting a proper bite.

Eyes: Large, round, set wide apart with the aperture in line with the base of the ear. Color ranges from gold to copper; copper preferred; the greater the depth and brilliance, the better.

Ears: Medium-sized, broad at the base and slightly rounded at the tips. Set well apart on a rounded skull and alert, tilting slightly forward.

Body: Medium, neither cobby nor rangy. Legs well proportioned to the body, with rounded feet. Muscular and deceptively heavy for its size.

Subject to penalty: Ranginess; fine bones; tail long, whippy; flat plane to forehead; snub profile.

Disqualifying fault: Lockets or spots; nose leather or paw pads not black; green eyes.

Basic genetic makeup of a homozygous Bombay:
aa BB CC DD LL *(see pages 142-151)*

Mating authorized with other breeds:
Yes, with Burmese.

TICA Standards	Points
Head and ears	25
Eyes	25
Body	30
Coat	20

British Shorthair

T his English vagabond or alley cat acquired its pedigree in the show ring. The standard was established to distinguish it from the Household Pet or non-pedigree cats.

A long history

The ancestors of the British Shorthair were brought to Northern Europe, and later to Britain, by Roman soldiers almost 2,000 years ago. For a long time they lived wild, multiplied rapidly, and bred without control. In the 19th century, English author and artist Harrison Weir, appreciating the sturdiness and intelligence of these street cats, began breeding the most outstanding specimens. Weir wrote the first standards of cat-show judging and his favourites, the shorthairs, were among the cats on show at the exhibition he organized at London's Crystal Palace in 1871.

Blues always popular

Blues were especially popular among the numerous British Shorthairs appearing in shows in the late 1800s. At Weir's bidding, a special category was established for British Blues. At the time they were compared to the Chartreux Blue. Breeders then began to work towards differentiating the two breeds, crossing the British Shorthairs with Persians to make them heavier and with a rounder head. This is the type that has persisted.

The British Shorthair was not recognized in North America until 1970, and then only blue cats of this breed were accepted—under the name of British Blue. Now all colours are accepted, and while blue is still the most popular, white and bicolour British Shorthairs are being seen more often at shows.

Fortunately breeders had the sense to maintain the original sturdy type of British Shorthair, with its calm, pleasing disposition.

AUS.	CAN.	N.Z.	S.AF.	U.K.	U.S.A.
●	●	●	●	●	●

Like its ancestors, the British Shorthair is a sturdy, powerful animal, and a particularly good hunter. Calm, patient, and good-natured, it can be entirely self-sufficient and independent, even rather distant. It is truly a problem-free pet.

Characteristics

General description: Very sturdy, medium to large cat. Body is semi-cobby, well-knit and powerful, especially in males. Shoulders broad and flat at the wither, and hips the same width. Head is broad with well-rounded contours when viewed from any angle. Cheeks are full, giving a chubby chipmunk appearance. Nose is short and snub with a change of direction at the bridge, giving a short, straight appearance. Coat is short, firm, crisp, plush, and dense, with a natural protective appearance.

Head: Medium to large, broad with well-rounded contours. Muzzle well-defined. Full cheeks and short nose with no break. Chin forms a perpendicular line with nose.

Ears: Broad at the base and rounded, medium sized, set wide apart, but not to extreme.

Eyes: Large, placed level in the head, wideset.

Body: Medium to large body; full-grown male should weigh 11-17 pounds (5 to 8 kg); females smaller. Broad at the shoulders, chest, and hips with deep chest and flank. Short, thick neck is heavily muscled, especially in males. Tail tapers slightly to a rounded tip, and should be two-thirds body length. Bones medium-heavy, muscles sturdy and solid.

Coat: Short but slightly longer than other short-hairs. Firm, crisp texture—plush and dense.

Colour: Ranges from black smoke and tabbies to bicolor (black and white, blue and white, red and white, cream and white).

Subject to penalty: Long or soft coat, light undercoat, delicate boning.

Disqualifying fault: White lockets.

Basic genetic makeup of a homozygous blue and white British Shorthair:
aa BB CC dd LL SS *(see pages 142-151)*

Mating authorized with other breeds:
Yes, with Scottish Fold and Manx (to improve the Manx).

TICA Standards	Points
Head	15
Neck	5
Ears	5
Eyes	5
Nose	5
Body	20
Legs and feet	5
Tail	5
Colour	10
Coat	15
Condition	5
Balance	5

Burmese

Few breeds of cat are as well documented in their origin as the Burmese. All are descended from one small brown queen named Wong Mau. In 1930, she was imported to the United States from Yangon, Myanmar (formerly Rangoon, Burma).

In San Francisco, Dr. Joseph Thompson, a retired ship's doctor, first mated Wong Mau to a seal point Siamese tom. Some of the resulting kittens were Siamese, the others were dark brown. When the brown kittens were mated to each other, or when one of the brown males was bred back to Wong Mau, they produced the even-coloured, darker kittens we now call Burmese.

AUS.	CAN.	N.Z.	S.AF.	U.K.	U.S.A.
●	●	●	●	●	●

The Burmese, though quite a reserved animal with a gentle and even timid nature, has retained the loud voice it probably inherited from its Siamese ancestors. This cat is intelligent, active, and a playful companion. As a kitten it is a hell-raiser. Burmese cats like to stay comfortably at home, and are faithful to their owners.

A rocky road to acceptance

The breed was established with great difficulty: the breeders of Siamese claimed that Wong Mau had been nothing but a poorly coloured Siamese, and that hybridization would result in litters of 'bastard' colours and types.

The Burmese breed was officially recognized in 1936, and the first club was founded that same year. Under great pressure from the Siamese breeders, however, the Cat Fanciers' Association (CFA), in 1947, decided to stop the Burmese from competing for championship events. The decision was taken because few Burmese could meet the CFA's strict requirement that they be descended from at least three generations of Burmese. But the breed and its devoted fanciers persevered until, in 1956, the CFA relented and once again allowed the Burmese to compete in sanctioned cat shows.

British breeders imported their first Burmese cats in 1947, and set about producing red, chocolate, lilac, and diluted shades of champagne, platinum, and blue coats. The breed was recognized in Britain in 1952. American breeders concentrated on 'typing'—changing the characteristics slightly to make the Burmese quite distinct from its progenitors. There are fanciers who prefer the older, oriental or English type, and those who like the newer, sturdier American type.

In the 1980s a Burmese queen played a feature role in starting yet another new breed when it mated with a Chinchilla thus producing the four founding kittens of the Burmilla breed (page 137).

Characteristics

General description: Of medium size and rich colour, with substantial bone structure, good muscular development, and surprising weight for its size. Expressive eyes and sweet face.

Head: Medium in size and pleasingly rounded, without flat planes. Face must be full, with considerable breadth between the eyes, tapering slightly to a short but well-developed muzzle. Muzzle and skull rounded. In profile, a visible nose break above the bridge between the eyes, with nose flowing gently into forehead. Rounded forehead, cheeks, and chin.

Ears: Medium in size and set well apart. Alert, tilting slightly forward, broad at the base. Slightly rounded tips. Ear hairs must be short and inside tufts sparse.

Eyes: Round and wide set, their aperture in line with the base of the ears. Colour from yellow to gold; the greater the depth and brilliance, the better. Green eyes a fault; blue eyes disqualify.

Body: Medium in size, muscular, and somewhat compact. Allowance made for larger size in males. Chest broad, ample, and rounded. Back level from shoulder to tail; hips the same width as shoulders. Overall bone structure must be strong,

with a broad rib cage. Well supported by hard and well-developed muscles. Surprisingly heavy for its size. Legs, with rounded feet, are well proportioned to body. Tail round and straight, thicker at its base and tapering to a blunt end.

Coat: Short, fine, and glossy, with a satin-like texture. Must lie very close to the body.

Colour: Colours include blue, chocolate, lilac, and sable. Should be rich and sound to the root, with slight lightening on the underparts. No smoke, barring, or pointed colouration.

Basic genetic makeup of a homozygous zibeline Burmese:
aa BB c^b c^b DD LL *(see pages 142-151)*

Mating authorized with other breeds:
Yes, with Bombay, Tonkinese, Siamese, and Burmilla.

TICA Standards	Points
Head and ears	25
Eyes	10
Body and tail	25
Colour	25
Coat	10
Condition	5

California Spangled Cat

Like the Bengal, this new breed dates from the 1970s. It was then that American breeder and scientist Paul Casey, on a visit to Tanzania, was impressed by sightings of magnificent wild leopards and determined to create miniature domestic replicas.

Not yet fully accepted

Although the first Spangled Cat was not created in a test tube, it was the result of careful calculations. Casey used eight different breeds, each chosen for certain characteristics, to establish the bloodline. Abyssinians were used for their leopard-like qualities and Siamese contributed their svelte and muscular characteristics, but even cats of no specific breed added personality or physical traits to the gene pool. By 1986 TICA had accepted the breed for registration in the New Breed category. In 1991 the American Cat Association followed suit.

A complex pedigree

Although the Spangled Cat is often confused with the Bengal, the look is very different. While both breeds are large and well muscled, their body structure and facial characteristics are quite different. As well, Bengal breeders work towards green eyes; Spangled breeders favour brown eye tones that complement most of the nine accepted coat colours. Only the leopard coat is favoured in the Bengals.

'Spangled' is an ornithological term meaning spotted, an apt description of this cat. California is part of its name because that is where the first such spangled cat was born.

AUS.	CAN.	N.Z.	S.AF.	U.K.	U.S.A.
	●				●

The Spangled Cat, which looks exactly like a miniature leopard, is slender, elegant, and graceful, but also highly muscled, athletic, and well proportioned. At first glance it looks like a wild creature, a hunter, and gives the impression of being bigger than it actually is. The males, considerably larger and more muscular than their mates, weigh up to 16½ pounds (7.5 kg), while the females weigh up to 11 pounds (5 kg).

This intelligent and energetic but gentle animal is renowned for its sociable, affectionate nature.

Characteristics

General description: First impression is of an unmistakably spotted cat with a long, strong, tubular body, and hunter-like quality to its gait. Its face should be expressive and well contoured, with prominent cheekbones and well-developed whisker pads. The Spangled should create the illusion of a much larger cat. It is known for its affectionate and social nature, along with athletic abilities and keen intelligence. Energetic without being aggressive.

Head: Sculpted, with wide cheekbones. Of medium length and width, with forehead slightly domed. Muzzle must be full and well developed, chin and jaw strong. In profile, a gentle stop between forehead and nose, with a slightly raised and rounded cranium. Whisker pads, pale in colour, must be well developed to create a broad, medium-length muzzle, especially in adult males.

Ears: Base and height of each ear must be approximately equal. Ears are medium in size and have rounded tips. Placed high and back from the face.

Eyes: Medium-large eyes should be open and almond in shape, placed wide and gently sloping, accentuated by the cheekbones, which are wide and prominent, giving the eyes a sculpted setting.

Body: Long, lean, muscular body must be well supported. Carriage is typically low and even, giving the cat a hunter-like stance. Should have ample bone without undue bulk, and muscles must be well developed overall. Cylindrical neck is well-defined, and muscular. Medium-length tail must be full end to end, with a blunt tip. In typical attitudes the forelegs, which are long in the forearm, are carried at nearly a 90-degree angle at the elbow, setting them well back of the breastbone and allowing the body to ride low. However, they have long extension when stretched or 'sitting tall.' Rear legs are muscular in the thigh, and long when extended but must also appear shorter to carry the body low. This allows the body a low carriage when the cat is walking or running. The legs must be strong, and the muscles particularly well developed in the thigh. Feet are of medium size with tactile toes and a distinctly 'usable' appearance. Long, solid, and tight body must appear heavier than it actually is. In general, adult males are larger, heavier, and more muscular than females; males average from 13 to 17 pounds (6 to 8 kg), females 9 to 11 pounds (4 to 5 kg).

Coat: Short and close across back, sides, neck, and face; short but slightly longer on tail and underbelly. Coat soft and short, except on tail and underbelly, where fur is longer, giving a fullness to the otherwise sleek appearance. Spotting covers back and sides of body, while striping extends from between the ears, down back of neck to shoulders. Definite dark bar marks the top of each foreleg. Tail is well furred, ending in one to three dark rings.

Subject to penalty: Cobbiness. Lack of bone or musculature. Long or whip-like tail. Pointed or low-set ears. Narrow or bony rib cage. Green eyes. White toe markings. Longish or fluffy coat, or hard bristly coat. Lack of standard pattern. 'Fish-scale' pattern. Lack of contrast in pattern-to-ground colour. Excessive ticking. Bad temperament.

Disqualifying fault: Any general barred or striped appearance. Any random white patch markings. Elongated or foreshortened skull. Light-tipped tail. Roundness of head. Narrow or pointed muzzle. Lack of chin and jaw development. Lack of sturdiness in physique. However, a 'bib mark' is not considered a patch mark.

Basic genetic makeup of a homozygous bronze spotted tabby California Spangled:
AA BB CC DD LL t^s t^s *(see pages 142-151)*

Mating authorized with other breeds:
No.

TICA Standards	Points
Head	20
Eyes	5
Ears	5
Neck	5
Body	20
Tail	6
Legs	6
Feet	5
Pattern	20
Coat	8

Chartreux

Also known as the Monastery Cat or the Blue Cat of France, the Chartreux is the natural breed of France, descended from one of the earliest breeds. It is also the subject of many legends. One claims that in 1558 Carthusian monks were already breeding the cats because of their hunting skills. The animals were also needed to protect the abbey's stores of wheat from hungry rodents. The Chartreux has scarcely changed since this time, a rare phenomenon in the world of animal husbandry.

Originating in the Middle East, the Chartreux probably arrived in Europe on merchant ships some 450 years ago. The breed was much exploited by the fur trade, since Chartreux coats could be cut and dyed to look like otter pelts.

Confusion with British Blues

Even though the Chartreux owes a great deal to French writer Colette (1873-1954), whose frequent references aroused new interest in the breed, the first breeders of record are the Léger sisters of Brittany. They discovered a large population of cats on Belle-Isle-sur-Mer off Brittany, and in 1931 became the first to exhibit these cats in France. In the 1940s, the war caused many pedigree cats to go homeless: during those lean years some Chartreux were undoubtedly killed for food; others may have died because their plush coats could be sold.

Breeders in the 1950s outcrossed Chartreux to Blue Persians to achieve a paler shade of blue, more intensely gold eyes, and a sturdier bone structure. This explains why Chartreux were con-

AUS.	CAN.	N.Z.	S.AF.	U.K.	U.S.A.
●	●				●

The Chartreux, a sturdy, hardy, well-coordinated cat, is a swift and deadly hunter. It has an independent nature and is calm and well-disposed. It is known as the smiling cat, and has an engagingly rounded appearance. It becomes much attached to its owner and especially to its home, and is prone to laziness—until a rodent appears.

fused with British Blues, and why the hybrids were later crossbred to them. A single litter may contain British, Chartreux, and long-haired kittens. American breeders, however, who only began to take an interest in the Chartreux in 1970, are more purist than the Europeans. They maintain two distinctly different standards, and never cross Chartreux with British Blues. In recent years, French breeders have followed suit.

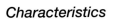

Characteristics

General description: A sturdy French breed coveted since antiquity for its hunting prowess and dense, water-repellent fur. Its type is sometimes called primitive, being neither cobby nor classic domestic. Though large, the Chartreux is extremely supple, refined, and agile. Males are much larger than females and slower to mature. Coat texture, coat colour, and eye colour are affected by sex, age, and other natural factors. The qualities of strength, intelligence, and amenability that enabled the breed to survive unaided should be evident in exhibition animals and preserved through careful selection.

Head: Comparatively large but not broad, rounded but not a sphere. Medium, straight nose with a slight stop permitted. Muzzle is narrow in relation to the head but not pointed. Cheeks are well developed in adult cats. Jaw is powerful, especially in mature adult males. In profile, a high, softly contoured forehead with a slight stop permitted.

Ears: Small to medium, minimal flare at base, slightly rounded tips. High on the head; erect.

Eyes: Rounded eyes must be open, alert, and expressive; wide set and large, but not over-powering. Colour should be gold to copper; clear, deep, brilliant orange is preferred.

Body: Robust, large, and well proportioned, but never gross. Strong shoulders with a deep, well-developed chest, giving a solid, sturdy appearance. Mature males weigh from 11 to 15 pounds (5 to 7 kg); mature females at least 6½ to 10 pounds (3 to 4.5 kg). Bone structure must be strong and sturdy, muscles dense and solid.

Neck is short, strong, and heavy-set. Tail heavier at the base, tapering slightly to an oval tip, and must be lively and flexible. Legs are straight, fine-boned and comparatively short. Muscles vary according to the gender: the upper portion of the leg is heavier for mature studs. Feet must be round and small.

Coat: Medium-short, dense and slightly woolly. Silkier, thinner coat permitted for females.

Colour: Any shade of blue-grey from ash to slate. Tips may be lightly brushed with silver. Preferred tone is a bright, unblemished blue with an overall iridescent sheen. Nose leather slate grey; lips blue; paw pads rose-taupe. Allowance for ghost barring and tail rings in juveniles.

Subject to penalty: Severe nose stop. Snubbed, humped, or upturned nose. Broad, heavy muzzle. Almond-shaped eyes. Eyes too close set. Green eyes or white locket disqualify.

Basic genetic makeup of a homozygous Chartreux: aa BB CC dd LL *(see pages 142-151)*

Mating authorized with other breeds: No.

TICA Standards	Points
Head	15
Ears	10
Eyes	10
Neck	4
Body	20
Tail	4
Legs and feet	8
Coat	14
Colour	15

Cornish Rex

The Cornish Rex has the suppleness, agility, speed, and elegant lines of a gazelle, an Italian greyhound, or a butterfly, but is 100 percent cat and a lively one at that.

This extraordinary creature—though it may look like it came from Venus or Mars—arose in the Duchy of Cornwall in England. On July 21, 1950, a perfectly ordinary cat named Serena had a perfectly ordinary litter, except for one frizzy little 'ugly duckling.' Serena's owner, Nina Ennismore, was a breeder of curly-haired Astrex rabbits and realized immediately that she had something unique on her hands. The wavy coat was confirmed as being a true recessive mutation. The name was easy: Cornish for the kitten's birthplace, and Rex for its wavy fur's resemblance to that of the Astrex rabbit.

A new breed that almost disappeared

The mutant kitten, a cream tabby male with curly hair, was named Kallibunker. Because the wavy-haired gene was recessive, geneticists advised his owner to mate him with Serena, his tricolour mother. (To have the wavy hair reappear, a kitten would have to inherit two copies of the gene that produced it—one from each parent. In this case both mother and son carried the wavy hair gene.) In 1952 Serena had another litter consisting of one female with a normal coat and two Rex toms. One of the toms died while still young; the survivor, a blue tabby, was named Poldhu.

Later Poldhu was accidentally rendered sterile, and the new breed seemed in danger of disappearing. Kallibunker had already died, and only one of his descendants, a cream and white male called Sham Pain Chas, was left. In efforts to

AUS.	CAN.	N.Z.	S.AF.	U.K.	U.S.A.
●	●	●	●	●	●

TWO TYPES

The English Cornish Rex, bred from Burmese and British, is a heavy, stocky cat, with a triangular skull and a relatively straight profile. Its ears are set widely apart, and its eyes are large. The American Cornish Rex is lighter, more fragile, with an oval head, enormous ears, and the lean look of a long-distance runner.

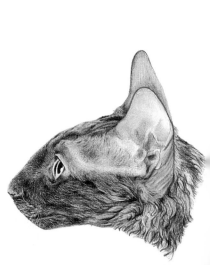

save the mutant gene, this tom was outcrossed to British Shorthairs and Burmese. This outcrossing also avoided inbreeding, provided a wider colour range, and helped establish the future standard for the Cornish Rex.

In 1957 a daughter of Poldhu, Lamorna Cove, was exported to America. She soon had four kittens and launched the breed on a new continent. It developed rapidly through the enthusiasm of breeders and the public alike, and began to win awards, trophies, and rosettes. But that was not the end of the story. Once again, the Americans elected to be different from the British, producing their own type of Cornish Rex by outcrossing to Siamese, Orientals, and other fine-boned breeds.

In 1981, Dali, the first American Rex exhibited in France, created a quandary for judges. They were forced to choose between an American and a British kind of Rex. In the end, they awarded Dali the prize. Despite some criticism, Dali gained admirers, and had kittens by Anna, a seal-point Cornish Rex, and Tiggy, a red tabby. Later, two other cats—Devil, a black and white like Dali, and Isabeau—had litters that became the basis for the now well-recognized American Rex breed.

The Cornish Rex, a well-coordinated, athletic cat, is a born acrobat with a lively intelligence. It is happy and affectionate, has a piercing voice, and eats like a horse despite its delicate appearance. It is no more demanding than any other cat, and requires no special care. The breed has several traits that make it unique:
• slightly curly hair all over its body in regular waves like a crimped coiffure; even the whiskers and eyelashes are wavy;
• a long, egg-shaped skull with no flat planes, all long curves;
• a lively and mobile expression with large, round eyes that always look surprised or questioning;
• at birth the Cornish Rex looks like a baby bat, with its enormous ears, or like a spider, because of its long, spindly legs; it is born all curly, like an astrakhan lamb.

Characteristics

General description: A curly-coated, fine-boned cat standing high on its legs. Distinctive arched back and tuck-up resembling a greyhound. Hard, muscular body that is warm to the touch. The coat quality, texture, waviness, and distinctive body type are of prime importance.

Head: Skull must be egg-shaped with a pronounced roundness at the back, and longer than it is wide. Muzzle break must be definite. Roman profile, but there can be a slight change of direction. Straight line from nose to chin. High, prominent bridge.

Ears: Large, highly placed; conical appearance, modified point. Outer surface often bald.

Eyes: Medium-sized, oval, with a slight upward slant. Colour in keeping with coat colour.

Body: Rib cage must be full and deep. Trunk follows upwards curve of backbone, forming a 'tuck-up.' Hips rounded and somewhat heavy. Fine, long bone structure; hard muscles. Long, slender tail tapers slightly from body to end. Fine, dense hair with waves preferred, but no penalty for bareness on upper surface. Long, fine-boned, firmly muscled legs. Small, oval feet.

Coat: Deep, even waves extending to the head, legs, and tail desirable. Hair short and fine; soft, dense texture; velvet pile on head and legs. All colours are recognized.

Subject to penalty: Lack of definite muzzle break. Extreme wedge-shaped head. Bareness on large portion of body, except ears and tail.

Disqualifying fault: Presence of coarse hairs.

Basic genetic makeup of a homozygous white and black smoke Cornish Rex:
aa BB CC DD LL I^{sm} I^{sm} LL rr SS
(see pages 142-151)

Mating authorized with other breeds: No.

TICA Standards	Points
Head	12
Ears	5
Eyes	5
Neck	4
Body	15
Tail	4
Legs and feet	5
Coat	36
Colour and markings	5

Devon Rex

An elf, a clown, an extraterrestrial, a cartoon cat—everyone has a special description for the Devon Rex. It sports bat-like ears, the curly hair of a poodle or a lamb, has a lively intelligence, and an endearing expression.

In 1960, an English woman, Beryl Cox, found a cat with a strangely curly coat near an abandoned mine in Devonshire. A mating with a tricolour female produced one tom, Kirlee, as curly-haired as his sire. Since the Coxes knew about the Cornish Rex, which had been developed during the previous decade in neighbouring Cornwall, they bred Kirlee to several Cornish females expecting to obtain litters of the curly-haired kittens.

AUS.	CAN.	N.Z.	S.AF.	U.K.	U.S.A.
●	●	●	●	●	●

The Devon Rex might be described as a 'poodle-lamb-puss.' Attractive, intelligent, playful, loving, agile, and lively, it has extraordinary eyes. However, the most seductive characteristic of this creature is its remarkable coat, which is as soft as its voice.

Two spontaneous mutations

To their disappointment, all the offspring of Kirlee and the Cornish queens had normal, straight hair. It was evident that the mutations producing the Cornish Rex and the Devon Rex had nothing in common. The genes were recessive yet different, even though they had produced much the same result. So, in this unusual way, two new spontaneous mutations were discovered. As breeding progressed, the Cornish and the Devon each became more typed.

Because of the rarity of Devon Rexes, and since the Devon could not mix with the Cornish, a lot of inbreeding was necessary at first to preserve the mutant gene. Unfortunately, this produced a rare disorder that Devon breeders call the spasticity syndrome.

A breed under close surveillance

Because the spastic gene is recessive, a kitten will not get the disease unless it inherits two of the genes—one from each parent. The Devon breed is being closely followed in Europe by two couples: Mr. and Mrs. Rey du Boissieu of France and Mr. and Mrs. Scholten-Klein of the Netherlands. Their data banks contain the pedigrees of all registered Devon Rex cats, and every kitten's pedigree indicates the eventual risk of a handicap, if any. Their record-keeping is helping the breed to stay healthy.

The Devon Rex began competing in American cat shows in the early 1970s: it had arrived there some 10 years before. Because the breed's gene pool is limited, American breeders have been able to outcross to other shorthairs, including Burmese, Bombay, and Siamese.

Characteristics

General description: An alert and active cat, the Devon shows a lively interest in its surroundings. Its large eyes, short muzzle, prominent cheekbones, and huge low-set ears create a characteristic elfin look. Viewed from the front, the head is delineated by a narrowing series of three distinct convex curves: the outer edges of the ears, cheeks, and whisker pads. Males may be up to 25 percent larger than females.

Head: Comparatively small head must be a modified wedge. In profile there should be a strongly marked stop. Muzzle short and well developed, its break strong, with prominent whisker pads. Forehead curves from the stop to the flat skull. Chin strong and well developed, the cheeks full.

Ears: Large and low-set at the base, tapering to rounded tips. Well covered with fine fur, though their insides should be sparse. Ear muffs and tufts may or may not be present. Sparse hair on the temples not considered a fault.

Eyes: Large, oval and wide set. Opening should slope towards the outer edge of the ear. Colour must conform to the colour of the coat.

Body: Slender and of medium length. Must be carried high on the legs. Chest should be broad, muscles hard. Long and tapering tail is medium-fine in size and well covered with short fur. Legs are long with medium-fine bones. Length of the hind legs must be emphasized. Small oval feet.

Coat: Well covered with short, full-bodied, wavy fur. Coat has a distinctive texture—the mutation causing its wavy coat is found in no other breed. Devons may have down on underparts of the body; this is not bareness. Allowances made for lack of full coat on kittens with very good type, over fully-coated lesser types. Short coat must have a fine and wavy texture. Full-bodied Rex should appear to be without guard hairs.

Colour: White lockets or buttons are permitted.

Subject to penalty: Narrow, long, or domestic head; ears too small or set too high; short, bare or bushy tail; straight or shaggy coats.

Disqualifying fault: Weak hind legs or excessive baldness.

Basic genetic makeup of a homozygous brown spotted tabby Devon:
AA BB CC DD re re t^s t^s
(see pages 142-151)

Mating authorized with other breeds: No.

TICA Standards	Points
Head	30
Body	30
Coat	35
Colour	5

Egyptian Mau

Mau meant cat in ancient Egypt. This animal is the descendant of the legendary cat of the pyramids, which was deified and worshipped in ancient times.

Today's Egyptian Mau looks extraordinarily like its ancestors, depicted in papyri, sculptures, and frescoes dating from the age of the pharaohs. Few breeds can boast such nobility or such a glorious past. This cat was the constant companion to Cleopatra, enjoyed the protection of the temples, was an integral part of a whole culture, and held pride of place in every home in that ancient civilization. This is the cat that survived through the centuries to become, today, the incarnation of the great art works of antiquity.

A princess and the ambassador's cat

Despite its long history, however, the Mau's contemporary reputation dates from 1953 in Rome, where Russian Princess Natalie Troubetskoy became the first modern admirer of the Mau. Entranced with a Mau belonging to Italy's ambassador to Egypt, she obtained a female named Baba. The ambassador's cat and Baba produced a bronze-coloured male, who was later mated with his mother to produce Lisa. This female was shown in Rome in 1955.

In 1956, the princess took her three Maus to the United States. There, in 1957, Baba became the first of the breed to be exhibited in North America. During the same period, some British breeders were attempting to obtain a replica of the Mau without actually importing one. (Importation was undesirable because of Britain's six-month quarantine of animals.) They crossed

AUS.	CAN.	N.Z.	S.AF.	U.K.	U.S.A.
✳	●	✳		✳	●

✳ In these countries the Egyptian Mau may be recognized under different names (Oriental Shorthair Tabby, Spotted Oriental, Oriental Spotted Tabby or Chocolate Oriental Spotted Tabby). Check with local cat associations.

ANOTHER FAMOUS VINTAGE

Both the Mau and the Abyssinian are living replicas of early cat images. They are also the only pure breeds that can claim Egyptian ancestry. The only difference between the two breeds is in the coat: the colouring of the Abyssinian is similar to that of the puma, while the Mau's colouring is closer to that of the ocelot.

The Mau is healthy, hardy, good-tempered, calm—even a little shy and reserved—and loyal. It is also extremely agile, a good hunter, and well able to look after itself. This friendly animal makes an excellent companion.

Abyssinians, Tabbies, and Siamese, but did not successfully achieve complete resemblance to the true Mau. These various attempts did, however, produce the Oriental Spotted Tabby. There has been confusion between the two breeds ever since.

Characteristics

General description: The Egyptian Mau is the only natural domestic breed of spotted cat. Its body is graceful, showing well-developed muscular strength. Striking a balance between the heftiness of the cobby and the svelteness of the oriental types, it is an alert, active, strong, colourful cat of medium size. It should be well balanced physically and temperamentally. General balance is more desirable than size.

Head: A modified, slightly rounded wedge without flat planes. Brow, cheek, and profile all show a gentle contour, with the cheeks less than full. Gentle rise from bridge of nose to forehead, flowing into arched neck without a break. Medium-sized muzzle is rounded, neither short nor pointed, and blends into overall head shape. Allow for broad head and jowls in mature males.

Ears: Moderately pointed, broad at the base. Medium to medium-large, upstanding, with ample width between them. Set well back on the head, and cupped forward in the alert position. Ear hair short and close-lying. Lynx tips are allowed.

Eyes: Rounded, almond-shaped eyes are large and level in the head, with a slight upward slant to the lower lid. Neither round nor oriental. A light gooseberry-green colour is preferred. Allow for slow colour development; an amber cast is acceptable in kittens and young adults up to 18 months of age.

Body: A balance between the sturdy cobby and foreign types. Bone structure must be medium with high, angulated shoulder blades. Body should be medium in length and size. Well-developed muscles. Though muscular, especially in male cats, the neck must be arched. Medium-length tail has a slight taper. Legs are medium in length, but hind legs should be proportionately longer. Leg muscles well developed and the bone structure medium. Feet should be slightly oval, almost round. Though the feet are small, toes are very long on back feet.

Coat: The medium-length coat must be long enough to carry two bands of ticking. Close-lying with a fine, silky, and resilient texture.

Colour: There should be good contrast between pale ground colour and deeper markings. Forehead has characteristic tabby M and brown lines between ears and down back of neck, which become elongated spots along spine. On the haunches the spine lines meld into a dorsal stripe, which continues to tip of tail. Tail is banded, the tip dark. Cheeks have mascara lines from corner of the eye along the contour of the cheek. Shoulder markings are a transition between stripes and spots. Upper legs are heavily barred but do not necessarily match. Spots on body are random and in various shapes and sizes.

Subject to penalty: Short or round head; pointed muzzle; full cheeks, small ears; small, round or oriental eyes; cobby or oriental body, short or whippy tail; body spots that run together; unbroken necklaces.

Disqualifying fault: Lack of spots; wrong eye colour; white locket or white spots; lack of ticking in silver or bronze coats; ticking in smoke; red colouring in bronze. Lack of grey undercoat in bronze.

Basic genetic makeup of a homozygous silver Mau:
AA BB CC DD LL S^i S^i t^s t^s *(see pages 142-151)*

Mating authorized with other breeds: No.

TICA Standards	Points
Head	10
Ears	5
Eyes	10
Body	15
Legs and feet	10
Colour	15
Coat	10
Pattern	25

Exotic Shorthair

Sometimes called the Persian in pyjamas (because of its scaled down Persian coat) the Exotic Shorthair is one of the most popular show cats. A gorgeous plush coat is no doubt part of its charm. But many of its fans find the endearing expression of its round, snub-nosed face equally captivating.

This American breed was acknowledged officially in 1967 after considerable debate within various cat associations about just how a well-bred Exotic Shorthair should be received. Prior to this, many breeders had obtained Exotic Shorthairs accidentally, when Persians mated with short-haired cats, or when they were trying to create a new colour of Persian.

This was what happened to breeder Carolyn Bussey, who was hoping to produce a chocolate Persian. She mated a Persian queen to a chocolate Burmese, but the litter all had short hair because the Persian's long hair results from a recessive gene. Her disappointment was short-lived, however; faced with the magnificent little bears of the first litter, she decided to produce short-haired Persians.

Her first attempts produced mixtures of Persian and Burmese, Persian and American Shorthair, Persian and British Shorthair. Finally she succeeded by breeding a Persian to a short-haired cat with a stocky body and a round head. Cat show judge Jane Martinke recommended the name include 'exotic' to reflect the use of non-American breeds in its development. From 1967, however,

AUS.	CAN.	N.Z.	S.AF.	U.K.	U.S.A.
●	●	●	●	●	●

The Exotic Shorthair has the Persian's gentle manner together with some of the liveliness and playfulness of the short-hair breeds. It loves comfort, peace, and quiet, but it is more playful, active, and inquisitive than the Persian. Many of its admirers consider it to be the perfect apartment cat.

only Persians and American Shorthairs could be used to produce Exotic Shorthairs.

Meantime, the breed continues to win fans worldwide. An undemanding pet, it is easy to groom, good with other pets and with children, and completely at home in the show ring.

Classifying the newcomer

Showing the cat outside North America has its problems, however. The European system, for example, divides all breeds into three categories: longhairs, semi-longhairs, and shorthairs. Within that framework, the Exotic Shorthair is difficult to classify. Some clubs place it among the shorthairs, which it is—genetically speaking. Others put it with the longhairs because it has the Persian conformation, though not the coat.

Judging presents similar problems. If an Exotic Shorthair competes with longhairs, it looks less striking than the Persians. If it wins, however, the owners of Persians complain: they have spent hours grooming their cats, whereas the Exotic Shorthair requires only a shampoo. And when this cat competes with true shorthairs, it is also the exception.

> In competition, a Persian's coat can hide faults: an over-long body or too-big ears. But adroit combing of the long coat can mask these problems. Similar camouflage is impossible in the Exotic Shorthair. Grooming will not hide flaws from the judges.

Characteristics

General description: The head should be round and massive with a great breadth of skull. The face should be round with a sweet expression, and round underlying bone structure. The jaws are broad and powerful with full, prominent cheeks and perfect tooth occlusion.

Head: The medium-large head should be broad round, and domed, in proportion to body, the skull round and having great breadth. In profile, there should be a short snub nose with a definite break between the eyes. The forehead, nose, and chin should be in a straight line. The muzzle should be short, broad, and full, the jaws broad and powerful. The cheeks should be full and prominent, the chin strong, full, and well-developed, and fitting into the face. The small ears should be round tipped with a not-unduly open base. They should be set wide apart, fitting into the contour of the head. The large eyes should be round and full and set wide apart. They should conform to the coat colour.

Body: Medium-large, cobby, firm, and rounded in the midsection. The back should be short and level. The bone structure should be sturdy and large, muscles firm and well-developed. The tail should be short, but in proportion to the body. The legs should be short and straight with sturdy bones and well-developed muscles. Feet are large and round; toes are short.

Coat: The coat should be short, but slightly longer than in other shorthairs. The texture should be soft, dense, plush, and luxurious, and it should stand away from the body.

Condition: Should reflect excellent health with good muscle tone. All parts of the body should be in proportion.

Subject to penalty: The Exotic must not have a long, narrow head or a long Roman nose. A thin muzzle, severe overshot or undershot jaws, and bite deformities are all faults, as are large, pointed ears, a narrow chest, or long back.

Disqualifying fault: Overall lack of merit. Appearance of any lockets or buttons.

Basic genetic makeup of a homozygous white Exotic Shorthair:
BB CC DD LL WW *(see pages 142-151)*

Mating authorized with other breeds:
Yes, with Persians.

TICA Standards	Points
Head	30
Eyes	10
Body	30
Coat and colour	20
Condition	10

Havana Brown

The Havana Brown is a shy cat that prefers to have only one owner. It dislikes being handled by strangers and appreciates quiet and comfort.

Havana Browns, created in England in the 1950s, are so named because their colour resembles the tobacco in Havana cigars. Because the name led to confusion about the breed's origins, British breeders once called this cat the Chestnut Brown, but the original name prevailed. The American Havana is sturdier than the British Havana.

AUS.	CAN.	N.Z.	S.AF.	U.K.	U.S.A.
✷	●	●	✷	●	●

✷ In these countries the Havana Brown may be known as a variety of Oriental, Brown Oriental, Oriental Brown, or Oriental Shorthair. Check with local associations.

Characteristics

General description: Overall, this is a medium-sized cat. Males are larger and more heavily boned than females. Stud jowls in males and tabby markings in kittens are acceptable. The Havana should be clear-eyed and firm of body, the coat should have a pronounced glossy shine. The cat should be gentle and amenable.

Head: The head should be longer than wide, and in proportion. In profile, there should be a definite stop at the eyes. The end of the muzzle should appear almost square, with a definite break behind the whisker pad. The chin should be strong, the skull slightly rounded. Round-tipped ears should be large and wide-set, but not flaring, and pricked slightly forward on the alert. Little hair on outside of ear; inside, almost none. Oval eyes should appear large but not bugged and should begin at the top of the nose. Any vivid shade of green and changes in eye colour are permissible until the cat is one year old.

Body: The medium-sized body should be neither cobby nor runty. The bone structure should be medium, the muscles firm. The slender medi-um-length tail should taper. Legs should be long for the size of the cat. The bone structure should be slim, but not fine. The oval feet should be compact in size.

Coat: Short, with a smooth and soft-to-the-touch texture. Lilacs may have fuller coats.

Subject to penalty: Absence of muzzle break. Bad temperament. Weak chin.

Disqualifying fault: White locket. Wrong eye colour.

Basic genetic makeup of a homozygous Havana Brown: aa bb CC DD LL
(see pages 142-151)

Mating authorized with other breeds: No.

TICA Standards	Points
Head	30
Body	35
Coat and colour	19
Condition and balance	16

Himalayan

Placid and easy-going, the Himalayan is simple to care for—apartment life suits it perfectly. A top performer, too, it has been named Best in Show many times.

AUS.	CAN.	N.Z.	S.AF.	U.K.	U.S.A.
✶	●		✶	✶	●

✶ In these countries the Himalayan may be known as Colourpoint Persian, Colourpoint Longhair, or Pointed Persian. Check with local associations.

The classification of the Himalayan (some cat associations call it the Colourpoint Longhair or the Exotic Shorthair) is a matter of controversy. In fact, the Himalayan, a light-coloured, luxuriously-coated, blue-eyed cat with mask, ears, legs, feet, and tail darker than the rest of its body, is a Siamese version of the Persian. It is named for the Himalayan rabbit, which has similar coloration.

Even though the idea of a Persian with Siamese colouring was not to everyone's taste initially, Swedish breeders began working on the concept in 1922, American breeders a decade later. The first U.S. pointed longhair was born at Harvard Medical School in 1935.

Pedigree breeding of the Himalayan began in the 1950s. American breeder Margaret Goforth, Briton Brian Stirling-Webb, and Canadians Ben and Ann Borrett were among pioneers of the cross-breeding that produced the Himalayan as we know it today.

Physically it retains Persian characteristics: its hair, for example, is spectacularly long and as thick as the Persian's. Yet it has as broad a range of colours as the Siamese. Point markings are barely visible at birth and may take up to 18 months to develop fully. All varieties have the Siamese's sapphire blue eyes.

Affectionate, gentle, and intelligent, the Himalayan needs a lot of attention. It becomes devoted to its owner, whom it may follow around the house.

Characteristics

Head: Round, broad, domed, and massive. In profile a break between the eyes. Broad muzzle; strong chin. Full, prominent cheeks. Ears round-tipped, small, and wide-set. Eyes round, large, wide-set; intense blue preferred.

Body: Cobby, medium to large, heavy bone structure, firm muscles. Thick, short, powerful neck. Short, tail is heavier at base, tapering to full plume or bush. Short, straight legs with heavy bone structure. Large, round feet. The coat is soft and silky.

Basic genetic makeup of a homozygous Himalayan: aa BB c^s c^s DD ll *(see pages 142-151)*

Mating authorized with other breeds: Yes, with Persians and Exotic Shorthairs (all colours).

TICA Standards	Points
Head	30
Body	30
Coat and colour	30
Condition	10

Household Pet

This is the alley cat, the farm cat, the cat from an animal shelter—any cat without a pedigree or authenticated blood line. Such cats are the basis for all the breeds that have come about through careful breeding, mutations, and processes of selection. Thanks to its native intelligence and adaptability, the Household Pet has survived through the centuries—in spite of wars, diseases, and human cruelty.

AUS.	CAN.	N.Z.	S.AF.	U.K.	U.S.A.
✶	●	✶	●	●	●

✶ In these countries the Household Pet may be known as Moggy, Domestic, Domestic Shorthair, or Domestic Longhair. Check with local associations.

Show ring stars

The absence of aristocratic forebears from their genealogical tree does not prevent household pets from appearing in large numbers at cat shows everywhere, but especially in the United States. This should come as no surprise. Cats are now easing out dogs as North America's favourite pet. And only a small minority of those cat owners have pedigreed cats.

Besides, the Household Pet category accommodates every kind of conformation and colour, hair of every length, colour or combinations of colours, tails of every length and shape, eyes of every colour and shape. They must, however, be neutered for competition.

Balance, proportion, good grooming, and condition are the essential factors. In addition, the cat should seem content and have a healthy coat. Beyond these considerations, the judge's decision is personal.

Non-pedigreed Household Pets are very popular with visitors to shows, since they are not an exaggerated kind of cat but look just like the cats seen in any neighbourhood. Often these cats have more beautiful colouring and more striking markings than some aristocratic felines who can boast long pedigrees.

Characteristics

General description: All coat and eye colours, all coat and tail lengths acceptable. Must be clean, well-fed, and healthy. It should be alert and easy to handle. No penalties for crossed eyes, kinked tails, extra toes, etc.

Disqualifying fault: Poor condition.

Basic genetic makeup of a homozygous Household Pet: none.

Mating authorized with other breeds: No; must be neutered for competition.

TICA Standards	Points
Beauty	20
Personality	25
Condition	55

Japanese Bobtail

Despite its name, this breed originated in China, migrating to Japan centuries ago. It appears in numerous ancient works of Japanese art—statues, prints, and paintings. The breed is said to have once saved the Japanese silk industry from hordes of rodents who were devouring its silkworms.

Japanese Bobtails reached the United States in 1968 and breed standards were set there in the 1970s. The colour pattern most sought after is the *mi-ke* (pronounced *mee-kay*), large red and black patches on a white background.

AUS.	CAN.	N.Z.	S.AF.	U.K.	U.S.A.
	●				●

TICA Standards	Points
Head	20
Type	30
Tail	20
Colour and markings	20
Coat	10

Characteristics

General description: Should present an overall impression of medium size with long clean lines and bone structure. The unique set of its eyes, combined with high cheekbones and a long parallel nose, lends a distinctive cast to its face. The hair on its short tail should fan out in a pompon.

Head: Appears long and finely chiselled; forms an equilateral triangle with gentle curving lines, high cheekbones and noticeable whisker break. Fairly broad muzzle, rounding into whisker break. Long nose, well-defined by two parallel lines from tip to brow. Large, upright ears, wide-set but at right angles to the head. Eyes are large, oval, wide, alert; set into skull at a pronounced slant.

Body: Medium-sized, long, lean; well-muscled, long, slender legs. Hind legs longer than forelegs. Torso is nearly level. Oval paw pads. Coat is medium-long, soft, silky, no real undercoat.

Tail: The short tail is usually carried upright when cat is relaxed. The tail hair somewhat longer and thicker than body hair, growing outward to create the pompon. The tail bone is usually strong and rigid, except at the base. It may be straight or composed of one or more curves and angles.

Subject to penalty: A short, round head or a cobby body.

Disqualifying fault: Tail absent or too long; lack of pompon.

Basic genetic makeup of a homozygous tricolour Japanese Bobtail:
aa BB CC LL Oo SS *(see pages 142-151)*

Mating authorized with other breeds: No.

101

Japanese Bobtail
Longhair

T he first recorded instance of a long-haired version of the Japanese Bobtail was in Japan in 1954. However, the longhairs existed in Japanese street cat populations, especially in the northern provinces, long before that.

Even though the Longhair may seem bigger than the traditional Bobtail, the animals are exactly the same except for the hair length. Newborns of both breeds tend to be exceptionally large.

AUS.	CAN.	N.Z.	S.AF.	U.K.	U.S.A.
	●				●

Friendly, easy-going, intelligent, charming, both kinds of Japanese Bobtails have soft voices and a wide range of tone. Some people say they sing.

Characteristics

General description: TICA standards and characteristics for the Japanese Bobtail Longhair featured on this page are the same as those for the Japanese Bobtail on the previous page. The two cats have the same basic standards. The longhair gene is recessive and in breeding two shorthairs who carry the gene, the ratio of longhairs in the litter will be one in four. Comparing the two cats, you might get the impression that the Longhair is the bigger cat, but this is mainly due to the Longhair's coat; this version of the Japanese Bobtail also sports a ruff.

There has been some disagreement among cat associations about whether these two cats are really different breeds. In May 1991, however, TICA accepted the Longhairs as a separate breed and gave the short-haired Bobtails a slightly more specific set of standards when it came to their coats.

The essential difference is the obvious length of coat hairs. The Japanese Bobtail lacks the ruff on the chest of the Longhair. Another difference is that the legs of the short-haired Bobtail are finely covered with hair, while the Longhair's coat lies fairly flat and then may flow into hairy 'pantaloons' on the hind legs.

Like the short-haired variety, the Longhair lacks any noticeable undercoat. While the short-haired coat is medium in length, soft and silky, and relatively non-shedding, the Longhair's is medium-long to long and sheds.

Basic genetic makeup of a homozygous tortie and white Japanese Bobtail Longhair:
aa BB CC II DD Oo SS

Mating authorized with other breeds:
No

Korat

Astonishingly powerful, intelligent, shy, and somewhat reserved, the Korat has a very soft voice. It is a well-behaved, calm, friendly animal, and very faithful.

One of the oldest natural breeds, the Korat dates from 14th-century Thailand. The Thais regard this cat they call Si-Sawat (pronounced *see-sah-what*) as a symbol of good fortune, and often presented a pair to a bride to ensure wedded bliss. Two cats sent to the United States in 1959 were the first true Korats to reach the West.

Korats have extraordinary hearing, sight, and sense of smell. Unlike other cats, their hair does not float loose with petting. As a result, people who are ordinarily allergic to cats can tolerate a Korat in their homes.

AUS.	CAN.	N.Z.	S.AF.	U.K.	U.S.A.
●	●	●	●	●	●

TICA Standards	Points
Head	18
Ears	7
Eyes	18
Neck	2
Body	15
Tail	3
Legs and feet	4
Coat	13
Colour	20

Characteristics

General description: Heart-shaped head and face with breadth between and across eyes. Eyebrow ridges form upper curves of the heart; gentle curve to a well-developed muzzle.

Head: The forehead is large and flat with an indentation or crease, predominantly in the male. There should be a slight stop between forehead and nose, and the nose has a lion-like downward curve. Chin and jaw are well developed. Ears are large with rounded tips and flare at base, set high on the head in an alert position. Eyes are fully rounded when open, with an Asian slant; they should be oversized for the face. A luminous green is preferred; amber cast is acceptable.

Body: Semi-cobby, well-muscled, and powerful; semblance of hard-coiled spring power and unexpected weight. Females are smaller and daintier. Tail is heavier at base, tapering to a rounded tip. Legs should be in proportion to body; front legs slightly shorter than back. Bone structure should be medium strong. Feet should be oval.

Coat: Short to medium; fine, glossy, and satiny.

Basic genetic makeup of a homozygous Korat: aa BB CC dd LL *(see pages 142-151)*

Mating authorized with other breeds: No.

Maine Coon

Admirers use superlatives to describe the Maine Coon Cat, the oldest American breed. To its fans, this is the big one, the head honcho, the boss cat. One story maintains that this impressive beast is descended from matings between raccoons and wildcats of the U.S. forests. (Even though early specimens had tabby in their coats and round ring markings on their tails—something like those of the raccoon—geneticists say such a mating is biologically impossible.) Fuelling this wild legend is the fact that the Maine Coon Cat has large snowshoe feet with large, round, and well-tufted paws, which help it cross the winter snows that fall in abundance in Maine and other parts of the northeastern United States.

Another legend endows the breed with French blood from Marie-Antoinette's Angora cats. She is said to have given some to the Marquis de Lafayette on one of his trips to the New World during the American War of Independence (1775-1783). Once in America, the Angoras mated with local cats.

The first 'purebred American'

In fact, the Maine Coon is the result of interbreeding between Angora cats imported by British sailors and the semi-wild cats of Maine's forests. Thus, it is the first truly American breed. Maine Coon cats were appearing in shows as early as 1860 and became immensely popular. A brown tabby Maine Coon took Best in Show at Madison Square Gardens, New York, in 1895. With the arrival of Persians, Siamese, and other 'purebreds' in the New World, however, the Maine Coon's glory went into eclipse for almost 50 years. But

AUS.	CAN.	N.Z.	S.AF.	U.K.	U.S.A.
●	●		●	●	●

Elegant yet rugged, gentle yet wild, the Maine Coon is also loving, faithful, and self-confident. It has a noble bearing, is extremely healthy, and is an excellent family cat. Even though it enjoys being indoors, it needs access to a backyard or other open space where it can romp. The Maine Coon has a particularly soft voice.

A MIGHTY HUNTER

The Maine Coon is not afraid of water, and hunting is its favourite occupation. It can fend for itself when necessary—proof that it has not forsaken its free-roaming ancestry, and that breeders were wise to adhere to its original size and build. Good specimens often weigh as much as 30 pounds (14 kg).

in the early 1950s a Maine Coon club was founded, followed in 1976 by the formation of the International Society for the Preservation of the Maine Coon. As a result, the breed has regained all of its former prestige.

North American farmers always recognized the Maine Coon's hunting skills. In so doing, they helped to conserve the breed. The Maine Coon can adapt to any climate and to the toughest terrain, and is an exceptionally powerful cat. The legs are long and heavily muscled, ending in paws that are almost like hands, with very long, widely spaced toes that are astonishingly prehensile.

Maine Coons were introduced to Britain in 1983. In North America, this gentle giant with the lynx-like face continues to be a people pleaser in the home as well as in the show ring.

Characteristics

General description: The Maine Coon was developed as a 'working cat' who could fend for itself in rough, woody terrain and under extreme climatic conditions. Today it is a show cat, but a sturdy-looking one with an amiable disposition. Maine Coons are large with big ears, broad chest, substantial boning, a long, hard muscled, rectangular body, and a long flowing tail. Good muscle tone and density give the cat the appearance of power. Females are significantly smaller than males and can weigh about 5 1/2 pounds (2.5 kg) less.

Head: A broad, modified wedge, with a medium profile and gentle concave slope with a slight bump at the end. The forehead should be a gentle curve; high, prominent cheekbones with distinct stop under them. Square muzzle, firm chin in line with the nose and upper lip. Mature males can have larger, broader heads than females.

Ears: The large, tall ears should be wide at the base, with the lower part just slightly further back than the upper one. Moderately pointed; high on the head with a very slight outward tilt, bases no more than an ear's width apart. Lynx tips should extend vertically from the top back of the ear, the furnishings extending horizontally beyond outer edge of the ear.

Eyes: Large, wide-set, slightly oval, appearing round when wide open. The opening is slightly oblique and towards the outer base of the ear. Any shade of green and/or gold; blue and odd eyes accepted in white cats. No relationship between coat and eye colours.

Body: The large body should be long and rectangular, but not slender. The bone structure

should be substantial and the muscles powerful. Tail is wide at the base and tapering to the tip with full, flowing hair; it should be at least as long as the body from the shoulders to its base.

Legs: The legs are large, rounded, of medium size, and should form a rectangle with the body. Bone structure and muscles substantial; toes well tufted.

Coat: All-weather coat should be of uneven length, shorter on shoulders, gradually lengthening. There should be a frontal ruff, long shaggy britches and belly fur. The coat has distinct body, falling smoothly all along, and there should be a slight, but definite, undercoat.

Colour: White trim around eyes, lips, and chin, except in solid colours. All colours allowed.

Subject to penalty: Pronounced whisker pads. Undershot chin. Nose break or severe bump at end. Lack of slight undercoat. Buttons, lockets, or spots. Straight nose profile. Wide, flared ears. Long stilty legs. Slanted, almond-shaped eyes. Flat tops on eye openings. Short tail. Rounded head. Overall even coat. Lack of belly shag. Short, cobby body. Fine, light boning. Overall small cat.

Basic genetic makeup of a homozygous brown and white classic tabby Maine Coon: AA BB CC DD II SS t^b t^b *(see pages 142-151)*

Mating authorized with other breeds: No.

TICA Standards	Points
Head	35
Body and tail	40
Coat and colour	25

Manx

The Isle of Man, in the Irish Sea between England and Ireland, is world famous for its tailless cats. According to one legend, the Manx slipped onto Noah's Ark just as the door was closing—in time to sail, but too late to save its tail. Another says that a few tailless cats escaped from galleons when the Spanish Armada was shipwrecked offshore in 1588. The cats sheltered on what is now called Spanish Rock until low tide, then made their way to the island. Restricted to that small space, with little opportunity for intermingling with other cats, they bred among themselves. Thus, the gene causing their taillessness was widely propagated.

What is much more likely is that tailless cats began as a natural mutation of the island's domestic breeds. Since the responsible gene is dominant—it can be passed on even if only one parent has it—one mutant cat could easily have founded a whole strain of look-alikes in that isolated environment.

It runs like a hare

The Manx has a distinctive gait; it runs like a hare. This is due to long hind legs, and not as another myth claims: that it mated with rabbits. The true Manx has a hollow or dimple where a tail would ordinarily grow, and is known as a Rumpy. One with the remnant of a tail is called a Stumpy. Breeding Manx can be a problem. Mating can result in malformed kittens that may be stillborn or die soon after birth (see lower box). This may be why some unscrupulous breeders dock kittens' tails and pass them off as genuine Manxes.

AUS.	CAN.	N.Z.	S.AF.	U.K.	U.S.A.
●	●	●		●	●

A fine hunter, lively, active, and speedy, the Manx is somewhat like a dog in temperament. It is extremely faithful to its owner and can even be taken for walks on a leash. It is patient with children, lives quite cheerfully with other animals, is a good companion, accepts training, and can easily be taught a few tricks.

Because of a lethal gene that sometimes crops up in litters when a Manx is bred to a Manx, some British breeders believe breeding should be prohibited and the Manx allowed to die out.

A less drastic approach is to breed a Manx to an American or a British Shorthair, the two breeds that the Manx most resembles—apart from the tail. Not all kittens in the ensuing litter will be Manxes, but some undoubtedly will be tailless. Today, the Manx breed, though still associated with the Isle of Man, has spread throughout the world.

Characteristics

General description: The Manx/Cymric has a round head with a firm muzzle and prominent cheeks, short front legs, high hindquarters, a great depth of flank, and a short back that forms a smooth continuous arch from the shoulders to the round rump. The overall appearance should be that of a medium-sized, compact, and muscular cat. These cats are slow to mature.

The Manx/Cymric cat should appear tailless. The flank should have greater depth than in any other breed.

Head: The medium-sized, round head should be slightly longer than broad. In profile there should be a gentle nose dip. The forehead should be moderately rounded, and the muzzle slightly longer than broad with definite muzzle break. Large, round whisker pads; strong chin, prominent cheeks. Short, thick neck.

Ears: Rather wide at the base, medium-sized, tapering to the tip. They should be placed wide apart and, when viewed from behind, resemble the rocker of a cradle. The hair may be tufted, the furnishings sparse.

Eyes: The round eyes should be large; the aperture should be at a slight angle. The colouring should conform to coat colour, but should only be considered if all other points are equal.

Body: The body should be cobby and of medium size, well-muscled and sturdily boned. Forelegs should be shorter than hind legs. The round rump should be higher than the shoulders. The hind legs should have substantial bone and should be straight when viewed from behind.

Tail: Appears tailless. No penalty for a rise of bone or cartilage which does not stop the judge's hand when the palm is stroked down the back and over the rump.

Feet: The round feet should be medium size.

Subject to penalty: Eyes set straight across in head; rangy body; level back; short hind legs, fine bone, bowed or knock-kneed hind legs.

Disqualifying fault: Any congenital deformity. Weak hindquarters causing inability to stand or walk properly.

Basic genetic makeup of a red and white male Manx:
BB CC DD LL Mx mx OO SS
(see pages 142-151)

Mating authorized with other breeds:
Yes, with European Shorthair, British Shorthair, American Shorthair. Also the rumpy Manx may be bred with the three other categories of Manx (see list of four categories below), but never rumpy mating with rumpy because of a gene that causes lethal spinal abnormalities.

The four categories of Manx:

- The rumpy, the top-rated Manx, has no tail.

- The rumpy riser has one to three vertebrae connected to the last bone of the spine (sacrum).

- The stumpy has one to three tail (caudal) vertebrae.

- The longy, or tailed Manx, has a kinked or normal tail.

TICA Standards	Points
Head and ears	25
Eyes	10
Body	30
Legs and feet	15
Coat	15
Colour and markings	5

Cymric

The Cymric is simply the long-haired version of the Manx. It is a relative newcomer, first appearing in litters of pedigreed short-haired Manxes in Canada in the 1960s. When the new long-haired cats were bred together, the breed held true.

The standard Cymric is affectionate, intelligent, happiest when active, and is identical in every respect to its forebears, except for the coat.

The fur of the Cymric is long, soft, silky, and double, with a thick undercoat. The ruff and hind legs are thickly furred, and the cat sports distinctive tufts of hair on both its cheeks and its ears.

Mating and TICA Standards: As above.

Basic genetic makeup of a homozygous brown mackerel tabby Cymric:
AA BB CC DD II Mx mx TT

Norwegian

Norse legend describes this sturdy cat as mysterious and enchanting. Known in its native land as Norsk Skogskatt (Norwegian Forest Cat), its ancestors were Angora cats adopted by Viking sailors in the Near East to serve as rat-catchers, pets, and sometimes as ships' mascots.

The early Norwegian cats lived wild in Norway's rugged forests. According to a legend, Thor, strongest of all the Norse gods, was unable to lift one off the ground. A pure white pair pulled the chariot of Freyja, the goddess of battle, death, fertility, and love.

Life in the wild

As protection against Norway's heavy winter snows and harsh winds, the Norwegian has a double coat—the undercoat thick and woolly, the guard hairs long and water-resistant. Like any good insulation, it keeps the cat warm in winter, cool in summer. Its water-repellent guard hairs, which are 5 inches (12 cm) long, can dry out 15 minutes after being soaked. These cats are solidly built and well proportioned, strong walkers and skilful climbers, qualities guaranteed to ensure their success as hunters.

Norwegians were first exhibited in Norway in the 1930's, but because of a ban on their export they were not recognized internationally for another 40 years. The efforts of a Norwegian cat fancier, Carl-Fredrik Nordane, are credited with saving the breed from extinction because of the side effects of inbreeding. Grateful cat lovers paraded in Oslo in his honour in 1977, after a Paris meeting of the Feline International Federation of Europe admitted the Norwegian Forest Cat to championship competition.

AUS.	CAN.	N.Z.	S.AF.	U.K.	U.S.A.
●	●		●	●	●

The Norwegian is affectionate, confident, and calm, and has a faithful nature. It loves the outdoors and is an effective hunter. The 'Wegie,' as it is sometimes called, is hardy and self-sufficient and, if an outdoors cat, can endure the extremely cold temperatures of Norway's harsh northern climate.

SUMMER AND WINTER COATS

When showing these cats, the changing seasons must be taken into account. The length and thickness of the fur vary considerably depending on the temperature. In summer, the only really long fur that remains is on the tail and the tufts in the ears and between the toes.

The coat of the Norwegian is so dense that you need a generous amount of shampoo to make sure the lather gets through the water-repellent guard hairs. The thicker hairs on the back make it almost waterproof. In winter, the undercoat is extremely thick.

Characteristics

General description: The appearance is an alert, healthy, firm, muscular, and well-proportioned cat. Males are large; females can be considerably smaller. The boning should be substantial, with good muscle tone and no evidence of obesity or emaciation. Overall appearance in a mature cat in full coat is square. Temperamentally, they should be gentle and amenable to handling.

Head: The rather triangular head should be in proportion to body size. The nose in profile should be straight from the top of the forehead to the tip of the nose. There should be no break, and the muzzle should follow the line of the head, with no evidence of pinch or snippiness. The front of the skull should be flat and the chin firm.

Ears: Wide at the base; medium to large and slightly rounded at the tip. The lower outer edge should follow the line of the head down to the chin and should be arched forward as if listening. Tufts: lynx tips are desirable; furnishings: extend beyond outer edge of the ear.

Eyes: Moderately large and set medium-wide, with the aperture slightly angled and the outer corner slightly higher than the inner corner.

Body: The body should be sturdy, moderate in length and have substantial boning; it should be full-chested and have considerable girth, but not be fat. There is also considerable depth of flank. The neck should be muscular and medium in length.

Legs: Medium to long, in proportion to the body, the hind legs longer than the front ones.

Heavy bone structure. Thighs must be heavily muscled and lower legs substantially muscled. Legs should be straight when viewed from the rear. Feet must be rounded, large, and be well tufted.

Tail: Wide at the base, the tail should taper towards the end. It should be bushy and as long as the body.

Coat: The coat should be of uneven length. The coarse texture gives the cat a double coat that has a feeling of heaviness and depth covered by water-repellent guard hairs. In summer the overall coat is shorter and lacks both muttonchops and bib; only the tail, ear and toe tufts distinguish the cat as a longhair. Buttons, lockets, and spots are allowed in all colours. White or off-white is allowed on chin, breast, and stomach of tabbies.

Subject to penalty: Legs not in proportion to the body; a cobby or extremely long body; nose with a break; round or square head; small ears; short tail; delicate bone structure.

Basic genetic makeup of a homozygous brown and white classic tabby Norwegian:
AA BB CC DD II SS t^b t^b *(see pages 142-151)*

Mating authorized with other breeds: No.

TICA Standards	Points
Head	30
Body	20
Tail	10
Coat	20
Colour and markings	5
Condition and performance	15

Ocicat

This wild-looking animal possesses a temperament that seems almost half-cat, half-dog. Its 'doggy' half can be trained to fetch, sit, and respond to human commands; it will eagerly go for a walk on a leash.

As a pet, the Ocicat is loyal, affectionate, playful, and even-tempered. It combines the liveliness and speed of the Abyssinian with the gentleness of the Siamese—minus the harsh voice.

The first Ocicat appeared in the United States in 1964 during experiments to create Abyssinian-pointed Siamese. The successful litter also produced one spotted kitten that breeder Virginia Daly called Tonga. Her daughter, seeing the resemblance to an ocelot, called him an ocicat. Tonga was sold as a pet, but news of him piqued cat fanciers' interest and the mating that produced him was repeated.

AUS.	CAN.	N.Z.	S.AF.	U.K.	U.S.A.
●	●	●		●	●

TICA Standards	Point
Head	20
Body	30
Tail	5
Coat and colour	20
Pattern	25

Characteristics

General description: The Ocicat is a large, well-spotted cat of moderate type. It displays the look of an athletic animal, being powerful, well-muscled and solid, graceful and lithe, yet with a fullness of body and chest. It is alert to its surroundings and shows great vitality. The Ocicat is bred in many colours, and is particularly noted for its 'wild' appearance.

Head: The head is a modified wedge. In profile, there should be a visible but gentle rise from the bridge of the nose to the brow. The well-defined muzzle should have a suggestion of squareness; in profile it shows good length; no snippiness. Chin should be strong and there should be a slight curve from the muzzle to the cheek. Ears are moderately large. Lynx tips, when present, are a bonus. The neck should be arched.

Eyes: Almond-shaped, wide-set, the opening angled slightly upwards towards the ears. All eye colours allowed except blue; there is no relationship between coat and eye colours.

Body: The large body is semi-foreign in length. The bone structure is fairly heavy and the muscles are substantial yet with athletic appearance. The chest is deep with some ribs slightly sprung; the back goes from level to slightly higher in the rear with the flanks reasonably level. The tail should be fairly long, medium-slim and have a slight taper with a dark tip. Legs should be medium-long and in good proportion to body. They should be well-muscled with a substantial bone structure. Oval feet should be in proportion to the legs.

Coat: The coat should be long enough to carry several bands of ticking, and should be fine, thick, tight, and close-lying.

Basic genetic makeup of a homozygous chocolate spotted tabby Ocicat:
AA bb CC DD LL t^s t^s *(see pages 142-151)*

Mating authorized with other breeds: Yes, with Abyssinians after three or four generations.

Oriental Longhair

The Oriental Longhair, sometimes called the Mandarin, is actually semi-long-haired—a Siamese in a Persian coat. Like its short-haired relative (see pages 112-113), its ancestry includes Siamese and other pedigreed breeds. It inherited many of their best features—intelligence, grace, curiosity, a strong body, a trusting, affectionate nature.

The fine dense texture of this cat's coat makes it seem less angular than the Oriental Shorthair. Beneath the coat nonetheless is the same elegant form and high carriage.

Lively, energetic, and intensely curious about everything and everyone, the Oriental Longhair makes an excellent pet. It is easily groomed, devoted to its owner, yet gets along well with other household pets.

AUS.	CAN.	N.Z.	S.AF.	U.K.	U.S.A.
✶	●	●	●	✶	●

✶ In these countries the Oriental Longhair may also be known as the Angora, Oriental, Javanese, or Balinese.

TICA Standards	Points
Head and ears	15
Eyes	10
Body	25
Coat	25
Colour	10
Balance	10

Characteristics

General description: A semi-long-haired cat with distinctive long tapering lines. It is svelte, refined, and very lithe, but strong and muscular. The coat should be fine, silky, and lie close to the body. The tail plume should be long and feathery. The head and neck should both be long. The cat should be in excellent physical condition.

Subject to penalty: Short or cobby body.

Basic genetic makeup of a homozygous black Oriental Longhair: aa BB CC DD ll *(see pages 142-151)*

Mating authorized with other breeds: Yes, with Oriental Shorthairs, Siamese, and Balinese.

Oriental Shorthair

Of all cat breeds, the Oriental Shorthair is the most dog-like in appearance and devotion to its owner. Because of its long, elegant body, it is often referred to as the greyhound of cats.

Known as Oriental Shorthairs in Canada and the United Sates, they are called simply Oriental or Foreign in other countries, notably in Australia, Britain, New Zealand, and South Africa.

Ancestors of all Oriental or Foreign breeds, whether Siamese or those resulting from Siamese and Korat (or Russian Blue) interbreeding, came from Thailand, formerly Siam. Known in Arab countries for centuries, the Oriental breeds arrived in Britain in the late 1800s, and reached North America some time later.

Relatives all

Cats known as Foreign or Oriental Shorthairs are the newest of three short-haired varieties. The other two—the British Shorthairs and the American Shorthairs—were used to develop the new strain.

The first of these new shorthairs appeared in England in the 1950s. A queen named Our Miss Smith had two short-haired kittens that looked like Siamese except that their eyes were green and their coats solidly brown. Over the next two decades various British breeders produced other cats with Siamese bodies but in white or other solid colours.

In 1972, U.S. breeders Peter and Vicky Marksten visited Britain and discovered these Siamese-looking full-colour cats. Later the Markstens were instrumental in having all Foreign Shorthairs in

AUS.	CAN.	N.Z.	S.AF.	U.K.	U.S.A.
✶	●	●	●	●	●

✶ In Australia the Oriental Shorthair may be called Oriental or solid-coloured Siamese. Check with local associations.

Lively, curious, and intelligent, the Oriental Shorthair does not like to be left alone. It demands attention by draping itself around one's feet or neck.

The Oriental Shorthair has the enduring muscle strength of a long-distance runner. These cats mature quite early, breed easily, and produce larger-than-average litters.

To ensure that this cat retains its slim elegance, it must be fed a diet that is virtually fat-free.

North America combined in one category, Oriental Shorthairs. With myriad colour combinations thus established, Oriental Shorthairs probably have the most varied colours and patterns of any cat breed. (Outside North America, individual colours continue to be registered as separate breeds.)

The shape of the Oriental Shorthair continues to be identical to the Siamese. Only the colouring of the coat and eyes differentiates the two. The Siamese is only coloured at the points and its eyes are green. The Oriental Shorthair has a full-colour coat and its eyes are green. Mating between the two breeds is common.

Characteristics

General description: A lithe, svelte cat with long tapering lines. It should be hard and muscular with no indication of fat or emaciation—in fact, it should have an appearance of health and vitality. Its coat should be short, fine-textured, glossy, and lie close to the body.

Head: The head is a long, tapering wedge that starts at the nose and flares out in straight lines to the tip of the ears, forming a triangle with no break at the whiskers. The skull is flat. In profile, a long straight line is seen from the top of the head to the tip of the nose. The nose is long and straight, a continuation of the forehead with no break. The muzzle is fine and wedge-shaped. The chin and jaw are medium-sized. When the whiskers are smoothed back, the underlying bone structure is apparent. The head is medium in size, and in good proportion to the body. Neck is long and slender. Ears are strikingly large and wide at the base.

Eyes: The almond-shaped eyes are medium in size and are slanted towards the nose in harmony with the lines of the wedge. There is no less than the width of an eye between the eyes.

Body: The medium-sized body is long and svelte, a distinctive combination of fine, firm bones and firm muscles. The shoulder and hips continue the sleek lines of the tubular body. The hips should never be wider than the shoulders; the abdomen should be tight. Legs are long and slim, in good proportion to the body, with hind legs longer than the front ones. The oval-shaped paws are small.

Tail: Narrow at the base, thin, long, and tapering to a fine point.

Subject to penalty: Round or broad head. Short or broad muzzle. Bulge over eyes. Dip in nose. Receding or massive chin. Small, round, bulging or receding eyes; unslanted eye aperture. Cobby, short, thick, or flabby body; belly pouch. Short legs, heavy leg bones; large or round feet.

Basic genetic makeup of a homozygous fawn Oriental Shorthair:
aa $b^l b^l$ CC DD LL *(see pages 142-151)*

Mating authorized with other breeds:
Yes, with Siamese, Balinese, and Oriental Longhairs.

TICA Standards	Points
Head	15
Ears	5
Eyes	15
Body	25
Coat and colour	20

Persians

A Calico or Tortoiseshell-and-White Persian.

Persians or Longhairs, the most plentiful and most prized of all pedigree cats, are descended from various breeds introduced to Europe from Afghanistan, Iran, Turkey, and Russia from the 1600s on. Before Pietro della Valle (1586-1652) brought several pairs from Persia (present-day Iran) to Italy in 1620, there were no long-haired breeds in Europe. Other early imports were by French scholar and politician Nicholas-Claude Fabri de Peiresc (1580-1637), who brought cats from Angora (present-day Ankara), Turkey, to France. (When this breed appeared in England, Britons called it the French cat.)

By the late 1800s, British cat owners had begun selective breeding of the various strains. By the early 1900s, two distinct breeds were emerging. The more powerful, most impressive of the two became known as a Longhair or Persian. Its immense popularity eclipsed the lighter-framed and lighter-coated breed, which became the Turkish Angora (see page 135).

The new breed was as commonly called Longhaired as Persian at the outset. Then owners formed clubs based on cat colour. Blue was one of the most popular shades. Even Queen Victoria had a blue pair, and 100 blues were exhibited at the London Cat Show of 1899. When Britain's Governing Council of Cat Fancy was organized in 1910, it decreed that Persians would be called Longhairs and that each colour type would be a different breed. This is still the case in Britain.

The new long-haired breed was equally popular in the United States, but there the breed is known as the Persian and the colours are a variety. American breeders also produced a cat with a chunkier build, shorter body, and a rounder head than the British Longhair. This is how the Peke Face (see page 139) came into being. But whereas the Peke Face may be encouraged in

AUS.	CAN.	N.Z.	S.AF.	U.K.	U.S.A.
✳	●	●	●	●	●

✳ In Australia Persians may be known as Longhairs. Check with local associations.

A ROYAL CAT

In the early 1600s, Italian traveller and writer Pietro della Valle returned home with a species of cat never before seen in Europe. They had long, grey silver hair and came from the Chorazan Province of Persia (present-day Iran). Ordinarily these cats were reserved for the aristocracy. Eastern rulers sent some as gifts to French notables, including King Louis XV.

The Persian retains its 'aristocratic' connections, continuing to be associated with luxury, silken cushions and high living. Even in less illustrious households, it relinquishes none of its regal habits. It also has acquired a wide range of coat colours.

The Persian remains one of the breeds most affected by changes in fashion and, as a result, has been much altered over the years. Its appearance can be modified easily in only a few generations.

Smoke Persian

Red Persian

Black Persian

North America, British breeders tend to regard it as a deformed breed. U.S. breeders settled on a less extreme type that has the nose and the very deep break in the same place.

The difference between American and British Persians is marked. European breeders are free to import Persians from either Britain or the United States and to develop one type rather than another. At shows, however, their choice is not necessarily that of the judges, who have their own preferences. Show results vary widely and often spark heated debate. Perhaps there will come a time when one Persian will combine the beauty of the American version with the sumptuous colours of the British.

> Placid, good-tempered, and extremely easy-going, the Persian is upset by virtually nothing. It is indeed a charming and decorative addition to any household. A modern Persian cannot hunt and is therefore quite incapable of looking after itself. Persians are extremely expensive, largely because they achieve sexual maturity relatively late and their litters are often very small.

Cameo Persian

Brown Tabby
Persian

Golden Persian

Tortoiseshell
Persian

IMPORTANT DAILY CARE

A Persian's grooming must never be neglected. Tangles and knots form easily and can be impossible to remove. To prevent this happening, the coat must be combed and brushed every day. A thorough brushing needn't be a trial, however. It can serve as a time of pleasant closeness between an animal and its owner. The eyes, which weep easily, must also be cleaned daily.

Before welcoming such a marvellous bundle of fur into the home, potential owners should realize that keeping this magnificent cat happy, clean, and at ease in its luxurious coat lies entirely in their hands. However beautiful it may be to start with, however proud and majestic, an animal of this breed can soon become an unattractive mass. There is no more pathetic sight than an ill-kept Persian.

Grooming for exhibition can take hours. All breeders have their own secret tips for making their animals look their very best on the judge's table.

Characteristics

General description: The cat should be firm in flesh but not fat; well balanced physically and temperamentally, gentle and amenable to handling. It should give the impression of power.

Head: The head should be round and massive with great breadth of skull, the face round with a sweet expression and round underlying bone structure. The jaws should be broad and powerful with full, prominent cheeks and teeth meeting perfectly. The short nose should be almost as broad as it is long, with a definite break between the eyes. The short neck should provide adequate support for the big head. The small ears should be set low on the head, fitting into the rounded contour.

Eyes: Large, round, wide-set, and expressive, with eye colour conforming to coat colour. The deeper and richer the eye colour, the better.

Body: The chest is to be deep and massive across the shoulders and rump, with a short, well-rounded abdomen and a level back. In the front view the forelegs should be short and straight from breadth of the chest. When viewed from the rear, the legs should be straight. Feet are fairly large and round. The tail should be short and carried at an angle lower than the back, but neither curved nor trailing.

Coat: The coat should be full and long all over the body, including the shoulders. The ruff should be immense and continue in a deep frill between the front legs. Seasonal variations in coat.

Subject to penalty: Long, narrow head; long Roman nose; thin muzzle, severe overshot or undershot jaw; bite deformity. Small eyes set on a bias or close together; pale eye colour. Large, pointed ears, slanting out from head or set too close together. Narrow chest, long back; long, thin neck; disproportionately long tail; light, long legs, bow legs; oval feet or separated toes; poor muscle tone.

Disqualifying faults: Overall lack of merit. Lockets or buttons; kinked tail; bad bite; extremely asymmetric face; slanted eyes; poor condition; totally unamenable to handling.

Basic genetic makeup of a homozygous black Persian:
aa BB CC DD ll *(see pages 142-151)*

Mating authorized with other breeds:
Yes, with Himalayans (which are another colour of Persian) and the Exotic Shorthair.

TICA Standards	Points
Head	30
Eyes	10
Body	30
Coat and colour	20
Condition and balance	10

Ragdoll

The name aptly describes this docile cat's most renowned characteristic—its propensity to lie limp and relaxed in its owner's arms, just like a rag doll. The semi-long-haired breed was developed in California in the 1960s, the progeny of Josephine, a White Persian queen, and her consort, Daddy Warbucks. According to breeder Ann Baker, the pregnant Josephine was hit by a car and all kittens in the subsequent litter exhibited the limpness for which the breed is named. A similar trait did not occur in Josephine's preaccident kittens.

Geneticists, however, dismiss the accident theory, and attribute the trait to the breed's gentle, even-tempered nature, the result of selective breeding.

Another Ragdoll myth is that they have a high tolerance to pain. People who know the cats say their pain threshold is similar to that of other cats, and that the Ragdolls' injuries often go unnoticed because of the animal's uncomplaining nature. For this reason, it is better kept indoors.

The Ragdoll rivals the Maine Coon in size, length, and strength. It is a tall cat with a long, muscular body, with the hind legs longer than the front. It does not attain its full size until it is 4 years old. The breed is fairly rare outside the United States.

AUS.	CAN.	N.Z.	S.AF.	U.K.	U.S.A.
●	●	●		●	●

The Ragdoll is the essence of sweetness and gentleness. Cats of this breed seem to have perfect self-control, never showing the slightest sign of aggression or impatience.

Characteristics

General description: The ideal Ragdoll grows exceptionally large and heavy. The cat should be firm and muscular with no fat except on the lower abdomen. Females are noticeably smaller than males. Colour maturity is not achieved until 2 years old; full weight and size for at least 4 years.

Head: The medium-sized head should be a broad modified wedge with appearance of a flat plane between the ears; the muzzle is round and medium in length with a gentle stop and a well-developed chin. Neck should be short, heavy and strong. The oval eyes should be large. Medium-sized ears should be set to form a continuation of the modified wedge. They should be broad and tilt slightly forward.

Body: The long, large body should have a full chest, as broad at the shoulders as it is at the hindquarters where muscles should be heavier. A fat pad on the lower abdomen is acceptable. The long tail should be in proportion to the body length and have a slight taper. The legs should

be medium-heavy, the back legs higher than front. Round feet should be large with tufting.

Coat: Plush, silky, medium-long to long, with longer preferred. It breaks as the cat moves and is longest around the neck and the face.

Subject to penalty: Short tail or legs; pointed ears; long thick legs; cobby body; Roman nose.

Disqualifying fault: Non-blue eyes. Short coat.

Basic genetic makeup of a homozygous white seal point Ragdoll:
aa BB c^S c^S DD ll SS *(see pages 142-151)*

Mating authorized with other breeds: No.

TICA Standards	Points
Head	30
Type	30
Colour and pattern	20
Coat	10
Legs, feet and balance	10

Russian Blue

The origins of the Russian Blue are uncertain, but it is believed that sailors docking at Archangel on the White Sea collected grey cats for sale in Britain. Cats similar to today's breed were often seen at British shows in the late 1800s. They had yellowish eyes, were heavier and bigger than today's specimens, and were known not only as Russian Blues but also as Archangel cats, Maltese cats, Spanish Blues, and American Blues. (Introduced to the United States in the 1900s, they were known there as Maltese cats.) Until 1912, when British cat fanciers recognized the Russian Blues as a separate class, they were shown alongside British Blues, Chartreux Blues, and other blue shorthairs.

Two world wars led to the breed's decline in Europe. After World War II there were revitalization attempts using British Blue and Siamese outcrosses, with mixed results. Around the same time, U.S. breeders imported Russian Blues from Britain and Sweden, and the combined strains produced graceful cats with silver blue coats.

By the late 1960s the breed had been revived in Britain, where breeders began developing Russian Whites and Russian Blacks. The Russian Blue itself continues to be popular in North America.

This elegant cat has a gentle expression. Its fur is short, thick, and lustrous—like a seal's pelt but in a shimmering pale grey with a silvery cast. Stroking one is like stroking a piece of silk, and to see one is to fall under the spell of its intense green eyes.

AUS.	CAN.	N.Z.	S.AF.	U.K.	U.S.A.
✶	●	●	●	●	●

✶ In Australia the Russian Blue may be known as Russian, Russian Black, Russian White, or Russian Red. Check with local associations.

Timid, reserved, soft-voiced, and easily upset, the Russian Blue is affectionate, but needs quiet. It attaches itself to one person only, and will wait for that person for hours without budging. Towards other animals, however, it is demonstrative and friendly.

119

Characteristics

General description: Distinctively elegant with foreign-body type and an angular, modified wedge-shaped head consisting of seven flat planes. It is a gentle, shy cat with a soft, sweet voice; it is easily startled and prefers being handled delicately. Its most outstanding characteristic is its double coat: short, silky and upstanding, like the coat of a seal or beaver, with silver tipping on the guard hairs that gives the fur a silvery sheen.

Head: The head should be a modified wedge with flat planes, with the straight nose and flat forehead forming two planes. The medium muzzle should have no break. The forehead should be high, the chin a flat vertical plane from the tip of the nose to the bottom of the chin. The ears should be pointed and have slightly rounded tips, set far apart, as much on the side as on top of the head. The slender neck should be long but may appear shorter due to dense fur. The rather large eyes should be set far apart and be just oval enough to show an oriental slant. Colour should be green; in kittens, changing from yellow to green.

Body: The long body should have a foreign shape; males larger than females. The coat gives the cat a chunky appearance, but the body should be finely boned and have lithe muscles. The long tail should be straight, tapering from a rather thick base to a slender tip. Legs are long and the feet are small and well-rounded. The cat seems to stand and walk on tiptoe.

Coat: The dense, plush double coat should be fine, soft, and silky.

Subject to penalty: Weak chin. Full penalty for eyes with no green.

Basic genetic makeup of a homozygous Russian Blue:
aa BB CC dd LL *(see pages 142-151)*

Mating authorized with other breeds:
No.

TICA Standards	Points
Head	20
Eyes	10
Neck	3
Tail	5
Body	15
Legs and feet	7
Colour	20
Coat	20

Nebelung

The Nebelung is a very gentle, quiet, timid, calm, and reserved cat. As the breed is still being developed, the standard is not yet definitively established. The only Nebelungs in existence are in the United States.

The Nebelung conformation is the same as that of the Russian Blue, from which it was bred. In lengthening the hair of the Russian Blue, breeders created a double coat of thick fur which is very soft to the touch. The fur is a very pale blue-grey with a silvery sheen as if spangled.

The Nebelung is an elegant cat, slim and streamlined despite its long hair.

Colours
Both blue and white are recognized.
• Blue: regular, without tabby markings, shining and glossy; the lighter the colour the better; a slight silvery sheen is desirable; pads and muzzle, pinkish grey.
• White: pure white and glossy; muzzle, lips, and pads pink.

Eye colour: Eye colour is very important; the eyes should be the brightest possible green at maturity. Nebelung kitten eyes change rapidly through yellow to green. By 4 months, a green ring should appear around the pupil.

Colour description: The coat is an even bright blue throughout with lighter colour preferred. The guard hairs are silver tipped, giving the coat a lustrous appearance. Ghost tabby markings permitted on kittens. The nose leather is charcoal grey; paw pads rose flesh pink.

Subject to penalty: Weak chin; insufficiently long fur; not sufficiently Russian Blue in type; white patches in the blue; eyes insufficiently green. Amount of penalty determined by quantity and vividness of green. Full penalty given for non-green eyes.

Genotype of a blue homozygote Nebelung:
BB CC dd ll *(see pages 142-151)*

Mating authorized with other breeds:
Yes, with Russian Blues.

Scottish Fold

At first glance, the Scottish Fold looks owlish, teddy bearish even, with its saucer-like eyes and rounded head set off by forward-folding ears. It first came to attention in Perthshire, Scotland, in 1961, when Susie, a white kitten with folded ears, the result of a spontaneous mutation, was born on the McRae's Tayside farm. Two years later, the mutant Susie had an identical kitten, which the McRaes gave to William and Mary Ross, a local shepherd family that had long been enamoured of Susie. They named their kitten Snooks.

From Scotland to England to the United States

Within a few years, the Rosses were taking their unusual cats—by now Snooks had produced Snowball, a white male kitten with folded ears—to local shows. They caught the eye of English breeder Pat Turner who introduced the Folds to England. It became evident that when Folds are bred to cats with straight ears, half the litter will have folded ears. Matings of Fold to Fold, however, can produce kittens with skeletal abnormalities such as curved hocks.

In 1970, several Scottish Folds arrived in Massachusetts, where Dr. Neil Todd was researching carnivore genetics. Dr. Todd gave one of the cats to Sally Wolfe Peters, a Pennsylvania breeder. She produced Wyola Jed Gallant, the first Fold registered in the United States (1973). Five years later, Folds were admitted to championship competition.

In Britain meantime, registration of the Scottish Fold was halted. Those in charge of the British conformation were concerned about the frequency of ear mange and the high level of deafness among

Rather slow moving, the Scottish Fold is extremely good-tempered, affectionate, well-balanced, alert, and intelligent. The voice is soft and undemanding. This cat can very quickly become an important member of the household, whether this be a home of sedate retirees or one that is noisy and full of children.

The ears, more or less straight at birth, begin to fold when the kitten is 2 or 3 weeks old.

The fold may be single or double, and not all Scottish Folds have folded ears. The straight-eared Folds are known as pink-eared Folds.

To prevent skeletal abnormalities, Folds must never be interbred, but always outcrossed with another breed such as a British or American Shorthair.

these animals. In fact, the Governing Council of Cat Fancy, Britain's oldest and largest cat association, has never recognized the Fold. Until 1983, when the Cat Association of Britain added the breed to its register, British breeders could not register this cat.

Experience has shown that this breed can be treated for mange in the same way as any other breed, and the deafness is associated with a white coloration, not breed. But there is a real difficulty associated with the dominant gene of this mutation. Kittens born to two Folds may suffer a bone disorder in which the vertebrae of the tail become fused and cartilage grows around the joints of the paws. The disorder may be caused by the gene responsible for the unusual ears.

TICA Standards	Points
Head	15
Ears	30
Tail	20
Eyes	15
Body	10
Colour	10

Characteristics

Head: Rounded, with a firm chin and jaw. The broad, short nose has a gentle curve, and a slight stop is permitted. Muzzle should be well-rounded. Jowly appearance is allowed in males. The large eyes should be well-rounded and separated by a broad nose. Colour should conform to coat colour.

Ears: The small-to-medium ears should be folded forward and downwards, the tips rounded. A smaller. tightly folded ear is preferred over a loose fold and large ear.

Body: The body should be medium size (females slightly smaller), rounded and even from shoulder to pelvic girdle. Body should be well-padded with medium bone structure and sturdy muscles. No short, coarse legs. Tapering

tail should be flexible and at least two-thirds the length of the body.

Coat: The short coat should be very dense and resilient.

Subject to penalty: Tail that is foreshortened, or that is lacking in flexibility due to abnormally thick vertebrae. Definite nose break.

Basic genetic makeup of a homozygous blue cream Scottish Fold:
AA BB DD Fd fd LL Oo t^b t^b
(see pages 142-151)

Mating authorized with other breeds:
Yes, mandatory to obtain pedigree. Can be bred with British, Exotic, and American Shorthairs.

Scottish Fold Longhair

Head: Rounded, with a firm chin and jaw. The nose should have a gentle curve, with a slight stop permitted; the muzzle should be well-rounded, as should the whisker pads; the cheeks should be rounded too. Males should have a prominent jowl, and a broad, short nose. Well-rounded, large eyes should be separated by the broad nose.

Ears: The small-to-medium ears should be folded forward and downwards, the tips rounded, and set in a cap-like fashion to expose a rounded cranium; a smaller, tightly folded ear preferred.

Body: Medium size (females slightly smaller). Muscles sturdy, bones medium. Tapering tail; no shorter than two-thirds length of the body.

Coat: Semi-long, standing away from the body; ruff and breeches desirable; soft and full of life.

Basic genetic makeup of a homozygous white and brown mackerel tabby Scottish Fold Longhair:
AA BB CC DD Fd fd II SS TT
(see pages 142-151)

Mating authorized with other breeds:
Yes, with American and British Shorthairs.

Siamese

Once a wild species of the Far East, the Siamese cat was refined at the royal court of Siam (now Thailand). Its earliest depiction appears in the manuscript of the *Cat-Book Poems*, a Thai literary treasure, now preserved in the National Library at Bangkok. The poems describe a feline with the features of today's seal point–a white body, and dark ears, feet and tail. The manuscript survived the destruction of the ancient Thai capital, Ayuthia, by Burmese invaders in 1767. The great age of the manuscript, thought to date from the 1500s or earlier, suggests the Siamese was centuries old even in 1767.

AUS.	CAN.	N.Z.	S.AF.	U.K.	U.S.A.
●	●	●	●	●	●

A ROYAL TALE

A kinked tail is considered a flaw in a Siamese cat. But legend says the flaw is a sign of service to royalty. Before Thai princesses bathed, they put their jewels on the tail of their favourite cat, which curved the tip to keep the rich burden from falling off.

Cats of palace and plain

According to Thai tradition, only royalty was permitted to own Siamese cats. The tradition began with an early Thai monarch, who was so entranced by the cats that he threatened to execute anyone who attempted to steal one. His successors honoured his wish to preserve the purity of the breed and confined the cats within the palace walls. They became cherished pets, and according to Buddhist belief, the inheritors of the souls of dead royalty headed for the afterlife. To obtain one of the revered cats was difficult: to receive one as a royal gift was a great honour.

The Siamese was also seen in regions far from its hot, humid homeland in southeast Asia. A German naturalist, Peter Simon Pallas (1741-1811), observed the cat while travelling across the plains of Russian central Asia during the 1770s. Pallas described the colour of its body as light chestnut, rather than white, with dark extremities. Some experts wonder whether the cat was a genetic oddity. But others believe it may have been the offspring of an imported cat. In which case, the colour difference was due to the colder, harsher climate of central Asia. (As a rule, outdoor exposure during the winter darkens the colour of a Siamese cat.)

A gift of royal cats

The first genuine 'Royal Cats of Siam' appeared in Britain at the London cat show of 1885. They were a pair of seal points–known as Pho and Mia–presented by King Chulalongkorn to Owen Gould, the departing British consul general in Bangkok. (Chulalongkorn, Thai ruler from 1868 to 1910, was the son of Mongkut, whose story is told in the Rodgers and Hammerstein's musical play, *The King and I*.) Gould gave the pair to his sister, a Mrs. Veley, who exhibited them with success.

Unfortunately, later imports were too sickly to survive in their new home. Some British cat fanciers of the 1890s wondered whether the Siamese would ever become popular. By the decade's end, once breeders had resolved the rearing problems, the cats were proliferating.

After 1900, the popularity of the Siamese cat spread to the United States, where British imports were used to develop the American breed. (The first Siamese had arrived there in 1878. David Stickles, the American consul in Bangkok, had also received a gift of royal cats, which were eventually given to the wife of President Rutherford B. Hayes.)

In Great Britain, the United States, and elsewhere, the demand for Siamese cats peaked in the 1950s and 1960s. But the increase in numbers brought about a significant decline in quality, which breeders have attempted to reverse in recent decades.

Nevertheless, the Siamese is an enduring favourite. Its intelligent and affectionate nature, as well as its beautiful blue eyes, lithe body, and graceful movements, ensure its continuing popularity. It is the only purebred instantly recognized by people whose experience of cats is limited to mixed household types.

The four classic Siamese varieties include: the seal point (a fawn coat with seal brown to almost black markings); the blue point (a bluish-grey coat with deeper blue markings); the chocolate point (an ivory coat with milk-chocolate markings); and the lilac point (a very white coat with frosty grey markings).

For many years, the seal point was the only desirable kind of Siamese. The blue point was

A ONE-MASTER CAT

The Siamese is characterized by a frank, steady gaze, accurate, and controlled movements, unequalled flexibility and grace, and such steadfast loyalty that an animal can become ill if it is abandoned. The Siamese is a one-master cat, but owners must be wary, because it can easily take control of the household. The cat adores children, treating them with gentleness and patience. Its charm and lively intelligence quickly win admirers. However, it is extremely vocal, and its ear-splitting voice may strike some as disagreeably strident. Sometimes Siamese talk noisily with their owners, who seem to understand perfectly. The eyes, which can be any shade of blue, are also very expressive. Siamese get on well with other cats. But with their lively nature, they invariably dominate such relationships. The females are reputedly highly sexed and in heat more frequently than those of other breeds. They are efficient, attentive mothers.

recognized by the United States in 1932, and by Britain, in 1936. The chocolate point received its accolade in the early 1950s; and the lilac point, during the mid-1950s in the United States, and in Great Britain in 1960.

In North America, only the four classic varieties are considered Siamese. All the other varieties are members of the colourpoint short-hair breed. In Britain, a number of different Tabby Points, Tortie Tabby Points, Red Points, Tortie Points, and Cream Points are members of the Siamese breed.

The original British breed standards (1889) called for bent or kinked tails and crossed eyes. Today, these features—as well as the round or 'apple' head—are considered genetic defects, which are unsuitable in show cats, although owners may find them endearing in a pet.

Characteristics

General description: The ideal Siamese is svelte, graceful, refined, of medium size with long tapering lines. It should be in excellent condition, very strong, lithe and muscular.

Head: Should be a long tapering wedge, of medium size, in good proportion to the body. The wedge is created by straight lines extending from the nose to the tips of the ears, forming a triangle, with no break at the whiskers. When whiskers are smoothed back, the underlying bone structure is apparent. Allowance must be made for jowls in the stud. The desirable profile may be seen as a long, flat, straight line extending from the top of the head to the tip of the nose, with no dip at the nose, and in a straight line from the tip of the nose to the tip of the chin. The neck should be long and slender. The ears are strikingly large, but in proportion to the head. Wide at the base, they are set so as to be in a continuing line with the wedge, neither too high nor too flared.

Eyes: The eyes are almond-shaped, of medium size, set in an oriental slant towards the nose with less than an eye's width between them.

Body: The body is long, tubular, hard and muscular giving the sensation of solid weight without excessive bulk. The overall body structure is finely boned and well-muscled like a swimmer. Males in general are proportionately larger than females. The bone structure should be fine, the muscles very firm. While the breed is considered 'medium' in size, balance and proportion are to be considered of greater consequence; the cat should 'fit together.' The tail is long and thin, tapering to a fine point, adding to the overall appearance of length.

Legs: The legs are long, slim, and fine-boned in proportion to the overall size of the cat. The hind legs are longer than the front legs. The feet are small and dainty, oval in shape.

Coat: The coat should be very short, tight, and close-lying and of a fine texture.

Colour: Even colour on the body with any shading to be in the colour of the points. Allowance for darker body shading in older cats; however, definite contrast between body and points must exist. Lack of leg and tail barring desirable, except in lynx points. Lack of body barring desirable in all patterns.

Subject to penalty: Malocclusions. Receding or excessively massive chin. Sanded or shaved coat. Belly spots and/or flank spots. Crossed eyes. Visible protrusion of the cartilage at the end of the breastbone. Any evidence of poor condition. Allow for incomplete mask in kittens and young adults to 18 months; dip above the eyes in kittens and young adults to 18 months; ghost barring of the tail and flanks in kittens and young adults to 18 months. Full penalty for evidence of poor health, emaciation, visible tail fault, white toes and feet, or patches of white in the points, except in particolour points.

Basic genetic makeup of a homozygous cinnamon point Siamese:
aa b^l b^l c^s c^s DD LL *(see pages 142-151)*

Mating authorized with other breeds:
Yes, with the Balinese, Oriental, Oriental Longhair, and the Burmese to obtain Tonkinese.

TICA Standards	Points
Head	24
Eyes	10
Body	40
Coat	10
Colour	16

Singapura

This rare breed hails from Singapore, the tiny prosperous island republic and port city located at the southern tip of the Malay peninsula. In the city's streets, the Singapura roams wild, sometimes seeking shelter in drains and sewers, where it hides during the day, before emerging at night to feed on restaurant throwaways. Local disdain for the animals is summed up in the disparaging nickname—'drain cats'.

AUS.	CAN.	N.Z.	S.AF.	U.K.	U.S.A.
●	●			●	●

Calm, even-tempered, quiet, and alert, the Singapura possesses a beautifully soft voice that it hardly ever uses. It makes itself understood through the candid expression of its large eyes. When it comes to hunting, this charming animal has the speed and talent of a judo expert.

From street to show ring

The rise of the Singapura breed from its lowly origins has been remarkably swift. In 1974, an American couple, Hal Meadows and his wife, Tommy, found three cats in the streets of Singapore. The following year, the cats were brought back by the Meadows to the United States for breeding purposes. Seven years later the Singapura was accepted for registration by the Cat Fanciers' Association. The breed entered the championship show ring in 1988. During the second show season, 22 Singapuras achieved grand-champion titles—a noteworthy feat for a breed with fewer than 1000 specimens in the United States, England, Europe, and Japan.

The perfectly proportioned Singapura cat is small to medium in size, with an average adult weighing only about 6½ pounds (3 kg). In contrast to the dainty body, the ears and eyes are strikingly large, as might be expected in an animal whose senses must be keen for nocturnal foraging.

The preferred eye colours—essential for the show-class Singapura—are hazel, green, or yellow. The silky, short, and close-lying coat has an old or yellowed ivory background colour with dark brown ticking.

A lovable pest

According to Tommy Meadows, Singapuras are 'intelligent, loving, people-oriented cats.' From kittenhood to old age, they retain their playful nature and delight in toys and games. They are quite at home in the company of strangers and at parties, where they look for a welcoming lap to sit on. A bit of a pest, sometimes; but a lovable one, always.

> **BUYERS BEWARE!**
>
> There have been attempts to create 'counterfeit' Singapuras. The aim is to produce the breed in great numbers without reducing the cost. The efforts of unethical breeders failed because their look-alikes did not meet the breed standards. Genuine Singapuras are few, but their origins are well-documented.

Characteristics

Head: The skull should be rounded and well-balanced with the rest of the cat.

Muzzle: The muzzle should be medium-short in length and broad, and with a blunt nose. There should be a definite though not extreme whisker break. The chin is well-developed, rounded and not noticeably receding or projecting. Allowance for jowls in adult cats. In profile, there should be a short, curved rise to the nose between the brow and muzzle with a very slight stop below eye level. Not to be considered a break, this is a slight indentation marking the transition to the muzzle.

Ears: Large with an alert appearance, the ears should be slightly to moderately pointed and wide open at the base with a deep cup. Set is medium-broad. Definite light-coloured ear furnishings.

Eyes: Large eyes in an almond setting, neither protruding nor recessing, giving neither a rounded nor an oriental appearance. The eyes should be accented by a darker lid skin encircled by a light-coloured area and facial markings highlighting the eyes. Eyes set not less than an eye's width apart. Colour shading celadon green, hazel, green, gold or copper with brilliance preferred. Blue eyes are not permitted.

Body: Medium to small, moderately stocky and muscular, solid to the feel, neither cobby nor rangy. The body and legs should form a square with the floor when viewed from the shoulder blades to the base of the tail. Mid-section not tucked but firm. Rib cage rounded, back slightly arched.

Neck: Short and thick.

Legs and feet: Legs heavy and well-muscled at the body, tapering to a fine lower leg boning with small, short, oval feet.

Tail: Length to be short of the shoulder when laid along the torso. It tends towards slender but is not whippy and ends with a blunt tip.

Coat texture: Fine texture, not plush or springy, lying close to the body. Not an oriental 'painted on coat,' but one which can carry sufficient bands of ticking. Woolliness undesirable. Coat is longest at the spine where the ticking is most intense.

Ticking: Four or more alternating bands of light and dark colour. At least two bands of dark with the outer tip band dark and the lightest band next to the skin. Outer part of the body has less noticeable ticking. The most intense ticking is across the upper back allowing for a fully ticked, dark spine line. The space between ears can be dark but must be ticked. Underside of body usually unticked. Ticking should exhibit intense contrast and is a most important feature.

Subject to penalty: Small ears, small eyes, springy or plush coat, coldness and predominant grey tones, lack of leg barring, prominent outer front leg barring, dark necklaces, protruding eyes, too short a muzzle, anything more than a slight indentation as a nose stop, non-visible tail faults.

Disqualifying fault: Unbroken necklaces and circular leg bracelets, barring on the tail, white lockets, visibly kinked tail, definite blue eyes, unticked top of head, removed ear furnishings.

Basic genetic makeup of a Singapura:
AA BB $c^b c^b$ DD LL $T^a T^a$ *(see pages 142-151)*

TICA Standards	Points
Head	20
Eyes	10
Body, legs, and tail	20
Coat and texture	10
Colour pattern	40

Snowshoe

The Snowshoe has inherited a positive personality and a gentle and friendly nature from its ancestors. It is a lively creature and a good hunter, affectionate and faithful, and fond of the company of humans.

AUS.	CAN.	N.Z.	S.AF.	U.K.	U.S.A.
	●				●

Another new and still rare North American breed, the Snowshoe was developed in the late 1960s by breeding Siamese with bicoloured American Shorthairs. Its striking physical features are Siamese-type points combined with the white feet of the Birman. It blends the grace, elegance, and refinement of the Siamese, with the muscularity and coordination of the Shorthair.

TICA Standards	Points
Head	25
Body type, colour	25
Tail, legs, feet	10
Point colour	5
Colour pattern	20
Coat	5
Condition/balance	10

Characteristics

General description: A medium-to-large cat that combines the heftiness of its American Shorthair ancestors with the length of its oriental ancestors. It is a well-balanced cat overall, firm and muscular. It gives the appearance of great power and agility. The unique combination of the pointed pattern, the white spotting and the moderate body type sets the Snowshoe apart.

Head: Medium-sized, almost an equilateral triangle; in proportion to the body. The nose should be straight in profile, with a slight rise at the bridge. Medium-length muzzle has no break; forehead should be flat, cheekbones high. Large pointed ears should be broad at the base, set forward from outside of the head, and held alert.

Eyes: The large, walnut eyes should be slanted towards the base of the ears. They should be blue, bright and sparkling.

Body: The rectangular body should be medium-to-large, long but not too extreme, well-boned and well-muscled. The males are to be powerful and heavily built, while the females should not be frail or dainty. The tail is thick at

the base, tapering slightly and gradually to the end. It should be medium-to-long. The well-muscled legs should be a good length. The bone structure should be medium-to-heavy, but not as heavy as the American Shorthair.

Coat: Short and of medium texture.

Subject to penalty: Head: long or narrow; long Roman nose; thin muzzle, severe overshot or undershot jaw. Ears that are large, pointed; slanting out from the head or set too close together. Body that has a narrow chest, long back, slab flanks and long, thin neck; disproportionately long tail; light long legs, bow legs; oval feet or separated toes, poor muscle tone. Small eyes, set on a bias or close together; pale colour.

Disqualifying fault: Overall lack of merit; lockets or buttons; kinked tail; difficult to handle.

Basic genetic makeup of a homozygous seal point Snowshoe:
aa BB c^S c^S DD LL SS *(see pages 142-151)*

Mating authorized with other breeds: No.

Somali

Playful, active, and highly interested in everything that is going on around it, the soft-voiced Somali is a lively, muscular, and intelligent cat, as well as gentle and easy to handle. It is also a fine hunter.

The wild-looking Somali is a long-haired Abyssinian that was bred in the United States in the 1960s. Its sumptuous coat is soft, richly coloured and slightly shaggy; its tail is long, bushy, and fox-like. A thick ring of fur encircles its neck. The Somali is intelligent, even-tempered, and playful. Initially, it may be reserved about showing affection towards its owners. This cat grows restless if closely confined indoors, but thrives in gardens or yards.

AUS.	CAN.	N.Z.	S.AF.	U.K.	U.S.A.
●	●	●	●	●	●

Characteristics

General: The overall impression of the ideal Somali is a medium cat, regal in appearance. The Somali is a foreign shorthair in type. The males are proportionately larger than the females, the females being finer boned and usually more active than the male. The Somali shows firm muscular development and should be lithe and panther-like in activity, showing a lively interest in all its surroundings. The coat of the Somali has an iridescent quality reflecting warmth of colour and should be very soft to the touch, with preference given to a cat with ruff and breeches. The Somali should be of sound health and vigour, well-balanced physically and temperamentally, and amenable to handling.

Subject to penalty: Colour faults; slick coat or excessive plushness; wrong colour or patching in pads. Full penalty given for white lockets; unbroken necklace; and reversed ticking.

Basic genetic makeup of a homozygous fawn Somali:
AA BB CC DD II T^a T^a *(see pages 142-151)*

Mating authorized with other breeds:
Yes, with the Abyssinian.

TICA Standards	Points
Head	30
Coat and texture	10
Body	35
Colour and pattern	20
Eye colour	5

Sphynx

The public is divided in its opinion of the Sphynx. Some people find it attractive and fascinating. They liken it to E.T., the enchanting extraterrestrial of Steven Spielberg's popular 1982 movie. Others recoil with shock, possibly because the Sphynx runs counter to their idea of what a cat should be. Whatever the reaction, there can be no doubt that the Sphynx is always going to be an attention-getter.

Soft, pliable, and warm

The Sphynx is said to be hairless. However, its wrinkled skin–with a texture as soft and pliable as suede or chamois leather–has a covering of short, fine down. In some specimens, the down may be almost imperceptible. The degrees of coverage vary; but more down, rather than less, is preferable.

There should also be short, tightly packed soft hair at the extremities–the ears, feet, muzzle, and testicles. A tiny tassel of hair may appear at the end of the tail. Whiskers and eyebrows–either whole or incomplete–may also be present. The skin can have any recognized coat colour or pattern; the colour of the eyes should complement that of the coat.

Despite the lack of a thick, insulating fur, the Sphynx is warm to the touch. The unprotected creature has a system that compensates by producing body temperatures that are much higher than those of other breeds. (As a result, the Sphynx

AUS.	CAN.	N.Z.	S.AF.	U.K.	U.S.A.
	•		•		•

GENESIS AND GENES

To produce the Sphynx, its parents should be hairless or carriers of a recessive gene. Advocates of the cat claim that the presence of the gene neither affects the cat's life expectancy nor predisposes it to specific defects or weaknesses.

A word of warning: some Birman and Persian kittens born hairless due to a defective gene soon die. There is, however,. no cause for alarm if Orientals descended from the Cornish Rex are born hairless. They will grow hair in adulthood.

has sometimes been called the 'suede hot-water bottle'.)

Unlike other breeds, the Sphynx sweats and, with no thick coat to absorb natural oils, it must be bathed or sponged often. Although the cat is suited to a temperate climate, it is best kept indoors at all times, because it responds poorly to changes in temperature and may become ill.

The Sphynx's temperament is a blend of gentleness, gallantry, intelligence, and mischief. Owners claim that it is extraordinarily agile and as faithful as a dog. It is no more finicky about food than other less exotic breeds, but it must eat well to fuel its high body temperature. It is sociable and affectionate, although it does not like to be clasped or cuddled.

Sphynx of past and present

Cats resembling the present-day Sphynx are depicted in the stone engravings on the monuments built by Aztec and other Indian civilizations in Mexico and central America. The early 19th-century German historian and naturalist Johann Rudolph Rengger described hairless cats in *A Natural History of the Mammals of Paraguay*, published in 1830. A breed known as the New Mexican Hairless cat was reputedly exhibited for a short time about 1900.

During the remainder of the 20th century, reports about hairless cats circulated from time to time, only to be treated skeptically or ignored. The modern Sphynx appeared in an otherwise normal litter of short-haired kittens in Canada in the late 1960s.

The road to recognition

Efforts to gain recognition for the breed have not met with complete success. The Cat Fanciers' Association (CFA) gave provisional status in 1970. But there has been no further progress, because CFA board members have been concerned about the breeds' health problems, particularly the fragility of its immune system.

In the early 1990s, The International Cat Association (TICA) was the only registry in North America with championship classes in which the Sphynx could compete.

Today, the Sphynx is rare outside North America. Nevertheless, other countries have worked at its development and improvement. For example, France has had success with the breed. In the early 1980s, the cat excited public interest when it was exhibited at Paris. Two years later, French breeders Aline and Philippe Noel imported a pair from Holland—Mogwai (a black-and-white female) and Gyzmo (a brown-and-white

IS IT A CAT OR IS IT ART?

Any cat show with a Sphynx is sure to be a success. It usually draws crowds of cat fanciers and curiosity–seekers who ask: What is this creature with a hairless body, a snake's head, a rat's tail, and ears like bats' wings? A few observers have been known to admire it as a work of fine art, comparable to a painting or a sculpture.

tabby male). Because the cats came from different litters, they reproduced without difficulty. (Other breeders had not been so fortunate with inbred Sphynxes.)

The news of the Noels' success sparked interest among American breeders, who began to import the French Sphynx. In 1988, the Noels' black-and-white female called Amenophis Clone took the Best Cat in Show at TICA's exhibition at Madison Square Garden, New York.

Characteristics

General description: The Sphynx is sweet-tempered, lively and intelligent and, above all, amenable to handling. It is not absolutely hairless; it may be covered with very fine down that is almost imperceptible to both the eye and the touch. On the ears, muzzle, tail, feet and breastbone, short, soft, fine hair is allowed. The skin should have the texture of chamois, and the lack of a coat makes the cat quite warm to the touch. Whiskers and eyebrows may be present, either whole or broken. A lion's tail, a puff of hair on the tip of the tail, is acceptable. The skin is very wrinkled in kittens; adults should ideally keep as many wrinkles as possible, especially on the head.

Head: The head should be slightly longer than it is wide, with prominent cheekbones and a distinct whisker break. The profile should have a slight-to-moderate stop at the bridge of the nose.

Eyes: The eyes are a large, rounded lemon in shape and slant towards the outer corner of the ear. There should be slightly more than the width of an eye between the eyes.

Ears: The ears are very large, broad at the base and open, with no interior hair. They are upright, neither low set nor on top of the head.

Neck: The neck is medium, well-muscled and rounded, arching from the shoulders to the base of the skull. The neck is powerful, especially in males.

Body: The body is medium to medium-long, well-rounded, thick through the abdomen, and should have the appearance of having eaten a large meal; but it should not be fat. The chest is broad, and may tend towards being barrel-chested. Males may be up to 25 percent larger

so long as proper proportions are maintained. This is a very hard and muscular cat with medium bone structure; it should not be too small or dainty.

Tail: The tail should be whippy, tapering from the body to the tip of the tail; the tail length should be in proportion to the body.

Legs: The length of the legs is in proportion to the body; legs should be firm and muscular. Female's legs may be more slender than those of the males. Hind legs should be slightly longer than the front, the forelegs widely set. Paws are oval, with long, slender toes and paw pads are thicker than in other breeds, giving the appearance that the cat is walking on air cushions.

Subject to penalty: Overall small cat; body that is too thin, frail, delicate or fine-boned; too cobby or foreign. Lack of wrinkles on the head. Straight profile, narrow head. Non-amenable disposition. Significant amounts of hair above the ankle.

Disqualifying fault: Any indication of wavy hair or suggestion of the Devon Rex or Cornish Rex in moult; any evidence of plucking, shaving or clipping or any other means of hair removal.

Basic genetic makeup of a homozygous white and brown mackerel tabby Sphynx: AA BB CC DD hr hr LLSS TT *(see pages 142-151)*

Mating authorized with other breeds: No.

TICA Standards	Points
Head	35
Body	35
Coat and skin	25
Colour	5

Tonkinese

Neither a natural breed nor a true random mutation, the Tonkinese is the result of complex genetics, and the product of mating Siamese to Burmese. Developed in the 1960s by Margaret Conroy, a Canadian cat fancier, it is the first pedigree breed to originate in Canada. In 1965, the Canadian Cat Association recognized it as a separate breed with its own standard.

History repeated

For the first few years, these cats were called Golden Siamese. Ironically they had also been developed, albeit unofficially, some 10 years earlier under that identical name. Milan Greer, a New York pet shop owner, had begun crossing Siamese and Burmese in the 1950s, and produced several generations of 'Golden Siamese.' But his cats attracted little attention, and he later stopped the experiment.

The Tonkinese was warmly received the second time around. (Its admirers recommended the new name to distance the breed from both the Siamese and the Burmese.) In 1972, the now defunct U.S. Independent Cat Federation admitted Tonkinese for championship competition and other cat registries followed.

The charm of the past

Mating breeds as different as the present-day slender, tubular Siamese and the contemporary heavily built, short-bodied Burmese is unthinkable today. But when the Tonkinese was created, Siamese cats were quite rounded, with light eyes, a thick tail, and fairly heavy bones. The Burmese were big-boned, but not so rounded as they are

AUS.	CAN.	N.Z.	S.AF.	U.K.	U.S.A.
●	●			●	●

A nicely balanced cat in all respects with quite beautiful colouring, the Tonkinese is also a very lovable animal. Intelligent, lively, and devoted to its owner, it has all the good traits of both its ancestors, and seems to have escaped their small faults.

today. They had a less round head, paler eyes, slightly bigger ears, and a longer nose. Today's Tonkinese appeals especially to cat lovers who miss the old-style Siamese and Burmese.

The Tonkinese enjoys another legacy from its breed founders. It has magnificent eyes that range from aquamarine to turquoise—a blend of the Siamese blue and the Burmese gold. This extremely inquisitive cat is also one of the most affectionate. It enjoys play and outdoor exercise, and enough attention from its owner to be assured that its affection is returned.

An excellent traveller, it seems to enjoy looking out at the passing scene. A rub with a dampened gloved hand is usually sufficient to keep its soft shiny coat looking its best.

The Tonkinese is a healthy cat with a long life expectancy. However, its curiosity and interest in people lead it to investigate moving cars, which can lead to tragic results.

TICA Standards	Points
Head	27
Body and tail	27
Coat	9
Colour	27
Condition	5
Balance/temperament	5

Characteristics

Head: Medium-sized, modified wedge with clean, gently curved contours, and just slightly longer than wide. Head and ears should give the impression of an equilateral triangle when viewed from the front. In profile, there should be a slight convex curve from the top of the head to just above the eyes, dipping to a gentle stop at or just below eye level with no appearance of a break. The nose should have the slightest convex curvature, neither ruler-straight nor humped. Cheekbones should be high and gently planed, the muzzle of medium length, a good width at the jaw hinge, tapering gently to a blunt finish. The chin should be firmly curved, neither prominent nor weak.

Ears: Medium-sized ears should be slightly longer than wide on a broad base with oval tips, and set as much on the side of the head as the top, and pricked forward. The hair to be very short and close-lying; skin may show.

Eyes: The medium-sized eyes should be half almond on top, slightly more rounded on the bottom—the shape of a peach pit. They should be set well apart, at least one eye width apart, and slanted towards outer edge of ear.

Body: The semi-foreign body should be neither stocky nor rangy. Torso should be a medium-length rectangle, chest medium width rounding gently in front with the ribs slightly curved, the flanks level, the back rising slightly from shoulders to rump. A refined medium bone structure; well-developed muscles. The tail should not be thick, and should taper gently to a slightly blunted tip. Medium to medium-long, it should be equal to body length from rump to shoulders.

Legs: The legs should be medium-long, proportionate to the body, the hind legs slightly longer than front. The oval feet should be trim.

Coat: The coat should be medium-short with a fine texture, soft and silky with a lustrous sheen. The density should be luxuriant but close-lying.

Subject to penalty: Round eyes. Barring on body.

Disqualifying fault: Round head with protuberant round eyes, short muzzle, and nose break. Cobby or oriental type. Miniaturization. Rapid oscillation of eyes; depressed or protruding breastbone.

Basic genetic makeup of a natural mink Tonkinese: aa BB c^b c^s DD LL *(see pages 142-151)*

Mating authorized with other breeds: Yes, with Siamese, Burmese. There are no long-hair Tonkinese.

Turkish Angora

For many years, the Angora was considered aggressive, difficult to handle, and anti-social. However, these disagreeable traits were the result of poor selection and excessive inbreeding. Today, these problems have been rectified, and the animal is now a good companion–quick-witted, lively, playful, mischievous, and friendly.

The Turkish Angora, famous for its long, thick silky coat, came to Europe from Ankara (then called Angora), Turkey, in the early 1600s. The breed helped create the Persian (see page 114), which became so popular that the Angora became all but extinct in Britain and the United States. It became a protected species in its native Turkey. Revived in the United States after World War II, the Turkish Angora made a strong comeback there in the 1960s, when Liesa Grant imported a pair, Yildiz (Star) and Yildizcik (Starlet), from the Ankara zoo.

AUS.	CAN.	N.Z.	S.AF.	U.K.	U.S.A.
✱	●				●

✱ In Australia the breed may be considered a variety of Turkish Van.

TICA Standards	Points
Head	30
Body	30
Colour	10
Eye colour	5
Coat	10
Condition	5
Balance	10

Characteristics

General description: A medium-to-small cat, it is long and svelte with all of the features combining in balance to give an impression of graceful, flowing motion. The Turkish Angora is not fully mature until 2 years of age.

Head: The medium-sized head is a modified wedge, small-to-medium in proportion to the body. The top of the skull is medium wide, flat and long with a smooth taper to the chin. Stud jowls in mature males. Medium-long nose, gently sloped, but with no break. The neck is lithe and graceful, medium in length. The ears are wide at the base, tall, pointed and tufted, and are set high on the head. The eyes are large, almond shaped and slanting slightly upwards.

Body: Narrow, deep chest, never rounded. Hips never wider than the shoulders. Tight abdomen. Long, slender legs; hind legs higher than forelegs, making the rump high. Paws in proportion to the legs; tufts between toes. Long, tapering tail, in proportion to body length; full plume.

Coat: Medium-long, longer at the ruff, breeches, and underbody. The texture is silky and fine, with a slight undercoat; wavy on stomach.

Subject to penalty: Coarseness; broad chest, hips, or shoulders; heavy bones, any hint of stubbiness.

Disqualifying fault: Cobby body; an oriental head type.

Basic genetic makeup of a homozygous white Turkish Angora :
BB CC DD ll WW (see pages 142-151)

Mating authorized with other breeds: No.

Turkish Van

The Turkish Van's temperament has been modified by breeders. Once an aggressive cat, it is now friendly and very faithful. It is also called 'the swimming cat,' as it delights in going for a swim.

In 1955 Laura Lushington and Sonia Halliday returned to England from a Turkish vacation with a couple of cats from the Lake Van area. Four years later, they brought home two more. The cats' white kittens with auburn markings launched the Turkish Van. It was registered in Britain in 1969 and in North America in 1985.

AUS.	CAN.	N.Z.	S.AF.	U.K.	U.S.A.
✱	●	●	●	●	●

✱ In Australia this breed may also be known as the Turkish.

Characteristics

General description: A solidly built, semi-long-haired cat with a seasonal coat, and great breadth to chest and hips. The strength and power of the breed can be seen in the substantial body and powerful legs. The breed also has unique pattern, an assertive temperament, and affectionate nature. Males are large and imposing, females medium-to-large.

Head: A modified wedge, broad in males and semi-broad in females, and about as long as it is broad. The muzzle is neat, rounded, and proportionate to head, with a definite but not sharp whisker break. Bite is even, chin is rounded. The face should not look foxy. The cheekbones are high, and the profile is sculpted with a dip or gentle stop at eye level. Nose has a downwards curve. The neck is medium-short and muscular. Ears are large and set relatively high on the head. Height is equal to separation width. Ears turn slightly to the side in set. Eyes are large and expressive, peach pit/walnut in shape, set midway in the face, slightly oblique. Colour is blue, amber, or odd, and green is permissible.

Body: Long, large, and substantial. The rib cage is somewhat rounded; chest is full and broad, and the body tapers slightly to a strong pelvis.

Strong muscle development. The cat should feel heavy and firm. Allow for loose skin between back legs. Legs are set wide, medium in length and boning. Back legs are longer than front. Neat, rounded feet; tufted toes. Tail is a brush or plume, medium length, in proportion to the cat. Colour should be continuous from base to tip. Soft-textured, waterproof coat has seasonal semi-long hair.

Subject to penalty: Yellowed white; auburn colour over more than 20 percent of the cat; lack of facial blaze.

Disqualifying fault: Poor condition; bicolour patterning.

Basic genetic makeup of an auburn and white Turkish Van:
aa BB CC DD II OO SS *(see pages 142-151)*

Mating authorized with other breeds: No.

TICA Standards	Points
Head	30
Body, tail	40
Colour and pattern	15
Coat	15

RARE BREEDS

Burmilla

Also called the Silver Burmese, the delicately coloured, handsome Burmilla has become one of the most popular new British breeds and a great favourite in Australia.

A blending of gold and silver

This breed began in England in 1981 through the accidental mating of a lilac Burmese queen and a Silver (Chinchilla) Persian stud–hence the name Burmilla. The cats, owned by Baroness Miranda von Kirchberg, produced four kittens with the body conformation of the Burmese, but with tipped coats. The baroness saw the potential for a new breed in this tipped silver shorthair of foreign (tubular) body type, and the Burmilla Cat Club was launched. Appearances at shows further boosted the breed, which was granted preliminary championship status in Britain in 1990.

Part of the Burmilla's attraction is its luminous coat–the ground colour may be silver or golden–gently tipped in black, brown, or other standard Burmese colours. But an equal pop-ularity factor is its even disposition.

Head and body standards for the Burmilla are the same as for the Burmese. The Burmilla's body is lithe and muscular. Its coat is slightly longer than the Burmese, but smooth, soft, flat, and glossy. Its tail, ringed in the same colour as the tipping, tapers to a round end. The Burmilla's hind legs are slightly longer than its forelegs; the paws are neat with pads corresponding in colour to the tipping. Green eyes are set well apart in a gently rounded head. Its medium-to-large ears tilt forward slightly. A short nose ends in a terra-cotta nose pad. Pencilling around the eyes, lips, and nose is the same colour as the tipping.

Difficult to achieve

Even though the Burmilla has many admirers, few British or American breeders are developing the breed. Obtaining the Burmilla's requisite Burmese conformation, fur texture, eye colour, and chinchilla colour is a considerable challenge. When a breeder does succeed, however, the result is spectacular.

German Rex

In 1951, Dr. Rose Scheuer-Karpin adopted a stray cat that was wandering around the Hufeland Hospital in what was then East Germany. The black curly-haired cat had a couple of unspectacular litters sired by local toms. But when she was bred to one of her sons, two of the four kittens that resulted had their mother's wavy hair.

The kittens' astrakhan-style coats fascinated French cat fancier Étienne Letard, who imported one to France. For a time, Professor Letard and Dr. Scheuer-Karpin continued developing German Rex kittens, unaware that English breeders were also experimenting with Rex cats (see pages 90 and 92). Despite their efforts, the German Rex is almost unobtainable today. The type has remained the same over two decades: fairly heavy bone structure, roundish head, wide-set ears and a thick tail. The fur is dense, longer than that of the Cornish Rex and curling all over in irregular waves.

There is no recognized standard.

Munchkin Cat

The latest American novelty cat could well be called the dachshund cat. It is in fact a natural breed of the Household Pet, except that it is characterized by very short legs. It began with a spontaneous mutation in a cat's genetic code that introduced a gene similar to the one that produces dachshunds, basset hounds, and corgis. The Munchkin is therefore a product of nature that appeared without any help from man. Since the gene is dominant, any cat carrying it will produce short-legged offspring.

The first Munchkin Cat was discovered at a TICA show in Madison Square Gardens in 1991. However, there were cats of this type in England in the 1930s, and four generations of them were in the care of veterinarians in 1944. British Munchkins may have died out during the war, as happened to many breeds. A Munchkin was also reported in Stalingrad, Russia, in 1953.

The Munchkin Cats presently registered all come from Louisiana. All are descended from a black queen called Blackberry.

A ROBUST BASSET

While some basset hounds have problems in the lumbar region, the Munchkin Cat does not. A cat's spine is constructed differently to a dog's, and cats, even the long-bodied slender breeds such as the Cornish Rex, the Siamese, and the Oriental, suffer relatively little from back problems.

Ojos Azules

Despite its lovely Spanish name, the Ojos Azules (Blue Eyes) is an American cat of recent vintage. This comparatively rare breed dates from 1984 when Cornflower, a tortie female, was discovered in New Mexico.

Cornflower's most remarkable characteristic was her blue eyes. Dark pools of intense blue, they were such that even the bluest blue-eyed Siamese might envy.

A puzzle for the geneticists

Geneticists do not yet fully understand how the genes responsible for eye colour sometimes do the unexpected. For example, from a genetic standpoint, only white cats with white or colour point genes can have blue eyes. Yet one can find black, auburn, tortie, blue, silver, and blue cream cats with blue eyes. Is it then possible to produce a jet-black cat with dark-blue eyes, an auburn cat with blue-green eyes, or a tortoise-shell with sapphire eyes? Such unusual colour combinations would indeed be staggeringly beautiful. Research carried out on the Ojos Azules did not yield these answers. It did reveal that the cat's blue eyes resulted from a spontaneous mutation. Since the responsible gene was dominant, all Cornflower's kittens had magnificent blue eyes.

The standard for Ojos Azules has not yet been fully defined. Only about 10 of the breed had been registered in 1992.

GOOD HEARING AND NOT A SQUINT IN SIGHT

Although some blue-eyed white cats are deaf, to date no Ojos Azules has had this handicap, and while some Siamese have a pronounced squint, no Ojos Azules is cross-eyed.

Peke Face

The Peke Face Persian, a spontaneous mutation of the Red Persian, is named for its resemblance to a Pekingese dog. Controversy surrounds the breed, which tends to have skin problems, and because its facial features—deformities some say—contribute to eating and breathing difficulties. Some breeders have pushed experiments with the breed so far that the cats' faces have a piggy look.

The Peke Face has a Persian's long coat, but has long legs and a long body. Most differences between it and other Persians relate to the head. The head is square rather than round; the jaw long, narrow, and very undershot. Poor occlusion of the jaws makes it hard for the cat to chew and swallow.

An ultra-snub-nose

The Peke Face's snub-nose, set back in a furrowed muzzle, is so short that it is practically nonexistent; narrow nostrils are level with the eyes. Breathing through such a nose is hard work at the best of times, and almost impossible if the animal has a cold. Because of its squished facial features, the skull seems flat, and the round, tufted ears, set not on the sides of the head but on top of the skull, seem disproportionately big and flat, the eyes tend to be particularly prominent, or may appear deep-set and half-closed. Running eyes are often a problem because the eye ducts may be distorted. There is a distinct indentation, almost a hole, between the eyes. It is particularly prominent in young cats.

Shunned by some breeders

Most British breeders consider the breed's compressed features a deformity and have relegated it to the ranks of those to avoid. It is still encouraged in North America. An affectionate, sociable cat, the Peke Face prefers an indoor life. Generally calm, it usually gets along well with other cats. Its thick, silky fur, with red or red tabby colouring, requires daily grooming.

Oregon Rex and Ohio Rex

Mutations produced both these cats, one born in Oregon, the other born in Ohio, in 1944. In each case, the mutation is believed similar to that which produced the Cornish Rex in England some six years later. These American cats resembled the British mutant in type and colour (see page 90). But the doom and gloom of World War II overshadowed 1940s life, and few people took any interest in developing the feline oddities. Inevitably the Oregon Rex and the Ohio Rex disappeared from the cat scene.

Selkirk Rex

Looking like an animated stuffed toy, the Selkirk Rex is another of the rare curly-haired breeds, the result of spontaneous mutation. Cat fanciers say that the Cornish Rex looks like a greyhound, the Devon Rex like the lovable alien in the Steven Spielberg film, *E.T.*, and the Selkirk Rex like an ordinary cat that got too close to the fire and ended up singed and frizzy.

A sheep in cat's clothing?

Each hair on the Selkirk Rex is curly, giving it the look of a poodle. And because the top coat, the awn hairs, and the down hairs are affected, the coat appears extremely thick. But it's not just the coat that curls: no part of this cat's body is smooth. Brow tufts, whiskers, and ear tufts are all curly. No wonder some people call it a 'sheepcat.'

The Selkirk Rex first appeared in the United States in 1987 and has not yet been recognized officially by any cat association. However, The International Cat Association has given it provisional recognition, a first step on the road to registration as a separate breed.

Chance mating

Until a curly-haired kitten arrived (it became known as Miss Pesto), there was nothing exceptional about the straight-haired founding queen of the Selkirk Rex. Miss Pesto was the result of a chance mating in Wyoming with a unknown tom. Jeri Newmann, a Montana breeder of Persians, adopted Miss Pesto and mated her to Photo Finish, a black Persian. On July 4, 1988, Miss Pesto produced six kittens. Three of them had curly hair: a black-and-white tom, a black female, and a tortie female. In all three, their curly coats were thick, soft, and beautiful.

Inbreeding was necessary to produce more curly-haired kittens, since this is the only way to fix a type or a gene. A year later Miss Pesto was pregnant by one of her sons. Of the four kittens in the litter, three had beautiful curly coats, and the breed came into being.

According to geneticists, the gene that produced these cats is dominant; a single Selkirk parent produces Selkirk kittens. The responsible gene is quite different from three other curly-haired breeds.

Siberian Cat

This rarity from Russia takes its name from the Asian part of the country that extends from the Ural Mountains to the Pacific Ocean.

From St. Petersburg to Berlin

The first registered members of the breed came from the city of St. Petersburg (formerly Leningrad). The names of the pair were Mussa, a red-and-white tabby female (born in 1987 and discovered in a Leningrad market), and Tima, a tom of the same age from the same city.

Both cats arrived in Berlin in September 1987. Several months later, they produced a litter of five kittens: three males, a red tabby female, and a cream female. The litter was eventually moved to Plettenberg, near the city of Wuppertal, in what was then West Germany. By April 1990, five males and nine females were registered in different European countries. Most of the offspring had been born in what was once the East German Republic.

The only Russian club with an accepted birth registry for the Siberian breed is the Kotofej in St. Petersburg. Be wary of counterfeit, and check for identification papers showing the cat's pedigree and Russian ancestry.

The Siberian cat is similar to Norwegian Forest and Maine Coon cats, which also hail from wooded northern regions. The resemblance to these breeds may explain the reluctance of the clubs to accept Siberians in championship classes.

As a protection against the cold, harsh climate, the Siberian has long, dense fur, which thickens in winter. Another distinguishing characteristic is its powerful bone structure.

A GENTLE GIANT

The Siberian Cat has charm, quiet strength, and gentleness. Its soft voice is in tune with its slightly shy nature. It is a big, powerfully built cat: females can weigh almost 13 pounds (6 kg) and males almost 24 pounds (11 kg). Despite their weight, Siberian cats are agile, lively, and good hunters.

York Chocolate

This is a newcomer to the world of the purebred cat. The breed takes its name from New York State, where it first saw the light of day (in 1983) on a farm belonging to Janet Chiefari. The second part of its name celebrates the rich brown colour of its semi-long coat.

Cool reception

This new American cat was a spontaneous mutation—that is, a naturally occurring specimen. However, the breed has received a cool welcome from cat fanciers and geneticists. By late 1992, it had not yet received full recognition. Some cat associations want to see more examples of the York Chocolate before making a decision about the breed's future. Moreover, many geneticists consider the breeding programme unacceptable.

Siamese background

The parents of the first York Chocolate kittens were merely household cats with a trace of Siamese in an otherwise uncertain ancestral background. The sire was a long-haired black cat; and the dam, a long-haired black-and-white. The Siamese ancestry common to both of the parents introduced the chocolate-coloured gene that has become the defining factor in the breed's makeup.

The cat comes in a wide variety of chocolate colours, including solid chocolate, chocolate and white, solid lilac lavender, and lilac lavender and white. The colouring of the cat develops slowly. Therefore the kittens are much lighter than the adults. The kittens may have a few tabby markings or tipping. However, these defects are acceptable under the age of 18 months.

Some Chocolate traits

The York Chocolate is bigger than the Siamese. An adult York weighs between 15 and 17 pounds (7-8 kg). However, the structure of the head and of the body is similar to the Siamese.

By the early 1990s, there were only about 100 York Chocolates in existence. A programme of interbreeding guarantees a 100 percent pure York Chocolate pedigree.

Cheerful and lively, agile, and healthy, the York Chocolate is also very attentive to its owner's wishes. It is enthusiastic, energetic, playful, and a good hunter.

Elements of feline genetics

Genetics is the part of biology that deals with heredity—the transmission of characteristics via genes from parents to offspring. Genetics applies to all living things, including cats.

Genes are contained within the nucleus of a cell. They direct the manufacture of proteins, which build the body's cells and tissues, and enzymes, which are essential for the body's growth and function.

Cells

A domestic cat's life starts with a single fertilized sex cell—or zygote—too small to be seen without a microscope. That cell contains a structure called the nucleus. Within the nucleus are 38 tiny structures called chromosomes, which contain the genes. These genes are arranged in a predestined order and position—or locus—along the length of the chromosomes.

The physical differences between cats—eyes, hair type and colour—are caused by differences in the genes controlling the development of these traits. These genes may be dominant or recessive.

Half of a cat's genes come from its father, the other half from its mother, by way of the sperm and egg respectively. Each parent provides a different mixture of genes that accounts for each cat's different characteristics, whether in its appearance (phenotype) or in its health.

If the offspring received identical genes from both its parents, the genetic makeup of the offspring would be pure (denoted by the symbols AA or aa) and the kittens would be called homozygotes. If one parent contributed a dominant gene and the other a recessive gene, the offspring would have a mixed genotype (Aa) and would be called heterozygotes.

Two recessive genes for a characteristic are required before the characteristic can express itself. Either the dominant or the recessive gene can be passed on by a heterozygotic cat to its progeny. A recessive gene can be carried for several generations without being expressed.

The gene for a characteristic that can be seen in a heterozygotic kitten is dominant; it is symbolized by the capital letter (A). The other gene for that characteristic has no effect on the kitten's appearance when combined with the dominant gene; it is recessive, symbolized by the small letter (a).

Determining the sex

The domestic cat carries 38 chromosomes, 19 of which came from the father via the sperm and the other 19 from the mother via the ovum. When the ovum is fertilized by the sperm and becomes a zygote, it therefore carries 19 pairs of chromosomes. Each chromosome of a pair carries genes at identical loci to its mate. Eighteen of these pairs are identical, but one pair, the sex chromosomes, is different in the two sexes. This different pair decides a kitten's sex. Females carry two X chromosomes, males carry an X and a Y chromosome. A kitten inherits one of its mother's X chromosomes and either an X or a Y from the father. If it inherits two X genes, it is a female; if it receives an X and a Y, it is a male.

Pattern and shade

Some genes located at different loci on the chromosomes often interact and modify each other's expression. These are called polygenes and modifiers. They have a strong influence on traits such as colour and appearance, or conformation. They are the cause of variations of pattern and shade in the cat's fur.

Epistatic or masking genes prevent or mask the expression of other genes in the same cat. For instance, the dominant white gene (W) prevents colour cells from reaching the skin and masks the presence of the pigments eumelanin, which appears as black and brown, and phaeomelanin, which appears as red, orange and yellow.

Pigmentation

Melanin

Melanin is a pigment produced by cells called melanocytes that are spread throughout the top layer of the skin and the hair follicles. It gives colour to the hair, skin, and eyes.

There are two types of melanin: eumelanin and phaeomelanin. Granules of eumelanin, which are spherical in shape, absorb almost all light. Granules of phaeomelanin, which are longer and oval, refract light in the red-orange-yellow range. Depending on the variety of enzyme in the melanin, the colour will change in heat and light. The less sensitive the enzyme is to heat and light, the darker the colour will be. So a black coat will be less sensitive to heat than a chocolate one.

Intensity of pigmentation

Density of pigmentation is determined by a pair of dominant (DD) genes or recessive (dd) ones. The fur of cats with the dominant genes absorbs light across the whole surface, resulting in a darker colour, such as black, chocolate, or cinnamon (for skin containing eumelanin) and red (for skin with phaeomelanin). The dd genes cause a scattered pigmentation. Light is less well absorbed, resulting in a lighter colour, such as blue, lilac, or fawn for eumelanin, and cream for phaeomelanin.

Agouti

The agouti (A) gene is responsible for the banding or ticking that produces the tabby pattern. Each hair has alternate bands of light and dark colour, ending with a dark point.

Non-agouti

The presence of the non-agouti (aa) gene prevents the yellow band from being produced on the hair, and so allows an uninterrupted distribution of eumelanin on the hair shaft. This gives the cat a solid-coloured coat.

It is practically impossible to obtain a solid red or cream coat, however. All red or cream cats have a tabby pattern to a greater or lesser degree.

Colour expression

The C gene is responsible for a coloured coat. All coloured cats carry at least one C gene. White cats fall into another category, which will be described later.

A lack of colour can be caused by more than one genetic arrangement. One of them is the absence of a C gene at the C locus. Various mutant forms of the C gene are known, including the c^b gene. This is responsible for the so-called sepia factor that reduces the colour on the body (in a graduated way) but not at the points (ears, mask, legs and tail). This phenomenon is clearest on the Burmese breeds. The c^s gene determines the colour point pattern, in which pigmentation occurs only at the points. This can be seen in the Siamese, Himalayans, and Balinese.

The combination of the c^b and c^s genes has produced another colour, mink, which is characteristic of the Tonkinese. In this breed, the two colour genes are co-dominant, meaning that the sepia does not dominate the colour point, and vice versa.

Also in this genetic series is the c^a gene which produces an albino cat with blue eyes. When the c gene occurs homozygotically (cc), it produces an albino cat with red eyes. This combination was believed to be fatal. However, occasionally an albino with red eyes does survive.

Particolour

The white spotting gene, symbolized by the letter S, is responsible for coloured coats with a varying degree of white. These white areas contain no pigment cells, or melanocytes, at all. White spotting takes various forms: for example, in Birmans (which have white feet), or bi-coloured or harlequin (tri-coloured) cats, or Van cats (coloured only on head and tail).

Dominant white

Unlike the white spotting gene, the dominant white gene, represented by the letter W, masks all other colours and patterns and produces completely white fur. The fur of cats carrying the W gene has no pigments because there are no melanocytes in the skin. The white is therefore not a colour, but an absence of colour. The W gene causes blue, green, copper, or odd-coloured eyes. It also produces deafness in one or both ears.

Silver

The silver colour is due to a dominant inhibiting gene that eliminates all yellow pigmentation from the hair shaft and influences the amount of melanin deposited at the tip of the hair. Its symbol is Si.

Breed-specific mutations

Various recessive mutant genes have been selected by breeders to establish special breeds. A good example of the true breeding genotype is the Siamese, $c^s c^s$.

However, some dominant mutant genes have also been used to establish breeds. For example, the American Curl carries a dominant gene that affects the shape of the ears, causing them to curl towards the back of the head. And taillessness, as in the Manx breed, results from the dominant M gene. This gene is lethal in the homozygous form, since it prevents proper development of the spinal cord.

GENETIC SYMBOLS

Wild type		Mutation	
A	Agouti	a	Non-agouti
B	Black pigment	b	Chocolate
		b^l	Cinnamon
C	Full colour	c^b	Sepia
		c^s	Pointed
		$c^b c^s$	Mink
D	Dense pigmentation	d	Maltesing
fd	Normal ears	Fd	Folded ears
Hr	Normal coat	hr	Hairless
i	Normal pigmentation	I	Inhibitor
		I_{ch}	Chinchilla
		I_{sh}	Shaded
		I_{sm}	Smoked
L	Short hair	l	Longhair
m	Normal tail	M	Absent or short tail
o	Normal colour	O	Sex-linked red
R	Normal coat	r	Cornish Rex
Re	Normal coat	re	Devon Rex
s	Normal colour	S	White spotting
si	Non-silver	Si	Silver
T	Mackerel tabby	T^a	Ticked tabby
		t^b	Blotched or classic tabby
		T_{sp}	Spotted tabby
w	Normal colour	W	Dominant white
wh	Normal coat	Wh	Wirehair

Colour descriptions

Obvious and hidden colours

When breeding cats it is important to remember that a cat of a certain colour may carry genes for other colours. A black cat, for example, may genetically be BB (having two dominant genes for black), or Bb or Bb^l (in which chocolate and cinnamon respectively are carried by the recessive b gene). This means that a black cat bred to a black cat may produce black, chocolate, or cinnamon offspring, depending on the colour genes they carry.

A black cat may also carry dd—the recessive maltesing or dilution gene that is responsible for paler colours. If this cat is bred with another black cat carrying the maltesing gene, their kittens may be black, or blue, lilac, or fawn. This same genetic principle applies to any other recessive colour or pattern genes and means that each of the basic colours may appear in practically any breed.

When colour descriptions are written in genetic terms, sometimes the capital letter of the dominant gene is paired with a hyphen rather than with a letter, for example: A- . The dash indicates that there must be another gene accompanying the dominant one; this second paired gene may be dominant or recessive.

Eumelanin (black-based) colours

Black (B-, C-, D-)

Most standards require a lustrous jet-black coat, black from roots to tip, with no reddish shading and no white or grey hairs. This coat is difficult to maintain, because both the sun and the cat's saliva tend to redden the colouring somewhat.

Black Persian kittens are born with a grey ruff that is often so pale they are taken for smokes. The grey disappears with moulting, and is not considered a fault in young cats. In adults, the head, front legs, top of the back, and tail are shiny black, while ruff, hind legs and belly are more mat, since these areas are woollier. Orientals and Bombays, especially, can have a coat that is so intensely jet black that it looks blue-black.

The eyes of black cats range from gold to orange to deep copper, except for Orientals where green is accepted. The nose leather, lips, and paw pads are a deep charcoal or brownish black.

Blue (B-, C-, dd)

This colour is quite common. In fact, blue is included as an accepted colour in many breeds of cats. The shade varies depending on the length and thickness of the fur, although some standards do not take into account these differences. It requires a grey that is as pale as possible, with no brownish shading. These do occur on some blues, because, as with black fur, the sun and saliva both have a reddening effect.

Blue kittens are born a very pale blue, but darken a little with age, especially on the back, head, and upper surface of the tail. The woollier lower leg areas remain pale. Short-haired breeds display a more even blue colouring than long-haired ones. A few tabby ghost markings may be visible in certain young cats.

The eyes are gold, except for Orientals, Korats, and Russian Blues, in which they are green. The nose leather, lips, and paw pads are slate grey.

Chocolate (bb, C-, D-)

A rare, highly sought-after colour, the chocolate required by the standard is a rich, deep shade of medium to dark chocolate-brown or milk-chocolate or coffee-bean colour. It should be as even as possible with no ghost markings. In Persians, the thickly furred areas are paler. The colour is more common among Orientals and the Havana (Browns). In short-haired breeds, the brown is darker, but very shiny and smooth.

The eyes vary from gold to orange and deep copper; green in Orientals and Havanas. The nose leather, lips, and paw pads are a similar shade to the fur but with a slight rosy flush.

Cinnamon (b^{l}b^l, C-, D-)

This rare, very warm, and attractive colour is found mostly in Orientals. It has different shades, from a medium, reddish-brown, lighter in colour than chocolate, to terracotta or burnt sienna, to a cocoa powder colour.

The eyes are gold to orange and deep copper; gold, hazel, or green for sorrel Abyssinians and Somalis. The nose leather, lips and paw pads are a pinkish tan.

Lilac (bb, C-, dd)

This too is a rare colour and ranges from an even frost-grey or dove to light taupe grey, or French grey. It should have no ghost markings. Lilacs are very pale in the belly, ruff, and tail regions. The fur may be thick and woolly.

The eyes are gold to orange and deep copper, but green in Orientals. Kittens and young adult shorthairs may often display ghost tabby markings and may have a slightly darker colour. The nose leather, lips, and paw pads are lavender pink.

Fawn (b^{l}b^l, C-, dd)

Fawn can mean a warm taupe to a mushroom tan with a pink overlay, somewhat reminiscent of a brown paper bag, or a warm pinkish buff. Eyes are gold to orange to deep copper. Abyssinians and Somalis may have gold, copper, hazel or green eyes; green is preferred in Orientals. The nose leather, lips, and paw pads are dusty rose to pink.

Phaeomelanin (red-based) colours (OO)

For a red to be solid, both genes must be dominant and homozygous (OO). If they were Oo, the cat would be a tortie. Although most colour standards require an even, deep warm, clear solid red or cream, this is in fact almost a genetic impossibility. Tabby markings are almost always evident in reds and creams.

Red (B-, C-, D-, OO)

The standard red is an extremely rich, deep red colour. In red longhairs, the colour may be darker on the back, head, legs, and top of the tail, because the fur may be coarser in these areas; the ruff and belly may be paler and may tend to mat. All shades of red are accepted, but richer, darker colours are preferred. The eyes are gold to orange and copper except for Orientals, in which they are green. The nose leather, lips, and paw pads are a rosy pink.

Cream (B-, C-, dd, OO)

A very pale beige, or buff cream, this colour rarely occurs naturally. It is quite common among Persians, some of which are born so pale as to appear to be smokes. They darken with the effects of age, light, saliva, and reproduction. The ruff, tail, and belly, where the fur is longer, thicker and woollier, then appear much paler. The top of the tail and back, the legs, and the head are darker because the hair there is shorter.

The standard requires a pale, uniform, sound cream colour. Tabby markings may be more visible on short-haired breeds.

The eyes are gold to orange and copper, but green for Orientals. The nose leather, lips, and paw pads are a rosy pink.

Dominant white (W-)

White is the most difficult colour to achieve. This is because the standard requires that it should be absolutely pure. But saliva and tears (in Persians) tend to tint the fur a yellow-brown, and the genital area, feet, and hocks all tend to become discoloured.

Many white kittens are born with a patch of colour on the head. This is a trace of the genetically masked colour of which they are carriers, and it disappears with age. It is not penalized in kittens and young adults.

The eyes may be gold to copper, blue or odd-coloured. The nose leather, lips, and paw pads are pink.

Genetically speaking, white is not considered a colour, but a factor that masks another colour. In order to determine the possible colours of the future offspring of a white cat, it may be necessary to consult its pedigree. This will not necessarily reveal much, because recessive genes may be in the pedigree many generations back. They may not show up on a common five-generation pedigree. Breeding a white cat to a white cat may produce any colour or pattern the cats are carrying.

Tortoiseshell (Oo)

The tortoiseshells can be full-coloured, sepia, mink, or pointed. A blaze, a distinct streak of phaeomelanin colour, is desirable on the nose. The nose leather and paw pads should be the same colour as either or both of the two solid colours. And often a speckled or patched, mottled pattern is seen on the pads.

Tabby markings may be present in red or cream areas, especially on the extremities of the cat, but will not be present on the body if the cat's gene mixture contains the agouti tabby gene. If the eumelanin patches have any tabby patterning, the cat is a torbie (and is called a patched tabby or tortie tabby).

Red and black tortie (aa, B-, C-, D-, Oo)

This unusual colouring, found mostly in females, consists of a mosaic of small patches of red and black. There are two opinions about torties: British standards require a perfect and regular mixture of red and black, whereas some American standards accept a less uniform appearance. The ideal coat consists of red and black patches of colour. Brindling, or scattered red and black hairs, may be allowed in certain breed standards.

The eyes are gold to copper, except for Orientals, in which they are green. The nose leather, lips, and paw pads are mottled pink and black.

Blue tortie (Blue cream) (aa, B-, C-, dd, Oo)

This is a dilution of a red and black tortie, in which the red has become cream and the black has become blue. The colours should be pale, but displayed in the same proportion and mixture as for the red and black tortie. The fur in longhairs may be thick, woolly, dense and mat, and may become easily tangled.

The eyes are gold to orange to deep copper, except for Orientals, in which they are green. The nose leather, lips, and paw pads are a mottled pink and grey.

Chocolate tortie (aa, bb, C-, D-, Oo)

A combination of chocolate-brown hairs and red hairs creates this very warm colour.

The eyes are gold to orange to deep copper, except for Orientals, in which they are green. The nose leather, lips, and paw pads are a mottled brown and pink.

Cinnamon tortie (aa, b^{l}b^l, C-, D-, Oo)

Cinnamon and red, with a marked tint-on-tint effect, produce this rare colour.

The eyes are shaded gold to orange to deep copper, except for Orientals, in which they are green. The nose leather, lips, and paw pads are a mottled red and cinnamon.

Lilac tortie (Lilac cream) (aa, bb, C-, dd, Oo)

This pinkish beige is a subtle blend of cream and lilac, which produces a very delicate tint-on-tint look.

The eyes are gold to copper, except for Orientals, in which they are green. The nose leather, lips, and paw pads are a mottled pink and pale grey.

Fawn tortie (aa, b^{l}b^l, C-, dd, Oo)

This very delicate and rare colour is a dilution of cinnamon tortie, which has become a honey gold, whereas the red has become cream.

The eyes are gold to orange to deep copper, except for Orientals, in which they are green. The nose leather, lips, and paw pads are pink speckled with a pinkish brown-grey.

Tabbies

Four tabby patterns are recognized: ticked, mackerel, classic, and spotted. Like tortoiseshells, tabbies exist in all colours and in all gradations, from full colour to sepia, mink, and pointed. If the colour of the tabby is in question, the colour on the tip of the tail should determine the accurate colour. Only the patterns of the tabbies are described here.

In long-haired cats, the markings are always less obvious than in the short-haired cats because of the length and thickness of the fur, which tends to blur the pattern slightly. The markings are clearer on the head, legs and along the tail, where the fur is shorter.

All tabby cats have a paler chin colour, which should not be positioned too low on the breastbone. A pale chin is not considered a fault, but is an indication that the animal is genetically a true tabby. A red self-coloured cat with tabby markings, for example, has a red chin, indicating that it is not a tabby.

The nose leather is either the same colour as the marking colour or may be pinkish towards the centre and outlined in the marking colour. Lips and paw pads are the same shade as the marking colour.

Whatever the pattern or the colour, the goal is to achieve the greatest contrast between the markings and the ground colour.

Ticked tabby (A-, T^a-)

Abyssinians and Somalis are excellent examples of the ticked tabby. Each hair (with the exception of those on the belly and the inside of the legs) is marked with a band of yellow that separates the darker band of eumelanin colour. The yellow band in these two breeds has become apricot (or rufused), giving these cats a reddish-brown appearance.

In other breeds, the yellow band may or may not be rufused, and separates eumelanin or phaeomelanin pigment. What we see is a yellow band alternating with a coloured band repeatedly. The tip of the hair should be coloured with the marking or indicative colour, with the lower part of the hair shaft ending with a paler yellow band. The more bands of colour there are on an individual hair, the better and more clearly defined the ticking.

The belly and inside of the legs are not ticked or banded. Necklace and bracelet tracings are considered faults in Abyssinians but are accepted and even desired in the other ticked breeds (especially the Singapura).

Mackerel tabby (A-, T-)

The legs and tail should be evenly marked with fine rings and there should be at least one complete necklace. The M on the forehead, the frown marks extending between the ears and down the back of the neck, and the spine lines should all be continuous, close together and parallel. The flanks, shoulders, and haunches show either markings like the rib bones of a fish (hence the name 'mackerel tabby') or fine, regular parallel lines. The belly should show rows of the spots of the dark marking colour commonly referred to as 'vest buttons.'

Classic tabby or blotched tabby (A-, $t^b t^b$)

The rings encircling the tail and legs are quite broad and well spaced, and wide necklace tracings appear on the neck. The M on the forehead and the parallel head lines should also be broad. The swirl on the side of the body should be an unbroken circle centred with a spot of marking colour surrounded by the ground colour.

The spine lines consist of three broad parallel stripes running from the base of the neck to the tip of the tail. The shoulders are marked with a pattern like a butterfly with open wings. The belly should have 'vest buttons.'

Spotted tabby (A-, T_{SP} or t^b_{SP})

The legs and tail are barred with fine, close lines, and there should be necklace tracings. The forehead should be marked with an M, and the head and neck lines should be parallel and close together.

A stripe runs down the length of the back to the tip of the tail, and is ideally composed of spots. The flanks, shoulders, and legs are also marked by spots; these may vary in size and shape, but the standard prefers round, evenly distributed spots, which should be quite distinct. The spots are sometimes separate but arranged in lines; this is called the interrupted mackerel or classic tabby pattern. The belly should display rows of spots or 'vest buttons.'

Torbie or tortie tabby

A tortie that has been tabbied is called a torbie. All the torties, if they have the agouti gene (A-) instead of the non-agouti (aa), can appear in any of the four tabby patterns. The colour combinations remain the same. But wherever the cat has eumelanistic patches of colour, those patches are now tabby, and the markings are more obvious on the legs and head.

Silver tabby

All torbies that are silvered are called silver torbies. This is a particularly attractive combination because of its sparkling, contrasting colours. Cats of this type should combine the colours of the torties, the markings of a tabby and a brilliant silver ground colour.

Any of the tabby and torbie patterns may be silvered. The ground colour should be silvered in all areas, including the chin and lips, and the marking colour should be dense. Paw pads and nose leathers should be the same colours as in the corresponding tabbies, that is, of the marking colour.

All the patterns of tabby previously mentioned can exist in silver. In this case the tabby markings are exactly the same, but the ground colour (including the chin and lips) must be a brilliant, silver white, which should be as pure as possible. The contrast should be extremely sharp, so that the markings are very clear. Paw pads and nose leathers should be the same as the marking colour.

Green is the preferred eye colour, but the eyes may appear gold-green in kittens and young adults, as full green pigmentation is slow to develop.

Silver tabbies are highly valued, especially those with the spotted and classic patterns, which make the cat look as if it had been handpainted. The silver spotted, silver classic, silver mackerel, and silver ticked tabby patterns are seen mostly in Orientals, British Shorthairs, American Shorthairs, Persians, Manx and the Scottish Folds.

Chinchilla and shaded

Chinchilla silver (A-, I_{CH}-, Si-, T^a-)

The name chinchilla comes from a small rodent that has hair tipped with black and with a white undercolour. This colouring is seen more frequently in long-haired than in short-haired cats. The tipping effect is less marked than in shaded cats, as only one-eighth of the hair is pigmented, the rest being a brilliant, sparkling, silver white. The colour contrast is barely perceptible, especially if the cat is pale. If the chinchilla colour is slightly too dark, the cat can easily be confused with a shaded silver. The same confusion can occur in summer, when the cat has no undercoat and the tipping becomes more apparent. Chinchilla has emerged as a distinct colour pattern, following breeder's manipulation of the modifying effects of polygenes.

Black chinchilla is the most common colour. The animal looks like a white cat that has been dusted with very fine coal dust. The black tipping appears only on the back flanks, tail, neck, ears, and head, though the head is hardly marked at all. The chest and inside of the legs are a brilliant white.

The nose leather is brick red, although the lips and paw pads are black, and there is 'makeup' round the eyes and nose. The eyes are an emerald green, which is particularly distinctive in chinchilla silvers.

Chinchilla silvers come in all colour gradations: full, sepia, mink, and pointed. Chinchilla colouring is much sought-after in Persians. However, breeders have had some difficulty achieving it in the Persian type because they tend to lose the emerald-green eye colour, and the bone structure tends to be a little lighter.

Shaded silver
(A-, I$_{SH}$-, Si-, T- or t^{b}t^b)

Shaded silvers come in all colour gradations: full colour, sepia, mink and pointed, as well as shaded torbies.

Shaded silvers may be difficult to distinguish from chinchilla silvers, depending on the age of the cat and the season. The shaded silver is silvery white, evenly shaded with the indicative colour. The hair from the foot pads to the joint or hocks may be shaded, or may be as dark as the marking colour. The undercolour is generally silvery white, although the legs are shaded. The chin, ear tufts and stomach are silver white, and the nose leather should be brick red outlined with the marking colour. The visible skin of the eyelids and the paw pads should be the same colour as the marking colour.

A black shaded silver is coloured with a form of tipping. The individual hair is a brilliant silver white for up to half its length, starting at the root. The rest of the hair, including the tip, is black for at least one-eighth and at most one-half of its length.

This colouring is very common among Persians in Europe and Japan. The contrast between the two colours, a very important element, must be sharp. The face may seem to be sprinkled with ash, the hocks are grey to black. The tipping must be regular, without clear tabby markings. The top of the tail is very dark; the ears should also be tipped. The belly, inside of the legs and chest must be a brilliant white. The cat should give the impression of having been generously but evenly sprinkled with coal dust.

Chinchilla or shaded silver torbie
(A-, B-, C-, D-, I$_{CH}$-, T^a-, or I$_{SH}$-, T-, or t^{b}t^b, Si-, Oo)

In this form, the tip of the hair is coloured with the torbie pattern colours from one-eighth to one-half of its length; the rest is silver white. The varieties are blue, chocolate, cinnamon, lilac, and fawn.

The nose leather, lips, and paw pads are pink speckled with black.

Chinchilla golden
(A-, I$_{CH}$-, sisi, T^a-)

In this cat the hair is chinchilla tipped with eumelanin or phaeomelanin (the marking colour). The undercolour should be apricot to deep gold, though a deep apricot is preferred. The chin may be of a lighter colour, and the belly may also be a lighter shade than the back. The rims of the eyes and the nose should be outlined with the marking colour and the centre of the nose is brick red. Paw pads are the same as the marking colour or a shade lighter. The tip of the tail should be of the marking colour, as though dipped in ink.

Chinchilla goldens come in black, blue, chocolate, cinnamon, lilac, fawn, red and cream, as well as in torbie patterns.

Shaded golden
(A-, I$_{SH}$-, sisi, T- or t^{b}t^b)

The hair of this cat is shaded—tipped with eumelanin or phaeomelanin (the marking colour). The undercolour must be apricot to deep gold, with deep apricot the preferred shade. All other markings, colours and descriptions are the same as for the Chinchilla golden. A shaded golden torbie is also a genetic possibility.

Smokes

The smokes come in full, sepia, mink, and pointed colours.

In solid-coloured cats the colour could be black, blue, chocolate, cinnamon, lilac, fawn, red, or cream. Tortie smokes can appear in black and red, blue and cream, chocolate and red, cinnamon and red, lilac and cream, and fawn and cream.

Each hair is tipped from about half to 80 percent of its length. The rest of the hair is a brilliant, silver white. Long-haired black smokes are the most striking, because they appear to be a solid colour until they move. Then the hair ripples, revealing the brilliant, white undercolour beneath. For judges, this contrast is extremely important. It is most obvious in long-haired cats. For this reason, Persian smokes are shown only in the winter, when their coat is at its longest and thickest. In this condition, it shows all the desired contrast and good colour proportion.

Ghost tabby markings may appear in kittens and young adults. These will vanish when the cat reaches maturity, unless the cat is specifically bred to retain them.

Colour points

This is a restricted colour pattern in which the pigmentation is confined to the points only—the ears, mask, legs, and tail—and the body colour is a paler shade of the indicative colour. The eye colour must be blue—the deeper the better.

Solid point

In these cats, the ears, mask, tail, and legs are dark, well-defined and contrast with the body colour, which is much lighter, with each hair a uniform colour from the roots to the tip. Body shading should harmonize with the point colour. In longhairs, the chest and ruff may be paler than in shorthairs.

Seal point (aa, B-, $c^s c^s$ D-, oo) This is the best known, best loved, and most common of the Siamese varieties. The body colour should be an even pale fawn or cream, shading gradually into a lighter colour on the belly and chest. The points should be a dense, deep seal brown. If these cats are allowed outside in the cold, adult seal points tend to darken very markedly in the hip and shoulder areas.

Seal point colouring occurs too in Himalayans and Birmans, but the tail fur of these cats is much longer and is lighter than on the legs, ears, and mask.

The nose leather, lips, and paw pads are seal brown.

Blue point (aa, B-, $c^s c^s$, dd, oo) The points should be a cool, grey-blue. The very pale body should show only a very light platinum shading in adults.

The tail fur of Himalayans and Birmans is much longer and lighter than on the legs, ears, and mask. The nose leather, lips, and paw pads are dark blue-grey.

Chocolate point (aa, bb $c^s c^s$, D-, oo) The points are a warm milk-chocolate colour, the body a pale ivory. The long-haired chocolate points (Himalayan, Birman) have a paler tail because of the added length of the fur.

The charm of this colour lies in its warmth. The contrast between the points and the body is marked and should persist even in adulthood. However, 'spectacles' of paler hairs outlining the eyes are frequent. The eyes are as dark a blue as possible, with a rosy aura (tending towards violet in the Siamese and Birmans). The nose leather and lips are a burnt rose, and the paw pads a salmon pink colour.

Cinnamon point (aa, $b^l b^l$, $c^s c^s$, D-, oo) The points should be an extremely warm, reddish, cinnamon brown. The pale body colour ranges from buff to ivory. As in the chocolate point, there is generally a marked contrast between the body and the points. This rare colour is now seen primarily in the Siamese.

The eyes are the darkest blue possible. The nose leather and lips are a burnt rose, and the paw pads a salmon-pink colour.

Lilac point (aa, bb, $c^s c^s$, dd, oo) The points should be a lilac-grey or pinkish tone, the pinker the shade the better. The body colour ranges from milk-white to an extremely pale old ivory; there is a marked tint-on-tint effect, which gives a rather 'dull' but very delicate look, especially in Himalayans and Birmans, which seem even paler because of their long fur.

The eyes are as dark a blue as possible. The nose leather, lips, and paw pads are coral pink.

Fawn point (aa, $b^l b^l$, $c^s c^s$, dd, oo) The body should be an even milk-white, rather like a magnolia shade. The points should be a pale dove to light taupe-grey and may have light fawn tones or a pinkish lavender cast. Eyes are as dark blue as possible. Paw pads are an ash-rose to lavender-pink, and the nose leather is a lavender-pink to lavender-grey.

Red point (B-, $c^s c^s$, D-, OO) The points should be a deep orange-red, a 'hot' colour, the deeper the better. The body should be a warm, even white, with delicate creamy shading on the haunches and shoulders. Adult cats, breeding animals, and cats allowed outside in the cold tend to lose this contrast and become almost entirely red.

All red points show some tabby markings, and although the standard theoretically forbids them, they may not be considered a fault by all standards. These markings cannot be totally eliminated as the red gene has no effect on the non-agouti gene. The eyes are as dark a blue as possible, the nose leather, lips, and paw pads hot pink; black spots are common on the lips and nose.

Cream point (B-, c^{s}c^s dd, OO) The points may be any shade of cream, from deep cream to pale cream. The body should be an even white all over; the overall colour should be sufficiently 'dull' to distinguish it from the red point.

The eyes are deep blue, as dark a blue as is possible, and the nose leather, lips, and paw pads are rosy pink.

Tortie point (aa, B-, c^{s}c^s, D-, Oo)

The tortie point is a mixture of eumelanin and phaeomelanin: seal, chocolate, cinnamon and red pointed colours; blue, lilac, or fawn, and cream pointed colours. These colours appear on the points only. The body, as the cat ages, may have the mottled pattern of the tortie, which may be only a shade lighter than the points. This colouring is found in Siamese, Birmans, and Himalayans, among others.

Lynx point (A-, B-, c^{s}c^s, D-, Si- or sisi, T-, Oo or oo)

This cat has a body colour that is a shade lighter than the point colour, and the points may display one of the tabby patterns. Most standards require that there is no tabby pattern on the body. Torbie points are also shown with the Lynx points. The Lynx point may or may not be silvered.

Particolour points (c^{s}c^s, Ss or SS with any pointed colour and/or pattern)

The ears, mask, and tail of particolour points are of the marking colour. If the cat is bicolour, it may have an inverted V or a white blaze running from the point of the nose to between the eyes. The body, legs, and feet may have white patches, which indicate the presence of the white spotting gene. If there are spots of white on the body, the body may be only a slightly paler shade than the points.

The action of the white spotting gene causes the body shade to be darker than in most colour point cats. If the white spotting gene is not present, the body colour will be a very pale version of the points.

The nose leather, lips, and paw pads may be in the indicative colour, mottled, or pink.

Certain breed standards, such as those for Birmans, Ragdolls, and Snowshoes, specify the exact placement of the white.

Particolours (Ss or SS)

These are cats that have the white spotting gene, which creates white areas of various sizes, mixed with one or more other colours.

There are three levels of white: mitted (a low grade of white and a colour and/or pattern), bicolour (a medium grade of white spotting and a colour and/or pattern), and harlequin or Van (a high grade of white spotting and a colour and/or pattern).

For all particolours, the nose leather, lips, and paw pads are either pink (because of the white gene), mottled, or the same as the indicative colour.

Mitted (Ss)

This is a predominantly coloured cat with the white limited to the paws, the back legs, belly, chin, and chest. The exception is the Birmans. The standard for that breed does not allow any white on the belly, chest, or chin. Mitted cats are typically about one-quarter white.

Bicolour (Ss)

A bicoloured cat has a coloured head, back, and tail, with white on its legs, feet, underside, and lower flanks. A white blaze such as the inverted V pattern is often seen. Various markings of white and pigment may occur, but the cat is generally one-third to two-thirds white.

Harlequin or Van (SS)

This is a predominantly white cat with coloured patches. The coloured patches are usually found on the head and tail with two or three separate patches permitted on the back. The Van pattern (below) has a coloured cap and tail and is an extreme expression of the white spotting gene.

Calico or tortoiseshell and white
(aa, B-, C-, D-, Ss, Oo)

These cats have black and red patches of colour surrounded by white, which makes the colour seem very vivid. Tortoiseshells are usually females, but occasionally a tortie male is found.

Dilute calico or blue tortie and white
(aa, B-, C-, dd, Ss, Oo)

Blue and cream patches of colour surrounded by white define these attractive cats.

BODY TYPES

Cobby
Short, sturdy: Burmese, Cymric, Exotic Shorthair, Himalayan, Manx, Persian.

Semi-cobby
Slightly longer and not as sturdy as the cobby: American Shorthair, American Wirehair, Bombay, British Shorthair, Korat, Scottish Fold, Birman, Norwegian.

Foreign
Long, elegant: Abyssinian, Turkish Angora, Russian Blue, Somali.

Semi-foreign
Quite long, but with a slightly heavier boning than foreign: American Curl, Devon Rex, Havana, Egyptian Mau, Singapura, Tonkinese. Semi-foreign and sturdy: Bengal, Ocicat.

Oriental
Very long and elegant: Balinese, Cornish Rex, Oriental, Siamese.

Long and substantial
Maine Coon, Ragdoll, Turkish Van.

Out of Balance
Chartreux (semi-cobby with slender legs); Sphynx (semi-foreign with a full belly).

SEPIA ($c^b c^b$)

Eye colour is yellow or gold, chartreux to amber, depending on the requirements of the standard.

Seal sepia (B-, $c^b c^b$, D-, oo)
A rich, warm seal brown or bitter chocolate; may have ruddy tones.

Blue sepia (B-, $c^b c^b$, dd, oo)
Medium-to-slate blue, often with warm fawn tones

Chocolate sepia (bb, $c^b c^b$, D-, oo)
Warm, milk-chocolate or coffee-bean brown.

Cinnamon sepia ($b^l b^l$, $c^b c^b$, D-, oo)
Warm, red-brown, light ruddy tan, soft cinnamon or terracotta colour.

Lilac sepia (bb, $c^b c^b$, dd, oo)
Pale, delicate dove grey, with a slightly pinkish cast giving a faded effect.

Fawn sepia ($b^l b^l$, $c^b c^b$, dd, oo)
Warm pinkish buff, with pale lavender-grey undertones, a light mocha or cocoa powder shade.

Red sepia (B-, $c^b c^b$, D-, OO)
A tangerine colour.

Cream sepia (B-, $c^b c^b$, dd, OO)
A rich cream or apricot colour.

Any of the above sepias may also appear in tortie, tabby, torbie, silvered, golden, chinchilla, shaded, smoke, or particolour versions.

MINK ($c^s c^s$)

Points are darker than body colour.

Seal mink (B-, $c^b c^s$, D-, oo)
Body: a rich seal brown or bitter chocolate; may have ruddy tones. Points: bitter chocolate to seal brown.

Blue mink (B-, $c^b c^s$, dd, oo)
Body: soft blue-grey to medium blue. Points: medium blue to slate blue.

Chocolate mink (bb, $c^b c^s$, D-, oo)
Body: buff cream-to-light tan. Points: golden tan to warm milk-chocolate or coffee-bean brown.

Cinnamon mink ($b^l b^l$ $c^b c^s$, D-, oo)
Body: light coppery amber, strawberry blond. Points: light ruddy tan, muted burnt sienna, or sorrel.

Lilac mink (bb, $c^b c^s$, dd, oo)
Body: pale silver-to-light pearl grey. Points: light pewter to taupe-grey with pinkish-lavender cast.

Fawn mink ($b^l b^l$, $c^b c^s$, dd, oo)
Body: light warm sandy beige, rosy sand beige, or pale mushroom. Points: warm pinkish buff, light mocha, or cocoa powder; lavender undertones.

Red mink (B-, $c^b c^s$, dd, OO)
Body: pale peach beige. Points: apricot.

Cream mink (B-, $c^b c^s$, dd, OO)
Body: pale cream or apricot cream. Points: peach.

Any of the above minks may also appear in tortie, tabby, torbie, silvered, golden, chinchilla, shaded, smoke, or particolour versions.

Glossary

This glossary gives the definitions of a number of terms used in cat breeding and showing. Words followed by an asterisk (*) have their own alphabetical entry.

Agouti: Hairs 'ticked'* with alternate bands of light and dark colour, ending with a dark tip, or the colouring between stripes. This colour formation creates a tabby* pattern.

Albinism: The total lack of pigmentation and therefore of colour, due to a c gene. This gene is lethal* when carried by homozygous* cats, creating red-eyed albinos that rarely survive.

Alopecia: A skin condition that causes hair to fall out in patches.

Anurous: Used to describe a cat without a tail.

Awn hairs: The coarser of two secondary types of hair composing a cat's coat; the awn hairs form an insulating layer of varying thickness.

Balance: A cat's physical and mental balance. A cat is said to be 'out of balance' when the physical parts of the body are not in proportion. (The Chartreux is a breed out of balance in that the body is robust while the legs are slender.)

Best: An award presented in cat shows.

Bicoloured: Said of a cat showing one of various markings formed by white and another colour (black, blue, red, tabby, cream, etc.).

Blaze: A marking on the centre of the forehead between the eyes and which can run down the nose.

Blotched or classic tabby: One form of the tabby* pattern showing large solid-colour areas on the flanks and broad lines on the back and legs.

Bracelet: The ringed marking encircling the legs in the tabby* pattern.

Brachygnathism: A malformation of the jaws that prevents them from closing properly. The lower jaw is too narrow and set back, and the upper teeth are sometimes actually visible.

Break: An indentation of the nose at about eye level or between the eyes (see also stop*).

Breastplate: The region of the body stretching from the lower part of the chin to the chest and between the front legs.

Breeches: Longer, thicker hair on the back of upper hind legs.

Brindle (brindled, brindling): A scattering of 'wrong' coloured hairs in a colour (usually in the tail or mask*).

Brown: The colour of certain breeds; genetically speaking, though, it is black.

Calico: Tortoiseshell* and white, showing clearly defined patches of black, red, and white.

Cameo (shell, shaded*, or smoke*): The tip of the hair is red, cream or tortie*, the remainder being a brilliant silver white.

Carrier: An animal able to transmit to its descendants a colour, an illness, a fur type, etc., other than those it expresses itself. A heterozygous* animal capable of passing on a recessive* gene.

Cat association/club/federation: Groups of breeders, fanciers, and judges possessing at least a chairperson, a treasurer, and a secretary. Most are non-profit-making organizations. They organize exhibitions and seminars and keep a stud* book.

Cattery: The place where cats are kept at a breeder's. The name of the cattery becomes the family name or prefix of all the kittens born at that breeder's establishment; it is valid for 30 years.

Chinchilla: The tip of the hair is black, the rest a brilliant silver white; this is the weakest degree of tipping*.

Chocolate: A rich shade of deep brown.

Cinnamon: A reddish-brown, cocoa colour.

Classic tabby: see Blotched* tabby.

Cloven (Forked): Said of a deformed foot in which the toes are stuck together in twos. It is a disqualifying fault for all breeds.

Cobby: A short, compact, sturdy body with broad shoulders and rump (seen in Persians, Himalayans, Exotics and Manxes).

Co-dominance: The situation in which two colour genes are equally dominant. For example, the Tonkinese, which results from a combination of the c^s Siamese genes and the c^b Burmese genes, constitutes a third breed $c^b c^s$.

Colour point: Coloured only at the extremities, or points*; the eyes are always blue (as in Siamese, Birmans, Himalayans, etc.).

Cryptorchidism: The obvious absence of a testicle (a disqualifying fault for all breeds). In this condition, the testicle remains within the abdominal cavity.

Curling: The regular crimping of the fur displayed by Rex breeds, especially the Cornish.

Dam: the female parent of a cat.

Depigmentation: A lack of colour in the skin, which causes pink spots on the paw pads or nose leather.

Dilute calico: A colour with patches of blue, cream, and white.

Dilution: A paler version of a basic colour; for example, dilute black gives blue, dilute chocolate gives lilac*.

Diploma: An award given by judges during a show in accordance with the standard* of perfection for the breed. Some examples: European Champion, International Champion, Grand International Champion.

Disqualification: Elimination from a competition due to a fault sufficiently serious to prevent a shown cat from winning a prize.

Dome: Rounded forehead.

Domestic type: A non-pedigreed cat, usually a short-hair, native to a particular country. It is usually heavier boned than many of the foreign* types.

Dominant: Describes a gene that prevails over another, such as the agouti* over the non-agouti gene.

Donkey's ears: Straight ears set close together.

Double coat: A thick coat in which the awn* hairs are as long as the outer, guard* hairs.

Down hairs: Soft, slightly wavy secondary hairs (around the ears and toes)

Dutch agouti: A golden* shaded* breed with gold eyes.

Fawn: Dilution* of cinnamon*; refers to a 'coffee and milk,' vanilla fudge or warm pinkish buff colour.

Flabby cheeks: Especially developed cheeks in adult males caused by a heavier musculature and a thickening of the skin in this area.

Fontanelle: A space above the forehead covered by membrane; the skull, thought to be open while the cat is young, gradually closes due to ossification.

Foreign: A body type characterized by a long, elegant shape: seen in Orientals, Siamese, etc.

Frill: A ruff that extends down between the front legs.

Fur ball: A collection of dead hairs swallowed by a cat while grooming itself.

Genotype: The hereditary characteristics of an individual, expressed or not.

Ghost markings: Faint tabby* markings seen in some genetically solid-coloured animals, particularly when young; these marks disappear with age and moulting.

Gold/golden: A golden apricot shade.

Guard hairs: The longest of the three types of hair making up the cat's coat. They form the outer layer, giving the coat its shine and colour.

Hairlessness: This condition is never absolute. Even in the Sphynx breed, there is some hair on the points* and the body is covered with a light down*.

Harlequin: A predominantly white cat with colour patches usually restricted to the extremities, but sometimes with a few body spots, usually on the lower back.

Havana: A recognized breed in North America; a colour (warm chocolate brown) in Europe and other countries.

Heterozygous: Possessing two dissimilar genes for a particular trait, one received from each parent. One is dominant*, the other recessive*. In the case of Aa or Bb, the cat shows a dominant colour (black, for example), but is the carrier of a dilution* (blue or lilac*).

Himalayan or colour point*: A pointed Persian.

Homozygous: Possessing two identical genes for a particular trait. In the case of AA or BB, the cat displays a colour and does not carry a gene for any other.

Hybridization: The crossing of two distinct breeds.

Inhibitor gene: The gene responsible for the inhibition of pigment, and therefore causing chinchilla*, shaded*, smoked* or tipped* colours.

Lavender: See lilac*.

Lethal gene: A gene that in the homozygous* state leads to the death of the foetus or newborn.

Lilac: Also known as lavender; a pale pinky-beige shade.

Lynx point: Describes a cat whose points* are coloured with tabby* markings.

Lynx tips or tipping*: The extension of hairs from the tips of the ears; a desired characteristic in Maine Coons and Norwegians; discouraged in Persians and Exotics.

Mackerel tabby: A type of tabby* pattern with fine stripes.

Maltesing: Also called dilution*: caused by pigment granules clumping together in the hair shaft to produce a pale colour.

Marbled: A tabby* pattern used only to describe the Bengal cat. The pattern is a variation of the classic* tabby pattern.

Markings: Tabby* markings, such as the frown lines, the 'M' on the forehead, necklaces*, bracelets*, tail rings, and body markings.

Mask: A darker region on the face, including the nose, whisker pads, chin and around the eyes, stopping between the ears.

Masking, or epistasis: The masking of the phenotype*. When a gene masks, or hides, another; for example, the W gene produces a white cat but masks another colour which may appear in that cat's offspring. Masking is more visible in ghost markings*, which appear on solid-coloured cats.

Mink: A colour of fur that results from the combination of the Siamese pointed and Burmese sepia genes. The mink cat has stronger colouring at the points* and on the back, while the main and lower body regions tend to be lighter (although still coloured). See Co-dominance*.

Mittens: The pure white feet of certain cats (as in Birmans).

Monorchism: The presence of only one testicle (a disqualifying fault for all breeds).

Mutation: A sudden change in genotype* having no relation to the individual's ancestry.

Muzzle: The projecting part of the head, including the nose, whisker pads, chin, mouth, and cheeks.

Muzzle break: Indentation where the muzzle* is attached to the skull; also a whisker break.

Necklace: Tabby* markings around the neck.

New breed: Used to describe a breed that is in the process of being created and whose standard* has not yet been perfected.

Nodosity: A slight deformation of the end of the tail (thickening of the last vertebra).

Odd-eyed: Having eyes of different colours: for example, one blue and the other gold, as in white Persians.

Oriental slant: A particular slanted setting of the eye (seen in Siamese and Orientals, for example).

Oriental type: A long, lean body type like that of the Siamese. See also Foreign.*

Particolour: Displaying one or more colours or patterns, and white; for example, black and white, tortie* and white, tabby* and white.

Pattern: Refers to colour distribution that forms a pattern, such as the tabby* pattern, or colour and white distribution such as the mitted*, bicolour*, harlequin* or van* patterns.

Paw pads: The furless padded area under the feet.

Pedigree: A document or certificate showing the names, breeds, and colours of a cat's ancestors; a family tree.

Pewter: A silver shaded* breed with gold eyes.

Phenotype: The physical appearance of an individual.

Points: The extremities of a cat's body: the mask*, ears, tail, and legs.

Polydactyly: A malformation in which there are more toes than normal: either six or seven instead of five on the front feet, and five or six instead of four on the back feet (a disqualifying fault for all breeds).

Prognathism: A malformation in which the lower jaw juts too far forward; the lower teeth may actually be visible (seen in Persians, etc.).

Recessive: Describes a gene which is usually masked by a dominant* gene; it must be present on both members of a pair of chromosomes in order to be expressed.

Roman profile: Said of a profile that displays a downward curve, as in Birmans and, in a more pronounced form, in the Cornish Rex.

Ruddy: The colour name given to Abyssinians and Somalis; a brown ticked* tabby that has a high degree of red.

Ruff: A mass of long, thick fur around the neck.

Self-coloured: Solid-coloured.

Shaded or shading: Colour change at the tip of the hair or in certain areas (particularly the upper legs).

Silver: Refers to the silver ground colour of a tipped* cat; a brilliant silver white caused by the elimination of yellow pigmentation.

Sire: The male parent of a cat.

Slip: Darker markings around the hip area on a colour* point (as in Siamese, Himalayans and Birmans).

Smoke: Colouring of 50 percent to 80 percent of the hair shaft, the rest being silver.*

Sorrel: A colour name given to Abyssinians or Somalis. A cinnamon* ticked* tabby that has a high degree of red. Sometimes referred to as 'Red,' which is a misnomer in that it is not a true red and does not have OO in the genotype*.

Spectacles: A lighter area surrounding the eyes in a coloured mask* (as in Siamese, Birmans, and Himalayans).

Spotted: A pattern displaying clearly defined spots of a darker colour; a type of tabby* marking.

Spread: The distance between the ears or eyes.

Spur: A white area seen on the back of the feet in Birmans.

Standard: The detailed description of each breed, describing the ultimate in 'perfection.' Used by judges as the criteria against which to evaluate individual animals.

Sternum: The breastbone. If it sticks out and is obvious to the touch this is a disqualifying fault for all breeds.

Stop: The short incline between the forepart of the skull and the muzzle,* or a concave curve occurring in the nose at or just below eye level; may be slight or very marked.

Stud book: A book of breeds prepared by an organization that establishes pedigrees.

Tabby or agouti*: Refers to any of the tabby patterns. The agouti gene must be present for full expression of a tabby pattern.

Thumbprint: A round mark found on the upper part of the back of the ears in tabbies*; this darker patch actually shows the ground colour.

Ticked tabby: The most extreme form of tabby;* each hair is banded in alternately dark and light colours.

Tipping: A form of tabby* in which only the tip of the hair is coloured (chinchilla*).

Torbie: Usually a female cat; refers to a tortie* (red and black or cream and blue) that has turned tabby* (spotted*, mackerel*, classic,* or ticked*).

Tortie: See tortoiseshell.*

Tortoiseshell: A mixture of red and black or blue and cream displayed as a rule only in females, although the rare male tortoiseshell has been produced. Any male with this colouring is usually sterile.

Triangle: Used to describe a particular head shape seen in some breeds, such as Siamese and Orientals.

Undercoat: The woolly or down hairs that are the finest of the three types of hair of which a cat's coat is composed.

Van pattern: A particoloured pattern; the most extreme expression of the white* spotting gene. Usually exhibits a coloured cap and tail, although a few small spots may appear on the lower back near the base of the tail.

Wedge: Used to describe a particular type of head formed by straight lines running from the outer ear bases along the sides of the muzzle,* without a break in the jaw line at the whiskers. The skull is flat and the straight nose a continuation of the forehead.

Whippy: Describes a type of long, slender, flexible tail: seen in the Cornish Rex, Siamese, Orientals, and Sphynx.

Whisker pad: The fleshy part of the upper lip on either side of the nose, from which the whiskers grow.

White spotting (S) gene: The gene responsible for white with colour patterns; has incomplete dominance in the heterozygous* form (when it produces mitted and bicolour patterns).

YOUR CAT'S PHYSIOLOGY

How the body functions

Physiology deals with body functions—the activities of the organs and systems, and the way they interact. Physiologically the cat is similar to other mammals, including humans. This section focuses on what is specific to the cat's physiology, and discusses the animal's body functions in detail.

Whiskers are one of the cat's most distinctive features.

The senses

Vision

The retina and pupil of the domestic cat's eye, although much the same as those of other mammals, do differ in important ways. All retinas contain light receptor cells: cones and rods. The cones detect colour and fine detail, but require a lot of light to function; they don't react in dusk. The rods, however, give black-and-white vision and are sensitive to dim light.

The cat, a nocturnal animal, has evolved a retina with a greater proportion of rods than most other animals. To boot, layers of reflective cells, the *tapetum lucidum*, form a mirror behind the rods and cones, which bounces light back to them for a second hit. (This is why we see a cat's eyes glowing in the dark.) Thus the cat's night vision is particularly strong (see page 54).

The cat's vision is perfectly adapted to different light conditions. The pupils are narrow slits in bright light, but become round at night or in dim light.

When it is dark, the pupil opens into a large circle, letting in whatever glimmer of light there might be. In bright light the pupil contracts—to a tiny circle in most animals—limiting the light that enters the eye. The cat's round pupil shrinks to a thin vertical slit in bright light. The slit pupil closes more completely than a circular one, protecting the cat's highly sensitive retina.

Cats have stereoscopic vision. This means that when a cat looks at a bird, for instance, it can judge the distance between itself and the bird very accurately. The bird, however, must look at the cat first with one eye, then the other, in order to judge how far away the cat is. By the time the bird has assessed this distance, chances are the cat will be on it. The cat's comparatively large eyes, deeply set in the sockets, face forward. This means that the cat must move its head, and sometimes its body, to see what is around it.

Touch

Vibrissae or whiskers—large stiff hairs growing in neat rows on either side of the upper lip—play a major role in the cat's acute sense of touch. Rooted in an inner layer of the skin called the dermis, the base of each whisker has many nerve endings that provide instant information about everything it brushes against and even about changes in air currents when anything moves. The cat finds its whiskers particularly useful in dim light or when stalking prey. Using powerful muscles at the whiskers' base, the cat projects them forward to discover obstacles in its path.

The eyebrows, cheek hairs, nose tip, and paws are other tactile-sensitive areas.

Smell

Cats generally have a very keen sense of smell, approximately 30 times more powerful than that of a human. This has two practical consequences.

A cat's meal will seem tasty or not depending on its smell, especially since cats have relatively few taste buds—473 in cats compared to 9000 in humans. (Cats generally prefer lukewarm food, for example, because it has a stronger aroma. And they are especially sensitive to odours of substances such as fish, which contain nitrogen.) A cat with nasal congestion may refuse to eat at all, simply because it cannot smell what is in its dish.

A cat marks out its territory chiefly through the use of smells. Both males and females use urine to make their marks, and sometimes excrement or secretions from the skin around the lips. A cat that rubs its cheeks against an object such as a door or a piece of furniture—or against its owner—is impregnating that object or person with its smell and in this way staking out its private property.

Hearing

Cats have a wider hearing range than humans, especially in the high frequencies, and therefore live in a different world of sound than we do. Like most mammals, cats have highly mobile ears that can swivel to detect sounds more clearly and to identify the location of those sounds.

With their highly developed senses of hearing and sight, cats are ideally suited for hunting at dusk and during the night, especially when the moon is shining. This is why even domestic cats are often more active at night than during the day.

Digestion

Cats are carnivores, their organs designed to handle a diet of raw meat. Their teeth are shaped to ready food for digestion: the incisors to grab prey, the pointed canines to kill it, and the premolars and molars to cut and tear it apart, after which it is swallowed in large chunks.

Stomach

The digestive process begins in the cat's mouth, then continues in the stomach. Large amounts of hydrochloric acid secreted there break down a meal into components the body can absorb.

Intestines

Most of the transformation of food into nutrients and all the absorption of nutrients take place in the small intestine. Fats can only be absorbed after they are converted into an emulsion by fluid from the bile. The enzymes required for digestion are supplied by the pancreas and the intestine, and these go to work in the neutralizing process. The stomach's contents are transformed from acidic to alkaline by bicarbonate supplied from large quantities of pancreatic juices.

Since a cat's digestive system is designed primarily for meat, the small intestine is very short. When a cat has diarrhoea, it can quickly become undernourished and lose weight.

Adapted as they are to a carnivorous diet, the digestive enzymes will not absorb vegetable foods properly. A diet too high in vegetable matter can reduce the cat's overall nutrition, and cause diarrhoea and gas production in the large intestine. Most veterinarians recommend a cat be fed high-quality animal protein and fat. All diet changes should be made gradually over several weeks because the cat's digestive system is comparatively fragile. When you find the particular diet that your cat thrives on—and likes—it's best to stick to it with little variation.

Metabolism and diet

Metabolism refers to the chemical reactions that make the digested food available for essential cell activities, and transform it into energy.

The prey that makes up a cat's natural diet contains all the nutrients its body requires. If the cat devours skin, muscle, bones, and entrails of small animals, it has very little need for other food. Thus the digestive system of the cat has a limited ability for metabolizing essential nutrients from carbohydrate or vegetable sources. For proper nutrition, therefore, the domestic cat's food should contain the same nutrients found in its natural diet.

Protein requirements

Cats must consume a great deal of protein. In fact it must make up at least 25 percent of the cat's energy supply or, in food terms, 25 to 30 percent of the dry content per serving. A diet of less than 19 percent protein may cause a deficiency in amino acids, the basic structural units in protein. A diet of 19 to 25 percent protein may lead to overeating as the cat attempts to consume sufficient protein; the result is often an unhealthy weight gain.

The diet of all animals must include 10 essential amino acids. The body cannot synthesize these—they must come from the diet. The amino acids are lysine, leucine, isoleucine, threonine, histidine, tryptophan, arginine, methionine, phenylalanine, and valine. Certain of these are of particular importance to the cat.

Arginine is necessary to convert ammonia, which is produced when protein is metabolized, into urea that can be easily eliminated from the body. This process is important in the cat because of its high protein intake. An inadequate supply of arginine can result in acute ammonia toxicity, which can lead to death; consequently it must account for about 1 percent of dry content in the cat's diet.

Lysine is important for growth. It is found in abundance in animal proteins, but it can be destroyed by overcooking. Taurine is also needed for feline growth—in fact, cats have a greater need for it than other animals, but they cannot synthesize sufficient amounts. A deficiency, over time, can cause irreversible degeneration of the retina, and eventually blindness. Cats fed a diet low in taurine can also develop reproductive problems and a form of heart disease called dilated cardiomyopathy. Plant products are poor sources of taurine, but meat and fish contain high levels of it. Although commercial cat foods are formulated with sufficient amounts of taurine, dog foods are not and should not be substituted for cat food.

Fat requirements

A carnivore can digest fats easily because it can secrete ample bile and lipase, a

When on the hunt, the cat uses all its senses for maximum effectiveness.

digestive enzyme produced in the pancreas. Fats can represent between 30 and 40 percent of its total food.

As with amino acids, there are also fatty acids essential to a cat's health.

Cats have a special need for arachidonic acid, which many other animals can synthesize from linoleic acid, found in many foods other than flesh. Arachidonic acid is found only in animal fats, especially fish oil. Consequently a cat's diet must contain a large proportion of fat, one of the principal components of living cells, and this fat must come from animal sources.

Vitamin requirements

Vitamin metabolism in cats differs from that of other animals in a number of ways. First, vitamin A occurs naturally only in animal tissue. Vitamin A precursors (B-carotene) are found in abundant supply in plants such as carrots. Most other mammals can convert B-carotene to vitamin A, an ability that cats lack.

Cats have a much greater need than most animals for the water-soluble B vitamins. In the case of pyridoxine (vitamin B_6) and niacin, for example, they require four times as much as dogs. They need pyridoxine to convert dietary protein into energy. Niacin is essential in metabolizing carbohydrates and fats, and for the general functioning of the digestive system. Yet unlike other animals, cats do not convert tryptophan (an essential amino acid) to niacin.

Feline metabolism

Cats are particularly vulnerable to poisoning. Their livers are unable to metabolize toxins and other chemicals efficiently, so even a small dose of poison is life-threatening. Cats are particularly sensitive to insecticides, preservatives used in food products, and medications. Since even common drugs such as aspirin and acetaminophen are eliminated very slowly, they can be toxic. Do not administer medicine to your cat without consulting a veterinarian.

Excretion

Urine is produced by the kidneys in two stages. A diluted urine consisting of water, urea, and various mineral salts is extracted from the blood by the million or so filtering units called nephrons that lie in the outer section of the kidneys. Since the kidneys' main role is to maintain the body's water balance, nearly all of this fluid and some of the other substances are subsequently reabsorbed into the blood. The excess water and other waste products are then transported to the bladder and eventually excreted as urine.

The ancestors of the cat lived in semi-desert areas and rarely drank water. They didn't have to: 60 to 70 percent of their prey's body weight was water.

Today's cats also drink very sparingly, but unlike their predecessors, their normal diet contains little water. This can lead to constipation, dehydration, and urinary tract problems. Without adequate quantities of water to flush waste matter from the body, for example, mineral salts in the urine will form stones in the urinary organs.

The formation of stones in the bladder can be influenced by other factors, too. When a cat eats, acidic gastric juices are secreted in quantities more or less proportional to the amount of food eaten. The blood becomes alkaline in order to neutralize the acid. Alkaline urine is then created, which can promote the formation of mineral salts and stones. For this reason, your cat may need a diet that does not produce alkaline urine. Ask your veterinarian's advice. It is also essential that the cat have ready access to water.

Residue waste from food is expelled from the anus as faeces.

Reproduction

Puberty and the seasons

In a typical male cat, the production of reproductive cells, a process called spermatogenesis, begins when the animal is about 5 months old. Although most cats will not yet be capable of fertilization, reproductive behaviour such as the marking of territory and the mounting of females can start as early as 4 months.

In the female, puberty is signalled by the first heat, the age varying with the breed. Domestics, Birmans, the Rex and the Sphynx breeds reach puberty around 6 to 9 months. Siamese, Orientals and Burmese are more precocious and their puberty begins at 4 to 6 months. Persians reach puberty later than most cats, when they are 12 months or even older.

The seasons of the year also have an important bearing. If a cat reaches puberty between October and December, it may not go into heat until the following spring.

Sexual activity in cats is largely governed by changes in the length of daylight hours, a phenomenon called photoperiodism. Shorter days will result in sexual dormancy in the female and lowered fertility in the male. Sexual activity peaks from January to October and occasionally stops altogether in the middle of the summer. These variations in sexual activity prevent the birth of kittens during the cold winter months.

Reproductive surgery

As cats reach sexual maturity, they often develop undesirable behaviour. Male cats tend to roam, fight with other cats, spray urine to mark territory, and become more aggressive towards people and other animals. Females will have heat cycles during which they are extremely vocal, and they will deposit urine markings. Early reproductive surgery typically prevents these objectionable behaviours.

Male cats generally are castrated, or neutered, by the removal of both testicles at 6 to 10 months of age. Most veterinarians recommend that a female cat have an ovariohysterectomy, or spay, before her first heat, and before she is 6 months old.

The female cat's cycle

All female mammals who have intermittent sexual activity have a cycle of several phases:
• anoestrus, a period in which the female will have little or no sexual activity;

Sunshine is more than a luxury; it is a physiological necessity.

• prooestrus, a period immediately before heat, which normally lasts about two days;
• oestrus, a period when the female is in heat and mates voluntarily, which generally lasts from five to eight days. There is great variety in the length of oestrus, but it may last anywhere from 3 to 20 days.

The female cat's behaviour when she is in heat is unmistakable. She is generally nervous, caterwauls and crouches, flattening her back while arching her pelvis upwards, then kneads with her hind legs and lifts her tail to the side.

In most species, ovulation occurs spontaneously during this phase. In the cat, it is triggered by coitus, which follows a definite pattern. The male sniffs the female's genital region while she crouches, then mounts her, biting her loose neck fur. Penetration lasts only a few seconds. The female emits a dramatic coital 'scream' and breaks the male's hold by turning and striking him with her paws. As the male withdraws, the female rolls and thrashes and licks her vulval area. Ovulation occurs about 24 to 48 hours later.

Sexual cycle of the cat

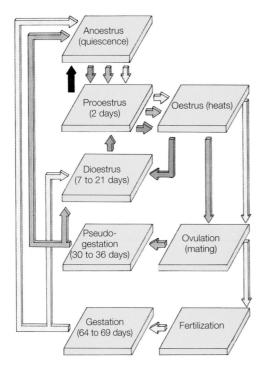

Fewer than 50 percent of female cats ovulate after a single encounter, so it is recommended that the male and female be left together for several days to ensure pregnancy. Suprafecundation (multiple impregnation) occurs when several toms sire a single litter.

After oestrus, there are three possible outcomes. If coitus did not occur, there will be no ovulation, and the cat will enter the period between two oestruses called dioestrus. On the other hand, if ovulation

A female cat in heat.

occurs without fertilization, there will be a false pregnancy. And if fertilization is successful, gestation will start.

Dioestrus is the interval between two oestruses when ovulation does not occur. It normally ranges from 3 to 14 days during the breeding season, but may be as long as 30 days.

Infrequently, and most commonly in older cats that have never given birth, a cat may show signs of continuous oestrus. This condition is often called nymphomania.

A false pregnancy, which lasts from 35 to 70 days, corresponds to the time during which progesterone, the hormone that supports pregnancy, is secreted by the corpus luteum, a structure that forms in the ovaries when ovulation has occurred.

This is followed by dioestrus, when the interval between two oestruses is extended. Some breeders use this technicality to control reproductive periods by artificially stimulating ovulation.

Gestation lasts from 64 to 69 days, with the average duration between 63 and 65 days, counting the first coupling as the starting date.

Implantation of the embryos within the uterus occurs approximately 13 days after mating. The placenta is the organ that unites the foetus to the uterus by way of the umbilical cord. In the cat the maternal and foetal tissues lie alongside each other and are not intermingled. Therefore the foetus does not receive antibodies from its mother prior to birth. This makes it particularly important for the newborn kitten to receive its first mother's milk, its colostrum, because it is rich in maternal antibodies.

Each foetus has its own placenta, and it is important that each of these placentas, or afterbirths, is expelled as the kittens are born. Otherwise the mother will have difficulties with the remaining births.

Pregnancy is usually diagnosed by a direct medical examination of the cat, and cannot be diagnosed by measuring hormone levels as with other species.

After the second or third week of pregnancy, the cat's nipples often enlarge. During the period between the third and fourth week, a veterinarian should be able

A queen waiting to give birth.

to feel the foetuses, because by now they should be between 0.6 and 0.8 inch (1.5 and 2 cm) in diameter.

Between the 36th and 38th day, the kittens' skeletons will show up on an X ray and the age of the foetuses can be determined from their measurements.

Giving birth

About 12 hours before the kittens are born, the mother cat's rectal temperature drops a few degrees below the normal of 100.4 to 101.2°F (38 to 38.4°C). The teats will then enlarge and often begin producing milk. But the surest sign that birth is imminent is a distinct change in the mother cat's behaviour.

She becomes nervous and, a few hours before giving birth, washes herself continuously. She will prepare a nest with her claws. She will start panting and, soon after, labour begins.

The first contractions of the uterus are barely noticeable. The mother cat will lie down and begin to purr.

Then the contractions become more violent, with labour lasting from 30 to 60 minutes until the first kitten is born. The afterbirth is expelled between 5 to 15 minutes after each kitten.

As soon as each kitten appears, the mother breaks the amniotic sac surrounding the kitten and licks the newborn. She immediately eats all the afterbirth.

The kittens are born at intervals of 5 to 90 minutes. In some cases, kittens may be born half a day or even a whole day after the first ones. These delays are no cause for alarm as long as the mother cat seems to be handling the births well and is no longer showing signs of imminent labour.

There is cause for alarm, though, if the mother stops eating 24 hours after giving birth, if she has a temperature above 103°F (39.4°C), or if she will neither groom nor nurse her kittens. If any of these events occur, you should call your veterinarian immediately.

Nursing begins soon after the kittens are born. The kittens will nurse frequently until they are weaned, about eight weeks after their birth. During this period, the mother eats two to three times more food than normal and needs a great deal of calcium. Cats, unlike other animals, can have heats during this stage, sometimes as early as one week after giving birth.

Although the delivery of healthy kittens can be a wonderful experience for the cat, and for her owners, it is important to realize that you are responsible for them. Newly born kittens are unable to look after themselves, as we shall see in the next section.

Growth of kittens

Kittens are born deaf and blind. From the top of the skull to the base of the tail, they measure about 5½ inches (14.5 cm) and usually weigh between 3 and 4 ounces (80 and 110 g).

The nursing box must be kept warm—a temperature of about 86°F (30°C) is recommended—until the kittens begin to suckle normally. The most frequent causes of kittens dying shortly after birth are hypothermia (a subnormal body temperature) and hypoglycemia (a decrease of sugar in the blood).

Determining the sex of kittens is not always easy. One way is to examine them from behind. The anus and genitals are always farther apart in males than females. At birth, the distance between the two in the male is about one-half inch (13 mm) and in the female about one-third inch (8 mm). The scrotum, the external pouch containing the testes, is more visible when

The newborn kitten needs colostrum immediately after birth.

a male kitten is still wet. At birth the testicles are normally in place, but occasionally they will not descend into the scrotum permanently until the 10th or 14th week.

A kitten should gain weight at a rate of one-third ounce (10 g) a day, and at three weeks will weigh between 10 and 12 ounces (300 and 350 g). It should reach 24 to 28 ounces (700 to 800 g) after six or seven weeks. The fewer kittens the mother has to suckle, the faster they will gain weight.

An average litter is four kittens. Siamese have larger litters. Queens giving birth for the first time may have only one kitten.

Soon after birth, the kittens will suckle about 0.10 fluid ounce (2 to 3 ml) of milk every three hours. As the days pass, they will suckle less often but will take more milk each time, reaching 0.35 fluid ounce (10 ml) of milk seven times a day at 1 month of age.

After each nursing session, the mother will lick the kittens' anogenital regions to make the kittens urinate and defecate: she then swallows the results.

During the second week, the kittens will open their eyes and, in the third week, they begin to play and leave the nest. By the fourth week, they can be given small cans of baby food or meat to wean them. Once weaned, they can be separated from their mother.

A newly weaned kitten will probably need five small meals a day to keep healthy. As it grows, and its capacity increases, it should have four larger meals each day. When the cat is 9 months old it should be well developed and have two good meals a day of about 4 or 5 ounces (110 to 140 g) of high-quality commercial cat food, either canned or dry.

When the average adult cat is fully grown, it will need 50 calories for each pound (450 g) of body weight daily, although this might vary according to how active the cat is. A nursing mother cat will need more food. Neutered cats generally need less since they tend to be less active.

From this brief survey of a cat's physiology, we can better understand the diseases that afflict them.

General disorders

Organic diseases

The cat is a secretive animal. When it is sick, it displays few symptoms. It concentrates on conserving its strength to fight its illness. Owners, therefore, must watch their cats carefully. Even the slightest change in the animal's activity could indicate that it is sick.

This section explores the disorders that can afflict the cat's internal systems, and how these disorders can lead to disease.

The cat is also prone to infectious diseases, most of them viral. An index at the end of this chapter (page 188) lists some of the common infections.

Cardiovascular system

Heart

The main cause of heart disease in cats is disorders of the cardiac muscle. These abnormalities, called cardiomyopathy, take several forms:
• Hypertrophic, where the ventricle walls in the chamber of the heart thicken and the volume of the cavities decreases;

• Dilated, where the ventricle walls become thin and tend to balloon out under pressure;
• Intermediate, in which the wall of the heart is affected by dilation and hypertrophy;
• Restrictive, which scars the inner lining of the heart, making it tough and fibrous.

In all these conditions, the volume of blood pumped into the arteries at each beat of the heart is lower than normal. Blood then pools in the ventricles, which can cause a blood clot, called a thrombus, to form. As the disease progresses, the body compensates for the lack of blood flow by increasing the heart rate. If this does not work, the tissues of the body do not receive enough oxygen. The cat's respiratory rate will increase, and it will tire from even the slightest effort. In many cases, there will be one of two fatal complications. The first is congestive heart failure caused by pooling of fluid in the lungs. The second occurs when the blood clot that has formed within the heart moves into the descending aorta and blocks key blood vessels; this can lead to kidney failure and/or paralysis of the cat's back legs.

Heart disease in cats is often fairly advanced before there are noticeable signs.

When treatment is started late in the course of the disease, the response can be disappointing. Unfortunately, the causes of most forms of feline heart disease are unknown.

Blood and anaemia

When the quantity of haemoglobin—the red, oxygen-carrying blood cells—is below normal, the cat is said to be anaemic. The first outward sign is pale mucous membranes, and in a cat this shows up on the gums. If the anaemia is severe, the cat will also suffer from rapid breathing (tachypnoea) and an accelerated heartbeat. Many problems can cause anaemia:

• Blood loss due to injury or poisoning by anticoagulants, especially rat poison;

• Abnormal haemolysis, a widespread destruction of red blood cells within the body. This can be caused by the blood parasite *Haemobartonella felis*, which is spread by biting insects; feline leukaemia virus (see page 184); poisoning; or an autoimmune disorder in which the body creates antibodies that attack its own red blood cells. Many of these conditions are treatable.

• Nonregeneration or inadequate production of red blood cells. This can be caused by chloramphenicol poisoning; by feline leukaemia virus; by a kidney disorder in its final stages (see page 168); by chronic inflammatory diseases including feline infectious peritonitis; and by the invasion of bone marrow by abnormal cells which may or may not be malignant.

Digestive system

The mouth and pharynx

The most common form of oral disease found in the cat is the gingivitis and periodontal disease caused by plaque and tartar buildup on the teeth. If left untreated, the gumline will become progressively inflamed and painful. In more serious cases cats may refuse to eat, may salivate excessively, and may even become aggressive. In cases of severe periodontal infection, when the gums recede and the roots are exposed, painful root tip abscesses can develop. Most veterinarians recommend routine dental care, which may include home care such as brushing, as well as regular cleanings by the veterinarian.

Possible tooth defects include cervical line lesions, or neck lesions—so-called because they occur at the gumline or neck of the tooth. They resemble human cavities, but do not have the same cause. Teeth affected by neck lesions can be quite painful if the lesion extends to the root. This also weakens the teeth making them susceptible to fracture.

Tooth fractures arising from accidents are also fairly common, especially with the long, narrow canine, or fang, teeth. If the fracture is spotted immediately, the tooth may be saved by performing a root canal treatment. Otherwise, the root of the tooth is susceptible to infection. If this occurs, the cat will likely develop a painful root tip abscess. For this reason, fractured teeth should usually be extracted.

There are other causes of severe gingivitis in the cat that are not completely understood. Feline immunodeficiency virus (FIV) is commonly associated with these very serious cases, as is chronic calicivirus infection. Calicivirus most commonly causes an upper respiratory infection. Most of these conditions seem to be triggered by a deficiency in the immune system. Treatments to make these cats more comfortable range from cortisone-type drugs and antibiotics to removal of all the cat's teeth.

Less frequently, cats may develop tumours within their mouths or throats. Biopsies should always be performed. Even though such lesions are frequently cancerous, some are benign and treatable. Unfortunately, cats hate having their mouths examined, and growths can become quite large before they are noticed. Often the first symptoms are eating difficulties and excessive salivation, frequently blood-tinged.

Many of the problems a domestic cat has with its teeth are a result of its diet. Cats that eat wild prey have less plaque and tartar and consequently less gingivitis and periodontal disease. Eating commercial dry food helps control the buildup of plaque and tartar.

Oesophagus

The oesophagus is a long, narrow, muscular tube that extends from the back of the throat to the stomach. Its purpose is to act as a conduit for food and fluid from the mouth to the stomach.

Gingivitis, a gum disease, combined with stomatitis, inflammation of the mucous membranes.

Because cats are fastidious eaters, the oesophagus is rarely obstructed by foreign objects. However, it is subject to a number of diseases and abnormalities which may make swallowing difficult, or may prevent it entirely.

Chief among those diseases is megaoesophagus. This occurs when food fails for whatever reason to pass into the stomach, and instead accumulates in an ever-ballooning pouch on the wall of the animal's oesophagus.

Common causes include thoracic tumours, failure of the sphincter (the circular muscle between the oesophagus and the stomach) to relax during swallowing to allow food into the stomach, and reflux of the stomach's acidic contents. Cats with this condition are liable to inhale regurgitated food. This in turn can lead to bronchopneumonia.

Disorders of the oesophagus may sometimes require surgery. In some cases, the veterinarian may recommend that you place the cat's food on top of an elevated platform in such a way that gravity aids the passage of food while the cat is actually eating.

Stomach

Gastritis, or inflammation of the lining of the stomach, is a common condition in cats. It may be caused by infection (see page 181), allergies, parasites, or ingestion of rancid food, wild animals, toxic chemicals or a foreign body, such as a toy or a piece of foil. Hair balls swallowed by the cat, too, can become so large that they cause stomach disorders.

In the case of gastritis, frothy, blood-stained vomit is the first symptom you are likely to see. This will be followed by diarrhoea. Be aware that this combination often leads to dehydration.

Vomiting is not always a symptom of any illness. Even healthy cats may vomit as often as once or twice a week, and gluttonous cats often throw up after eating too much too quickly.

Intestines

The intestinal tract, a major part of the digestive system, has two parts: the small intestine, where nutrients from food are absorbed into the body, and the large intestine where more fluid and additional nutrients are absorbed, and subsequently, where undigested food residue and other matter are stored until the cat has a bowel movement. Feline disease can affect either or both intestines. Cats with intestinal problems generally display diarrhoea or constipation.

Often, cats will develop diarrhoea after an abrupt change in diet, and the cure may simply be to return to the previous foods. Many cats cannot digest dairy products and will develop diarrhoea when given milk or cheese. This intolerance stems from the lack of lactase, the enzyme that breaks down milk sugar.

Diarrhoea can also be a reaction to antibiotics or other medicines. If your cat develops diarrhoea or begins vomiting after taking medicine, call your veterinarian. Most cases are easily treated by a 24- to 48-hour fast, often in combination with an anti-diarrhoeal medicine. However, some intestinal diseases can be fatal, so see your veterinarian if the constipation or diarrhoea does not clear up completely within a day or two.

Immediate veterinary intervention is essential in the case of an obstruction of the intestine. This usually occurs when the cat swallows an object that it can neither digest nor pass. Toys, particularly small balls, are common culprits, as are Christmas tree tinsel and yarn. Infrequently, a large hair ball can also cause an obstruction. The diagnosis is usually made with the aid of X rays, and treatment may include surgery.

Occasionally cats will swallow sewing thread attached to a needle. If one end of this thread becomes looped under the tongue, the cat develops what is known as string foreign body. The swallowed end of the thread will continue to move along with each contraction of the intestines, pulling the loops of the bowel tighter and tighter into an accordion-like mass. If the thread is not removed, necrosis of the bowel, in which tissue weakens and eventually dies, may result. The thread could then actually cut through the bowel and cause the intestines' contents to leak into the abdomen, which could cause a fatal case of peritonitis. Cats that are suffering from a string foreign body will vomit and generally refuse to eat. It is imperative that you do not try to remove the string by pulling as this will worsen the situation.

Sharp objects like sewing needles or toothpicks can perforate the intestines. If you know your cat has swallowed a sharp object, see your veterinarian immediately. Your cat will likely suffer a punctured peritoneum.

Intestinal diseases can be caused by viral infections such as panleucopenia, fungal infections, and bacterial infections such as salmonella and *Campylobacter jejuni*. These diseases cause severe diarrhoea and are particularly dangerous since they can be transmitted to humans.

Cats 7 years or older that suffer from diarrhoea and weight loss may have hyperthyroidism. This is caused by overproduction of a hormone, which controls the cat's metabolic rate. The diagnosis can be made following a blood test, and the disease is treatable.

Intestinal parasites are among the most common causes of intestinal diseases. Those affecting domestic cats include roundworms, hookworms, tapeworms, giardia and coccidia.

Roundworms, often called ascarids, are the most common. Two species, *Toxocara cati* and *Toxacaris leonina*, can infect cats. Infestation occurs if the cat ingests infected eggs which are usually found in the soil where an animal suffering from roundworms had a bowel movement. Kittens can catch the infection from their mother through her milk.

Roundworm eggs hatch into larvae in the intestine, then migrate through the liver and lungs of the infected cats, finally returning to the intestine where they become adult worms. Cats suffering from these parasites may lose weight and suffer from vomiting, diarrhoea, and abdominal distension.

Diagnosis of roundworms is made by spotting the long, spaghetti-shaped worms in the stools or vomit, or by microscopic examination of a stool specimen.

Two species of blood-sucking hookworms, the *Ancylostoma tubaeforma* and the *Ancylostoma braziliense*, commonly infect the cat. Infection can occur through ingestion of larvae, or through penetration of the skin. The immature larvae migrate through the lungs and eventually inhabit the intestine where a large infestation can consume considerable quantities of blood. This produces symptoms, such as anaemia and blood in the stool, that are related to this blood loss. Diagnosis is made by microscopic examination of the stool. Hookworms are quite rare in North America.

Most tapeworm infestations occur after a cat ingests an infected flea when grooming itself. Occasionally cats become infect-

ed after eating lizards and small mammals such as rodents and rabbits. The most noticeable clinical sign is the presence of tapeworm segments in the cat's stools or around its anus. These segments, called proglottids, are not the entire worm but are packets of eggs. Diagnosis is made by spotting the rice-shaped segments or by microscopic examination of the stool.

Giardiasis, an infection which can spread to humans, is contracted when a cat ingests single-celled *Giardia lamblia* found in the stool of infected animals. Giardia cause diarrhoea and weight loss. Diagnosis is made by observing the infec-

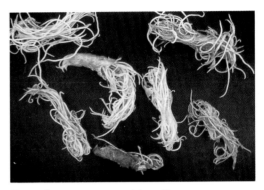
Roundworm, or ascarid, coils.

tion source microscopically or by the cat's response to treatment.

There are several kinds of coccidia that can affect the cat. All will likely cause diarrhoea. The most serious perhaps is *Toxoplasma gondii*. This infection can be spread among humans and is of particular risk to unborn children. Therefore pregnant women should guard against tooclose contact with their cat if it roams outdoors. Diagnosis of an infestation is made by microscopic examination of a stool specimen.

Cats can also develop cancer of the intestines as well as a number of other diseases that affect their ability to digest and absorb the nutrients in food. They can also suffer from inflammatory bowel diseases.

Liver

The liver has many complex and diverse functions. It manufactures and excretes bile, which is necessary for proper fat absorption, it detoxifies and excretes many potentially toxic substances, and it produces many blood proteins, including those necessary for normal blood clotting.

The most common symptom of severe liver disease, and the most noticeable, is jaundice. Cats that are jaundiced will have a yellowish cast to their skin, gums, and the sclera (white areas) of their eyes. Jaundice can occur with other disorders,

Rice-shaped egg packets around the anus are a sure sign of tapeworms.

but is seen in liver disease because of an increase in the yellow-brown bile pigment bilirubin in the cat's blood stream. The liver is responsible for excreting bilirubin, a product in the breakdown of red blood cells. When the liver is not functioning properly or if there is an obstruction to the flow of bile, which contains the bilirubin, the pigment will cause the animal to appear jaundiced.

Idiopathic hepatic lipidosis,or fatty liver syndrome, is one of the least understood of the diseases that affect the cat's liver. It usually occurs in obese cats. The most common clinical sign is a lack of appetite, which often lasts several weeks. Other symptoms include lethargy and intermittent vomiting and diarrhoea. Treatment requires forced feeding of a balanced cat food diet until the cat will eat on its own. Because this forced feeding may take several weeks, it is often necessary to have a feeding tube placed into the cat's stomach. Even with very intensive treatment, this condition is frequently fatal.

Cholangiohepatitis, simply defined, is an inflammatory disorder of the hepatobiliary system which includes both liver cells and the bile excretory system. The causes of cholangiohepatitis are not well understood, but some cases are probably caused by bacterial infections. The final stage of this condition is cirrhosis. Treatment usually consists of antibiotics and cortisone-type drugs.

Since the liver is responsible for the detoxification of many of the chemicals that enter the body, it is particularly susceptible to injury from these chemicals. Generally, treatment is specific for the poison and the cat's chances of a cure are usually related to the type and amount of toxin involved.

Cats can develop cancer of the liver. Cancer can be either primary, developing from cells in the liver, or it can be metastatic, involving cancer that initially developed elsewhere in the body.

Some cats are born with a congenital anomaly of the blood vessels of the liver called a portosystemic shunt. In this condition the vessels that generally lead into the liver from the intestines bypass the liver and go immediately into the circulation. Because the blood bypasses the liver where detoxification occurs, the kittens suffering from this condition have symptoms related to poisoning such as loss of appetite, excessive salivation, depression, blindness, abnormal behaviour and even seizures. Treatment involves surgical correction of any abnormal blood vessels.

Bile is excreted from the liver through the bile ducts. Occasionally these will become obstructed. The most common causes are gallstones and sludged bile, which is associated with cholangiohepatitis. Inflammation of the pancreas and bile duct cancer can also cause a bile duct obstruction. These cats are very ill, and surgery is the only way to remove the obstruction.

Cats are subject to a number of less frequently seen liver disorders such as bacterial abscesses, benign cysts, fungal and parasitic diseases, and trauma.

Pancreas

The pancreas is actually two totally separate glands occupying the same organ. The exocrine pancreas produces and excretes digestive enzymes. The endocrine pancreas consists of clusters of cells, called the islets of Langerhans. These clusters, dispersed among the exocrine cells, produce insulin.

Diseases of the exocrine pancreas are difficult to diagnose in the cat. Pancreatitis, or inflammation of the exocrine pancreas, is associated with a number of conditions such as cholangiohepatitis, pancreatic fluke infestations, and trauma, but the disease is still poorly understood. Symptoms can vary and are usually none too specific. Weight loss, depression, and loss of appetite are the most common complaints, with vomiting, increased thirst and diarrhoea occurring less frequently. Some cats have abdominal pain and/or enlarged livers. The diagnosis can generally be made during a surgical exploration of the abdomen, but sometimes it cannot be confirmed until after the cat has died. Treatment is directed at reversing the cause, if known, and at providing supportive and symptomatic care. Fluid replacement, antibiotics and withholding food and water when the cat is vomiting are usually recommended. Some veterinarians believe pancreatitis in cats is far more common than the number of diagnosed cases suggest. Many cats that have cyclical episodes of vomiting and general malaise followed by periods of normal health may have pancreatitis.

Occasionally a cat may develop exocrine pancreatic insufficiency (EZI). These cats' bodies lose the ability to manufacture the digestive enzymes produced by the exocrine pancreas. They generally have tremendous appetites, but tend to lose weight and have voluminous stools. Without the pancreatic enzymes, the food eaten by the cat cannot be absorbed and used for nutrition. A diagnosis is usually made if the cat responds appropriately to the treatment for EZI, which generally consists of adding pancreatic enzyme supplements to the diet. These supplements 'pre-digest' the cat's food, making it available for the animal's nourishment.

Cats are also susceptible to cancer of the pancreas.

Problems of movement

The skeleton

Cats are active, athletic creatures, and this puts them at risk of suffering broken bones. This is especially true of cats that are allowed out of doors.

Luckily, cat bones heal well and quickly. With proper treatment most fractures will heal in three to six weeks, unless they become infected.

Unfortunately, there are cases where the outlook is not so optimistic. Cats are susceptible to several forms of bone cancer that increase the risk of fractures without preceding injury. Such a fracture, commonly called a pathologic fracture, is usually diagnosed by X ray. This may be the first indication that the cat has cancer. The disease will interfere with normal healing.

Kittens fed an all-meat diet may be getting too little calcium and too much phosphorus, and may develop osteodystrophy, or nutritional secondary hyperparathyroidism. Kittens with this debilitating condition have paper-thin bones that can break easily. Deformities of the spinal column and pelvis are also common. Treatment is directed at correcting the nutritional imbalance. Generally the solution is to feed the kitten a good-quality commercial cat food.

Adult cats are also affected by this condition, but they generally do not develop skeletal deformities; instead, they suffer from pathological fractures brought on by thinned bones. Cats with impaired kidney function or renal secondary hyperparathyroidism may also develop symptoms of osteodystrophy.

Cats that are fed a diet composed primarily of liver may be consuming too much vitamin A. They may, as a result, develop exostoses, bony spurs around their joints. Exostoses are extremely painful, but the condition can be stopped by feeding a good commercial cat food. Unfortunately, bony spurs that already exist will remain.

Rickets, seen in animals fed a diet low in calcium, is very uncommon in the cat. Too much vitamin D on the other hand can be fatally toxic.

Those skeletal diseases related to imbalanced diets can be prevented by feeding a good quality commercial diet. Vitamin supplements should be used with caution and only with a veterinarian's approval.

Muscles

Most muscle disorders are associated with trauma: injuries due to lacerations, punctures, and bone fractures are fairly common. Bacterial infections sometimes result from such injuries and may have to be treated with antibiotics.

Cats are known to suffer from a disorder called polymyositis in which the muscles become inflamed. Cats that suffer from the disorder exhibit an abnormal head posture, weakness of the limbs, and muscle pain. The cause of this rare disorder is not

Drops often must be given for inflammations of the nose, but only on a vet's prescription.

known, but fortunately most cats do respond well to corticosteroid (cortisone-like drug) treatments.

Respiratory system

Rhinitis, which causes congestion and excessive discharges from the nostrils, is often seen in cats suffering from upper res-

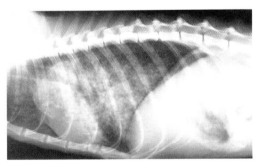

This X ray of the chest, or thoracic region, reveals lesions in the lung.

piratory infections (see page 181). Nose drops prescribed by your veterinarian may help relieve these symptoms.

Bronchopulmonary diseases

Bronchopulmonary diseases affect the lower airways and involve the pulmonary tissue below the level of the trachea. The most common affecting cats is bronchial asthma. This condition is not a single disease, but comprises a group of disorders with different causes and similar symptoms. One form is a familial immune-mediated disorder which can be passed along from generation to generation. Cats suffering from this disease will squat down, extend their necks and have a coughing fit. Some cats will vomit after an episode. About half of the cats with bronchial asthma have difficulty breathing and some 25 percent wheeze. Most cats respond well to corticosteroids.

Symptoms of heartworm disease, *Dirofilaria immitis*, a relatively rare disorder in cats, are similar to those of bronchial asthma. Treatment depends on the severity of the disease.

Cats infected with the feline lungworm, *Aelurostrongylus abstrusus*, generally have few if any symptoms. Some cats suffer labored breathing and require treatment.

Cats with severe upper respiratory disease may develop pneumonia. Unless treated quickly, the condition can be fatal.

Primary lung cancer is not common in the cat, but secondary malignant tumours (metastases) of the lung occur fairly frequently, as a result of primary cancer of some other organ.

Diseases of the pleura and pleural cavity

Inflammation of the pleurae, membranes that envelop the lungs and line the chest wall, produces fluid, called a pleural effusion. This compresses the lungs. (Pleural effusions may affect one or both sides of the chest.) As fluid accumulates in the pleural cavity, breathing becomes more difficult. If the condition goes untreated, the cat will die.

Different pleural effusions give rise to the following conditions:
• Haemothorax: an accumulation of blood in the pleural cavity. The condition is caused by physical injury, but it may also occur in cats suffering from anticoagulant poisoning or cancer;
• Chylothorax: an accumulation of chyle, lymphatic fluid, which can follow from cancer or heart disease;
• Pyothorax: an accumulation of pus caused by a bacterial infection. This usually follows a severe chest wound or a lung puncture;
• Hydrothorax: an accumulation of watery fluid, following a lung injury, diaphragmatic hernia (see below), heart failure, or cancer.

Pleural disease may also occur in cats suffering from feline infectious peritonitis (see page 185).

X rays are usually used to diagnose pleural diseases. The treatment for all pleural effusions is fundamentally the same. If a cat has difficulty breathing, fluid is removed from the pleural cavity. After the cat's conditon has stabilized, further treatment aims to find and cure the underlying disorder.

Diaphragmatic hernia

The diaphragm is a muscle that separates the abdominal organs from the heart and lungs. Its main function is to aid breathing. A cat may suffer a tear, called a diaphragmatic hernia, often as a result of an accident. For example, hernia may occur when a cat has been hit by a car. The seriousness of the condition depends on the size of the tear, and it may be complicated if the abdominal organs, such as liver, stomach, and intestines, intrude into the thorax. The treatment for a diaphragmatic hernia is surgical repair.

The urinary tract

Kidney disease

The kidneys filter toxins from the blood and maintain the fluid and electrolyte balance within the body. The end product of these functions is urine, which flows down small tubes called ureters into the bladder, where it is stored.

Feline congenital kidney diseases include polycystic renal disease, which occurs when large cysts develop in the kidneys and damage normal tissue, or when one kidney is missing.

Kidney stones occur in cats. The stones may remain within the kidney, or they may move down a ureter into the bladder. This problem becomes critical when the stone lodges within the ureter, stopping the flow of urine. Surgery is then necessary to remove the stones from the kidney or the ureter.

Glomerulonephritis is an inflammation of the kidney's filtering units (glomeruli). Although this condition is uncommon, it can hamper the removal of waste from the body, and cause death.

Infection of the kidneys, called pyelonephritis, can cause fever, lack of appetite, dehydration and weight loss. If not treated with antibiotics, pyelonephritis can lead to kidney failure.

Acute renal failure (ARF), characterized by an abrupt deterioration in renal function, leads to an inability to regulate water and electrolyte balance. This in turn leads to the development of uraemia—a buildup of toxins generally removed from the blood by the kidneys. There are three forms of ARF:

• Prerenal failure is caused by a reduction of the blood flow to the kidneys. This can occur as a result of a blood clot in the renal arteries, or a severe drop in blood pressure. Treatment of prerenal ARF aims at restoring normal kidney flow (perfusion). If the treatment does not succeed, one or both kidneys will soon fail.

• Intrarenal failure is caused by loss of blood supply and exposure to renal toxins. The most common cause of intrarenal failure in cats is the ingestion of ethylene glycol used in antifreeze.

• Postrenal failure may occur following an obstruction to the outflow of urine or a rupture with leakage of urine into the abdomen. The most common cause in the cat is urethral obstruction associated with feline lower urinary tract disease (FLUTD) (see next section).

Acute renal failure requires immediate veterinary help to restore the kidneys to their normal functions and to reverse the principal cause. Without this, the cat will undoubtedly die.

Chronic renal failure (CRF), which occurs with chronic interstitial nephritis, is the most common chronic renal disease of cats. Exactly what causes this condition is not yet known, but what is known is that there is a progressive loss of functional kidney tissue.

Cats in the critical stages of CRF are indifferent to food, vomit, and lose weight; they also drink water and urinate excessively. These cats are usually lethargic and dehydrated when first brought to the veterinarian. Often the owner of a cat that is in the earlier stages of CRF will notice the animal increasing its usual water consumption weeks or months before other symptoms appear.

This condition is common in cats that are 7 years of age or older. Veterinarians use blood tests and urine evaluation to diagnose CRF. Specifically, two blood tests, called the blood urea nitrogen (BUN) and creatinine, as well as an analysis of the specific gravity or concentration of the urine, are used to determine if CRF is indeed present.

Initial treatment of CRF tries to reverse dehydration with intravenous fluids. When the cat is in stable condition, long-term medical treatment begins. This includes dietary restriction of protein and phosphorus, and the administration of vitamin supplements, sodium bicarbonate, anabolic steroids, and control of vomiting. There are low-protein prescription diets available to help in the treatment of CRF, and these should be given to the cat if at all possible. These diets are often refused by finicky cats but home-made diets may be substituted.

Cats suffering from feline infectious peritonitis (see page 185) may also show signs of CRF.

Diseases of the lower urinary tract

The bladder stores the urine produced by the kidneys. It is subject to a number of disorders that are unique to the cat as well as to those found in other mammals.

Feline lower urinary tract disease (FLUTD), sometimes called feline urologic syndrome (FUS), encompasses a number of disorders with similar symptoms. Veterinarians have seldom been able to determine the basic cause of the disease in individual cats.

Those with FLUTD urinate small amounts frequently, have pain when they do, and scratch themselves extensively whenever they have to use their litter boxes. Often they don't even bother to seek out the litter box, but will urinate wherever they may happen to be, often in front of their owner.

As if to counteract burning or itching, cats suffering from this disorder lick themselves repeatedly.

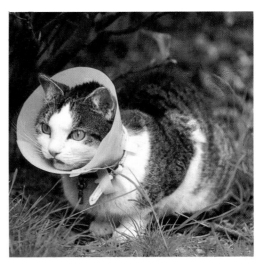

An Elizabethan collar prevents a cat with a bladder infection from licking itself.

Cats with FLUTD may suffer from one or more of the following:

• Urolithiasis, or stones in the bladder, which occurs when substances that are usually excreted in urine precipitate out of solution and form crystals within the bladder instead. This occurs when urine is saturated with various salts and low in fluids, something that occurs frequently in cats due to their tendency to drink very little water. Most bladder stones are composed of struvite, a combination of magnesium, ammonium, and phosphate. Urolithiasis occurs with equal frequency in male and female cats.

• Urinary tract infections (UTI) are most often caused by bacteria, but may also be activated by fungi and viruses. However, bacterial UTI is the most common by far. Bacterial infections can occur alone, or in conjunction with FLUTD disorders such as urolithiasis.

• Obstructed urinary flow can usually be traced to a urethral obstruction. The urethra is the canal which discharges urine from the bladder and urethral obstruction affects males almost exclusively. The male cat's urethra is much longer and narrower than a female's and so more subject to blockage. Obstruction can be caused by mucus, a blood clot, or sloughed fragments of tissue, but most commonly by struvite bladder stones. Blockage can also occur without the presence of material at the obstruction site. Swelling of the urethra, cancer, scar tissue, and prostate disease can interfere with urinary flow. Untreated urinary obstruction can cause postrenal acute renal failure, rupture of the bladder, and death.

Symptoms determine FLUTD treatment. A urinary obstruction requires emergency care. Most veterinarians will catheterize the urethra to remove the blockage and establish the flow of urine. Then they administer intravenous fluids to promote kidney function. If an infection is present, antibiotics will be prescribed.

Reoccurrences of FLUTD can be controlled with dietary changes. Although foods themselves do not cause this condition, some contribute to stone formation. Veterinarians have found that by limiting dietary magnesium and feeding cats diets that produce an acid urine, the incidence of FLUTD episodes can be reduced. Since magnesium is a component of struvite stone production, limiting the cat's intake, and thus decreasing magnesium in the urine, also decreases struvite crystallization. Struvite crystals form most readily in a nonacidic environment. The problem can be minimized by a diet that promotes an acidic urine.

Large bladder stones can be treated by a diet that dissolves them, or they can be removed surgically.

Skin

The most common fungal disease in cats is dermatophytosis, better known as ringworm. Infection occurs when several different fungi called dermatophytes invade the outer layers of the skin, the nails, and the hair. The results are bald spots, stub-

Ringworm, which affects many cats, occurs frequently in kittens.

bled hairs, and a scaling and crusting of the cat's skin that can cause itching. In severe cases, lesions may cover the whole body. Treatment includes oral and topical medications.

Parasitic dermatosis

Fleas infest cats to suck their blood. Yet most cats can harbour several dozen fleas without suffering anything more serious than itching. This is not the case, however, with kittens or cats already weakened by disease and those that are severely infected. They may develop flea anaemia, which can be fatal. Some cats are hypersensitive to flea saliva; reactions include varying degrees of itching, a reddened skin, and scabs. The cat and its surroundings—the entire home perhaps—should be treated with flea-control products.

Mites also cause problems for cats. Notoedric mange, for example, begins with intense and constant itching around the head and neck. The cat may get red scaly bald spots, especially on the ears and neck. Lesions may extend to the face, paws, and genitals. This mange may infect a whole litter of kittens.

The parasite *Otodectes cynotis* is the most common cause of external ear disease. Infected cats will get scabs on their ears from scratching. This mite can spread to other parts of the body, causing lesions on the head, neck, rump, and paws.

Demodectic mange, though rare, can occur in young and weakened cats. It produces bald spots, possibly with inflammation, scaling, and itching, usually on the head, ears, and neck.

Cheyletiellosis is also uncommon. The cheyletiella live on the dead surface of the skin and can sometimes be seen moving along the hairs of the cat; they are called 'walking dandruff.'

Grown chiggers are rarely seen on cats, but occasionally the larvae are found sucking tissue fluids. They are very small, vary in colour from red to orange and yellow, and are active during summer and fall. This parasite causes intense itching and scabs on the head, ears, and paws. Ticks, too, are rarely found on cats. Even when they do occur, the cat shows little evidence of irritation.

Mosquitoes and lice are other common parasites. Symptoms depend on their numbers as well as on the cat's particular sensitivity to them.

Allergy problems

Seasonal allergies are the main cause of most skin diseases that affect cats. All of them cause itching. Most affected cats suffer itch all over their bodies. In most cases, these cats will scratch themselves so much that their hair will break off or fall out in clumps.

Your veterinarian may call this hair-loss problem symmetric hypotrichosis, and recommend corticosteroids or the progesterone drug megestrol acetate.

A majority of cat skin disorders are due to allergies to fleas. Other allergies are caused by inhalants either in the home or in the outside air, and food.

Food allergies, for example, can result in highly itchy skin. If you suspect a food allergy, monitor your pet's diet. Your vet-

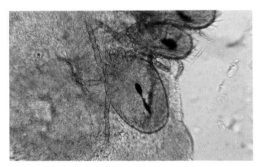

Chigger larvae (enlarged many times) are easily recognized by their orange colour.

erinarian may recommend that you try one of several available hypoallergenic diets for about three weeks.

Veterinarians generally do not recommend homemade diets for cats with allergies, since such diets may not be nutritionally balanced. Ask your veterinarian to recommend one of the foods being produced by cat-food manufacturers specifically for cats suffering from allergies. More and more of these foods are being sold commercially.

Cats suffering from food allergies will respond favourably to the right diet and the symptoms should then decrease, though it may be a gradual process. For a lasting solution to allergy problems, find

out what the cat is allergic to and eliminate it from your household or from the animal's diet. This may take some time, so a lot of patience is required.

Other skin diseases

Atopy is a common, hereditary disease that causes cats to itch. Airborne allergens trigger an attack.

Miliary dermatosis is a common feline reaction to food allergies, flea bites, atopy, and several other conditions. Cats suffering from this problem have small, seed-like scabs, and inflamed skin on their heads, necks, and rumps.

A number of rare autoimmune diseases, known collectively as pemphigus complex, make cats quite ill with fevers, depression, loss of appetite, a discernible weight loss, and skin lesions. Biopsies of skin tissue are needed before any diagnosis can be made.

Psychogenic alopecia is the term used for self-inflicted hair loss and skin lesions. Cats that do this may be reacting to pain or physical discomfort of some sort—an arthritic joint, for example—or they may have behavioural problems. Psychogenic alopecia occurs most often in the Siamese, Burmese, Himalayan, and Abyssinian breeds. Many cats with this condition are treated with behaviour-modifying drugs on a long-term basis.

Eosinophilic granuloma complex is a relatively common group of skin disorders whose cause is not always evident.

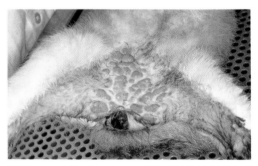

This angry-looking, pus-filled lesion is the result of eosinophilic plaque.

They can be divided into three groups:
• ulcers, red-brown sores found mainly in the mouth or on the upper lip;
• Eosinophilic plaques, fiery-red hairless lesions found anywhere, but 80 percent occur on the inside of the cat's thighs and on the abdomen. These lesions ooze pus (pruritus) and cause intense itching;
• Linear granuloma, long narrow lesions. Yellow or pink, they tend to form in a row, especially on the back of the thighs. These lesions also occur in the mouth.

Alopecia and acne

Many cats, especially Siamese and their crosses, have periauricular alopecia, areas of thin hair between their eyes and ears. Few cats, however, develop feline endocrine alopecia, a condition characterized by symmetrical areas of abnormally thin hair rather than complete baldness. It occurs in cats that were neutered at a young age—90 percent of those affected are males—and is believed to be related to sex hormone deficiencies or imbalances. Thin hair occurs in the genital area, the inner thighs, and abdomen. The condition does not cause itching nor does it damage the skin, and the cat is otherwise normal. Treatment is by sex hormone injections.

Stud tail (tail gland hyperplasia), another uncommon skin disease, is mostly seen in sexually active purebred male cats, although the condition sometimes occurs in castrated males and spayed females. Persian, Siamese, and Rex cats are particularly susceptible. (Some experts feel that stud tail affects all breeds equally, but that owners of pure-

Cats lacking protective pigmentation are prone to sunburn. It can lead to cancer.

breeds seek treatment for the condition more often than other cat owners.) The condition is characterized by blackheads, scaling, and yellow-to-black waxy debris on the skin and hairs near the base of the tail. It occurs when the supracaudal organ—the preen gland which produces the oily substance the cat uses to groom itself—becomes overactive. There is no particular treatment, although antiseborrheic shampoos may help.

Feline acne is fairly common. The most likely cause is the cat's failure to clean its chin properly. Affected cats have blackheads on their chin and lower lip and these may become infected. Bacterial infection may be suspected if there is swelling, pain, and itching, and antibiotics may be needed to clear it up. There is no particu-

lar treatment for the feline acne itself other than cleaning the area with a mild benzoyl peroxide preparation. Changing the cat's bedding may help control the acne. Checking the cat's forelegs might also be in order: a leg injury may have prevented the cat from cleaning its chin properly in the first place.

Cats with white ear tips and nose are susceptible to solar or actinic dermatitis. Without protective pigmentation at these points, they are prone to sunburn. Initially, there is mild reddening of the ear margins and occasionally of the eyelids, nose and lips. As the condition worsens, balding, scaling, and pus develop, along with curling of the ears. The lesions are at their worst in summer, then regress, or disappear entirely, during the winter, but return and become progressively worse each summer. This condition can progress into a skin cancer called squamous cell carcinoma, at which time the ear flaps may have to be amputated. Prevention, or treatment at the precancerous stage, consists of limiting exposure to the sun, and applying protective sunscreen before exposure.

After the lungs, the skin is the most common site of feline cancers. These vary greatly in malignancy. Therefore any tumour that develops on a cat's skin should be examined by a veterinarian. Squamous cell carcinoma occurs mostly in older cats and in white cats, most especially those with blue eyes. It generally appears on the head—the ears, lips, nose, and eyelids—as an irregularly shaped, crater-like, ulcerated tumour. Surgery or radiation are the most likely therapies.

Older cats are also the most likely to develop fibrosarcoma and the rarer cutaneous lymphosarcoma. Surgery is usually recommended for fibrosarcoma, but the condition may recur. Cutaneous lymphosarcoma, which spreads quickly to other parts of the body, is usually fatal within a few months.

Melanomas, well-defined brown or black tumours of the melanin-producing cells in the skin, may be removed surgically if diagnosed at an early stage of the disease. These tumours also spread quickly to other organs. By contrast, the fat-cell tumours known as liposarcomas seldom occur in cats, are slow to spread to other parts of the body, and can usually be effectively removed surgically.

Endocrine glands

All diseases of the endocrine glands disrupt hormonal production. The most common disorders are diabetes mellitus (sugar diabetes) and hyperthyroidism.

Diabetes mellitus

This disease occurs when the insulin-producing cells in the pancreas become impaired. Insulin is essential for glucose (sugar) metabolism, promoting its absorption into the muscle cells for energy and into the liver for storage. Reduction of insulin production can lead to increased levels of glucose in the blood. Cats younger than 8 years rarely develop diabetes mellitus, which affects older males and females equally.

Affected cats may be overweight at the onset of the disease, but become emaciated as it progresses. The most common symptoms of diabetes mellitus are excessive thirst and urination, accompanied by an increase in appetite and loss in weight. Other signs include soreness and swelling of the gums and tongue and a thinning of the coat. As the disease progresses, the symptoms become more severe and include weakness, vomiting, even more severe weight loss and, finally, coma and death. One unusual symptom is a weakness of the hind legs. Cats with this disorder will walk with their hocks touching the ground.

Diagnosis can be difficult. Even though a cat with this condition has an abnormally high glucose level, many cats develop unusually high blood glucose when nervous or stressed. Even a routine visit to the veterinarian may bring this about. It may be necessary, therefore, to test not only the cat's blood several times, but also its urine before a diagnosis is made. Normal cat urine should not contain any glucose; it is found only when the blood glucose is at an abnormally high level.

Treatment varies with the severity of the diabetes, and how ill the cat is. Inevitably, this disease makes tremendous demands on the cat's owner. Schedules must be observed. A missed meal or a delayed medication can have serious results. Even in not-so-critical cases, once- or twice-daily injections of long-acting insulin may be prescribed. Many veterinarians also recommend a change in diet; often, cats will require less insulin if they are fed a high-fiber diet.

Food content must be checked carefully. Products with a high sugar content, semi-moist cat food for example, should be avoided. Cats on insulin must also be monitored regularly to make sure they receive the proper dosage. To regulate this, many veterinarians recommend daily to weekly checks of the blood glucose. Once the dosage is regulated, the cat's blood glucose should be monitored every month or so. If the diabetes is well advanced and there is a risk the cat may die, the blood glucose may have to be monitored hourly. Dosages of short-acting insulin can be adjusted to the blood test results and administered after each test. The cat will also require intensive care to survive.

Ordinarily, however, full recovery is possible, provided the disease is diagnosed early, treatment is carried out consistently, and the cat is taken to the veterinarian for regular checkups.

There are many probable causes of diabetes mellitus in the cat. One common cause is long-term use of megestrol acetate, a progesterone drug sometimes used to treat cancer and allergies.

Hyperthyroidism

Hyperthyroidism is an increasingly common disorder, particularly in older cats. The thyroid gland, which is located in the neck, can become enlarged and produce excessive hormones. Hyperthyroidism may also cause enlarged nodules in the thyroid. These are usually benign, but may on rare occasions be cancerous. Cats with hyperthyroidism seem unable to rest and become hyperactive, pacing and grooming constantly. Despite the attention, the coat appears dull and unkempt. Most cats with the disease lose weight even though their appetite may be normal, sometimes even voracious. Other symptoms include tachycardia (increased heart rate), vomiting, diarrhoea, and excessively long nails. As the disease progresses, the cat will become thinner and more run-down.

Hyperthyroidism can also cause congestive heart failure. Heart problems related to the disease disappear once the hyperthyroidism is treated. Conversely, if the cat is left untreated, it will almost certainly die.

Hyperthyroidism is generally diagnosed by a blood test measuring the amount of thyroid hormones in the blood. One or both thyroid glands may be diseased although in nearly all instances of hyperthyroidism, both glands are affected. There are several effective treatments, including oral medication, surgery to remove part of the thyroid gland, and a dose of radioactive iodine. The veterinarian's recommendation will depend on the age and condition of the cat.

Eyes

Eye examination is particularly important because the eyes may present the first symptoms of diseases such as feline infectious peritonitis and feline leukaemia virus. Your veterinarian can examine the inside of the eye with an ophthalmoscope.

Conjunctivitis is quite common in cats.

Diseases of the orbit

The orbit is the bony cavity that protects the eye. Traumatic exophthalmos (abnormal protrusion of the eyeball) is fairly common in cats. It may be caused by an accident or a bite. A cat injured in this way must see a veterinarian quickly.

Abscesses behind the eye are common causes of bulging eyeballs. Often the abscess is due to a bite that became infected. Dental abscesses can also cause ulcers behind the eye. Treatment is essential.

There are also several forms of cancer that can develop within the orbit, especially in older cats. One or both eyeballs protrude gradually as the cancer grows.

Diseases of the eyelids

Coloboma—incomplete formation of the upper eyelid— is a congenital defect. Surgery is usually necessary.

Entropion, a rolling inward of the eyelids, is usually the result of injury. There is also a congenital entropion that afflicts some cats, Persians in particular. When the eyelids roll inwards, the eyelashes rub against the cornea, causing injury and discomfort. Surgery is the usual remedy.

Blepharitis (inflammation of the eyelids) may affect only the eyelids, or may accompany a generalized skin disorder. The underlying cause must be treated.

Lacerations of the eyelid may result from bites, scratches, or injuries. Early treatment will avoid complications that could interfere with eyelid function. Always consult your veterinarian about tumours of the cat's eyelids.

Diseases of the conjunctiva and nictitating membrane

The conjunctiva is a thin, semitransparent mucous membrane that covers the surface of the eyelids and the nictitating membranes (semicircular folds of conjunctiva between the globe and the lower lid). Conjunctivitis (inflammation of the conjunctiva) occurs frequently in cats. There are many causes, the most common being upper respiratory viruses and irritants such as dust and chemicals.

The nictitating membrane, also called the third eyelid, provides extra eye protection. The membrane, usually retracted into the corner of the eye, will sometimes protrude and partly cover the eye. This usually indicates that the cat is under the weather. Treatment and prognosis depend on the cause, whether injury, infection, cancer, severe weight loss, dehydration, congenital microphthalmia (smallness of one or both eyes), or a nerve disorder such as Horner's syndrome.

Diseases of the cornea

The cornea is the transparent part of the eye that covers the iris and pupil. This transparency is crucial to normal vision; any reduction is a sign of corneal disease. The cornea is particularly susceptible to injury, the eye being a favourite target when cats scratch each other. Such injuries are very painful, but ordinarily heal quickly.

Superficial corneal ulcers are treated with a topical antibiotic. If anterior uveitis is present (see next page), an atropine ophthalmic ointment may be recommended.

Deep corneal ulcers are serious; as the ulcer becomes deeper, the chances of the globe's rupturing increase. Deep corneal ulcers generally require surgery. Topical antibiotics and atropine should be applied for at least two weeks after surgery. Prognosis depends on the severity of the ulceration; some permanent corneal scarring is to be expected.

A form of keratitis (inflammation of the cornea) is seen in cats infected by feline herpesvirus. Herpetic keratitis occurs mainly in adult cats and may affect one or both eyes. Some cases display a telltale, irregular, branching ulceration. Treatment consists of a topical virostatic drug.

Cats can develop eosinophilic keratitis, a rapidly spreading corneal disease unique to felines. Raised pink masses appear on the cornea and adjacent conjunctiva. Immediate surgery is needed to remove the masses and the superficial layers of the cornea. A biopsy is essential to check for corneal cancers.

Corneal sequestrum, a black plaque on the cornea, is another lesion seen only in cats. It may be a response to chronic irritation from entropion or ulcerative keratitis. Treatment consists of surgical removal of the plaque and antibiotics.

Diseases of the uvea

The uvea is a pigmented structure consisting of the iris, ciliary body, and choroid, and is the middle, blood-vessel-containing layer of the eye. The iris is the thin, coloured membrane that separates the back and front chambers of the eye. The posterior uvea or choroid contains the large and small blood vessels in the back of the eye, and the tapetum lucidum (see page 54). The ciliary body is located between the iris and the choroid, and produces the transparent fluid, called the aqueous humour, found in the anterior chamber.

There are a number of congenital problems of the uvea, the most common being heterochromia, a difference in colour between the irides. This occurs mostly in white cats. Cysts sometimes develop on the iris at the margin of the pupil.

Uveitis, an inflammation of the uvea, may cause pain, excessive blinking, protrusion of the nictitating membrane, a change in the colour of the iris, and blood or protein deposits in the anterior chamber. Causes of uveitis include injury, corneal ulceration, feline leukaemia virus, feline immunodeficiency virus, feline infectious peritonitis, and toxoplasmosis. Atropine ointment, which dilates the pupil, will decrease pain and minimize potential adhesion of the iris to the cornea—a condition called synechia. A topical antibiotic/corticosteroid is generally prescribed as well.

Glaucoma occurs when the pressure of fluids in the eyeball becomes excessive. Owners may not observe anything amiss until there is irreversible damage. Causes include congenital abnormalities, injury, intraocular cancer, and feline infectious peritonitis. With early diagnosis, treatment can be effective. The eye may be removed if glaucoma has led to blindness. Removal of the eye is usually the best solution to most cancers of the uvea. The most common of these, lymphoma, can sometimes be seen on the iris.

Diseases of the retina

The retina is a semitransparent membrane made up of photoreceptors—the rods and cones that are the immediate instrument of vision.

Inherited retinal degeneration is progressive deterioration of both the rods and cones. Blindness is usually complete by 4 years of age.

Taurine deficiency (see page 196) causes feline central retinal degeneration. This is seen in cats fed taurine-deficient diets as well as in cats fed commercial dog food. If caught in its early stages, the condition is reversible with taurine supplementation. Advanced degeneration causes blindness.

Retinal inflammation is a side effect of choroiditis. Owners will notice that their cats, whose sight is failing, are bumping into things. Treatment is directed to controlling the choroiditis.

Retinal bleeding has several causes, including feline infectious peritonitis, feline leukaemia virus, systemic infections, and hypertension arising from renal (kidney) disease.

Retinal detachment occurs in cats suffering from feline infectious peritonitis, lymphoma, and systemic fungal infections. Blindness may occur if the retina separates completely from the back of the eye.

Reproduction disorders

Except for a few modifications, the feline reproductive system is similar to that of other mammals. Having your pet neutered will avoid problems in this area. With uncastrated cats, the most common problems are failure of toms to produce sperm and of females to conceive.

Reproductive diseases of the male cat

Male cats are usually born with both testicles in the scrotum. During development, the testes follow a complicated path from inside the abdomen into the scrotum. Occasionally a cat may be born with one or both testicles undescended. A cat with undescended testicles, a cryptorchid, is generally sterile, whereas a monorchid, a cat with one testicle, may be fertile and can transmit its condition to its offspring. Your veterinarian may recommend surgery in either instance. Even sterile monorchids and cryptorchids have all the characteristics of toms, including strong-smelling urine and an urge to use it liberally and regularly to mark their territories.

Because the role of the tom cat in the possible spread of infectious venereal diseases is unknown, a tom should be tested for feline leukaemia virus, feline immunodeficiency virus, feline infectious peritonitis, and toxoplasmosis before breeding.

Toms can transmit genital bacterial infections to female cats. If the females are suffering from genital discharges or infertility, the tom's semen should be cultured

175

for bacteria and breeding should be suspended until he is free of infections.

A hair ring may form around the base of the penis in long-haired uncastrated male cats. This makes mating difficult and very painful. If the tom does not remove this hair during its normal grooming, it should be removed by a veterinarian.

Some toms refuse to mate when they are under stress, or an inexperienced tom may be intimidated by an aggressive queen. In such cases, time and familiarization should alleviate the problem.

Poor libido and low sperm production have been linked to malnutrition, obesity, hypothyroidism, and hypervitamin-

---

NEUTERING A TOM

A male cat should be neutered when it is 6 to 8 months old. Late fall and early winter are best, when the tom is not sexually active. The operation to remove the testes is short, done under a general anaesthetic, and the cat should be able to return home the same day. Recovery should be fast. One thing: put shredded uninked newsprint (your local printer may have unused roll ends) in the litter box. Litter can get into the wounds and cause infection. Do not use newspaper or any printed paper (see page 199).

---

osis A, toxicity arising from too much Vitamin A (see page 167). Early diagnosis and treatment of underlying disorders may bring about a return to fertility.

Territorial fighting may result in bites on the scrotum and testes, commonly followed by fever and abscess formation. Proper treatment with antibiotics and surgical drainage of the abscess will generally conserve fertility.

A male tortoiseshell or calico cat is usually sterile, but a few have been reported to be fertile. The orange-and-black genes are found in the X chromosome and are therefore sex-linked. For a cat to have the tortoiseshell colour pattern, it must have two X chromosomes. The majority of tortoiseshell male cats have three sex chromosomes, XXY; these males exhibit small testes, poor libido and are sterile.

Reproductive diseases of the female cat

Prolonged anoestrus (see page 159) can be caused by malnutrition, genetics, hormonal imbalance, and disease. Cats that lack exposure to other cats or to at least 12 hours a day of light may not have normal heat cycles.

Precociousness, or early sexual maturity, can occur in kittens as young as 4 months of age. Good nutrition, adequate

light, and contact with older cats with normal heat cycles may result in early cycling–going in and out of heat regularly. It is not advisable to breed these very young females: small litter size, difficult labour and birth, and a greater incidence of birth defects are some of the many valid reasons to wait until the kitten is mature enough physically.

Nymphomania may occur in older females that have never had a litter. These cats usually have a disease called cystic endometrial hyperplasia-pyometra complex (see below). Nymphomania is characterized by heat cycles with excessive, frenzied, oestrus-related behaviour.

Pseudopregnancy (false pregnancy) may occur following a sterile mating, stimulation of the vulva of the cat, or spontaneous ovulation.

Because of the risk to the developing kittens, all medications, including vaccines, should be avoided during pregnancy. Griseofulvin, for example, a drug commonly used to treat ringworm, can cause birth defects.

Cats that are otherwise healthy but have recurrent miscarriages at the same point of gestation are thought to suffer from a progesterone hormone deficiency. Injections of progesterone may be helpful.

Bacterial and viral infections can cause infertility in the queen. Feline panleucopenia (see page 183), feline leukaemia virus, and feline infectious peritonitis have all been proven to do so.

The progressive condition called cystic endometrial hyperplasia-pyometra complex occurs in female cats aged 3 to 14. Mostly it affects cats over 5 years old that have never borne kittens.

Cystic hyperplasia, the first disorder of the complex to develop, involves a thickening of the uterus lining and cyst formation; victims usually display no symptoms except for infertility. Endometritis, an inflammation or infection of the lining of the uterus, can develop during or after cystic hyperplasia. Cats with endometritis often have no obvious signs of disease, although a vaginal discharge may be evident in some cases.

Untreated endometritis may develop into pyometra, an accumulation of pus in the uterus. As the disease progresses, the cat will appear steadily more ill. In the final stages, there will be a bloody uterine discharge, depression, and an elevated white blood cell count. Finally, infection throughout the body will lead to a rapid death.

The early stages of this disease complex may be treated successfully, but treatment becomes more difficult as the disease progresses. Unless the cat is essential for breeding purposes, an ovariohysterectomy (spay) is recommended.

Chronic infections of the cervix and vagina may cause infertility. A slight discharge may be evident, but is often overlooked due to the cat's normal cleaning habits. These infections usually occur following injury or difficult delivery of large kittens. If not treated, they may cause scarring and even closure of the cervix.

Foetal death and abortion

Foetal loss occurs frequently in cats. If the kittens are lost very early in gestation, the foetuses may be resorbed. Cats who are miscarrying may discharge bloody fluid containing foetal debris or whole dead foetuses. The kittens may appear normal, or may be mummified or decomposed.

The death of a foetus, depending on the cause, is not always followed by abortion. The rest of the kittens in the litter may not be affected and may be carried to full term. It is not unusual for a queen to deliver a dead foetus, in any stage of development, along with her otherwise healthy litter. This is most common when the foetus dies due to abnormalities in development.

Feline panleucopenia can result in death shortly after birth, mummification, stillbirth, weak newborns and malformations. Cerebellar hypoplasia, a common birth disorder of kittens associated with feline panleucopenia, causes a severe lack of coordination.

Feline viral rhinotracheitis (FVR) infections in utero can result in abortion or miscarriage, foetal death, and congenital foetal infections. Feline leukaemia virus (FeLV) is associated with many reproduction disorders. (Whether FeLV causes these disorders is not known.) Problems include infertility, foetal death and readsorption, abortion, stillbirth, endometritis, and the birth of fading kittens. Fading kitten syndrome refers to kittens that are lethargic and unusually small. They also have dry, lustreless coats.

Feline infectious peritonitis (FIP) is also associated with infertility and foetal death.

An infectious parasite, *Toxoplasma gondii* (see page 185), can cause abortions and miscarriages, and infections resulting in foetal death. The parasite can also affect kittens.

A bacterium, *Streptococcus canis*, can cause kitten death 7 to 10 days after birth. Kittens that acquire umbilical infections at birth, or shortly afterwards, can develop life-threatening infections. Dipping the umbilical cord in iodine immediately after delivery helps prevent this.

Cats used for breeding should be tested for feline leukaemia virus (see page 184), feline infectious peritonitis (see page 184), and toxoplasmosis (see page 185). The appearance of good health is no guarantee that a cat is free from these diseases.

Cats with access to the outdoors should

KITTEN MORTALITY

97.2% of litters are carried to term.

Of these, 10.5% of the kittens are stillborn.

Of the 89.5% that survive:
2.6% die between 1 and 3 weeks
4.6% die between 3 and 6 weeks
3.9% die between 6 weeks and 6 months
0.7% die between 6 months and 1 year.

The mortality rate among cats is high: Including the stillborn, a total of 22.3% of kittens die before they reach one year of age.

---

be kept away from breeding cats, as well as pregnant and nursing queens, and kittens should be isolated from all other cats. Show cats and cats not used for breeding should be denied direct contact with queens and kittens.

Reputable catteries and private breeders have standard procedures for preventing disease among their stock. Such precautions include immunization programmes and facilities for isolating or quarantining animals as needs arise. Good nutrition, ventilation, and hygiene are other essentials. Being cared for in such an environment will enhance both the general health of kittens and their chances of survival.

Many purebred cats that have been inbred with immediate family members or linebred with grandparents become carriers of birth defects. To prevent all such genetic or hereditary abnormalities, mate only unrelated cats or remove cats with defects from the breeding programme.

Disorders of parturition (queening)

The birthing process, or parturition, is called queening or kittening. This process starts with the contractions that signal the onset of labour and ends with the expulsion of the last placenta (afterbirth).

Cats, like other mammals, may have difficulty in giving birth. Dystocia, the term for difficult or abnormal labour, can be caused by complications associated with the queen, or the kittens, or both.

Healthy queens rarely have trouble giving birth. Inbred, sick, or nutritionally deficient queens may experience uterine inertia. They may not have the stamina to push strongly enough or their uterine contractions may be too weak, and they will need help to deliver their kittens.

Primary uterine inertia (not caused by disease) is most common in Persians. The tendency may be inherited, in which case these queens should not be bred again. However, sick or nutritionally deficient cats that have difficulty with one litter may have normal future deliveries if the underlying problem is corrected.

Pelvis size is often a factor in dystocia. A queen 5 months old or younger may be too small to deliver her kittens. Previous injuries or inadequate nutrition can also be a source of trouble. A cat that fractured her pelvis may have sustained a pelvic deformity that makes birthing difficult. This may also be the case if a queen has not been fed properly. In these cases, a caesarean section–surgery to ease delivery of the kittens–is usually necessary.

ORPHAN KITTENS

Sometimes a queen will not live through kittening. When this happens, the kittens must be cared for. Their body temperature must be kept at a precise temperature.

Birth to 7 days: 88-93°F (31-34°C)
8 to 14 days: 80-84°F (27-29°C)
15 to 28 days: 80°F (27°C)
29 to 35 days: 75°F (24°C)
After 35 days: 70°F (21°C)

Occasionally, a uterine torsion may cause dystocia. The feline uterus is divided into two horns. The twisting (torsion) of one horn a quarter to a full turn can cause dystocia, acute abdominal pain, uterine bleeding, or peritonitis. Immediate veterinary attention is necessary to preserve the queen's life.

First litters, particularly in young queens, may have only one or two large kittens. In such situation, it is not uncommon for a cat to have difficulty and require assistance. If a kitten in the birth canal cannot be delivered, it must be removed surgically to save the lives of the queen and remaining kittens.

Dystocia should be suspected if a kitten is not born within 30 minutes of the foetal membrane rupturing, or if two hours of unproductive labour pass. A veterinarian should be consulted immediately. A physical examination and X rays may be necessary to identify the difficulty.

Treatment may be a caesarian section or an injection of medication to stimulate contractions of the uterine muscles.

Postpartum disorders

Immediately after the birth of her kittens, the queen cleans and nurses her litter. Stillborn and placentas, unless removed, are usually eaten by the queen. Cannibalism is rare but is more likely after a first delivery by a highly nervous queen. Such cats should not be used for future breeding.

There is a normal, bloody discharge for 7 to 10 days after birth. Persistent foul-smelling discharges are signs of uterine infection. Persistent vaginal bleeding after three weeks may indicate a problem with normal uterine healing.

Generally speaking, postpartum disorders are uncommon in a healthy queen. Infections of the uterus associated with dystocia or a retained placenta are the most frequent problems. When one is present, the queen is listless and may be unable to nurse or care for the kittens. There is usually a foul-smelling discharge and a fever. Treatment with antibiotics may control the infection and restore the queen to health. Occasionally, it will be necessary to perform an ovariohysterectomy (spay) to remove the diseased uterus.

Occasionally, a postpartum queen develops a uterine prolapse, usually following a difficult delivery. In this condition, the uterus protrudes through the vagina. Uterine prolapse may be partial or complete (the entire uterus is expelled). Cats so afflicted are usually dehydrated and may be in shock. They are frequently restless and continue to strain as if in labour. Immediate veterinary attention is necessary to save the queen's life. The uterus may be salvageable, but an ovariohysterectomy may also be necessary.

Eclampsia, a life-threatening disease caused by an abrupt drop in the circulating calcium in a postpartum queen, is uncommon. The condition develops during the nursing period and usually occurs between two days and three weeks after giving birth.

The most noticeable symptoms are extreme weakness and an increased respiratory rate, followed by muscle tremors and loss of coordination. If the queen is left untreated, convulsions, coma, and death will inevitably follow. Treatment consists of a slow intravenous infusion of calcium. If at all possible, the kittens should be moved away from the queen and fed by hand.

In most cases, a mother cat will allow kittens to nurse without any fuss.
If not, the kittens must be nursed artificially.

When a queen develops postpartum disorders, it may be necessary to rear kittens by hand for a time. A commercial replacement for the queen's milk must be used. Cow's milk or infant formula does not provide adequate nutrition for kittens. It is also crucial to keep the kittens warm.

Disorders of the mammary glands

Most major disorders of the mammary glands tend to be related to infections or tumours. One infection, mastitis, is usually associated with queening and lactating. It occasionally occurs in pubescent queens, and is characterized by a benign enlargement of the mammary glands.

In bacterial mastitis, there is enlargement, or swelling, of the mammary glands, accompanied by heat, redness, and pain. The cat will also suffer from depression, fever, and lack of appetite. As a result, the queen may refuse to nurse, and the kittens will cry continuously from hunger and cold. Unless they are taken away from their mother and fed a milk substitute, they will die. They should also be examined for any signs of fever, lethargy, bloating, and diarrhoea. If they have been nursed by an infected queen, however briefly, they may need antibiotics. Meantime, the afflicted queen also requires treatment. Antibiotics, drainage of any abscesses, hot packing, and surgery may be necessary.

ARTIFICIAL NURSING

If the kittens require artificial nursing, they must be weaned young according to the following timetable:

At birth: 8 feedings a day
At 1 week: 5 feedings a day
At 2 weeks: 4 feedings a day
At 3 weeks: 3 feedings a day
At 4 weeks: 2 feedings a day
At 5 weeks: 1 feeding a day

The kitten must drink the equivalent of at least 25 to 30% of its weight in milk every day.

When bottle-feeding, be sure the kitten swallows properly and does not choke on the milk.

Tumours of the mammary glands are usually malignant. Therefore, any lump or mass should be examined by a veterinarian immediately. Malignancies can spread rapidly to the lungs, liver, and other internal organs. Surgery will be necessary to remove the tumour. An ovariohysterectomy (spay) may also be performed, if it has not yet been done.

Megestrol acetate, a synthetic progestin used to treat skin and behavioural problems, has been linked to benign and malignant mammary tumours. If this drug, or any other progestational drugs, is being taken by a cat with mammary tumours, discontinue its use.

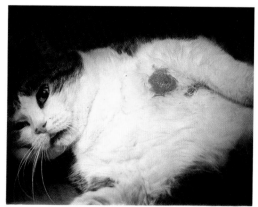

Tumours of the breasts can spread to the neighbouring nodes.

Pathology of the nervous system

Veterinarians usually distinguish between disorders of the brain, spinal cord, and peripheral nervous system.

The brain of a cat, like that of humans, is a complicated, even mysterious organ. Since the various regions of the brain have different functions, symptoms of disorders vary widely depending on the area of the brain that is affected.

Symptoms of brain disorders include such behavioural changes as abnormal sleep, aggression, excess docility, changes in litter-box behaviour, walking in circles, blindness, facial weakness or weakness of the limbs, tilting of the head, stumbling, dizziness, and episodes of falling. Treatment of these problems and prognosis vary depending on the cause.

Brain disorders may be classified as congenital, infectious, nutritional, metabolic, toxic, or cancerous.

Congenital brain disease generally results from a foetal injury, which prevents the normal development of one or more regions of the brain. Cerebellar hypoplasia, a disorder unique to cats, is the result of a foetal infection by the feline panleucopenia virus (see page 183), which prevents normal development of the cerebellum. Symptoms include an abnormal gait, tremors of the head, and a general lack of coordination. There is no treatment for this disorder.

Brain disorders also are caused by feline leukaemia virus, feline immunodeficiency virus, feline infectious peritonitis, and rabies. Pseudorabies, sometimes known as Aujesky's disease, is caused by a herpesvirus contracted as a result of eating infected raw pork. One symptom is an episode of intense scratching, during which the cat bites its own skin savagely. Unfortunately, death generally occurs within 24 hours because, there is no prevention nor any treatment.

Toxoplasmosis (see page 185) causes a parasitic brain disorder.

Occasionally, roundworm larvae (see page 165) may reach the brain and cause neurological disturbances.

Because of their small size and unique metabolism, cats are particularly susceptible to toxic, metabolic, and nutritional disorders such as lead poisoning and thiamine deficiency.

The symptoms and severity of spinal cord disorders, as well as their treatment and prognosis, depend on their cause. Physical injury, malformation of the vertebrae, infection of the intervertebral spinal discs, cancer of the spine, and intervertebral spinal disc disease are common causes of spinal cord disorders. Symptoms range from a general weakness to paralysis of the legs, especially the hind legs.

The main symptom of disorders of the peripheral nervous system is a general weakness of the animal. Such disorders include myasthenia gravis, diabetic polyneuropathy, and dysautonomia.

Cats suffering from diabetes mellitus (see page 173) develop an unusual walk: their hocks (ankles) touch the ground. Weakness of the tail is another symptom of diabetes.

Feline dysautonomia is a disease of the peripheral nerves. Its cause is unknown. It occurs often in Europe, but rarely in North America. Symptoms include a rapid onset of depression, appetite loss, constipation, decreased tear production, regurgitation of food, and dilated pupils. The disorder has a death rate of 70 percent.

Seizures are triggered by an abnormal discharge of energy from the brain. These electrical discharges will result in relatively brief, but disturbing, episodes of unusual activity. These spells may be

Diabetes often causes motor disorders, which may result in the cat walking on its ankles, or hocks.

brought about by feline infectious peritonitis, toxoplasmosis, fungal infections, rabies, cancer, trauma, or bacterial abscesses. Epilepsy with multiple seizures is still something of a mystery to veterinarians.

The severity and frequency of the episodes will dictate the kind of treatment your veterinarian will recommend. Mild seizures and infrequent seizures probably will not require treatment. Extensive grand mal seizures, which may last several minutes, probably will be treated with anticonvulsant drugs.

A SUGGESTED VACCINATION SCHEDULE FOR YOUR CAT

Feline distemper, calicivirus, herpesvirus, chlamydia vaccines

The first kitten booster shot should be given between 6 and 8 weeks and then every two to three weeks until the kitten is 14 weeks old. Then it should receive a booster shot annually.

Rabies

Laws for rabies shots vary between different parts of the world. Vaccinations are required by law every one to three years in many areas.

Feline leukaemia virus

Kittens should receive their first FeLV vaccine when they are 9 weeks old, and a booster three weeks later, followed by annual boosters. FeLV testing is recommended before vaccination.

Adult cats that have not been vaccinated, or whose medical history is unknown, should receive two boosters three weeks apart followed by annual boosters.

Feline infectious peritonitis

Kittens should receive their first FIP booster when they are 16 weeks old. This should be followed by a booster shot three weeks later. Adult cats who have not been vaccinated, or whose medical history is unknown, should receive two boosters three weeks apart, followed by annual boosters.

Principal infectious diseases

The most common causes of feline upper respiratory diseases are feline herpesvirus, which causes viral rhinotracheitis, and feline calicivirus.

Inflammation of the respiratory tract

Feline viral upper respiratory disease (VURD) usually occurs in kittens that are under 6 months of age. Kittens raised in catteries or in households where there are a number of other cats are particularly vulnerable. The most common method of transmission is direct cat-to-cat contact. But the virus may also be transmitted over short distances when an infected cat sneezes near another cat.

Feline infectious rhinotracheitis is caused by feline herpesvirus. The seriousness of the symptoms depends on the cat's immune status. The most acute form occurs in kittens at weaning, when the immunity provided by the queen's colostrum is lost. The disease causes fever, inflammation, sneezing, and a clear nasal secretion; bacterial

This 'dry eye' is the result of a severe cold.

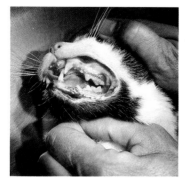

Gum disease caused by calicivirosis.

infection causes a purulent (pussy) nasal discharge. Irritation and inflammation of the mouth and throat, in turn, lead to anorexia, an inability or unwillingness to eat. Severe conjunctivitis combined with mild keratitis (see page 174) is common. Tracheitis (inflammation of the windpipe) causes coughing.

The incubation period, the time between exposure to feline infectious rhinotracheitis and the onset of symptoms, is two to six days. If the condition is not treated, side effects such as appetite loss and dehydration may cause blindness, even death. The acute stage of the disease generally lasts from two to three weeks. After that the cat either recovers or develops chronic rhinitis with a nasal discharge. Some cats, though no longer afflicted, remain chronic carriers. It is believed that up to 80 percent of cats who contract the disease become carriers.

Several strains of calicivirus cause symptoms with varying degrees of severity. The most acute form is seen in 6-month-old kittens.

Calicivirus infection appears as fever, inflammation of the eyes, inflammation and discharge from the nose, and ulcers on the gums and tongue. If kittens catch a virulent strain, they can develop tracheobronchitis and pneumonia, and die quickly. In general, though, the symptoms are less severe than those of rhinotracheitis. Again, most afflicted cats remain chronic carriers and develop a clear, watery inflammation of the eyes and gingivitis (gum disease).

In its mild form, calicivirus causes coughing, which is responsible for the spread of the virus. Because this virus can live outside as well as inside the cat's body, it may survive on surfaces used by other cats, which then become infected.

Chlamydiosis is caused by *Chlamydia psittaci*, a bacterial infection of the respiratory tract. The initial symptoms are an acute, severe conjunctivitis and runny eyes. Frequently, one eye is affected before the other. Other symptoms include sneezing and clear or purulent (pussy) nasal discharges. In its chronic form, chlamydiosis causes a thickening of the conjunctiva. The bacteria are generally transmitted from one cat to another by direct contact with infectious secretions.

Treatment of upper respiratory diseases depends on the symptoms. In the acute stage, good hygiene is essential. Gently remove discharges from the nose and eyes, and feed the sick cat by hand, making sure it drinks enough water. If necessary, use antibiotics, antihistamines, and decongestants to clear the nose. The treatment needs to be continued as long as your cat is sick. Most cats become chronic carriers, and this cannot be prevented except through prior vaccination (see box, page 181).

To prevent the spread of upper respiratory infection in a household with several cats, a comprehensive vaccination programme must be combined with strict isolation of all new cats and kittens for two weeks, and isolation or quarantining of sick cats.

Feline immunodeficiency virus

Feline immunodeficiency virus (FIV) is similar to human immunodeficiency virus (HIV), responsible for AIDS. It has become known only since the onset of the AIDS epidemic. However, FIV cannot be transmitted from cats to humans. Nor can it be easily passed between cats. FIV and HIV are both lentiviruses, which belong to the larger retrovirus family. When this type of virus enters the body, it may become active immediately or remain dormant for long periods.

In its active stage, FIV attacks T lymphocytes, white blood cells, that are essential for adequate immune response.

FIV develops in five distinct stages:

Stage 1 occurs just after infection and is limited to a slight fever that may last a few days or weeks. There may also be lymphadenopathy (enlargement of lymph nodes) for two to nine months. Some cats suffer from diarrhoea and depression. The death rate at this initial stage is low, but despite recovery, virtually all cats remain chronic carriers for life.

Stage 2, the dormant phase of the disease, may also last several weeks or years. There are no specific symptoms.

Stage 3 is characterized by recurrent fever, anaemia, and intermittent weight loss. Generally the cat looks thin and scruffy. Stage 3 FIV may last for years before progressing.

Stage 4 is marked by chronic secondary infections. Weight loss is common, and lymph node enlargement and other signs of illness occur. Chronic infections at this stage include: progressive infections of the mouth, upper respiratory tract infections, enteritis, bacterial infections of the kidneys and bladder, and skin disorders.

Stage 5, the final stage, is characterized by opportunistic infections. These are disorders that normally do not cause illness in healthy cats.

Secondary infections include chronic gum disease, inflammation of the mouth (stomatitis), rhinitis, conjunctivitis, enteritis, and recurring abscesses.

Opportunistic infections include haemobartonellosis, transmitted by biting insects (see page 163); feline infectious peritonitis (see page 185); systemic fungal infections (cryptococcosis); candidiasis (a yeast infection); toxoplasmosis (see page 186); and parasitic skin diseases (see page 170).

Chronic disorders include fever, loss of appetite and weight, anaemia, and autoimmune disorders.

Neurological disorders include: twitching movements of the face and tongue; behaviour disorders, such as excessive shyness or aggression; refusal to use the litter box; and compulsive roaming. Lack of coordination, convulsions, and tremors may also occur.

Experts believe that there is an increased incidence of certain cancers among FIV-infected cats. These cancers include lymphosarcomas, solid carcinomas, and sarcomas.

Feline immunodeficiency virus, like other lentiviruses, cannot survive outside the body of its host. Therefore, direct contact—usually by a bite—is the only known way to transmit the virus. The disease is most common in uncastrated male cats that fight more than neutered cats.

Blood tests are used to detect FIV antibodies. Kittens born to an FIV-positive queen may or may not be infected. Kittens with maternal antibodies will test positive. If the maternal antibodies are eliminated, the uninfected kittens may then test negative. The change from a positive to a negative result is called seroconversion. But this result is rare because the FIV virus causes life-long infection.

Treatment of FIV is limited to symptomatic care of opportunistic and secondary infections. The only effective prevention is to isolate a cat that tests positive. A safe and effective antiviral drug has not yet been made available.

Feline panleucopenia (feline distemper)

Feline panleucopenia is caused by feline parvovirus, which is excreted in the faeces of infected cats. Outside the body, feline panleucopenia may survive in the faeces at moderate temperatures for several months and is spread by oral contact with infected faeces. It has an affinity for the digestive tract, the lymphoid tissues, and bone marrow, where the severest symptoms of the disease appear. The death rate for cats with feline panleucopenia ranges from 50 to more than 90 percent.

The initial symptoms, which occur four to six days after exposure, are lethargy, anorexia, and persistent vomiting. Other symptoms include temperatures of 104°F (40°C) or higher and severe dehydration. Most cats develop diarrhoea and occasionally jaundice. The most important and consistent symptom is profound panleucopenia (an abnormal drop in the number of white blood cells), which begins two or three days after infection. It occurs when the virus suppresses the growth of white blood cells in the bone marrow. The extent of the drop is an indication of the severity of the disease and of its outcome.

Very few diseases can be transmitted from cats to children. (See Zoonoses, *page 186.)*

Subclinical infections (infection without symptoms of illness) affect adult cats in particular, but also occur in younger or other susceptible cats. In pregnant females, feline panleucopenia causes miscarriage, early neonatal death, and malformations.

Another form of this disease, chronic ataxia, occurs in kittens infected in utero or shortly after birth. The virus affects the kitten's developing cerebellum, the part of the brain concerned with balance and coordination. The disease becomes apparent when the kittens begin to walk at 3 to 4 weeks of age. Their unusually awkward gait is jerky, movements are exaggerated and falls frequent.

There is no specific treatment, only symptomatic and supportive care. This involves maintaining normal liquid intake, antibiotic therapy, and treatment for vomiting and diarrhoea.

Prevention of panleucopenia involves routine yearly vaccination. Live-virus vaccine is not recommended for pregnant queens. It may cause foetal deaths or cerebellar hypoplasia.

Regular examinations by a veterinarian can help prevent disease.

Feline leukaemia virus

Feline leukaemia virus (FeLV) is caused by a retrovirus which can lead to tumours. Sixty percent of all cats exposed to the virus develop a self-limiting infection and rarely become ill. About 30 percent of this group develop a transient viraemia. That is to say, the cat's immune system fights the virus. Five to 10 percent of exposed cats develop an atypical or sequestered infection. The cats test negative but the virus is, in effect, hiding undetected in their bodies. However, FeLV-related diseases may develop in the future. Persistent viraemia with progressive infection develops in about 30 percent of exposed cats.

FeLV infection leads to death within four to eight weeks, particularly in kittens. This is a result of the virus's suppressive effect on the immune system and is most common in kittens. Usually, FeLV-related diseases take months, even years, to develop. FeLV also causes cancerous (neoplastic) or noncancerous (nonneoplastic) disorders. Nonneoplastic disorders include nephritis (see page 168); a number of reproductive disorders such as miscarriage and disorders of the mammary glands (see page 179); disorders of the eye (see page 173); life-threatening anaemias; and chronic diarrhoea.

Neoplastic disorders include the leukaemias and cyto-proliferative diseases. The leukaemias (cancer of the blood cells) are less common. The cyto-proliferative diseases cause cancer of the lymph tissues. Lymphomagenesis is the most common neoplastic disease caused by FeLV. This disease may occur in three areas of the body. Thymic lymphoma occurs in the chest, just in front of the heart. Multicentric lymphoma manifests itself in the lymph nodes throughout the body. The third form, alimentary lymphoma, affects the intestine, intestinal lymph nodes, the kidneys, and the liver.

Some cats with FeLV develop neurological problems such as paralysis, behavioural disorders, walking difficulties, or general weakness.

FeLV is commonly transmitted to healthy cats by saliva or nasal secretions of infected cats. There is no cure for FeLV, which is more easily transmitted than FIV. Prevention consists of vaccination, and limiting exposure to cats suspected of being infected. Cats with FeLV should not be allowed to roam.

Feline infectious peritonitis

Feline infectious peritonitis (FIP) is caused by a feline coronavirus.

The number of cats that become ill with FIP is low, probably 1 percent or less. However, it is invariably fatal once a cat becomes ill. The virus is apparently spread among cat populations by oral exposure to the infected faeces, saliva, or urine.

FIP is subdivided into two forms based on symptoms: the first, a wet (effusive) FIP, characterized by fluid accumulations in the thorax (chest) and abdomen; the second, a dry (non-effusive) FIP, in which small pyogranulomas (a group of pus cells) develop in the abdominal organs.

The symptoms of wet FIP include poor appetite, weight loss, depression, abdominal swelling, and a chronic, recurrent fever that does not respond to antibiotics. If there is fluid in the thorax (pleural cavity), cats will have difficulty breathing.

Cats with dry FIP usually have a fluctuating fever, lethargy, and weight loss for 2 to 12 weeks or more. This form of FIP is considered to be a chronic condition. Many cats develop disorders of the eyes (see page 173) and of the nervous system (see page 180).

Diagnosis of FIP is difficult because no reliable laboratory test exists for this disease. The only available test measures the coronavirus antibody, but it cannot distinguish between the different kinds of coronaviruses. Microscopic examination of tissue is performed after death; surgical biopsies before death are rarely performed due to the severity of FIP-related illness.

The fluid in the wet FIP is high in protein, amber in colour, and thick. Many cats with FIP have an increased globulin (antibody protein) level in the blood.

Diagnosis of the dry form of FIP is even more difficult. It commonly goes undetected in weak, lethargic, feverish cats that have contracted minor diseases of the liver or kidneys.

The disease has no effective treatment. Cats that develop FIP-related diseases almost invariably die. Prevention is difficult because no accurate diagnostic test for FIP exists as yet. Therefore, healthy-looking cats with undetected FIP can easily spread the disease. Cats known to be infected should be isolated. The use of proper isolation techniques in catteries helps to prevent the spread of FIP.

FIP vaccine is available through veterinarians. Vaccination is particularly important in show and breeding cats.

Rabies

Rabies is a lethal disease caused by a virus (in the rhabdovirus family) that affects cats, humans, and many other animals, including the cat's favourite prey—birds. Most rabies infections result from a bite inflicted by a rabid animal, when saliva containing the virus gets underneath the skin (see *How to prevent zoonoses*, page 186).

The incubation period varies tremendously depending on the amount of virus transmitted and the area of the body affected. Generally, incubation lasts between 9 and 51 days.

Rabies has three progressive stages: prodromal, furious or dumb, and paralytic.

In the first stage, behaviour changes: outgoing cats may hide; shy cats become friendly. In the next phase, which lasts one to four days, unpredictably vicious behaviour predominates with the cat's muscles twitching. The cat becomes irritable, develops a hoarse voice, salivates, and gets progressively weaker. Paralysis, the final stage, lasts one to four days and ends in death. Most cats with rabies die within eight days.

Any cat displaying sudden unusual behaviour should be suspected of being rabid. However, if the affected cat survives

This cat has a swollen abdomen as a result of contracting FIP.

more than 10 days, it is unlikely that it has rabies. If it dies before that, the brain should be examined to confirm diagnosis.

Some jurisdictions require that all cats be vaccinated against rabies. Regardless of your local regulations, routine vaccination is highly recommended if you live in an area where rabies exist.

Toxoplasmosis

Toxoplasmosis is caused by the parasite *Toxoplasma gondii*. A cat is exposed to the parasite when it ingests raw meat or wild prey, such as rodents, whose flesh may be infected. Thereafter, the parasite multiplies in the cat's intestine and lives in its faeces. Generally, the parasite produces few signs of illness. But in severe cases, the parasite spreads rapidly through the cat's system, damaging body tissues. Symptoms depend on the areas affected.

Why some cats become ill, while most others remain well, is not clearly understood. Simultaneous infections, such as feline leukaemia virus, may make cats more susceptible to *Toxoplasma gondii* infection. Common symptoms include anorexia, lethargy, and breathing difficulties. Other symptoms include jaundice, vomiting, fever, diarrhoea, uveitis, enlarged abdomen, and neurological disorders.

Toxoplasmosis can be diagnosed by a test that measures the antibody level to *Toxoplasma gondii* in blood serum. Infected tissue can also be examined by microscope. The efficacy of drugs to treat toxoplasmosis remains unproven.

An affected cat can be a source of infection for pregnant women. The children of women infected by the disease while pregnant may have severe physical malformations.

Keeping a pet cat indoors and away from hunting wild prey is one sensible method of reducing the risk of exposure. A pet cat should be fed cooked food or commercial pet preparations. The cat's litter box should be emptied daily, preferably by someone not at risk.

The aging cat

Our present knowledge of the origin and development of many cat diseases is a long way from being complete. In many cases the symptoms that appear on the surface may mask other diseases underneath.

In the end, the cat has only one life—not nine, as folklore would have us believe. Especially as it gets older, the cat needs special attention and care. An elderly cat may want to eat less and drink more, and it may lose weight. A kind and helping hand may be necessary at home. Owners may have to help with grooming, keep a close watch on diet, keep the cat's favourite spot clean and warm, and enlist a veterinarian's careful attention to keep an animal companion in good health. The average domestic cat lives into its mid to late teens, and one English tabby queen is on record as living to the ripe old age of 34.

Zoonoses—and how to prevent them

Any infectious or parasitic animal disease that can be transferred to humans is called a zoonosis. Such diseases can be transmitted by insect vectors (mosquitoes), scavengers (rats), and animals used for food (chickens, pigs, cattle) or kept as pets (birds, turtles, dogs, cats). All developed countries have strict food hygiene regulations designed to limit infections from ani-

Life cycle of *Toxoplasma gondii*

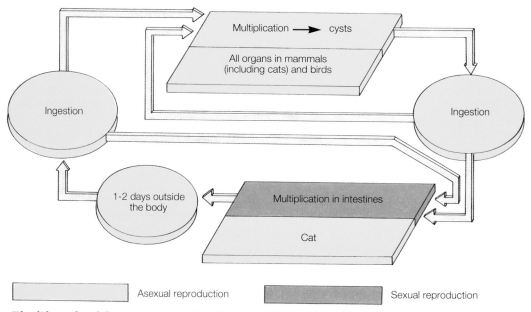

The life cycle of the toxoplasmosis infection is identical in all warm-blooded animals, but it may assume a specific form in cats.

A cat in perfect health brings joy to its owners.

mal food sources. Pet owners, however, must rely on their own good sense to make sure they and their families do not catch diseases from the family pet.

There are three routes of infection:
• bites and scratches—bacteria and other microorganisms in the cat's saliva and on its paws may be transmitted this way;
• direct contact—mites and fungi can be picked up from the cat's fur, and fleas can jump from the cat to the owner;
• faeces—worm eggs and parasites may contaminate fingers or food.

All bites and scratches should be washed and treated with antiseptics. Severe bites should always be seen by a physician. In areas such as North America that harbour the rabies virus, bites or scratches by a cat behaving abnormally should receive immediate medical attention. If indeed the cat had rabies, the victim will need postexposure immunization and delay could be fatal.

A small (unidentified) bacterium is suspected of causing cat-scratch fever, an uncommon disease that affects mostly children, mainly in fall and winter. The cat delivering the bite or scratch is not ill, doesn't need any treatment, and doesn't have to be destroyed.

The child, however, may show symptoms that include swollen lymph nodes or an infected blister near the scratch, fever, rash, and headache. Diagnosis is confirmed by a biopsy and skin tests. A severely infected node or blister may have to be drained. Painkillers may be needed for headaches and other discomfort, but the illness usually clears up in about two months.

Bites from fleas occur when fleas jump onto humans to feed. Fleas may have lodged in carpeting and upholstery, which must be treated if the infestation is to end.

Various fungal infections, scalp ringworm for instance, may be caused by cats. People who develop allergic reactions to dander from a cat's skin may develop hives or suffer asthmatic attacks when a cat is in the house. Cat faeces, or soil or sand contaminated by faeces, may carry eggs which produce infestations of threadlike worms, larvae of which can affect vision.

But all zoonoses can be avoided with a few simple precautions:
• Always wash your hands after touching a pet, its toys, dishes, bedding, and litter box. Teach children to do this from an early age, and discourage them from playing with pets until such practices have become second nature.
• Do not handle litter boxes when pregnant. Cover the children's sandbox when not in use.
• Make routine worming and flea treatments a regular part of your cat's health care. (See also *Human and cat diseases*, page 205.)

INDEX OF DISORDERS

THE CAT
AND ITS OWNER

The right cat for you

The Aristocats. © DISNEY. By special permission of The Walt Disney Company.

After enduring both its worship as a god-like figure in Ancient Egypt and unbelievable cruelty in the Middle Ages, the cat went on to become widely accepted as the world's best mouse-catcher. Today it is generally invited into our homes as a pet, and in recent years has also proven its value as a good companion to the sick and aged. Since the early 1980s, it has been recognized that the company of a domestic animal, particularly a cat, can influence the behaviour of adults and children alike. Stroking a cat's fur can soothe the nerves and reduce blood pressure; having the company of a friendly cat can sometimes speed one's recovery following a heart attack.

Establishing a mutually rewarding relationship with your pet requires certain skills and a little effort. Getting to know something of feline behaviour generally and the characteristics of particular breeds is a good way to begin. Purebred cats are quite predictable in looks and temperament, but cats with less impressive pedigrees, or no pedigrees at all, also make delightful pets. The ideal cat should be even-tempered and happy living with humans and possibly with other domestic species.

Before you get a cat, think about how it will fit into your household. Do you want an affectionate, companionable, cuddly cat or an independent-minded, outdoorsy feline that will roam the neighbourhood woods at will? Either way, a reputable breeder or knowledgeable cat fancier should be able to suggest a number of breeds that will meet your expectations.

A good way to see the different breeds is to attend shows and ask exhibitors about their animals. Visit breeders and pet shops to look at their stock. This will also give you some idea of prices.

Many people select cats for their beauty; others choose a cat over a dog, say, because it is easier to look after in a city. The cat is an ideal apartment pet: it is always clean, doesn't have to be walked, and can stay at home alone all weekend. It also costs little to maintain.

You will have to decide whether to get a male or a female, a long-haired or a short-haired cat. Unlike Persians and other long-haired cats, short-haired breeds such as Siamese and Manx won't require daily grooming.

There are certain behaviour patterns, too, which must be taken into account, particularly behaviours related to the cat's sexuality.

Neutering pays off

Pet owners who have their cats neutered at puberty avoid any number of problems. Often owners who intend to keep their cats indoors see no great need for this surgery and put it off indefinitely. But neutering makes sense even if your cat does not go out on the town. Living with an uncastrated male can be quite unpleasant due to its musky odour and the way it marks its territory by urinating on furniture, draperies, and clothing. And the wailing of a female cat in heat is likely to bring complaints from neighbours. In the long run, castration or spaying is the only solution.

Acquiring a cat

Kitten or grown cat? Buy or adopt? From shelter or breeder? Registered show breed or the friendly stray that wanders into the garden? Since acquiring a cat will affect the owner's life for a good many years, these are just the minor considerations. The nitty-gritty has to do with the responsibilities of owning a cat, and making a decision that's good for the pet as well as for the household.

Have you the time and temperament to play with the cat? Are you prepared to spend the money pet care requires—on food, veterinary care, and even boarding costs from time to time? And do you want a cat, or just a pet? Would you be just as happy with a goldfish?

Adopt or purchase?

Assuming you decide that you and a cat are right for each other, you're now ready to buy or adopt. Either way, you would be wise to first spend some time observing and playing with the cat of your choice. This is particularly important when adopting an adult cat, which will already have a well-established personality.

Adopting from an animal shelter

You can readily adopt a cat from your local pound or animal shelter and this humanitarian act may very well bring you one of the best friends you will ever have. Small communities may have only one such shelter, but large cities will likely have several. Where there is a choice, your veterinarian, and possibly local animal groomers and trainers, will be able to direct

An example of a clean, well-run cattery.

you to one that is well-run, where you have a good chance of finding a healthy, well-adjusted pet.

Keep in mind, however, that healthy animals may be given to shelters because of serious behavioural problems. This is one reason why you should spend as much time as possible playing with your prospective pet and observing its behaviour. Ask shelter employees about the cat's personality and litter-box habits. Try to visit a few times before taking the plunge.

Stop off at your veterinarian's on your way home from the shelter. You have to be sure that this new addition is healthy and free from both feline leukaemia and feline immunodeficiency infections, especially if you already have other cats.

Where to purchase?

From a breeder

If you have decided on a purebred cat, your best source is a breeder of the kind of cat you have in mind. Reputable breeders have an established clientele and a reputation to maintain. Some may be happy to put you in touch with their clients so that you can see some adult relatives of the kitten that interests you—a good indication of how the cat will develop.

Where can you find breeders? At cat shows, through your veterinarian or local cat association, or by word of mouth. Cat magazines are also a good source of breeders' names and cats for sale.

A word of warning: some breeders of pedigree cats rely on inbreeding to produce genuine specimens of a particular breed. Some kittens resulting from such matings are defective. This is particulary true of Manxes (see page 106) and Scottish Folds (see page 121).

From a pet store

Impulse more than sound reasoning sometimes governs pet store purchases. Often nobody there will know or be willing to tell you where the animals came from. With many animals confined together in such close quarters, disease can spread rapidly. If possible, check the store's reputation. Check it out yourself: look for premises that are clean and without unpleasant odours, cages that are clean and large enough for the animals, animals that are alert, bright-eyed, and well-groomed.

Privately

You will find cats advertised in the classified section of any newspaper. But be careful. You will have no idea where the cat came from and whether or not it will exhibit behavioural problems once home.

How to choose a cat

Good health should top your list of requirements in choosing a cat. This is no time to become sentimental over an unhappy-looking or sickly kitten. In fact one should avoid all cats from a litter, or a cattery, or a pet store where any cat seems sick. And your two best clues to the cat's good health are the condition of its coat and whether it is active and alert.

The coat should be smooth and without mats, fleas, or other pests. Ruffle the fur gently, watching for any black specks that could be flea droppings, and for scaly areas or fur loss that could indicate ringworm.

The cat should be lively, showing affection and curiosity about the world around it. (If one kitten in a litter bounds over to see you and takes an affectionate interest in your proffered hand, that is probably the one you should buy.) Check its eyes, ears, and nose. The eyes should be bright with no sign of the nictitating membrane (see page 55) and the ears and nose should be clean. There should be no discharge from either the eyes or the nose. Examine the anal area for signs of diarrhoea or tapeworm segments. Gently feel the abdomen. Potbellied cats may have worms.

Sale contract

Like all purebred animals, purebred cats vary considerably in price. Show animals, the cream of the breed, are priced accordingly. A 'pet quality' animal from the same litter, one that may be an excellent pet even though it does not meet show standards, will cost considerably less.

Some breeders may stipulate that cats purchased from them will be returned to the breeder at particular times for breeding and that they will not be mated otherwise. There may be stipulations from either party about ownership of future kittens.

A breeder may sell a cat on condition that it not be bred, with the purchaser agreeing to pay an additional sum if he doesn't provide proof that the cat has been neutered. A contract should also show if a cat was neutered before the sale. A vendor may also stipulate that the cat not be declawed—a controversial subject in some countries (see page 203).

The precise terms of any agreements between buyer and seller should be spelt out in a contract or certificate of sale. Read carefully before signing. The form of such contracts may vary from place to place but most begin by detailing the breed, sex, colour, identifying markings, and birth date of the cat, as well as the agreed-upon price. It should specify when the seller will give the buyer the cat's registration papers—usually within 90 days of receiving the purchase price. (Registration papers are proof that the animal is purebred and has been registered with the appropriate cat association. The breeder registers the entire litter within weeks of birth; each kitten is registered by name.) The registration document includes details of the kitten's breed, colour, birth date, and parentage.

A contract should also state that the cat is healthy, that it has been vaccinated, that it is guaranteed not to have any feline viral diseases, and that it is free of parasites, congenital malformations, and hereditary defects. If the cat is found to be in poor health, it can usually be returned for a full refund, provided the buyer has a veterinarian's written evaluation of the cat's health. Some contracts specify that health guarantees are void unless the cat is examined by a vet within 48 hours of purchase.

Duties

Once you have a cat, you must put some effort into seeing that it doesn't become a danger to itself and a nuisance to others. Ownership requires that we respect the freedom of others. So make sure your new arrival does not inflict itself on those who may not tolerate an animal's company.

Legislation on cats varies from jurisdiction to jurisdiction. Most is aimed at preventing neglect and cruelty. Some places set limits on the number of cats per household; others permit cats on streets only if leashed, or prosecute owners whose cats roam onto neighbouring properties.

But obeying legislation is only a minor part of responsible ownership. In fact responsible ownership involves looking out for the cat's well-being without imposing on family, friends, or neighbours. Set ground rules right from the start. Your cat will not understand why something that was all right yesterday is not permitted today. Say a firm 'No,' as you remove it from off-limits furniture or laps of visitors. Say an equally firm 'No' if it bites or scratches. Don't let it explore your yard if it is to be kept indoors. And if it is allowed outside, keep it leashed at first so that it doesn't go onto neighbours' flowerbeds.

Adapting to family life

Purebred or not, all kittens are lovable.

Ten house rules

First rule
Before you bring me home, pick up food and bedding for me

Make sure you have cat food and a place to sleep ready for your new cat. Since it may refuse an unfamiliar food, or suffer digestive problems from eating something new, find out what brand of food your cat was fed previously. The person from whom you're getting the cat may even give you a sample. This will ensure a very gradual transition in the cat's diet over at least a few days. You might also arrange to get some item of bedding that will carry home the odour of the litter and perhaps that of the mother too. In this way, the 'orphan' will have a sense of security in its new home.

Second rule
Let me take possession of the house and learn the ropes on my own

Your kitten will want to explore every part of its new domain. But prohibited rooms must be shut off from the outset; there is nothing more difficult than teaching a cat not to go somewhere it has already been allowed to venture.

Don't let the arrival of a kitten upset the family routine. Allowing children to stay home from school, for example, to spend the day with a new kitten would be a big mistake. There is no point in misleading the kitten into expecting that kind of attention all the time, since sooner or later it has to be left by itself. It would not want to sleep alone, either, after having been allowed to sleep on its owner's bed. And it would no longer want to eat alone on the floor after being accepted at the dinner table.

Third rule
Bring me into your home quietly

When your kitten arrives home, try not to be overenthusiastic. Undoubtedly everyone in the house will want to get to know the newest member, and as the kitten is passed around, some of the younger members may shriek in delight.

But you should remember that the kitten is already stressed by separation from its mother and litter mates. The shrieks of joy and the faces of all these strangers may terrify the kitten. So try to make the introductions gradually. Above all, make sure your children do not invite all their friends to visit the newcomer at once.

Fourth rule
Prepare a place for me to live, sleep and go about my toilet in peace

A quiet room—preferably not the kitchen—should be set aside for the new arrival during the first few days. A cardboard box turned on its side makes a fine temporary home. Place the familiar-smelling item of bedding that you brought from the kitten's previous home in or near the box. If the room is cold, a hot water bottle—not too hot—can be wrapped in a towel to provide warmth and help the kitten sleep. A ticking clock nearby is said to comfort and reassure a kitten.

Set out bowls for water and food at the other end of the room and, off in another corner, a litter box.

Fifth rule
Make sure I have plenty to eat and drink at all times

A kitten eats 8 to 10 times a day and also drinks more than an adult cat. Make sure its food and water bowls are always full. A weighted drinking bowl will prevent spills, or you can weigh the bowl down with a small clean rock. Keep special formula on hand—bought from a veterinarian—for any kitten you are weaning.

Sixth rule
Please be peaceful and don't rush around too much

The kitten will want to explore everywhere, but is easily frightened. Everyday activities—vacuuming for example—may scare it. And don't forget that even a young child will look like a giant to a tiny kitten. Too much caution over the kitten, on the other hand, will make it fearful or aggressive, characteristics that could last for life. Do not keep a kitten cooped up. It must make contact with its new surroundings gradually, even if they frighten the cat at first.

Seventh rule
Stow away potentially dangerous objects so I don't hurt myself

There are any number of objects that are irresistible to kittens—electrical cords and small objects that can be chewed on or swallowed, such as paper clips, thumbtacks, and coins. Young cats think these objects are their playthings, so never leave them in their path.

Eighth rule
Brush, comb, bathe me, inspect my ears, and cut my claws regularly

Even when such attention is not essential for good hygiene, going through the routine regularly makes a kitten easier to han-

dle in the long run. Think of it as a kind of behaviour modification. The grown cat will be more docile as a result of the attention. Because of such regular handling, it will be less stressed on veterinary visits and more willing to have its temperature taken when necessary, or to accept pills without a fuss.

The show animals exhibited by breeders in competitions have been accustomed to such attention from birth. These cats have their own distinct personalities, but remain calm when handled.

Ninth rule
Expose me gradually to the rigours of outdoor life

It is possible to take a kitten for walks in quiet streets where there is not much traffic, although it is not entirely necessary. However, a car ride—which can be necessary, if only for visits to the veterinarian—is different; if the first outings are kept short and sweet, car rides should never be disagreeable. But if those first rides are associated with fear and discomfort, it may be difficult, if not well-nigh impossible, to convince a cat to forget these early associations. On even the shortest car ride, a cat should either be safely ensconced in its carrying case or put on a leash and held securely on a passenger's lap. Left loose in a car, a cat—especially if it is upset or nervous—may distract the driver, or escape through an open window into traffic.

10th rule
Take me to the veterinarian within three days of my arrival

At first, everything is new and wonderful. But almost inevitably some problem will pop up. Call your veterinarian as quickly as possible with any questions you may have. Because you've now spent some time with your kitten, you will be able to make sense of the vet's answers and advice. If the kitten has to be vaccinated or wormed, you can take comfort in the fact that at least the acclimatization period is effectively over.

If particularly troubling symptoms occur, you must arrange to visit the veterinarian immediately, not only for the sake of the kitten, but also because any sale guarantees in the purchase contract are only good for a short time. After the examination, you can discuss health and training problems. By now the kitten should be showing its true character. You can tell whether it will be a lively or a sleepy cat, and whether or not it likes a lot of people around.

What will it eat?

The cat and its food

Strictly speaking, cats are not so much domestic animals as wild creatures that have been tamed. Many habits that set them apart from dogs are relics of their wild past.

This is particularly true in food matters. Cats left to roam outdoors, for example, become hunters, even though they do not always eat their prey. For fundamentally they remain the carnivorous forest animals they once were—creatures that survived for centuries on living prey. And even though a cat in 'captivity' will eat whatever is available, only meat, fish, and animal by-products truly satisfy its protein-craving body. Here again it differs from the dog, which gets adequate nutrition on half the protein essential for a cat.

However, cats themselves vary considerably both in their eating habits and caloric needs. To maintain its weight for example, a small but active cat may require as much food as a much larger sedentary cat. So keep such individual needs in mind when deciding daily food portions and feeding schedules.

You must decide between two types of feeding arrangements: free-choice feeding or scheduled feedings.

Many people who spend long days away from home find free-choice feeding the most convenient. With this method, food is available continuously and the cats can eat when and how much they want. This works well as long as all cats in the home have similar nutritional needs, but it fails if one or more cats in a multi-cat household require a special diet or overeat. And obesity is likely to be a problem if an extremely palatable, high-calorie food is always available to an inactive cat.

Most households have no problem feeding the cat twice a day, and most cats are quite happy with this arrangement. A measured amount of food can be fed at convenient times—typically morning and evening—and this way you can ensure that each cat eats the right food.

Switching from scheduled feedings to a free-choice system is rarely a problem. Doing the opposite may take a little time. Begin by putting down the appropriate rations in the morning, say. After 15 minutes, remove any food that remains. Repeat the procedure that evening, and so on. After two or three days, most cats will adjust to the new routine.

When all cats in a household can tolerate a similar diet, free-choice feeding is a convenient option—especially when family members are out all day.

The cat has an insatiable curiosity and, in a familiar environment, will always try something new. So you should have no hesitation varying a cat's food as long as you satisfy its dietary needs for fats and animal protein. (Any good-quality commercial cat food will do this.) Change foods, or brands, gradually however. Too abrupt a change may throw the cat off its food or upset its system.

A cat may also refuse to eat in a strange environment. When boarded or caged in a clinic, for example, a cat may not eat for several days.

Never be tempted to make a cat fast so that it will more readily eat a new food. Prolonged fasting can be dangerous, lest it lead to hepatic lipidosis, a more or less irreversible fatty degeneration of the liver.

Commercial cat foods come in dry, semimoist, and canned forms. Dry products are cheapest and will not spoil readily, but some veterinarians feel the higher mineral content may predispose some cats to urinary infections. Not all dry foods are alike, however. Some are specially formulated to actually dissolve some kinds of urinary tract stones.

Choosing the food

Cats have a reputation for being 'difficult' eaters. While they are curious about what is in their bowls and will pick at unfamiliar food, they will only regularly eat what they really like. And true carnivores that they are, their liking is often related to the fat and protein content of what is offered.

To satisfy their nutritional requirements, cat food has to be especially rich. Although dogs can get by very nicely on cat food, and on plant protein such as soya, cats cannot survive on dog food. They need a diet much richer in fats and digestible protein, one containing larger quantities of amino acids such as taurine and arginine (see pages 157-158). Adapted as they are to a carnivorous diet, their digestive enzymes can absorb only a limited amount of vegetable matter.

Adult cats can be fed between two and three times a day and be given about 30 calories per pound (500 g) of body weight a day to keep them healthy.

They need a diet heavy in protein (20 to 25 percent by weight of the day's total). This can be derived from fish, cheese, poultry, and eggs. Milk is also a good protein source, but few adult cats like it and some are milk-intolerant—they cannot drink milk and will be sick if they do. Most kittens, on the other hand, like milk.

Young kittens receive all the nutrients they require from their mother's milk during the first four weeks of life. After that they should be started on solid foods three to four times a day. (See *Balanced diet,* page 198.) Pound for pound, kilogram for kilogram, kittens need twice the nutrition of adult cats. They need a higher level of protein to develop their muscles and coat, and they need more calcium, phosphorus, and other minerals than adult cats for their developing bones and teeth. And because they are extremely active, kittens need more energy from their food than adult cats.

Varying the cat's food makes good sense in order to balance the diet and avoid mineral deficiencies. New items can be added gradually. Experts also recommend mixing some of the old food with the new when changing the diet to give the cat the idea of continuity. If the change is too drastic or too fast, the cat may stop eating. But by and large, plenty of meat and fish, whether as dry biscuits or the wet canned food, and chicken, kidney, heart, and muscle foods go down well with the adult cat.

Some cats prefer their food served at room temperature, possibly because the smell and flavour are more intense. They may either refuse or vomit cold food. Others, however, don't seem to mind cold food in the least and consume it with no problems. Sometimes a cat rejects its food because it has begun to spoil, and this is detected by the cat's highly sensitive nose.

Vitamin supplements should not be necessary if a cat is fed a properly balanced diet. Exceptions might be anaemic cats or pregnant or nursing queens. But these or any other medications should not be given without consultation with a veterinarian.

A few drops of mineral oil added to the food every few days will help prevent hair balls forming in the cat's stomach. Long-haired cats are particularly susceptible to these, especially in spring and fall when they shed most heavily. Commercial hair ball medication, though more expensive, is also available.

Quantity and quality

The quantity of food a cat needs largely depends on its age and weight. Most cats become accustomed to a certain quantity of food, regardless of its composition or energy value. Therefore, if a cat is overweight, increasing the cellulose (plant fibre) content in the diet may have positive results. Conversely, increasing the fat content can cause weight gain, although this may not occur with an active kitten, or when the cat is pregnant or nursing kittens.

But whatever the concerns about obesity, the cat owner must never lose sight of the fact that a cat's digestive system is designed primarily for meat and, as such, can only handle small quantities of vegetables. Otherwise, it gets inadequate nutrition and suffers from diarrhoea and gas. That being said, vegetables are certainly not off-limits, and in certain circumstances, such as obesity, they may even be desirable. Indeed some medically formulated diets to treat obesity have a high vegetable content.

Even though it is entirely possible to do so, it takes considerable time and effort to produce a well-balanced, home-prepared diet for your cat. If you are determined to do so nonetheless, one rule of thumb is to combine two parts (by weight) of protein foods with one part of vegetable or vegetable and carbohydrate filler. It also simplifies matters that cats like all meats, including organ meats and fish. Meat, fish, and other foods should be well cooked to prevent parasitosis and fish should always be deboned before serving.

But it is undeniably simpler, and more reliable, to feed your cat one of today's commercial cat foods. This way you can be sure it is getting a balanced diet. For desirable quantities of dry and canned foods, see page 198.

By nature, cats consume very little water. Domestic cats obtain 70 percent of the water they need from the meats and canned food they are fed. (Cats in the wild get it from the prey they catch.) Yet they are very demanding about the quality of the water they drink. If it is not clear or fresh enough, a cat will decline to drink, even when very thirsty.

Even though they are not big drinkers, cats must always have free access to their water bowls. But owners should not be alarmed if the water level stays the same for some time. Remember to wash out the bowl and change the water often.

A cat eating dry food will have to drink frequently, about 1½ tablespoons per pound (3 tablespoons per kilogram) of body weight. For the average cat weighing about 9 pounds (4 kg), this means 1 cup (¼ litre) per day.

Common misconceptions

Popular literature and art often portray a cat purring on its owner's couch as it gazes at its saucer of milk and dish of liver out of the corner of its eye. What is interesting about this image is that it depicts exactly what should be avoided in terms of diet if you want to keep your animal in good health.

If they drink milk at all, most cats will develop diarrhoea. This is unfortunate, because milk is an excellent complete food; but many cats, like dogs, are unable to digest lactose.

Other dairy products, however, including yogurt, are quite acceptable, because they have been fermented and contain lactobacteria.

Liver, while remarkably rich in proteins, trace elements, and vitamins, is also a strong laxative. Cooking will weaken its laxative effect somewhat, but very high concentrations of vitamin A make it extremely dangerous for cats. High doses of this vitamin can cause haemorrhagic periostitis (bleeding and inflammation of connective tissue covering bones), as well as painful bony spurs around the joints.

The problem with liver is that cats simply adore it and have been known to become fixated on it. They may then refuse to eat anything else. Some cats have even been known to go on a hunger strike until they get more liver.

How can you tell if your cat is not eating well? Its coat will become messy and dull, its eyes will be glazed, and its nose will be warm and dry. It will move slowly, appearing completely lethargic, and its breath will smell stale. If these signs continue for more than a few days, consult your veterinarian.

Yes, your cat can eat grass, and no, this does not mean it is sick. Contrary to popular belief, grass is quite good for your cat because it contains vitamins and it also helps the cat to eliminate hair balls. In fact, if you live in an apartment, or if your cat stays inside all the time, it might be a good idea to grow some grass in a pot or window box.

This cat is obese. To prevent or control excessive weight gain it may be necessary to decrease the volume of food, or to feed the cat a special weight-reducing diet.

GENERAL GUIDELINES

Small but frequent meals

Most cats are nibblers. They get by very nicely on several small meals a day. Some cats also do well on one or two larger meals, but others are gobblers, eating a large quantity of food very quickly. This leads to swelling of the stomach in the short run and, eventually, obesity. Obesity can start at a very early age.

Experiments with different foods should be tried when the cat is young. Later, being naturally curious, the cat will taste new dishes, but it will not become completely used to them and may even refuse them. It is therefore important to vary the menus while the cat is still young.

Gradual changes

Any sudden change in food could bring on diarrhoea. If you are planning a change in the cat's diet, do it gradually by varying the foods just a little or alternating meals of different consistencies. If you want to change from canned food which is very moist (more than 80 percent water) to a dry food, make sure the cat gets enough liquids, either by moistening the dry food, or getting the cat to drink extra water.

Fresh water

Cats insist on having fresh, clear water. One problem is that most tap water contains chemicals. Many communities have chlorinated water, which the cat does not like and will not drink until the water has settled; this can take 24 hours. This is why many cats refresh themselves from a pond or other body of stagnant water. They also prefer good quality fresh food. For example, they will spurn canned food that is beginning to dry out. Even dry food can become mouldy and unappetizing fairly quickly if it is improperly stored, and then your cat will refuse to eat it.

Balanced diet

A proper diet depends on the cat's age, its size, and how active it is, as well as the energy content of the particular food. Ask your veterinarian's advice.

For serving quantities per day, here are some rules of thumb per pound (500 g) of body weight: at 5 weeks of age, 125 calories; at 11 weeks, 75 calories; at 17 weeks, 55 calories; at 2l weeks, 50 calories; at 30 weeks, 48 calories; at 50 weeks or maturity, 30 calories.

Most veterinarians recommend dry foods for cats because they have a better energy balance than canned foods. They can also prevent dental problems, and urinary tract infections, a common cat ailment.

In serving commercially prepared foods, estimate about 1 percent of body weight per day for a 10 pound (4.5 kg) cat, and 1 to 3 percent of body weight for canned food.

A proper diet of home-prepared food should contain at least 50 percent of animal meat and fat—beef, chicken, and fish—served well cooked, 20 percent of well-cooked grains, 20 percent of cooked green vegetables, and 10 percent of vitamin and mineral complements, oil and dry yeast.

All meats and fish and other foods should be cooked well to prevent parasitosis.

Healthy food

A cat's dietary needs are totally different from a dog's, even though a cat may be curious enough to investigate a dog's food bowl. Neither animal's nutritional needs will be met if they eat each other's food. Nor is it a good idea to feed a cat table scraps because most cats do not fare well eating food prepared for people. A cat, unfortunately, has little self-control and will likely try anything. So it's up to the owner to decide what food is good for the cat.

Make absolutely certain that the cat does eat something if you are denying it certain kinds of food. A cat that does not eat for 48 hours may die. If your cat hasn't eaten for two days, consult your veterinarian. But remember to check first that your cat is not gorging itself on its favourite foods at a neighbour's.

Always chop up the food

A domestic cat, like its cousins in the wild, does not chew its food, but simply swallows it down in lumps, letting its strong gastric juices break it down. So when putting out your cat's food, eliminate any bones and cut up the rest in small pieces.

A good mix

When a cat eats wild prey, including birds and mice, it swallows a mixture of meat and bone, muscles and internal organs. A domestic cat eating a diet of canned food has to get the equivalent of that same mixture to get the right amount of protein and fat. It needs about 20 to 30 percent of protein and 40 percent of fat to stay healthy.

Eat better, live longer

To sum up, if a cat has a good diet, is active and playful, with a shiny coat, regular bowel movements with well-formed stools, correct weight and figure, it is well nourished.

Hygiene

Litter

The cat has been called the 'desert animal' because it needs very little water to survive. Because it consumes so little water, its urine is very concentrated. And because its diet is mainly meat, its urine tends to have a strong odour. So a good litter is very important.

The litter should be both absorbent and deodorizing and, since it must not be dangerous to humans or cats, should not contain poisons or powders. Most litter on the market today is made of clay.

The litter box should be made of plastic (wood retains odours) and should be large enough to hold the cat comfortably. It should be about 4 inches (10 cm) deep and the litter itself should be about 1½ inches (4 cm) deep in the tray. This will permit liquids to be absorbed and the cat can bury its solid waste out of sight.

Of the commercial products, dust-free litters are best. With all commercial litters, solid wastes become covered with fine particles, which quickly dry the stools and lock in odours. This is especially true of clumping litter. It has sand-like granules of absorbing ground clay that dries and completely absorbs a cat's liquid wastes.

You won't have to change the litter so often if droppings are removed daily. You can do this with a slotted litter scoop. The box itself should be disinfected regularly, but be careful to choose a disinfectant that is safe for cats. Avoid any with carbolic acid, phenol, or coal-tar ingredients.

Plant-based deodorant powders are now available in some stores. The powder, which can be placed under the layer of litter, both deodorizes and perfumes the air,

making life more pleasant for the cat owner. However, a few cats may be slightly offended by some perfumes and refuse to use their litter. Scented litters, too, should be used carefully for the same reason.

Sand and gravel are not good litter material because cats find them abrasive and they are neither absorbent nor deodorizing. They also promote bacterial growth and so are potentially dangerous for both humans and cats.

Sawdust is also unacceptable since it clings to the cat's fur, and the animal may ingest large quantities of it when it grooms. Another concern is the type of wood that created the sawdust. Some woods are treated with chemicals that can be poisonous or allergenic.

Newspapers, too, should be avoided. The chemicals in the ink may interact with urine to produce dangerous gases. Uninked newsprint, however, may be useful in some circumstances (see box, page 176).

Cats are very finicky about their litter box. They quickly become accustomed to one type of litter, and often insist on staying with the litter they used as kittens for the rest of their lives.

Cats are generally very clean. If a cat goes to the toilet outside the litter tray, it almost certainly has some kind of problem, and is letting the owner know. The odour may be new or offensive to the cat—or the litter may not be fresh. Sometimes a cat will also avoid using its litter box if somebody has teased it or handled it roughly or if it has been disturbed while in the litter. Cats are very private animals.

Whenever the cat goes to the toilet somewhere other than its litter box, clean the soiled area very carefully to avoid repeat soilings.

The basic clay-based litter, the most commonly used litter in most countries.

Clumping litter, which causes liquid wastes to form an easy-to-remove lump.

Brushing

Healthy cats can keep themselves reasonably clean, but a little assistance from their owners can contribute significantly to the cat's coat. A healthy coat will be shiny, neat, and clean, with dead hair and skin cells removed and the skin and circulation toned up. Whether your cat is a short-hair or a long-hair, its coat will need regular brushing; you cannot just let it groom itself.

Unlike their wild cousins, most domestic cats shed a little bit all year, but have two heavier sheds in spring and fall. Only particular circumstances such as illness, kittening, and stress will cause major hair loss, which can look like shedding.

When a cat grooms itself, it combs its coat, untangles its hair, and aerates its fur. It also regulates its body temperature by moistening its coat with its saliva. The air thus trapped in the fur provides thermal insulation, just like fibreglass between roof and ceilings insulates a house. Because the saliva evaporates when the cat is hot, it manages to maintain a comfortable body temperature.

When it licks itself, a cat swallows a certain amount of hair. This accumulates in the stomach, and from time to time the cat will bring up dark soggy masses known as hair-balls. If these are not regurgitated or excreted with faeces, they can create

A happy, healthy cat always grooms itself spontaneously.

an intestinal obstruction. In the most severe cases, surgery is the only solution.

This is another reason why grooming your cat is so important. Combing not only removes loose hair that might otherwise be swallowed and unsightly mats which cause itching, but it aerates the coat and massages the skin, thus stimulating further hair growth.

A metal comb is better than a brush, since brushes quickly fill up with hair after which they only scratch the surface of the coat. A comb, on the other hand, can penetrate right down to the skin. With a short-haired cat, use a fine-toothed comb and work from head to tail; on the tail itself, use a rubber brush.

For long-haired cats, try a pure bristle brush which does not cause static or break hairs. To remove snarls and tangles that are inevitable in a long-hair, use a fine-toothed comb, gently running it upwards through the hair. To finish the job, you will need a toothbrush for the ruff and to smoothe the short facial hairs without getting too close to the eyes.

Although surface mats can generally be removed with a blunt-nosed (surgical) scissors, seriously matted hair is another matter. If you try removing it with scissors, you risk cutting the cat's skin. Try to untangle it with your fingers. There are also commercial sprays for removing knotted fur and these can be quite effective.

As a last resort, consult your veterinarian about having the cat anaesthetized and shaved. This overall clipping can do no lasting harm, and a new coat, albeit a thicker one, will grow back within a few months.

In any well-groomed cat, long-haired or short-haired, a brisk stroking of the fingertips against the lay of the fur will get out a lot of dead hair without upsetting the animal. Why work against the lay? Because dead hair held in place by the rest of the fur can be removed easily this way, and the coat is fully aerated at the same time.

If you notice your cat grooming one spot of its fur over and over, check it out. More

Total body clipping may be required for a long-haired cat with severe matting.

than likely something has become stuck there—a burr or some tar.

Most kittens have learned to wash themselves by the time they are weaned, at which time the owner should get in on the act. The younger the cat when you begin grooming it, the easier it will be in the long run. This is doubly true of long-haired cats, that are not only more susceptible to matting than the short-haired breeds, but also have shorter tongues for doing the job themselves. Long-haired cats should be groomed every day; twice weekly is adequate for short-hairs.

From time to time, dust the animal with a flea or tick powder prescribed by your veterinarian. You can clean the cat's fur with household detergent if it has been

Shampooing is easier if the cat became accustomed to water at a very young age.

into some tar, paint, or chemicals. Or the fur in the affected area can be soaked in cooking oil until the foreign substance loosens enough to be washed off.

Bathing

Even though a few breeds of cat are quite at home in watery surroundings, most cats abhor water. So bath time could be a problem unless you accustom your cat to the practice early in life, preferably in the first few months—and provided you don't mind getting wet yourself! Since exhibitors like to wash cats before shows, good breeders try to get kittens used to water early on. Then, with luck, bath time will not be an ordeal when the cat is grown.

Apart from show cats, bathing is not essential on a regular basis. Cats, by their nature, keep themselves clean. But sometimes, whether for medical reasons or because the cat is badly soiled, a bath cannot be avoided.

If this is the cat's first bath, make a game of wetting it gradually, first with a washcloth and then a sponge which will work the water into the fur. Use a large washbowl, or the kitchen sink, filled with about 4 inches (10 cm) of lukewarm water, and fitted with a rubber mat so the cat won't slip out of your grip. Hold the cat firmly but don't restrain it anymore than you have to. Otherwise, it will struggle so much that shampooing will be extremely difficult. If possible have someone help you: one of you can hold the cat, talking to it reassuringly all the time; the other can apply the shampoo. (Make sure you use a cat shampoo: residues from human shampoos, when licked, could poison the cat.) Afterwards rinse thoroughly.

Dry the cat in a warm towel. A good rubdown will be fine for a short-haired cat but may result in tangles if you have a long-haired breed. In that case, blot firmly and confine the cat to some warm area until it is all dried out. Then finish the job with a good combing. Some people find an electric hair dryer on a low setting useful for drying the cat after its bath. But many cats are simply scared by the noise, which compounds an already stressful experience.

Baths are especially helpful in treating parasites and skin disorders. Male cats, for example, often suffer from 'stud tail,' an accumulation of sebum under the tail, especially near the base (see page 172). The hair may be so matted that only shampooing can restore its silky smooth appearance.

For those who find the bath time hassle too much, there is a way out—give your cat a dry bath. Use a standard pet-grooming powder, or a mixture of talcum powder and cornstarch. Shake the powder over the cat's entire coat, spread it around with your hands, and then brush it in using a pure-bristle brush. For a short-haired cat you can use 1 or 2 pounds (500 g-1 kg) of dry bran baked at 300°F (150°C) for 20 minutes. Massage the warm bran into the cat's fur, then comb it.

Cleaning the eyes and nose

As a rule, you do not have to wash a healthy cat's eyes. Should an eyewash become necessary, use cool, boiled water, a saline solution, or a product prescribed by a veterinarian.

A cat in good health never has a runny nose, but its muzzle is always moist because it licks itself there often, and its nostrils are moistened by tears flowing from the corners of the eyes down the lachrymal ducts. Therefore a dry or runny nose is a sign that something is wrong. Never tamper with a cat's nose, except on specific instructions from the veterinarian.

Cleaning the ears

The golden rule: the less you touch a cat's ears, the better. Inspect them carefully but don't poke with your fingers or cotton swabs. Both ears should be clean and clear, although the base of the pinna (see page 55) may be mildly greasy with cerumen, a yellow or brownish wax.

You can remove this with cotton balls dipped in warm olive or mineral oil and inserted into the outer ear; do not use a water-based cleanser or alcohol. Then pat the pinna with a dry cotton ball to remove the excess grease. Do not use cotton swabs. Although they can absorb much of the grease, they may push more of it back into the ear canal. There it can form a plug, which may have to be removed under general anaesthetic.

Don't be tempted to remove buildup too often. Every time you remove this wax, you exercise the cerumen glands, and in the long run the production of wax will actually increase.

If your cat runs away when you touch its ear, or stays put but is obviously in pain, it may have any number of problems ranging from ear mites and foreign bodies in the ear to middle ear infections. Sometimes the affected cat will actually lean against your hand as you clean its ear, seeking relief from the pain and itching. Deafness, staggering, and loss of balance are all symptoms of ear infections that require prompt veterinary attention.

Cleaning the mouth

A cat's breath is always strong, and you must learn to distinguish between strong breath and halitosis (bad breath). Halitosis

---

DENTAL HEALTH

The cat's mouth must be examined at least once a year by a veterinarian. The mouth is the body's front door, and consequently it can tell a great deal about an animal's general health. It is also the animal's 'hand,' its main grasping organ. A cat's teeth are not deeply rooted in the lower jaw and can easily come loose and fall out. They are also prone to disorders such as neck lesions or cervical line lesions. Although these resemble cavities, they are not the same.

These lesions, which develop at a point between the crown and the root, are hidden by the edge of the root and can only be diagnosed after careful examination. If left unattended too long, they eat away at the tooth under the gum, eventually causing the tooth to fracture.

Frequent removal of tartar helps maintain the tooth's support structure, and prevents premature loss of teeth. The short operation is done under a general anaesthetic that poses no danger to the cat, since modern anaesthetics are extremely reliable and risk-free, even for older animals.

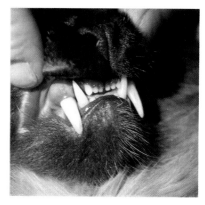

Broken teeth can now be repaired, thanks to new procedures in veterinary dentistry.

may be due to bacteria or to wastes that should be excreted by way of the kidneys instead of through the mouth. If a cat's kidneys fail, wastes that would ordinarily be extracted by the kidneys accumulate in the blood. In those circumstances, the cat will have breath that smells like urine. (The breath of a cat in good health merely smells stale.)

Problems with teeth and gums also produce putrid smelling breath. This commonly begins with tartar and food debris accumulating around the cat's teeth and gradually decomposing. Tartar buildup occurs as minerals in the saliva, food debris, and proliferated bacteria form a rough coating on the teeth. Older cats and those that are mainly fed soft foods are the most likely victims. Any bacteria or toxins in the mouth eventually find their way to the liver and kidneys. Because these organs are extremely fragile—liver and kidney disorders are the main cause of disease-related deaths in cats—it is easy to appreciate that a clean mouth is a key to good health.

There is no better way to keep a cat's mouth in good shape than by cleaning its teeth. But unless this was begun when the cat was quite young, it is unlikely to sit passively while you attempt it later on. It may work if you use a child's toothbrush and have somebody hold the cat's lips back while you do the brushing. Failing that, try a cotton swab or a strip of gauze bandaging wrapped around a fingertip; ordinary warm water is fine, with a final rinse in salt water. You may wish to use a special cat toothpaste. Never clean your cat's teeth with your own toothpaste: many such products contain detergents that are dangerous to cats. Some cats that are used to regular teeth cleaning may even tolerate having their mouths washed out with a stream of pressurized water. If your cat

thwarts all attempts at dental hygiene, you will have no choice but to take it to the veterinarian for an annual descaling. Good saliva circulation can be stimulated by frequent chewing on dried cowhide bones.

Check your cat's mouth regularly to make sure there is nothing stuck between its teeth. Mouth infections sometimes begin when a foreign body, such as a needle or a fish bone, gets lodged between the cat's back teeth. Check its tongue too. Cats are always licking things, and as a result may have adverse reactions to any number of chemicals.

Appetite loss, inflamed gums or tongue, ulcerous sores inside the mouth, and excessive salivating are all signs of mouth infections. See your veterinarian without delay. Most such disorders respond well to antibiotics.

Clipping the claws

One widely held misconception is that cats only strop their claws to sharpen them or to wear them down. Some observers

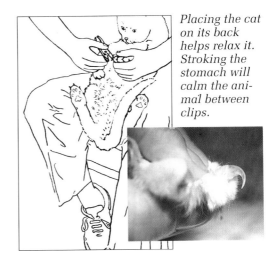

Placing the cat on its back helps relax it. Stroking the stomach will calm the animal between clips.

DECLAWING

Often those who have a scratching cat feel they must get rid of it when it becomes too aggressive or will not stop marking its territory with its claws. Surgical removal of the claws—a procedure many veterinarians will not perform—is viewed as a last resort by some owners. Many people are strongly opposed to declawing, and animal lovers in Britain want the practice made illegal. They point out that removing the cat's claws is too radical a solution, especially when a scratching problem can usually be cleared up with some behaviour therapy. Declawing is fairly widespread in North America, however, and several other countries.

Proponents of declawing say the declawed cat will not suffer insurmountable psychological problems and its behaviour will not change. The cat

should still be able to climb trees, but will have less of a grip. Opponents say declawing removes the cat's only defence against attacks by other, larger animals. Even those veterinarians who declaw cats recommend such animals be kept indoors for life.

Veterinarians who favour declawing say that the best time for this surgery is when the cat is 4 to 8 months old. They recommend that only the front claws be removed, since these are the ones that damage furniture and injure humans.

After the operation, the cat will be uncomfortable, but sedatives are generally prescribed to help it through the recovery period. The cat will still be able to do 'olfactory marking' with secretions produced between the paw pads.

suggest stropping actually produces the opposite effects.

They argue that when a cat 'sharpens' its claws, it is not honing its weaponry at all. It is merely giving notice that it has staked out—marked—the object or territory as its own. This, they point out, is why scratching posts designed to protect walls, sofas, and table legs frequently have little effect.

Cats do indeed leave scratch marks as territorial stakes. But it would also seem that cats confined indoors for long periods are beating boredom and thinking manicure when they attack your prized draperies or dining room suite. So put a scratching post at the cat's favourite attack site and thrust the cat at it whenever you find it sacking your home.

You can find all kinds of elaborate models at your local pet store, or you can make your own. (See *Scratching post*, page 205.) Even if the scratching post works, you would be wise to cut the tips off the cat's claws regularly. Then, even if it performs its rituals in all the wrong places, the stropping will cause less harm.

Once a month, sit down with the cat on its back, held firmly between your knees. With a pair of strong scissors or guillotine clippers, snip the tip off each claw just outside the pink nerve-containing quick. Clipping any closer to the bone will cause pain and considerable bleeding, an unpleasant experience a cat will remember. It is better to err on the side of caution, taking off less claw but clipping more often, and getting little resistance from the cat.

There is a positive side to these little exercises. They help develop good relations between owner and animal, especially important with cats which are always looking for ways to get more attention. Once again, a cat that is accustomed to pedicures at a young age will accept them more readily as years go by.

Nails should be inspected regularly to monitor their condition, the condition of the nail sheaths, and to catch problems at the earliest possible stages. This way amino acid deficiencies and bacterial or fungus infections can be spotted early.

Equipment and accessories

Litter box

Ideally the litter box should be about 4 inches (10 cm) deep and, depending on the size of the cat, about 20 inches (50 cm) by 16 inches (40 cm); a large cat will of course need a larger box. Essentially the box should be durable, it must be steady on the ground or wherever it is located, and it must be washable.

Some cats are more thorough about burying their excrement than others, and may scratch away vigorously with their hind paws. Cats with this habit should have a litter box with a high rim, or even one with an inward curving edge. Otherwise, you will have constant heaps of kitty litter all over your floor.

For the more fussy cat, a fully enclosed litter box will give the animal the impression that it is safe from prying eyes.

A litter scoop is also an essential part of the litter equipment. Buy a strong one, and it is useful to keep a spare. Faeces must be scooped out of the litter at least once a day, and preferably as soon as possible after the cat has used the litter.

Stores now sell litter tray liners, usually made of plastic, which are easily and quickly removed. A reminder: Don't locate the litter box near the cat's feeding area or the cat may refuse to eat or use its box.

This cat loves its classic wicker basket, but escape from it is fairly easy. The rigid plastic carrier (facing page) is much more reliable.

Cat carriers

The worst way to carry a cat is in a soft, open bag. Bags can collapse on the cat, are poorly ventilated and difficult to clean. They cannot be closed tightly, and an enterprising cat can easily escape from such carriers.

Rigid plastic cat carriers are far more practical. The best models come apart in the middle, and the bottom half can be used as a litter box. They are easy to clean, and the most practical ones open at the top like traditional wicker baskets. These traditional baskets are practical, but they tend to be draughty and fragile.

Placing a cat in a wire cage or a plexiglass box is real torture, because a cat enjoys crouching out of view to watch what's going on; it likes to lie in ambush rather than go out and look for prey. So when it is in a see-through enclosure, it feels exposed and knows it cannot hide. Opaque boxes with breathing holes for the cat are preferable. This way the cat can peek at its surroundings.

It's a good idea at first to leave the carrier where the cat can see it so it will seem less mysterious and not so frightening. Otherwise, every time the owner brings it out, the cat will fear the worst and make every effort to avoid being captured.

Bedding

As a rule, a cat will choose where it wants to sleep. It may even change places from time to time and won't really appreciate an elaborate bed. Nevertheless, some owners are tempted to give cats their own beds. If you decide to buy a cat bed, they can be found or made in a wide variety of designs from the fancy wicker basket to an ordinary cardboard box lined with paper or an old blanket. The bed must not contain any wool. Use cotton-covered foam cushions instead. Cats generally like these.

Feeding bowls

A cat should have its own dishes for eating. These should be shallow enough for the cat to eat without getting the food all over its nose—something it dislikes. The bowls should be well cleaned before each feeding, but use soap or dish detergent sparingly. Then rinse well; many detergents have ingredients harmful to cats.

Toys

Cats love to play, even when they are supposed to be staid and middle-aged. Just about anything will distract a cat, from the most sophisticated mechanical toys to a ball of paper on a string. Be very careful with sharp objects you may be using, like a sewing needle dangling from a piece of thread. A cat will play with the thread and may swallow it together with the needle, piercing its tongue or getting it stuck in its throat (see page 164).

Scratching post

It's a good idea to have a scratching post available for the cat and, with luck, the animal will rake its claws on it and not on pieces of furniture or drapes to which it has taken a fancy. Over a period of weeks, the post can be moved gradually to an out-of-the-way location if it is bothering anyone. You will need some sort of vertical pillar, since the cat usually stands on its hind legs when scratching. It may be free-standing as long as it is on a stable base, or it may be a panel attached to the wall. Either way, a log or piece of unplaned coarse-grained wood may do the trick, or you may want to fit it with some burlap or carpeting, which appeals to some cats.

Collar and leash

Never allow a cat outdoors unless it is wearing a collar to which your name, address, and telephone number are affixed. Should the cat become lost or injured, whoever finds it will be able to contact you. Ideally the collar should have an elastic section, so that the cat can free itself if the collar catches on anything. Get a leash when you buy the collar if you want to train the cat to go for walks with you.

Human-cat diseases

Fortunately, diseases that can be transmitted from cats to humans are rare and, in most cases, easy to control with good hygiene. Barring the cat's litter box from the kitchen, regular vacuuming, and keeping young children away from the cat's litter will prevent most problems. Sandboxes in public playgrounds are potentially hazardous. These are frequented by stray cats that are quite likely to be parasite carriers. (See *Zoonoses—how to prevent them*, page 186 for a fuller discussion.)

Signs of distress

General appearance and behaviour

Though cats proverbially have nine lives, in reality they can get sick and die. They are just as prone to diseases as other animals and from time to time face fights, falls, and risky adventures. There is not much an owner can do to curb a cat's natural curiosity, which often leads it onto distant windowsills and roofs or to the top of high trees in search of birds and squirrels.

Generally an owner can tell when something is bothering the cat—it may sleep all day or be aggressive or unusually listless. In those circumstances, a trip to the veterinarian is in order to make sure nothing is seriously wrong.

A sick cat will change its behaviour even to the point of misbehaving. In cases where the animal is suffering great pain, has a high fever, or is near death, it will disappear from sight. Cats hide when they are about to die.

If a cat usually goes outdoors, its range of movement must be restricted at the first sign that something is amiss. Any days that it spends away represent precious

Unkempt fur and a timorous crouching position are signs of a sick cat.

time lost to the veterinarian and can lessen its chances of recovery.

If the cat is in pain, perhaps suffering from a broken bone or a dislocation, it may well become aggressive. It may even try to intimidate its owner to avoid being handled and so having to suffer more. Because of this, it takes special skills to pick up or otherwise handle a cat that is suffering in any way. It is best to approach slowly, speaking calmly all the while in order to win its trust. Pick it up by the scruff of the neck, supporting its body weight with an arm under its rear legs. Carry the cat at arm's length, though, to avoid its sharp front claws.

Digestive and urinary disorders

If a cat has digestive problems, it will show its discomfort by becoming slovenly. It will go to the toilet outside its litter, often just beside the box, with frequent bouts of diarrhoea. It may suffer from cystitis, and in that case will also urinate outside the litter. Scolding won't help at all. The animal is already unhappy enough.

If it is constipated or has a urethral obstruction, it will spend its time in the litter box trying to go, but not succeeding. If it visits the box frequently and behaves this way, the alert owner will not waste precious time plying it with laxatives but will take it to the veterinarian immediately. A urethral obstruction can lead to life-threatening uremic poisoning.

Vomiting is not necessarily cause for alarm, since cats easily bring up a meal at the slightest gastric problem. Frequent vomiting should be investigated, though. If the cat vomits every day, or worse, several times a day, a visit to the veterinarian should be arranged without delay.

If the vomiting is merely a digestive problem, it is easily treated; vomiting due to infections, urinary or endocrine disorders or tumours can be serious, and may require veterinary intervention.

The cat's fur coat

A cat in good health spends much of its time grooming its coat. So dishevelled or matted hair, dandruff or a coat that feels greasy not only look unpleasant but are cause for alarm.

A poorly groomed coat reflects chronic suffering or heralds the approach of a serious disease, while an acute disorder will produce an abrupt, spectacular change of behaviour.

Often the coat's condition provides precise clues to whatever is wrong with the cat. Diffuse or localized thinning of the fur suggests a rash. This calls for a trip to the veterinarian, especially if there are scabs, any sign of parasites, fleas or ticks, or if the cat suffers from a hormonal imbalance.

Deterioration of the coat is sometimes due to vitamin deficiencies arising from inadequate nutrition or certain disorders. Sometimes the coat is matted and dry because the cat has failed to groom itself—possibly because it is exhausted, or

No special intelligence is needed to tell a sick cat (above) from a cat in good health (right). At the first signs of alarm, the owner should consult a veterinarian. If diagnosed in time, most diseases can be treated.

because stiff joints prevent it from moving its head and turning its body in order to reach, and clean, all parts of its coat.

When this is the case, the owner must lend a hand. With arthritic animals, you must be as gentle as possible and respect the cat's sense of pride.

Be especially careful when brushing any cat that is ill. The task will naturally be easier if the animal has been accustomed to regular brushing and combing. But even when you know the source of the illness or injury, you can't always be sure what parts of the cat are hurting. Play it safe, and use extremely gentle motions if you must brush its fur at this time.

Making sure the coat looks its best is only one aspect of coat care. What is more critical is ensuring that it is properly aerated and smoothed so that it insulates the cat from cold and humidity.

Appetite and thirst

A cat in good health does not necessarily have to drink a lot each day. If an animal seems inordinately thirsty for a single day, that is entirely acceptable; but if the quantity of water consumed increases each day, something must be wrong. It could signal some kind of serious problem, a fever or a metabolic disorder. Similarly, an excessive appetite may indicate the onset of diabetes. Anorexia, or loss of appetite, is more readily noted as a rule.

Generally, abrupt weight changes are serious warning signs.

Sensory organs

Eyes sealed shut with tears flowing, a grubby, runny nose, and dirty, foul-smelling ears are, in themselves, sufficiently obvious problems to warrant a visit to the vet-

erinarian. It is dangerous for owners to try to diagnose their pets themselves. For example, if the ear is especially painful, it is very important not to administer any medications since the wrong remedy may make certain ear disorders worse.

When the cat's eyes appear runny or have a blue or white film, the cat always needs professional attention.

Cats can catch a cold just as humans can, and the symptoms are similar. A bad cold may mean feline influenza, which requires a veterinarian's care.

A cat's breath, which is naturally strong, should not smell like urine. If it does, the owner should suspect a mouth infection or perhaps a kidney disease resulting in excessive wastes building up in the body.

Breathing

When a healthy cat is resting, you should barely see it breathing. An animal that is breathing heavily but has not been running, may have a cardiorespiratory disorder. If the nostrils are also dilating at each breath, waste no time in getting to the veterinarian. These are serious signs.

Like dogs, cats do not perspire through their skin, which has no pores. A cat may spread its saliva on its coat, perspire through its paw pads, or pant heavily. When an animal pants, its tongue hangs out and large quantities of air are drawn in and out of the throat and lungs and excess water evaporates from the tongue. These are not breathing motions, however. The amplitude is too small, so the air does not reach the sacs in the lungs. The cat may be panting and perspiring because the temperature is high or because it has just been running. More often, though, the cat is feverish or suffering from anxiety. If panting persists, the cat should be seen by a veterinarian.

Bodily changes

Just as a cat's behaviour is a good barometer of the cat's health, so too is its physical appearance.

An enlarged abdomen, for example, is often perceived as a weight gain. Since cats frequently have a layer of fat under the stomach, an inattentive owner may not notice the difference between a few extra layers of fat and a tummy that's bloated. Often the abdomen is distended because of an accumulation of liquid, frequently a symptom of feline infectious peritonitis and liver disorder. Since these conditions may be a secondary effect of heart disease, prompt treatment is essential.

Deformations or any signs of limb pain, limping for instance, should always be investigated. A young cat may have a growth disorder; an older cat may be suffering from arthrosis (stiffening of the joints). A thorn may have pierced the cat's paw or it may have sustained a wound that has abscessed.

SIGNS TO WATCH FOR

Good health

Temperature : normally between 101.5°F and 102.5°F (38.6°C and 39.2°C). No matter how big the cat, its temperature can be taken with a conventional medical thermometer smeared with a little oil. If it rises near 104°F (40°C), it is time to consult a veterinarian.

Colour : the best place to look is the conjunctival mucosa, the tissue around the eyes. It must be a light pink colour. If it is red, the cat is congested, and likely also has a fever. If it is dirty or yellowish, an organ such as the liver may be diseased.

Nose : should be shiny if the lachrymal canal is functioning normally, because tears keep the nostrils moist. To a lesser degree, the tongue fulfils this function as well. The cat regularly licks its nose, keeping it moist and cool.

Eyes : should not be blinking or red. Redness may be a sign of a simple conjunctivitis or may be caused by glaucoma, be a symptom of a serious general disease, or signal the presence of a piece of glass or other foreign body.

Hair : shiny hair indicates a good general state of health. There should be no dandruff or 'pepper'— flea faeces. Long hair can easily conceal a skin disease. If not properly groomed, it does not protect the cat against the cold.

Stools : even if the cat is fasting, it will produce stools, which consist mainly of cellular debris from the digestive tract.

Appetite : excessive appetite is not necessarily a sign of good health. It may indicate diabetes. Similarly, a poor appetite is not always a sign that something is physiologically wrong, but rather some behavioural pattern of the moment.

Drinking : if your cat drinks excessively, it may point to a kidney problem or diabetes.

Wheezing : if your cat wheezes and sneezes, it may simply have a cold. Discharges from the eyes and nose could mean the same thing, in which case, do what people do: wait until the cold goes away. But if the cat also has a fever, it may have bronchitis or asthma which will need professional help.

Worrying signs

Temperature : if it is below 100.5°F (38.6°C), check to see that the thermometer was put in far enough; grease it again and reinsert it gently a little farther. If the temperature is still low, see a veterinarian right away, since this could be a symptom of very serious problems.

Colour : the cat may be pale if it has just been stressed. A light colour is normal.

Nose : cracking may indicate a local nose or eye problem or general dehydration, a very serious situation. A nose that is dry, dull, and warm may be a sign of a temperature. Check to be sure.

Eye : if it is gummy, this may be due to simple conjunctivitis, or, worse, a dry kerato-conjunctivitis, which requires immediate medical attention.

Hair : the coat reflects general health, but it is a delayed indicator. At the onset of disease, the hair may still be deceptively shiny. Regardless of the cat's state of health, hair fallout may be due to climatic or hormonal factors, or to stress.

Stools : colour depends on food. If a cat eats too many carrots, orange stools should not be taken as a sign of intestinal haemorrhaging. Since parasite eggs are microscopic, any eggs visible on the surface of the stools are probably fly eggs.

Drinking : if a cat stares at its water dish but will not drink, there is a serious problem. It means the cat is thirsty but feels too sick to drink; it may be dying.

Straining : If your cat is straining in the litter box, but produces nothing, it could have a blockage. If your cat is unable to urinate, seek veterinary help immediately.

Changes in behaviour : despondency, irritability, trembling are serious signs of illness.

Care at home

There are several tell-tale signs that a cat is ill. Some are symptomatic of a particular disease. Others involve unusual behaviour by the cat because of the way the disease is affecting its body. And some signs point to malfunctioning organs or organic systems. Learn to distinguish between general, local, and functional symptoms.

General symptoms

Any change in the cat's general behaviour signals something is amiss. The cat may be despondent and sad, may not eat, and may try to hide from you.

Unexplained weight loss may be the first indication of a chronic, progressive disorder. Even if this prospect does not alarm you at first, such an illness is potentially more serious than an acute disorder. It reflects advanced deterioration of various organs and functions.

By itself, a warm nose may only mean the cat has not licked itself for a while. But a dry, cracked nose may be the result of either a general disorder or an eye disorder, since the tears that flow down the lachrymal canal are largely responsible for moistening and keeping the nose cool.

A cat in pain will not express this by crying. Instead it crouches to find a comfortable position, seeks an isolated corner, and may become aggressive.

Local symptoms

These appear at the site of an injury or infection, and thus can help locate the problem. Swelling may accompany a hernia, haematoma, abscess or tumour, while a deformation will indicate a fracture or dislocation. Pus from a wound usually indicates there is an abscess, or an abnormal passage, known as a fistula, between body parts. Nasal discharges suggest a case of rhinitis, and stuck eyelids or discharges from the eyes mean conjunctivitis; vaginal discharges accompany inflammation of the uterus or vagina. Hair loss or scabs indicate dermatitis. A change of colour of the mucous membranes is a local symptom of a general disorder: anaemia if they are pale, liver problems if they are yellow, heart and lung problems if they are dark or purple.

Functional symptoms

Generally these signs point to the cat's whole system being affected by disease.

Vomiting, for example, may originate in the oesophagus, stomach, pylorus (the lower outlet from the stomach), or the intestines. But it is just as likely to indicate overeating as a more serious condition.

Similarly, diarrhoea may indicate a digestive problem, a viral, parasitic, or degenerative disease of the pancreas, or even cancer.

If general, local, or functional symptoms persist, get your cat to a veterinarian quickly. The sooner an animal is seen professionally, the sooner a diagnosis can be made. Any instance of prolonged anorexia severely reduces a cat's chances of survival. Wise cat owners do not medicate their cats without veterinary advice. What works for humans can kill a cat. So too can the wrong cat medication administered for the wrong disease.

Before administering care, immobilize the cat

Cats do not take well to being restrained. Perhaps the most important rule in caring for a cat is to act fast and firmly, without being brutal. Exert enough pressure to dissuade the cat from putting up any resistance, but be flexible enough that you don't provoke defensive reactions.

The ideal way to hold a cat is to grab a handful of skin at the scruff of its neck. The cat will be disarmed by this, instinctively reacting passively like a kitten being carried by its mother and adopting a foetal position with paws folded under the body.

As well as being held by the scruff of the neck, the more recalcitrant animals should be pressed down on a table, with the front paws over the edge. The cat, which will then only be concerned with pulling forward to get to the floor, may not think of turning to use its claws.

When a cat is picked up by the scruff of the neck, it adopts a foetal position. It shows no anger and is passive and easy to handle.

Quick checks

If you suspect your cat is sick, listen to its breathing, take its temperature, and check its pulse. A healthy cat will take some 20 to 30 respirations per minute.

To check your cat's temperature, coat the end of the thermometer with vaseline or vegetable oil. Put your cat on a level surface and hold it steady between your body and arms. Lift the tail with one hand and gently but firmly push the thermometer into the cat's rectum for about 1½ inches (4 cm). A reading of between 101.5°F (38.6°C) and 102.5°F (39.2°C) is considered normal. Severe infections can drive the cat's temperature as high as 106°F (41°C). If the temperature gets anywhere near that high, call your veterinarian immediately.

If the temperature is registering below

Holding a cat by the scruff of its neck at the edge of a table should keep even the most stubborn feline still.

the normal 101.5°F (38.6°C), you may not be inserting the thermometer far enough into the rectum; very gently push it in farther. If the reading is still below normal, the cat may be suffering from hypothermia, a drop in body temperature that can lead to unconsciousness and death. Treatment depends on the cause. Is the cat taking any medication? Some drugs may induce the condition. Or has it been exposed to extreme cold or been immersed for a time in cold water?

Check your cat's pulse on the femoral artery, a major blood vessel on the inside of the hind leg close to the hip joint. Put your fingers over the artery where it comes close to the skin and you should be able

Keep those sharp claws under wraps in a towel.

to feel the pulse. Using your watch, count the number of beats for 15 seconds, then multiply that number by 4 and this will give you the pulse rate in beats per minute.

The normal pulse rate is between 100 and 180 beats; a higher rate may mean the cat is nervous or that your cat is sick. Check with your veterinarian.

Pulling a cat's head back causes it to open its mouth and swallow.

Administering pills

Pills are one form of medication a cat can take without too much trouble. Still, many people find liquid medications easier to deal with. Since a cat's claws are a far greater danger than its teeth, it may be a good idea to wrap a cat in a terry cloth towel preparatory to giving it pills or indeed any treatment. This effectively neutralizes the claws and works as long as being swaddled in this way doesn't make it too upset (see below, left).

Of course you can also administer a pill by placing the animal on a table, sitting on its haunches. Grip the head from behind with the left hand and pull it back (see above). The jaw should be vertical. The lower lip will automatically fall open. You can use the nail of the index finger of the right hand to pull the lower incisors and open the mouth wider, while you slide the thumb and middle finger of the left hand between its lips. If the cat tries to close its jaws, it will bite its cheeks and give up trying.

The pill, which you should hold between the thumb and middle finger of the right hand, can then be dropped between the palate and the back of the tongue. Then push firmly forward with the index finger of the same hand, forcing the cat to close its mouth. The head, with the muzzle still in the air, should not be released until the cat licks its nose—a sign that it has swallowed the pill. If this takes too long, you can rub its nose to make it dry. This triggers the licking reflex.

Administering liquids and pastes

Many veterinary medications are available as liquids and may be given to the cat easily and safely with an eyedropper.

You might also try mixing some of the liquid with one of the vitamin pastes available for cats. Pastes may be the pharmaceutical innovation of the future, at least as far as cats are concerned. They have all the advantages of powders mixed with

Liquids or pastes can be given with a syringe (minus the needle).

fresh cream, and can be prepared in a syringe before being injected between the animal's teeth.

Hold the head as if you were giving the animal a pill. But instead of pointing it upwards, the muzzle is kept horizontal to prevent gulping. The cat can bite down on the end of the syringe as the owner slowly depresses the plunger and the paste is being swallowed.

Some flavoured pastes can be mixed with food without requiring special handling, and it is a good bet that the cat will not reject them.

Administering suppositories

It takes two people to do this. One of them holds the animal down on the table by the scruff of the neck so that it cannot move. Using the left hand, the other takes the tail by the base and pulls it forward over the animal's back, exposing the anus. With the right hand, the suppository is inserted slowly and gently, and then the tail is lowered. Then the cat should be kept still for a few minutes.

Administering eyedrops

Hold the cat with its muzzle in the air, immobilized by the left hand's thumb and index finger, pulling the lower eyelid down with the middle finger. The right hand, which is holding the drop-per between the thumb, index and middle finger, is supported on the cat's forehead. Pull the upper eyelid upwards with the ring finger, and make sure the eyedrop falls on the cornea or into the corner of the eye. Ophthalmic ointments may be applied in the same way.

Administering ear drops

One person holds the cat in the position used for administering liquids and pastes (see left). The other pulls the pinna upwards and towards him, introducing the nozzle of the dropper into the open

To take a cat's temperature without fuss, lift the tail up over the back. The thermometer is then inserted gradually to the proper depth.

ear orifice, towards the outside and the nose. He should then massage the auditory canal for a long time, holding the pinna in the same position.

The home nurse

Nursing a sick cat requires a lot of patience and concern for a patient who cannot tell you how it is feeling. One of the essential things to bear in mind is that the cat will not behave as it usually does. It may lie there with dull eyes and exhibit absolutely no reactions. On the other hand, it may strike out with its claws and/or teeth.

The key to nursing a cat is to keep it clean, warm, and comfortable and, if possible, in a quiet environment. Have enough food and drink available and, if necessary, help it to eat and drink. Make sure its eating and drinking bowls are kept clean and away from other household equipment.

Always wash your hands both before and after handling a sick cat so that you don't transmit any disease or infection to or from the cat.

And if you really want to be a home nurse, talk to your cat in a reassuring way—it will appreciate that, even if it doesn't understand everything you say.

FIRST AID KIT

What to have

Cotton batting to clean wounds, and especially to make large compression bandages in case of haemorrhage or fracture.

A 4-inch- (10-cm-) wide bandage to wrap around the body, and other bandages for the limbs.

Sterile compresses to disinfect and protect a wound.

Wooden tongue depressors to devise a makeshift splint in the event of fracture or dislocation.

A 2-inch- (5-cm-) wide aerated adhesive tape to hold the crepe bandage covering the cotton, which is isolated from the wound by sterile compresses.

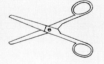

A pair of scissors, preferably blunt-ended, curved ones, to make dressings.

Hydrogen peroxide (3% or less) to clean wounds.

An antiseptic lotion to disinfect wounds. Saline solution to clean an irritated or injured eye.

Nail clippers in case the cat gets its claws caught in something.

Metal fine-toothed comb in case the cat gets tangled in the undergrowth or needs grooming.

An eyedropper in case you need to give the cat drops to keep an infected eye clean.

A disposable plastic syringe without the needle, in case you need to give the cat medication.

Medication to help stop diarrhoea—something your cat may catch if it is drinking water in different places.

Mineral oil or hair-ball medication to prevent hair balls from forming. This should only be given to the cat occasionally.

Pest spray made particularly for cats.

Blunt tweezers to probe safely in the cat's mouth or elsewhere where a sharp pair of scissors might cause injury.

Rectal thermometer to take the cat's temperature.

Not needed

Alcohol, which is a very poor disinfectant, damages tissues, and causes unnecessary suffering to the cat, which will be distrustful of further treatments.

A tourniquet, which is rarely used. Tourniquets must be loosened often at regular intervals. In case of haemorrhaging, a cotton compression bandage poses no danger to the animal's limb, even if it is not quite as effective at stopping the bleeding.

If your cat travels, pack these

The telephone number of your family veterinarian. Even if he or she is not available, a replacement will often provide good advice, and will have immediate access to the cat's medical records.

The cat's medical file, which will be helpful for a local veterinarian, though he will eventually contact the animal's usual veterinarian.

Water, which may be best carried in a bottle and put into a cat's bowl if needed.

A blanket to catch and immobilize the cat. In case of accident or pain, a cat will often refuse to be touched, even by those who know and love it.

Do not pack these

Medications that are not normally prescribed for the cat. Allergic reactions are frequent, and problems can occur if prescription drugs are exposed to the sun too long. If you are travelling with your cat, ask your veterinarian what medications you should take with you in case the cat falls ill.

UNDERSTANDING CATS

The territorial boundaries

Range and boundaries

Cats have received mixed reviews from the human race over the years. Many people think of them as antisocial creatures, solitary beings that refuse to share their territory with any other animal. But as most cat owners will testify, their feline friends form attachments to people, and even other pets. Under certain circumstances, cats can live with other cats in large groups. There are colonies of stray or feral cats in our cities living a communal life in parks, gardens, cemeteries, and even in the basement parking garages of high-rise buildings.

Every cat has a territory however small, and many cats lay claim to three. Two of these will be private domains, the third a communal ground, where some cats may gather regularly, others occasionally.

First among the territories is the private or central area, the cat's den, or lair. This is where it sleeps and where sometimes the female has her kittens. The cat will fight tooth and nail to defend that space against any intruder. Within its lair, a cat will sometimes even reject its owner's attentions.

The second territory might be called the cat's 'living space.' In an apartment, this will probably include every room. In a house, it usually includes both house and garden, and sometimes the gardens of neighbouring catless homes. A cat will share its living space with other animals in its household, but its resentment of any visiting cats and dogs will be unmistakable.

In urban areas, many cats share the same territory fairly peacefully.

The third territorial area, commonly held hunting and meeting grounds, relates mostly to feral cats, animals that have been domestic and returned to the wild through circumstances—such as abandonment—beyond their control. But cats with a tendency to stray from home and cats with a penchant for nightlife also lay claim to such territories, which they share with other animals they meet there. Open confrontations are rare in such an area. In fact, these feral cats manage not to confront one another, arranging their lives to avoid any unpleasant encounters.

The few fights that do occur in communal areas have to do with seniority, when a younger resident tries to oust an older one from its 'top cat' position. The confrontation is often limited to mutual glaring and intimidating growls, followed by the withdrawal of both parties.

Sexuality plays an important part in territorial rights. Within the private territories, which may be within the communal area or adjoining it, a neutered tom will make do with a much smaller living space than one that has not been neutered, and a queen with kittens will defend a broader living territory than one without offspring. But the more extensive communal territory is more a setting for social than sexual interaction. The several cats occupying a communal territory see it as an area that can be shared; consequently it is not defended as tenaciously as the den or living space. Such communal territories may cover some 50 acres (20 ha).

Cases where feral cats long reverted to the wild live alone in relatively uninhabited regions where food is scarce are rare. In such circumstances, a cat may prowl some 100 acres (40 ha), defending its boundaries against any other cat that ventures in. But obviously no one cat can defend such extensive boundaries 24 hours a day: it must pick and choose which transgressors to challenge.

All territories vary greatly in size. Of the several factors influencing this, food would seem to be the most important. Frequently, in urban areas where food is plentiful, many stray cats are found in a small area. Each has its tiny space or den, often not much bigger than itself, within a living area shared amicably with innumerable other cats.

Territorial marking

Territorial marking is of primary importance in the lives of many animals. This is especially true of cats, which are noted for leaving three different kinds of signals—two involving smell and one visual—to inform other cats of their presence.

A cat's sebaceous glands produce particular smells when rubbed against any object. The glands are found above the eyes on either side of the forehead, around the lips, and along the tail under the fur. When a cat rubs these parts of its body against a fence, a tree, or even its owner's legs, it is leaving its scent there. This is called marking.

Marking by smell constitutes a sort of 'visiting card' as well as a claim of territorial ownership. Other animals instantly

Cats leave smelly 'visiting cards' around their territory.

recognize the smell as belonging to a cat. Indeed, the smell provides very precise information on the sex of the cat that left the marking, on whether or not it was neutered, and possibly even on its state of health and temper. The sniffer can also deduce from the pungency how recently the mark was left.

Urine is also used for marking. All cats, whether male or female, neutered or not, mark their territory by leaving a few drops of urine in strategic places. This is distinctly at odds with the way they behave in the normal course of urination—when they spray on the ground, then cover it.

When marking with urine, the cat aims its spray not at the ground but higher up— roughly its own height. Thus the smell will readily reach the nose of any other cat passing by. This difference in the positioning of urine can provide useful information. If a cat has begun to mark in the house, its urine will be found on walls, curtains, and around the legs of chairs; but if the animal is simply incontinent because of a urinary infection, the urine will be found on the floor.

Cats also communicate with other animals by visual marking: they mark the places they use—tree trunks, upright posts, or furniture legs, for example—by scratching them with their claws. The cat finds it particularly soothing to produce visual markings because all the time it is scratching, it is also stretching and relaxing the whole body. Scratching hard surfaces is also useful in keeping the claws sharpened for hunting. Scratching is a very strong instinct that persists even in the most domesticated of domestic cats.

Since there is no fighting instinct involved in this kind of marking, it is best to try to limit the damage by sacrificing an old carpet or piece of furniture, or by buying or installing a scratching post (see page 205). Handling the problem of where the cat scratches can be very frustrating and difficult and may require the use of punishment (see page 231).

SEASONED TRAVELLER

When 15-year-old Kirsten Hicks of Adelaide, Australia, was going overseas with her family in 1977, she left her Persian cat, Howie, with her grandparents. So Howie settled in the Outback, some 1,000 miles (1610 km) from his former home. Then one day he disappeared.

A year later, back home in Adelaide, Kirsten was still mourning the lost Howie when a bleeding, bedraggled cat arrived on her doorstep. Neither she nor other family members recognized the cat at first. But when Kirsten picked it up, the animal snuggled into her arms, purring happily. No one had to wait until the cat was bathed to be convinced that Howie had come home. His incredible journey had spanned wide rivers, hot deserts, and the vast wilderness of the Australian Outback.

Obviously there will be times and places where you cannot permit the cat to mark as it sees fit. But it is important to realize that some marking behaviour is vital in a cat's life, enabling it to avoid confrontations and so live at peace in feline society.

Thanks to the 'visiting cards' it distributes around its territory, other animals recognize the resident cat's markings and, depending on the freshness of the marks, can tell if the cat is in the vicinity. In this way, cats organize their comings and goings as peacefully as they can, avoiding potentially unfriendly encounters.

This behavior illustrates a primary characteristic of feline social life, which is to avoid fighting and other domestic problems within a common living space.

Defending the territory

Although feline social life seems geared to avoiding fights whenever possible, cats can be quite resolute when it comes to defending their living space, especially their most private territory—their lairs or dens.

This defensive behaviour is most intense when a queen needs to protect her kittens. Motherhood gives her great courage, and to protect her offspring she is capable of attacking bigger cats, even dogs.

Territorial defence is more important for cats that remain unneutered than for neutered ones, and for wild or feral cats than for domestic cats. The arrival of an intruder does not necessarily lead to a fight.

On first meeting, cats take up threatening and intimidating postures. The protagonists begin staring at one another while padding slowly towards each other. They sniff each other's scent, and then the larger of the two attempts to control the other's movements, making various sorts of angry noises calculated to intimidate or at least 'test' its adversary. Its ears stand up and are turned slightly backwards, its whiskers bristle and point forward, its pupils contract and its forehead becomes wrinkled. Pursuing the advantage, the larger cat advances, staring the other cat in the eyes. The smaller cat cowers more, with pupils dilated and ears flattened. At this point, if it sees an avenue of escape, it will retreat slowly and resume a normal position a few cat-lengths away from its adversary.

Sometimes neither party retreats; then a fight begins, ending with the loser on its back and the victor on top, biting and scratching. The loser soon gives up and frees itself to run away.

Cats often defend their territory by threats alone. One animal usually backs down.

Fights, or even mere confrontations, are the basis of a fragile hierarchy; after a series of such encounters, the stronger cats attempt to extend their territory. But they do not necessarily gain supremacy, especially when they are far from home.

Often after several confrontations, two adversaries will come to a tacit agreement to respect one another's rights. This is most likely to happen if they are more or less equal in strength. However, size or status can change, and then hostilities resume until new borders are established.

Cats that share the same household relate to one another in a very similar way, but their confrontations are less violent and more ritualistic. Usually a hiss or a swift slash with a paw will settle matters.

Of course territorial defence extends beyond sibling cats to other house pets and even to people. This may explain why some domestic cats react aggressively when their owners entertain or have house guests. The cat regards the visitors as 'invaders,' but its attitude will become less chilly in the long run. It will warm all the sooner if the 'interlopers' do not back down or give the cat any reason to feel he has won any round in the 'Who's in charge?' wars.

You can count on about a month's adjustment whenever there is an addition to the household, whether this is a new baby, another cat or kitten, or some other pet. While a new balance of power is being established, the cat may do some posturing aimed at maintaining or even improving its status in the established pecking order. More often than not, peace returns.

Communal cats and their hierarchy

Feral cats and runaways often live on common territory in variously sized colonies. They prefer quiet fenced-off or otherwise secure areas with a good food supply, ideally an abundance of small wild prey and human food, especially thrown-away leftovers. Cemeteries, library and museum grounds, the basements of high-rise buildings, and alleyways behind retirement homes and hospitals are typical of places where such colonies spring up.

Cats in these colonies develop a very complex social structure, based in part on dominant and submissive roles. The concept of dominated and dominant cats is unfamiliar to most people, since by and large our knowledge of feline behaviour is limited to observation of one household pet. But people with two or more cats will have observed feline power struggles. And even in one-cat households, the pets try to dominate their owners. This is often the explanation for a cat's aggressiveness.

The dominant position in cat colonies is neither all encompassing nor permanent. A cat may exert power in some circumstances and be submissive in others. Generally a cat feels more confident the closer it is to home, and it will temper its behaviour accordingly. A healthy young cat will easily wrest power from an older

---

A SIX-YEAR SQUAT

Some cats, like some people, just want to be alone. Such seems to have been the case with Mincha, a black female that climbed a 40-foot (12-m) tree in Buenos Aires in the late 1940s and stayed there for more than six years. Local Argentinians used poles to provide her with daily rations. It also seems that a tom cat or two were granted visiting rights: Mincha had three litters in her tree-top home.

or weaker one. Unneutered cats will oust neutered ones, and cats neutered after reaching adulthood usually dominate those neutered before puberty.

A queen and her kittens form a dominant cohesive unit, resisting all intrusion by other cats. But within a single litter, some kittens will be more active and energetic than others simply because they are physically superior.

In groups of cats living free, the permanence of the hierarchy depends on the size of the territory, how extensively the ruling cat's authority is challenged, and how often he must fight to remain 'top cat.' (Feral cats are generally headed by the most powerful tom cat in the territory.) Hierarchical disputes are common, however, and fights occur often between the established occupants and young cats just reaching maturity that want to take over. Whenever the status quo is challenged, a number of confrontations, sometimes ending in fights, take place over several days until one cat is indisputably at the top of the heap.

Every now and then a ruling animal doesn't assert its prerogatives for a time, making way temporarily for a more submissive cat. When the former ruler wants to be reinstated, it will not openly attack its successor, although it will subject it to constant threats. Usually that's all it takes to get the more submissive cat to step down of its own accord.

With females, hierarchy is a function of reproduction. The older a queen and the

A group's stability is based on a hierarchy, but the pecking order often changes.

more litters she has had, the more power she exerts. There are clearly defined relationships between queen and daughter, or queen and granddaughter where they live together. The oldest female bosses her daughter, who in turn runs roughshod over the females of the next litter, and so on.

During courtship, a queen in heat calls the shots for the toms that pursue her,

becomes momentarily submissive in the act of mating, but within seconds resumes her snarling authoritarian manner. Paradoxically, the dominant male of a group does not necessarily have the right to mate with a queen in heat. She often prefers a less powerful, more submissive tom.

Cats that lord it over other cats not only have access to more territory than their 'subjects,' but also feed before the other cats and take first place in all the group's activities. Although age and sexual status are of great hierarchical importance, cats never yield to younger, more active, stronger cats until obliged to by age—at around 8 to 10 years of age—or when tired.

Not all feline relationships are determined by dominance or submisseveness, however. Within the group, cats also develop social, nonsexual preferences. They have grooming companions, playmates, and even 'friends' they prefer to sleep near.

The hunting instinct

Cats are predators, living off the prey they hunt down and kill. Since earliest times, their ability to reduce rodent populations has been recognized and it was largely for this reason that they were so venerated in ancient Egypt. By devouring huge quantities of rats and mice, they protected the stores of wheat that formed the major source of wealth for the peoples living along the banks of the Nile River delta. Cats kept European granaries rodent-free in the 1500s (see Chartreux, page 88) and, by devouring silk-worm-gobbling rodents, saved Japan's silk industry from annihilation (see Japanese Bobtail, page 101).

Nowadays wild and feral cats are still seen in European forests, living by hunting alone. They feed mainly on rodents, but also kill baby rabbits and fledgling birds taken from the nest, activities that do not endear them to bird and rabbit lovers.

Hunting behaviour is innate in kittens and is reinforced by teaching from the parent. Kittens at play are serving an apprenticeship. Observation brings instinctual patterns to the fore, prompting them to bat with their paws at anything that moves and bite anything resembling a mouse. These skills improve with practice, but initially are incorporated into play. A kitten is capable of hunting as soon as its neuro-muscular development is complete, at the age of 5 to 6 months. The kitten follows a parent and learns the basic tactics: lying in wait upwind, pouncing suddenly, immobilizing the prey with a bite to the neck.

Domestic cats no longer hunt out of necessity, since they are usually adequately fed. They hunt for pleasure, and are prone to proudly depositing their booty at the feet of their owners.

Long experience has taught us that a hunting carnivore's instinct to kill dimin-

Through the ages, cats have chased mice. Even in domestic cats, the instinct survives.

ishes as its appetite is sated. A hungry cat, seeing a mouse, will chase, kill, and eat it. A well-fed cat will still chase the mouse, but will take longer to catch it and will not eat it. The apparent cruelty with which a cat will toy with a captured rodent is actually due to lack of appetite. The cat's instinct has impelled it to catch the prey, but since it is not hungry, it plays with its victim without feeling the need to kill it.

The hunting instinct is still very strong, even in domestic cats. Toms especially carry out a sort of ritualized hunting behaviour involving their owners, attacking their legs, for example, as if they were legitimate prey. Such behaviour is often seen in tom cats living with elderly people. Perhaps the sound of shuffling feet, especially in slippers, resembles that of a prey fleeing through grass. This stimulus may

WILDCATS AND FERAL CATS

The world still supports a few rare specimens of wildcats of the species *Felis silvestris*. These are related to domestic cats descended from the Lybian wildcat. Domestic cats are probably a result of crosses between the two species.

The wildcat is stockier and stronger, with a striped tail like an alley cat and long thick hair of dark yellow. Unlike its domestic cousin, it has only one litter a year, which explains its rarity. A nocturnal predator, it owes its survival to its small size and night prowling habits, but it is becoming ever rarer and needs to be protected.

The domestic cat, although usually quite happy to live with human beings, sometimes feels a need to revert to the wild state. A cat that does this is called a feral cat. Queens who live out of doors sometimes have their litters there, and kittens born under such circumstances may later become domesticated by hanging around houses until they are adopted by the inhabitants. Other cats will refuse to return to civilization, preferring the wild life. They survive by preying on birds and various kinds of small animals.

These unneutered cats lead active sex lives and reproduce rapidly. The size of the territory they occupy depends on the amount of food available.

In the wild, feral cats become bigger and stronger than if they had remained domestic. The

Feral cats survive by hunting.

life they lead makes them more resistant to disease, especially to bacterial and viral infections. Not having been neutered, they continue to develop physically up to the age of 3 or 4. On the other hand, they are at risk from hunters and from other more powerful predators. They are often obliged to fight, and continual fighting weakens them. Their life expectancy rarely exceeds 8 to 10 years, almost half that of a house cat.

Populations of feral cats vary in size depending on living conditions and environment. Although they breed fast, many kittens succumb to disease or are killed by other animals. Within a given territory, the number of feral cats varies very little from year to year. Only those protected by humans in special areas increase in population.

This is the case with feral cats living in big-city cemeteries. They are safe from aggression, and people provide them with more food than they need. Animal welfare societies in some countries carry out sterilization campaigns.

Felis silvestris, the European wildcat.

unleash predatory behaviour in the cat, that pounces on passing legs with teeth and claws at the ready.

Although this is not truly aggression, owners should nevertheless refuse to tolerate such behaviour. It creates a special hazard for elderly people, who may trip and fall over a cat jousting at their ankles. The best solution is to distract the cat with previously established games.

The cat as 'landowner'

Within the cat's territory, be it a farm or a room, each cat in a sense owns a patch of 'land.' When there are several cats in one household, they often merge their territorial boundaries and join to 'defend' it. Outdoors, the scene is played out on a tougher scale: the city cat may defend an urban area only as large as a backyard, while a country cat may have to cover a huge area that also supports other wild animals. Within the territory the cat will stake out its favourite spots for keeping watch for marauders, and where it can sleep or relax in peace.

In the public territories, that is those not within households, backyards, or other private places where humans exert some control, the cats have a different and communal setup. One area may be designated for hunting, another for cats to meet, and yet another area left free for other animals, particularly dogs, to roam.

The indoor cat has no such gathering to attend and in some cases—especially if it was once an outdoor cat—it will become frustrated. Adding a second cat to the household is often the best solution.

Cats that wander over large areas of countryside not only defend their territory against all outsiders, but may also try to increase its size. However, they do this with noisy threats and aggressive behaviour rather than actual fighting. Sometimes they may try to encroach on a section of farmland, which the resident cat has trouble defending. Some male farm cats may try to protect as much as 150 acres (60 ha), but female farm cats tend to be content with one-tenth that space. Urban cats have the least space, and pets may be limited to their own and neighbouring yards. But such cats have no need to hunt for their food, so their limited territory is sufficient.

The ability of feral and domestic cats to thrive in such vastly different environments highlights their amazing adaptability. Rats in a maze will fight to the death to gain space, even when there is enough for each. Cats, however, survive well even in the most crowded conditions.

Social behaviour

Vocal communication

Since vocal communication is vital for human beings, we tend to be curious about the sounds made by other species. Do other animals understand these sounds? And what do they mean? Students of animal communication say that since cats emit sounds that have a specific meaning, these sounds constitute a kind of language. Cats, say the experts, use this language to communicate not only with their own kind, but also with people and even with dogs.

Experts divide cat noises into categories. One study by New York researcher Dr. Mildred Moelk separates cat sounds into three main groups: murmurings, vowels (calls), and high-intensity noises (cries).

Murmuring noises are low-intensity sounds made in peaceful situations with the mouth closed. The sounds are short and are usually made when the cat is enjoying something; perhaps when it is being stroked or groomed. They include a variety of purrs expressing moods ranging from anticipation and pleasure to dissatisfaction and distress.

The vowels, all variations of 'miaow,' are clear, easily differentiated noises made with the mouth opening and closing rapidly. Each vowel is used in a different situation—when the cat is asking for food or waiting for it, for example, or when it spies a pigeon out of reach on a nearby roof. A kitten's distress call when separated from its mother is one of the vowel sounds. Almost from birth, each kitten has its own

Each kitten has its own characteristic voice. A distress call alerts the mother, who will hurry to the rescue.

characteristic call, and in this way the mother can recognize which of her offspring is missing. Low growls are also included in the vowels category of sounds.

High-intensity sounds describe full growls, snarls, hisses, and various loud cries made in different situations. They are less specific and recognizable than the murmuring and vowel sounds, and are associated with normal events in everyday cat life. The cries made by tom cats in rut do not serve to attract females—their odour does—but seem spontaneously emitted. By the same token, the scream of a cat who has just received an injection is simply an instinctive expression of rage and fear.

Vocal communication is important in the relationships between people and cats. Neither cat nor owner will know exactly what is being communicated, but the mutual goodwill will be unmistakable. When trying to 'speak' to us, cats are attempting to get closer to us, who can never really know the feline world of smells, vibrations, and sounds. Domestication has enlarged their vocabulary of noises, and any owner can encourage a cat to 'talk' more. The more you do this, the better the response.

Body language and facial expressions

Like many other species, cats also communicate by means of body language and facial expressions. An animal's appearance, therefore, clearly expresses its feelings. The facial expressions, which a cat uses to communicate with its own kind or with its human companions, changes with the slightest shift in emotion. Not only do these expressions mirror the cat's mood, but they clearly communicate them to the world at large. And unlike people, cats cannot fake emotions. They only show what they really feel.

A happy, relaxed cat has a round face, upright ears, wide-open, normally dilated pupils and relaxed whiskers. An upset cat scowls, flattens its ears, narrows its eyes, and contracts its pupils.

The tail held straight up is a sign of welcome, but when the tail bushes up and flicks from side to side, it betrays agitation well on its way to becoming irritation. A cat with its tail between its legs is frightened and beaten, paralysed with fear. It probably will crouch on its belly next.

A happy cat arches its back when being stroked, and stretches to prolong the contact. However, an arched back and fluffed-up coat also occur in confrontations between cats. By standing its hair on end, the cat is hoping it will appear larger and more intimidating to its protagonists.

The forepaws can express a great deal. A light pat with the claws retracted is enough to quell a naughty kitten who is teasing its mother. A harder blow—with the claws out—is administered to an adversary or an owner who has scared it, or hurt it however unintentionally. Patting the owner's hand gently with the claws half extended is an invitation to play. It resembles the gesture of a cat playing with a toy.

All the signals used by domestic cats to communicate with their owners are the same signs they use for exchanging information with other cats. To understand them fully then, we must learn cat language, an effort they seem willing to make in reverse. They certainly observe us carefully and adapt their reactions to our behaviour.

Just how—and how much—cats 'talk' both to us and to other cats will probably never be known. What we do know is that cats have enough vocabulary—or perhaps it is the way they use it—to express many demands and emotions, from the obvious and persistent request to be petted or fed to the curious chatter made when a bird is spotted through the window.

Highly tuned senses

A cat has at least as many senses as human beings, and it certainly uses them for more purposes than simple survival. Apart from those pets that are never allowed outdoors, cats could not survive without their superb senses of smell, touch, hearing, and sight.

Vision

The cat's eyes, rounder than ours, are set in deep sockets and, like ours, protected by eyelids. But cats have a highly developed and mobile haw or third eyelid, called the nictitating membrane. In some illnesses, or when a cat is near exhaustion, this membrane may almost cover the eyeball.

A cat's vision is ideally adapted for hunting, an activity for which sharp eyesight is essential. Its eyes are wide enough apart to give it a total visual field of about 285 degrees, of which 130 degrees are three-dimensional vision. By comparison, the human visual field is 210 degrees, of which 120 degrees are binocular or three-dimensional vision: the cat's rounder eyeball gives it the wider angle of view.

Most cats see shapes almost as well as we do, and can judge distances with great accuracy. Siamese, however, tend to have less binocular ability—the capacity to focus both eyes on an object—than other breeds.

The many rods of a cat's retina are photosensitive in low light and provide excellent nighttime vision, although in rather soft focus. Under the microscope, various kinds of cells—primarily rods and cones—can be studied. The cones that are sensitive to blue and green are far fewer than in humans, and the cat has no cones that react to red. Because of this it was once thought that cats are almost colour-blind, seeing the world in predominantly pale blue. It is now believed, however, that cats can discriminate between large objects that are identical except for colour.

A cat's ability to see improves sixteen-fold between 2 and 10 weeks of age and cats retain good eyesight even in old age. Unlike dogs, they rarely develop cataracts or retinal degeneration. Only a progressive fading of colour in the iris betrays their age, and this does not imply any loss of function. The fading gives the iris a marbled look. Iris freckles are quite common in cats and are not cause for concern unless there is some change in their shape or size.

The sense of smell

All carnivores live primarily in a world of smells and, except for some hunting breeds, the sense of smell is as highly developed in cats as it is in dogs. It is clear from watching a cat approach an unfamiliar object that smell is of vital importance in identifying anything new.

Since kittens are born deaf and blind, their ears and eyes sealed, their sense of smell is paramount. It is the only tool they have for exploring their new world until they are almost 10 days old.

The mucous membrane lining the cat's nostrils is proportionately much more developed—and its surface area doubled—than the same membrane in humans. This membrane in cats contains some 19 million smell-related nerve endings compared to only about 5 million in humans.

The cat's smell organs include one that we do not have (although several other animals do): the vomeronasal organ, commonly called the Jacobson's organ after its discoverer. This small receptor-lined pouch on the roof of the mouth is also a prime example of the close links between the cat's senses of smell and taste. For the Jacobson's organ connects the cat's oral and nasal cavities and transmits messages to the hypothalamus, the section of the brain concerned with appetite and sexual behaviour.

It is pure myth that what we see as colour, cats see as pale blue: cats are not colour-blind.

When a cat presses its tongue against the roof of its mouth, the Jacobson's organ senses any solid particles the cat may have taken from the air. Should there be any pheromones (odour chemicals from urine and glandular secretions), the cat may react by *flehming*, appearing to grimace but actually savouring the smell. This often happens when a tom gets a whiff of a queen in heat. But the characteristic lip curling is also stimulated by other scents the cat enjoys, such as catnip (see box below).

The sense of smell helps cats find mates, identify friends and foes, tells them what cats and other animals are nearby, leads them to food and tells them which morsel is their favourite. Their noses are particularly sensitive to nitrogenous substances.

Hearing

Hearing is the third most important sense for a cat. Since cats often hunt very small animals that can easily hide from them, a cat needs more than good eyesight. The sounds of a small rodent attract a cat's attention, then its sharp sense of hearing enables the cat to unerringly find its prey.

CATNIP

Catmint or catnip *(Nepeta cataria)*, a sturdy perennial plant once used in cooking and for medicinal purposes, inspires odd behaviour in cats. This is caused by an oil the plant secretes to ward off insects that would otherwise eat its leaves. Cats may sniff at the plant or eat some leaves, but are most likely to indulge in ecstatic rubbing and rolling against the plant. In their excitement, some cats adopt the positions of an animal in heat. A few take up peculiar postures, remaining absolutely motionless for minutes at a time, and others indulge in imaginary hunts. Some observers have likened the effect of catnip on cats to that of psychedelic drugs on people.

Most domestic cats enjoy sampling other herbs besides catnip.

Cats' ears are small but very mobile. Some 10 different muscles enable the ears to turn 180 degrees to locate the origin of a sound. By analysing the delay between the reception of a sound in one ear and then in the other, the cat can determine within a paw's length where it originates.

The cat's hearing is similar to ours in the lower frequencies (around 20 cycles), but a cat can pick up much higher fre-

Especially outdoors, cats rely on their senses of sight, smell, hearing, and taste.

quencies than we can. They can receive sounds up into the 50,000-cycle range and are very sensitive to high piercing noises. Mice, however, can hear sounds up to 95,000 cycles, which is good enough to hear a cat approaching.

The ears also play an important part in communication between cats themselves. Flattened against the head they express fear; standing straight up they indicate good health and an even temper.

The cat's inner ears, like our own, are part of the balancing system that keeps the body upright and prevents falls and bumps any time the body moves or changes position.

The sense of taste

The sense of taste varies greatly from cat to cat and it may depend largely on where and how the animal lives. Like all good predators, cats seem able to eat just about everything they catch. However, domestic life may make them fussy, picky eaters.

All the cat's taste buds are found at the end of the tongue and along its sides. There are none on its surface, which carries only large, rough papillae used for licking and grooming. A few groups of taste buds at the back of the mouth complete the animal's tasting system.

The cat's innate tastes do not seem to vary much. Kittens have a natural appetite for their mother's milk, and are fond of other kinds of milk; most adult cats cannot digest milk at all, though some are very fond of it. Kittens especially seem to respond more to bitter, salt, and sour tastes than to anything sweet.

Cats also seem to be attracted by a number of foods that are bad for them. Most cats, for instance, adore lung tissue, which is of no nutritional value, and liver, which can be toxic in large doses. Regular daily consumption can bring on a very serious bone disease: rheumatoid spondylitis, a condition that may completely paralyse the animal and lead to an early death.

All cats prefer their protein in the form of meat or fish, are fond of foods with a high proportion of fats, and do not normally like vegetables or fibre. However, they should be fed a balanced diet (see page 198) since an all-meat or fish-only diet can cause severe health problems.

A cat's taste is formed early. A kitten that is always given the same kind of food will later have great difficulty adapting to others. On the other hand, if it is exposed to a number of different foods when young, its adult tastes will be more eclectic.

Cats may sometimes take a sudden aversion to previously relished food, rejecting it completely. It may be that the food made the cat sick, or it may associate it with some other unpleasant event. Either way the cat may continue making the cause-and-effect connection for six months or longer.

The sense of touch

Cats are sensual creatures that derive a great deal of pleasure from touch. When caressed, their whole bodies express delight and satisfaction. They love rubbing their bodies against their owner's legs and they devote a great deal of time to grooming themselves.

A cat's body is entirely covered with pressure and pain receptors that react to the lightest touch. Pressure on any hair is transmitted to sensory cells in the follicle and thence to the brain. Some hairs, stiffer and tougher than others—the guard hairs and especially the vibrissae—are particularly sensitive. These are mostly found as whiskers, but vibrissae also form the eye-

Tastes vary greatly from one cat to another.

brows, and grow in the elbows and the back of the paws above the pads in the forelegs. These bristles sense the movement of air, enabling the cat to 'feel' without touching and to make its way through the darkness without bumping into things.

The hairless areas of the cat's body—the nose and the foot pads—are the most sensitive. The nose reacts to the slightest sensations of heat or cold, particularly in food.

The skin of the foot pads registers the quality of the ground and any objects in the cat's path: it investigates by tapping lightly with its paws. The pads are also sensitive to sound waves or vibrations to the point that cats are generally believed to pick up tremors from impending earthquakes 10 to 15 minutes before people sense them.

Cats can tolerate more heat than we can and show no signs of being burnt up to a temperature of 120°F (about 50°C). Temperatures 10 degrees lower would cause people to feel burnt. This high tolerance for heat may explain why cats sometimes actually singe their fur by venturing too close to a fire in their search for heat. They are also much less sensitive to cold than we are, since they are protected by fur and have the ability to curl up to help retain heat. To get warm, they start to burn calories at a much lower body temperature than we do, at about 50°F (10°C).

The cat's sense of touch is vital to its survival. By providing information about danger, it reduces the risk of injuries. Touch is also very important in the relationships between people and cats, since a cat's evident enjoyment of its owner's caresses is one of its most endearing characteristics.

Purring

Kittens purr almost from birth in response to their mother's licking and grooming. Adult cats also purr to express pleasure, but a queen will sometimes purr during labour, and some cats purr when confronting a potential aggressor, when very ill or badly injured, and even when dying.

What causes purring? We still are not certain, but there are two main theories. The first and most likely maintains that the sound is caused by the vibration of two membranes, called false vocal cords, found in cats in the larynx behind the true vocal cords. Put your hand gently on the throat of a purring cat and you will be able to 'feel' the sound coming from near the voice box. However, this theory fails to explain why the purring seems to come from the animal's entire body.

According to the second theory, purring is the sound of the blood's turbulence when

The cat's hair- less nose leather is one of the areas most sensitive to touch and temperature.

the superior vena cava (the large vein extending from the top of the chest to the heart) is compressed by the cat when it arches its back.

Whatever the true explanation, purring is one of a cat's most unusual and endearing characteristics. Many people are charmed when a cat purrs at their proffered friendship, considering it proof that the animal is happy to live alongside them.

But although purring often seems a pleasurable response to the owner's attentions, its primary function may be communication among cats, especially between a mother cat and her kittens. The sound helps the kittens find their mother in the first weeks before their eyes open. And although newborn kittens will not purr when stroked by people, they do purr when they are suckling. This way the queen knows that all her kittens are feeding well.

Purring also seems to have a calming effect in feline confrontations. Some people feel it actually has a tranquillizing effect on the producer of the purr, which would explain the purring of an injured cat or why a queen in labour purrs between contractions.

The sound, then, remains something of a mystery.

Few other animal species purr, although bear cubs have purrs as loud as motorbike motors when they are nursing.

Cats can communicate

Purring of course is just one form of cat communication. Fear or dissatisfaction, for example, may be succinctly expressed by snarls, spits, and hisses. And cat fanciers also believe that cats have a wide vocabulary of miaows that mean different things depending on the way they are produced— long or short, soft or loud, relaxed or intense.

Studies of feline vocalization suggest a cat's vocabulary contains up to 100 different sounds, some of which are vowel sounds, others consonants. Queens use a particular chirruping sound to recall kittens to the nest, and other distinctive sounds to let her offspring know whether the prey they are hunting is a mouse or a larger rodent.

Nevertheless, some cats rarely 'talk' at all, except for a peremptory miaow when they want something. Other cats become quite agitated when trying to communicate, and keep on miaowing with intensity until someone responds to their needs. Often, a cat's miaowing, like a baby's cries, is simply its way of saying it is hungry.

Cats under stress—during a visit to the veterinarian, for example—tend to emit a continuous series of long moans quite unlike any sound they produce at other times. And different breeds tend not only to have different cat 'dialects,' but distinctive communication styles. The Persian, for instance, issues short sharp bursts of sound that might be interpreted as: 'Come on, dear owner, I need....' Siamese on the other hand tend to be chatterers, using a combination of sound and body language to grab the owner's attention.

Then there is the peculiar shuddering sound a cat makes when it is indoors watching a wholesome-looking bird outside, in territory the cat regards as its own. It occurs when the cat's jaws begin to shudder in a mechanical and strange-sounding way. This may be the cat's inherent killer instinct taking over. As it watches the out-of-reach prey, it automatically goes through the lethal motions required to down a juicy dinner, although it will likely have to content itself with eating its regular cat food in the family kitchen.

But while the cat's vocalization is not always easy to interpret, its body language is generally unmistakable. Above all tail and tummy are instant giveaways. A swishing tail is a sign of an unhappy cat, whereas a cat with tail aloft and curving slightly is confident and content. A cat at peace with the world will relax on its back and offer its tummy for stroking. A cat with fur bristling is on the defensive, and the whole world can tell that one with lashing tail, smooth fur, and pricked ears is poised for the attack.

Purring is one of the cat's most distinctive characteristics, endearing the animal to its human companions.

CAT NAPS

Cats are great sleepers. An adult cat, in good physical condition and fully active, spends 60 percent of its time sleeping. However, a cat's sleep pattern differs from that of humans. The cat does not sleep for a period of six to eight hours. Instead it sleeps for short stretches which alternate with periods of wakefulness scattered throughout the 24 hours of the day.

The cat's sleep is divided into two quite distinct periods. Phases of light sleep last from 10 to 30 minutes. Electroencephalograph recordings taken during a cat's light sleep show a slow, irregular, wavelike pattern. Although the cat is lying down during light sleep, its muscles are not completely relaxed, and it is quickly awakened by even the slightest sound.

Periods of deep sleep are shorter, each lasting a maximum of 10 minutes. Electroencephalograph recordings taken during deep sleep resemble those from periods of wakefulness, showing periodic bursts of low-amplitude, high-frequency waves of electrical activity. The cat's body, which is extremely relaxed, may be observed twitching briefly and occasionally, and its legs may move. Deep sleep is also characterized by rapid eye movements, which is called REM sleep.

Human beings dream, an activity essential to our mental well-being. Humans prevented from dreaming can suffer hallucinations and other aberrations. As for cats, their brain activity during their phases of deep sleep is similar to that of dreaming humans.

There is no way, however, of establishing the content of their dreams. It is tempting, of course, to imagine that as a sleeping cat growls and moves its paws it is in swift pursuit of some idealized dream-mouse. But we have no way of knowing what goes on in a cat's mind.

Owners have their own interpretations of the sounds and movements their cats make during periods of deep sleep. But these interpretations are usually projections of the owner's own dreams.

One thing is certain: cats do dream. This is reflected in brain activity that has been observed during laboratory tests. This activity has been found to be similar to that of humans in the same state.

The sleeping pattern of the domestic cat sometimes varies slightly according to the situation it is living in at the time.

An animal left alone during the day in an apartment, for example, sleeps a good part of that day. It becomes more active in the evening and at night when its owner is home to pay it some attention. Cat owners, however fond they may be of their pets, do not always appreciate this increased activity.

Older cats sleep more and more, often lying around for long periods as they did when they were kittens, when they spent up to 80 percent of their time sleeping.

Social life

Sexuality

Puberty

Female cats, or queens, become sexually mature between 7 and 12 months of age. Males, or toms, reach puberty at about 9 months. Purebred cats or cats kept indoors may reach puberty later. Health and nutritional status are other factors that influence the onset of puberty.

The female cat experiences the feline heat cycle—oestrus—when she is ready and willing to mate. The cycle lasts two to three days and occurs at two-week intervals. It is repeated during a specific season of the year. For example, in northern temperate regions, the season extends from February to October, with peaks in March or April, June, and September. Generally, the cycles cease between October and December. The cessation may be due to the reduced light levels at that time. Daylight and weather conditions are known to stimulate the hormones that control feline sexual function.

Just before heat begins, a queen is extremely affectionate, rubbing and rolling on the floor with enthusiasm. When heat begins, she becomes restless, howls and calls stridently, and tries to get out of the house to search for a mate. If the queen in heat is stroked, she may take up the mating position: front end pressed to the ground and rear end raised in the air with the tail stiffly bent to one side. If mating does not occur, the queen eventually relaxes until the next cycle begins. If mating occurs, she will produce a litter two months later.

After males reach puberty, they can reproduce for the rest of their lives without interruption. (However, sexual activity may diminish in the autumn.) This is the time when the male begins wandering and fighting with other toms for the attention of females. The tom also marks his territory with a pungent spray, which is a mixture of urine and anal-gland secretion. It is a sexual attractant. Meantime the female produces odorous secretions, known as pheromones, which serve to attract male cats.

Mating and fertilization

In female cats, an ovum (egg) is released from the ovaries only in response to the sexual act. The feline reproductive system differs from the human system, where ovulation occurs regardless of sexual intercourse. (Cats are known as reflex ovulators; humans, spontaneous ovulators.)

A queen in heat stimulates the male's interest by her scent and her inviting calls. Initially, she repels his overtures by clawing and snarling. The tom accepts the rejection, but renews his advances. After several advances and retreats, the queen relents and begins purring and rolling

The mating relationship between cats involves courtship rituals and sexual aggression.

provocatively. Eventually, the queen assumes the mating position. The tom mounts the queen from behind and grasps the scruff of her neck between his teeth. The neck bite, together with the stimulation of the male's bony, spiny penis, triggers the process of ovulation. Almost as soon as the penis is introduced, ejaculation occurs. It may be accompanied by a short, sharp howl from the queen.

The sexual act lasts no more than a few seconds. When it is ended, the queen wrenches away from her partner, often sending him on his way with a swipe of her claws. The tom moves off a little way, where he sits or lies watching the queen and grooming himself. At the same time, the queen goes through a display of rolling, rubbing, and stretching. Five or 10 minutes later, the cats resume mating.

Cats may mate up to eight or 10 times an hour. Sometimes the female may mate with several partners, one after the other, until all are exhausted. If fertilization occurs as a result of the mating, heat immediately stops. The queen's litter appears about two months later.

In female cats, the prime years for fertility last from two to seven; in males,

from two to eight. Experts advise using a queen for breeding only after she is 1 year old. A queen can produce on average two litters of two to six kittens a year. The litter sizes diminish as the queen grows older. Cat owners who wish to prevent pregnancies are advised to have a female neutered (spayed) at 4 months. If cat owners wish to keep a male cat, particularly for indoor living, it is best to have him castrated at 6 months. Castration inhibits urine spraying.

Development

Birth and maternal behaviour

The gestation period for queens lasts on average 65 days. The most common sign of pregnancy is a change in the colour of the queen's nipples from light to rosy pink, which occurs about the third week of pregnancy. At this stage, veterinarians can diagnose the pregnancy by careful abdominal palpation and by ultrasound. They may also use X rays in the sixth week of pregnancy.

During the first month, the pregnant queen seems physically unchanged. However, she grows quieter and eats more than usual. During the second month, her abdomen is noticeably larger. Physical changes may restrict the queen's activi-

The minute they are born, kittens are protected and cared for efficiently by their mother.

ty in the final stages of pregnancy. But daily light exercise will help to maintain good muscle tone, essential for easy birth.

Preparing for birth

A pregnant queen needs a well-balanced diet. The feeding instructions on commercial cat food products should be followed carefully. The veterinarian may recommend vitamins, minerals, or other supplements. Medication, vaccination, and worming should be avoided during pregnancy.

A large kittening box in a warm, comfortable, and secluded area should be prepared about 10 days before birth. However, the queen may reject it for a quiet spot of her own choice. Some queens give birth in a discreet corner of the house; others prefer places, such as their owner's bedroom, where they can be near people.

During the last weeks of pregnancy, the queen's mammary glands swell. Milk secretions can be seen just before birth. Owners are advised to start taking the cat's rectal temperature from the 55th day onwards. When the temperature falls from 101.5°F (38.5°C) to 98.6°F (37°C), delivery follows within 48 hours.

Stages of labour

The first stage of labour lasts up to six hours. It begins when the cervix opens up and a plug of foetal tissue passes into it from the uterus. At this point, a clear vaginal fluid may appear. When this happens, involuntary contractions of the uterine muscles begin. The queen heads for the kittening nest, where she breathes rapidly, purring and panting, but in no distress.

The second stage lasts 10 to 30 minutes. The queen intensifies the involuntary uterine contractions with voluntary contractions or straining ('bearing down'). Eventually, the birth sac—the fluid-filled membrane enveloping a kitten—appears at the opening of the vulva. With a few more contractions, the queen pushes out the kitten. The placenta or afterbirth, which has nourished the embryo, is quickly expelled thereafter.

The kitten usually appears head first, but the breech position (tail end first) is also normal. As soon as the kitten is born, the mother bursts the birth sac and begins to lick the kitten's head so that it can breathe. She bites off the umbilical cord about 1 to 2 inches (2.5-5 cm) from the navel. In the meantime, the kitten makes its way to its mother's nipple and settles down to suckle in peace.

The birth of successive kittens in the litter follows the same pattern. At the end of each birth, the queen eats the placenta. This instinctive habit was originally developed to ward off predators, but it still provides nourishment for the mother until she leaves the litter.

The time between the births varies considerably. It may be as brief as five minutes or as long as two hours. In some cases, a queen delivers half a litter and stops for 12 to 24 hours before completing the delivery.

Labour problems

Cats rarely have trouble giving birth. Generally, cat owners should tactfully oversee but not interfere with a delivery. Too much human meddling may distract a young queen. If labour problems occur, contact the veterinarian immediately. This is essential if a queen fails to deliver kittens after bearing down for more than two hours, or if she stops bearing down altogether. In an extreme emergency, put the queen in a warm padded box and take her by car to the veterinarian.

The kitten's development

At birth, the kitten weighs about 3.5 ounces (100 g)—2.5 ounces (70 g) at least, 5.3 ounces (150 g) at most. It is born deaf and blind, possessing only the senses of taste and touch. The kitten has just enough sense of smell to find its mother's teat. Hearing develops at about the fourth day, although the auditory canals are not open completely until the end of the second week. The eyes open in 7 to 10 days. Sight and hearing are fully developed only by the third month.

Immediately after birth, a kitten finds its own particular teat on the mother's breast that it uses until weaned. The teat has a characteristic scent. Avoid bathing the mother because it washes away the scent. If this happens, the kittens become confused and start to fight.

During the first two weeks of life, the kitten lacks strength, coordination, and mobility. The kitten remains in the bed-

The socialization of the kitten starts with play and games in the first weeks of life.

ding area, cuddled against its mother, sleeping for nine-tenths of the day.

At first, a kitten is extremely sensitive to cold, because it cannot regulate its temperature. The mechanisms for regulating temperature—muscular shivering and the bristling of the fur (piloerection)—start to develop about the third week. By the sixth week, they are completely effective.

The kitten is able to walk and get back to its den after the third week. It regularly leaves the sleeping den to explore its surroundings during the fifth week. At this stage, it also begins to climb. The kitten is completely mobile by roughly the eighth week.

Nourishment for kittens

During the first month, kittens rely on their mother's milk for nourishment. By pushing their forepaws against the mother's breast, the kittens trigger the reflex that provides the milk. Some mothers cannot always provide enough milk for their offspring. In these cases, the fretful kittens cry a lot. A veterinarian can correct the problem with a hormone injection.

If a queen dies or shows no interest in her offspring, ask a veterinarian for milk replacements. Cow's milk is unsatisfactory because the nutritional balance is not right for kittens. There are commercial formulas that match the queen's milk.

At 3 weeks of age, the kitten can start eating solid food. A commercially prepared kitten food can be used. If the queen's supply of milk is inadequate, mix solid food with a milk replacement. This will speed up the weaning process. By two months weaning should be complete.

The kitten learns cleanliness from its mother. In the first days of life, the mother licks the kittens vigorously, which stimulates defecation and urination. She keeps the sleeping den clean by swallowing all waste. Once the kittens are mobile, they are encouraged to relieve themselves somewhere away from the den. Towards the end of the third week, they begin burying their own waste, covering it over with litter or earth.

The socialization of the kitten

The behaviour of the adult cat depends on the kind of attention that it received as a kitten. When proper stimulus is lacking, there is a risk of excessive aggression, anxiety, and other behavioural problems in adulthood.

At 2 months of age, kittens are fearless and full of curiosity about the world. Fears born out of experience have yet to take root. Now is the time to undertake the kitten's social education. In a calm atmosphere, introduce the kitten to any other animals living in the same house. If a kitten is meeting a dog for the first time, make sure each is under control.

Put orphan kittens in contact with other mature cats as soon as possible. Orphans deprived of early contact with their own kind frequently show fear and aggression towards other felines. Early introductions help orphans to learn the behaviour pattern of their own species.

Similarly, introduce other human beings to establish a sound pattern for good future relations. It is best if several different people gently stroke or hold the kitten several times a day.

Kittens' games teach basic feline skills.

Lessons learned from mother

During the first weeks, the mother cat instils in her kittens the principles of feline life. By washing her kittens, she implants the lesson of keeping their living area clean. Her licking also stimulates urination and defecation. Reflex control of these functions develops quickly. By the third week, a kitten learns control and relieves itself well away from the sleeping area.

The mother's licking also keeps the kittens' fur in good condition. The sheer pleasure of the experience encourages kittens to groom themselves. The habit of grooming, starting the first week of life, is purely personal at first. At a later stage, it becomes a shared experience. By grooming each other, kittens reinforce group ties.

The mother also provides lessons in hunting and food-finding techniques. By a process of imitation, observation, and play, kittens acquire all the skills to survive as adult cats.

Learning through play

A kitten born in a litter is rarely alone. With its brothers and sisters, the kitten experiences a wide range of play activities, such as chases, fights, and even surprise attacks on the mother. Kittens learn by playing with simple household objects: empty thread spools, corks, or ping-pong balls. There is a wide range of special cat toys available. For example, a toy bird may satisfy the kitten's awakening hunting instinct.

Play is the essence of the feline learning process. Boisterous games sharpen physical and mental abilities. Fighting between kittens rarely results in injuries or loss of blood. Play also furthers muscular development. It heightens the animal's awareness of the dangers in its surroundings. This, in turn, awakens prudence and circumspection. Finally, play increases the social skills and sociability of the kitten. A kitten's development is rapid during its first six months, which is roughly equivalent to the first 10 years of human life (see page 235). What a kitten learns through play in its formative months cannot be taught later. Orphans, or kittens without brothers or sisters, that are denied contact with other cats, usually grow up fearful, nervous, and antisocial.

Grooming behaviour

Cats spend much of their time grooming. The habit is the basis of their reputation for extreme cleanliness. Some people believe they can predict the weather by watching a grooming cat. A common sight is a cat passing a licked paw behind its ears. According to folklore, if a cat spends a long time washing behind its ears, the weather will be fine. (Other people believe the same activity foretells a storm.)

Grooming keeps the cat's fur in good condition and calms its nerves. The cat combs its fur by licking. A few drops of saliva dampens the fur and keeps it shiny and in good condition. It is the cat's saliva, not its fur, that sets off human allergic reactions.

Licking removes dust, small bits of vegetation, and parasites, and smooths out tangled fur. Old cats unable to reach certain body areas due to arthritis or obesity may have tangled fur. Knotted fur becomes extremely dense and damages the underlying layer of skin. Owners can ease the problem by careful grooming of the old cat. In the long-haired breeds, such as Angoras, the fine fur tangles easily. Daily grooming with a soft brush keeps the fur in top condition.

The grooming habit is passed from the mother cat to her kittens in the earliest days of life. At birth, she licks away the birth fluids. Later, she cleans their bottoms to encourage regular bowel movements and urination. Once the kittens are mobile, they start to lick each other. The activity strengthens bonds between litter members and reinforces group relationships. Gradually, the kittens acquire grooming skills. By the age of 5 or 6 weeks, they have become completely responsible for their own toilet.

Grooming also has a calming effect. When the cat licks itself, it becomes peaceful and relaxed, impervious to outside disturbance. After a prolonged washing, the soothed cat falls asleep.

Grooming problems

A smooth and shiny coat and a normal grooming behaviour are signs of good health and psychological well-being. However, owners should watch grooming behaviour carefully. It is the basic indicator of their pet's overall condition.

Cats with behavioural problems often groom excessively, spending virtually all their waking hours washing. Such activity causes skin irritation which stimulates the desire to lick more. It may cause serious skin lesions and result in self-mutilation. If a cat develops these symptoms, consult a veterinarian immediately.

Toilet training

From an early age, cats are naturally clean. As soon as they can, kittens leave the sleeping den to excrete. This instinctive behaviour is reinforced by the fastidious care the mother devotes to her offspring during the early weeks of life. Thanks to her, their bedding den is never dirty. The kittens learn to follow her example.

Cat owners appreciate their pet's clean habits. Few owners would be prepared to run round their house or apartment cleaning up after a cat. Kittens aged between 2 and 3 months learn quickly, in a few days at most, to use a litter box.

If the kitten has already been trained by its mother, all the owner has to do is show it where the box is. You can also put the kitten in the box and move its paws in a digging motion. In the case of an untrained kitten, just pick the animal up gently and place it in the box.

For successful toilet training, put the litter box in a quiet spot where the kitten feels comfortable and private. Never chastise a cat if it has an 'accident' during toilet training. It is important to instil positive attitudes about the litter box. A kitten may reject the box if it is confused or upset by punishment.

Cats prefer different kinds of litter. Owners can choose the best kind for a particular cat from a wide range of commercial litters (see pages 199-200).

When using litter boxes, follow these rules: First, keep the box away from where cats eat. Avoid any high-traffic areas in your household where people pass by frequently.

Grooming always has a soothing effect.

Kittens are easily toilet-trained

Second, provide mineral litter. After cats relieve themselves, they cover their wastes by scratching around the immediate area. Modern mineral litters enable cats to gratify this instinctive behaviour.

Never fill the box with excess litter, or leave the litter unchanged for a long period. Clean out solid waste every day. This prevents an unpleasant smell from permeating the house.

Change litter completely every week or 10 days, depending on the amount of soiling. If a dirty litter box is left unchanged, a cat may eventually refuse to use it and relieve itself elsewhere in the house.

If a cat suddenly starts soiling, it may be ill or experiencing some other kind of distress. When the problem arises, consult a veterinarian as soon as possible.

Keeping a house clean is easy if there is only one cat about. Problems may arise if the number of cats increases beyond three or four. To ensure the house stays clean and odour-free, install several litter boxes. If some of the cats are unneutered males, the smell of their spray may spread throughout the house. It is best to have the males neutered to curb spraying and to reduce combative behaviour. Domestic female cats rarely spray indoors, except under stress.

Training a cat

It is often said that humans cannot train cats. The animals are said to be too independent to accept even the slightest constraint. This is simply not true. With gentleness and patience, cats can be taught to live as pleasant companions in houses and apartments. However, it is unrealistic to expect that the animals can be trained as police cats or watchcats. Unlike dogs, cats are not inclined to obey a leader. Only kindness and gentle persuasion will win their co-operation.

Getting to know a mature cat

Before any training begins, it is best to get to know your cat. A newly arrived, adopted or stray animal sometimes has problems adjusting to its changed circumstances. A mature cat with well-established habits and traits is likely to be upset when it enters new territory and meets unknown people. By contrast, a kitten, whose only training has come from its mother, is usually fearless and ready to learn whatever its human companions wish to teach it.

If a mature cat is defensive in its new home, it is unwise to create further stress by imposing a training programme at the outset. There is usually a period of adjustment, which lasts roughly two or three weeks.

During this period, owners should ensure the animal is properly fed and its litter box kept clean. It is best to set aside time to observe the cat and to consider which habits should be encouraged or curbed.

The mature cat will also assess its new family and learn which reactions elicit approval and disapproval. The future domestic relationship between cat and owners depends on the outcome of this period of assessment.

The mature cat sometimes reacts badly to change. For example, if owners switch furniture around, the animal may be disoriented. When guests arrive, it may take a dislike to them and act up. Such bad behaviour may continue until the visitors leave. Careful training may eventually modify some of these minor, but unnerving behavioural excesses.

Getting to know a kitten

Training a cat requires time and patience. But the process is usually easier with a kitten. Unlike dogs, cats are not inclined to accept or obey a leader. However, a kitten may see its new owner as a mother substitute, who must receive the same obedient response as the mother cat.

At the age of 2 or 3 months, a kitten is rarely afraid of anything. It usually arrives in the new household with the basic skills imparted by its mother. These skills can sometimes startle its new owner. If a kitten is the offspring of farm cats, it knows how to catch mice. During its first weeks, it watched its mother stalk, attack, and kill mice and other prey. A kitten reared in this way may carry on the hunting tradition and seek its owner's approbation by depositing prey at his or her feet.

Hazards and heights

If a kitten is settling into a new home, leave it to explore its new territory in peace. Close the door and windows to prevent the kitten from straying outside.

In a calm and relaxed atmosphere, introduce other people or animals in the

However far a cat falls, it gracefully arches its back and always lands on its feet.

In high rises, today's kittens face an unexpected danger. Nothing in their short experience can prepare them for the phenomenon of great height. 'Parachute cats' are often reported falling from high balconies and open windows. Some survive, but not all. Owners who live in high rises must be careful that their pets avoid this fate.

Success with reinforcement

The success of any cat-training programme depends on discouraging unsuitable behaviour and teaching the animal to do whatever you want it to do. This is best done by reinforcing—or rewarding—acceptable behaviour. Reinforcement with occasional tidbits is effective, particularly if a cat is hungry. But it loses much of its impact if the animal is spoilt, overfed, or obese. Social reinforcement—caresses, games, and tender words—demonstrates love and appreciation, and strengthens the ties between cat and owner. A stroke, a tickle under the chin, or a light massage of the neck are excellent ways of reinforcing good behaviour.

You must decide what reinforcement works for your cat after observing its conduct. Reinforcement must be effective to maintain a balanced and well-integrated relationship with the cat.

Discouraging bad behaviour

A gentle reproof may be all the punishment that is needed to keep a cat in line. A cat quickly learns the mood and tone of displeasure in your voice. It will respond appropriately if admonished firmly. If, as sometimes happens, you are amused at the same time, a cat may detect this and not take you too seriously.

To ensure good behaviour, follow these rules:

Discourage unwanted behaviour as soon as it occurs. A cat only associates a reproof with an activity that it is doing. Never admonish a cat for some misdeed

house to the kitten. Use play and games to train the cat, and mild reproofs only if its curiosity leads to mischief or danger. Painful experiences will teach the kitten where household hazards are—a stove ring burns its paw, or a door slams shut on its tail.

long past—for example, if you discover the cat scratched the furniture or stole food from a cupboard while you were at work.

Use indirect means to discourage the cat. For example, rattle a rolled newspaper while saying 'No!' firmly. You can use the paper to tap the cat lightly on the nose, or to thump the floor near the cat. (*Never* strike the animal.) A water pistol or water spray is another effective deterrent.

Try to dissociate yourself from the reproof. If the cat associates you with a water pistol, it may misbehave if you are not around to squirt some water its way as a means of enforcing good conduct.

Avoid any anger that may instil fear in the cat. In some cases, the cat may not understand why it is being admonished. If repeated, your anger may awaken its aggressive instincts.

Finally, apply reproof systematically until the unacceptable conduct has disappeared.

Controlling natural behaviour

Unacceptable feline behaviour—digging up the soil of potted plants, scratching wood or upholstered furniture, or stealing food—is nevertheless quite normal. It would be absolutely essential to the animal's survival in the wild. It is therefore dangerous to suppress this behaviour entirely, because other more serious problems, less easily resolved, may surface afterwards.

A cat must be allowed to indulge in its instinctive behaviour, but in a place especially reserved for the purpose where it will not be punished. For example, if the animal starts sharpening its claws on carpets, furniture, drapes, wallcoverings or anything else, provide a scratching post for the purpose (see page 205). A log or an old piece of wood may serve just as well. Or, if possible, take the cat outdoors where it can scratch trees or fences without causing any damage.

Making your cat happy

Some cats always seem calm, relaxed, and satisfied, whereas others are nervous, unapproachable, and aggressive. The owner of a difficult cat may be at wit's end trying to understand and deal with a problem animal. In desperation, he or she may consult a veterinarian. The outcome may be a realization that owner and cat are simply not made to live together.

Some people are just not suited to sharing life with a cat. This can be true even when external conditions seem ideal: a

---

TRICKS AND TELEPATHY

If you are going to teach your cat tricks, it is best to begin the training as early as possible. You can build on some instinctive activity that the cat already enjoys, such as hunting, retrieving, or jumping. For example, if you want the cat to jump through a hoop, start off with the hoop at floor level. Try to get the cat to walk through the hoop by tempting it with a favourite tidbit. Gradually raise the hoop until you can get the cat to jump through at the desired height. Training takes time and patience but, if successful, the cat may delight you and your guests with its stellar jump.

Do not expect miracles of performing skill from cats. You can teach them tricks, but getting them to perform on cue is another matter. Few cats have succeeded as stage or circus entertainers. During the 16th century, the citizens of Brussels devised an 'organ of cats' (see page 40) as part of a royal procession. The infamous musical contrivance amused a public whose only idea of entertainment was taunting and torturing cats. Its popularity faded in the late 18th century. Cat concerts, also known as 'Maiulique' shows, were staged at French fairs during the 1700s. A cat opera was performed near London's Haymarket in 1758. In our modern times, the Moscow State Circus has included feline stars. The Russian trainer Yuri Kouklachev claimed he took three years to teach his cats how to jump over hurdles, do handstands, and play chess.

You can probably learn as much from cats as they can from you. They delight in playing games—according to their rules—which involve chasing or retrieving. Frequently, cats initiate an activity to catch your attention—for example, sitting on the open pages of the book you are reading.

Some of the ploys cats use in play are essential for their survival. It may be amusing when a cat summons its owners by rattling objects, tapping on doors, or leaping up to push a doorbell. But these skills may help to alert owners to a problem. Cats always find their way home, no matter how far afield they wander, and some even have the ability to open the front door of the house when they get back. For a cat's convenience, it might however be best to install a flap door. According to some experts, cat's everyday skills are supplemented by a sixth sense. For example, cats detect vibrations better than humans can. In a quiet house, a cat raises its hackles in alarm as if reacting to vibrations or sounds we cannot hear. Some say cats have telepathic powers. However, it may simply be that their senses are more acute and efficient than ours.

---

quiet home atmosphere, adequate food, and lots of affection and caresses. And yet, the animal is not happy.

Sometimes it seems that it takes more than good living conditions and kind owners to make a cat content. Cats require certain other subtle and often imperceptible qualities from their human companions. A kind of telepathy may exist between cats and humans: it certainly seems that some people communicate better with cats than others. They are more sensitive to the animals and understand them better.

Respect is one key to making a cat happy. We shouldn't force our affections on our pets. Some cats dislike excessive caressing and fondling. If your cat is like this, wait until it approaches you before stroking and petting it.

Another key to the cat's happiness is providing a certain amount of outdoor freedom. Many cats enjoy basking in an enclosed sun porch or patio. Some cat owners have constructed special outdoor houses or gazebos for their feline companions to enjoy the outdoors.

The solitary cat

Since the beginning of the 19th century, the domestic cat has become a much beloved pet in households everywhere. By throwing in its lot with humans, the cat evolved from a wild animal to a companion. However, a companion is sometimes a prisoner in its owners' home.

Some cat fanciers believe the tame cat, unlike its wild relative, was easily domesticated because it never attained full adulthood. Eternally young, the domestic cat has attached itself to humans to ensure its survival. Nevertheless, the domestic cat needs a social life. It needs to meet and to play

The solitary cat develops a close relationship with its owners in the absence of any interchanges with other cats.

with its own species, other animals, and people.

However, a cat's life is often solitary. If it starts life as a kitten in an apartment, its social contact is strictly limited to its relationship with its owner. Some cat

lovers consider the situation unnatural. Yet, cats raised in these circumstances usually adapt perfectly and show no signs of disturbed behaviour. This may be because the animal has never known anything else. Without other life experiences, the cat moulds itself to the nearest available person, and appears satisfied with whatever its companion has to offer. However, a cat quickly reverts to the independent, instinctive ways of its species. If it returns to the wild it will adapt with little difficulty.

Sleep and games

A solitary cat may become bored, particularly if it is entirely dependent on its owner or its own imagination for diversion. It sleeps more than other cats and compensates for its lack of activity by eating too much. Eventually, it becomes fat and out of condition, and devotes most of its waking hours to asking for food.

A solitary cat frequently invents its own games. It tears up cloth scraps, chases dust balls that accumulate under furniture, or just sits in the window watching the birds. It may also make ritual attacks on its owner's ankles. Male cats living alone with the elderly sometimes do this. Outdoors, this kind of aggressive behaviour is usually directed against real prey.

Owners who are concerned about the well-being of their solitary cat may decide to provide it with a companion. This excellent idea has drawbacks. Problems occur when owners introduce a cat of a differ-

Cats can share cramped quarters but they may be uncomfortable and unhappy.

ent age, or an animal of another species, into a household where a pet is on its own. The pet is unlikely to be pleased when it sees its territory invaded by a stranger. In these cases, there is always a crisis of adaptation. The original animal acts aggressively towards the newcomer, sulks, and goes off to hide somewhere in the house. This difficult period lasts a few weeks. But, in some cases, it continues as long as the two animals share the same household.

The best solution is to adopt a pair of kittens of the same sex at the same time. They can grow and play together from the start, and establish a sound relationship for life. Owners who adopt two cats of the same sex avoid problems arising from the development of feline sexuality, which begins at the age of about 8 months.

Too many cats?

Some owners opt for several cats—sometimes too many. They love cats and, as long as they can provide food and care, they are happy to live in a household overflowing with cats. Unfortunately, the cats themselves may be unhappy, particularly if space is limited. Nevertheless, they can adapt to crowded quarters. For example, they will organize a hierarchy to avoid repeated fights.

Too many cats can create problems. The household may slip into a dirty, messy, and smelly state. Such uncomfortable conditions are undesirable for people and cats.

WHEN CATS WORK

Cats were workers before they became companions. In ancient Egypt and mediaeval Europe, farmers employed 'the harmless, necessary cat,' as Shakespeare called it, to protect the grain supply from the depredations of rats and mice. In the Far East, cats kept rodents from chewing sacred scrolls and books in libraries.

Today cats are on rodent patrol in offices, factories, storehouses, museums, and other public buildings. The champion of the lot is Towser, who was born in a Scottish distillery in 1963, where he continued working until he died in 1986. According to the *Guinness Book of Records*, Towser caught some 28,889 mice—an average of three a day—during his lifetime. (See also Awesome exterminators, page 219.)

The elderly cat

Until the age of 8 or 10, a cat normally enjoys excellent health. From that time onwards, the cat begins to experience the first problems related to advancing age. It may suffer arthritic pains and kidney disorders, and its muscles will begin to atrophy. All these physical problems can obviously affect a cat's behaviour.

As a cat ages, it becomes more placid, and it also begins to sleep more. The cat spends about three-quarters of its time sleeping as it nears the end of its life. It moves about slowly and embarks on new adventures reluctantly. Usually, it prefers to stay safe in its favourite spot, on top of a cupboard or on a windowsill. With age comes a concern for physical comfort. The cat often chooses to sit in a sunny spot or near a radiator or heat vent, where it can warm its old bones and muscles.

Changes in mood and appetite

An elderly cat may become finicky about food. With a diminishing appetite, the cat may sort through its meals, picking out only the choicest bits. In other cases, aging cats become bulimic. That is, they eat incessantly and demand food continually.

Grooming habits change with age. An elderly cat no longer maintains its coat with the same care. Its fur may become dry, damaged, and tangled. The cat's mood, too, may deteriorate. It becomes more bad-tempered, irritable, and less tolerant of strangers. When the cat meets unfamiliar animals, it may become aggressive. Or, as is often the case, it may become conscious of its physical deficiencies and slink away to an isolated corner to sleep.

From time to time, unneutered males go prowling in an attempt to recapture something of the sexual excitement of their youth. However, they are likely to be losers in confrontations with younger, stronger toms. They often return home scratched and bitten. To end these exhausting battles, it is best to have the old males neutered. (If owners want a male cat for indoor living, it is preferable to have him neutered (castrated) at about 5 to 6 months of age. The operation reduces urine spraying, which begins with the onset of puberty.)

Female cats continue to experience oestrus—the feline heat cycle—until they die. However, the cycles occur further apart with advancing age. An old female cat can give birth to kittens, but her litters grow smaller and smaller, sometimes consisting of only a single kitten. The litters in later life put a great deal of stress on the female cat's whole body. Therefore, a veterinarian may recommend an ovariectomy (spay). This operation enables the female cat to finish her days in peace and under good conditions.

In old age, a cat needs care from all members of the household, a continual assessment of its state of health, and a suitable diet to make the final years a time of serenity and comfort.

Cats and children

It is easy to understand a child's fascination with a kitten—a little ball of fur that miaows and jumps around, and is so soft to stroke. A child likes the animal's independence and curiosity. Nothing amuses a child more than watching a kitten struggling with its first piece of meat or playing with a ball of paper or a piece of string. Moreover, a child quickly learns to respect a kitten after receiving a quick swipe from its claws.

The cat is frequently a solitary creature. It provides the kind of companionship particularly appreciated by children. The cat also serves an educational purpose. Unlike an inanimate doll or a teddy bear, it not only receives attention and affection, it also returns it. Its demands are few: some caresses and a kind word or two.

Learning from cats

The presence of a cat introduces the child to the animal world. Moreover, it helps the child to develop a sense of responsibility for another living creature. In return, the cat offers its warmth, softness, and playfulness.

A cat can also bring children together. It acts as a kind of social go-between when a child entertains: visiting young friends may wish to play with the creature, or

A cat is an ideal companion and playmate for a young child.

simply touch or admire it. The cat's beauty and elegant movements also provide an early lesson in aesthetics.

If a female cat in the family household is used for breeding, the arrival of a litter is always an exciting event for children. It is the perfect opportunity to observe the miracle of birth. Even very young children want to lend their support when a litter arrives. Later, nursing and raising of kittens put such children in close contact with other facts of life and growth.

AS CATS AND PEOPLE AGE

Compared to people, cats have short lives. A cat of 20 is very old. This table shows an approximate comparison of cat and human ages:

Cat's age	1	2	4	7	10	15	20
Your age	15	25	40	50	60	75	105

And a cat has only one life—not nine!

Some parental concerns

Nevertheless, some parents worry about keeping cats, fearing that cats and children together may simply create havoc in the house. They may also be afraid of cats because they believe some of the myths once used to perpetuate an anti-cat prejudice. According to one myth, a female cat will jump into the cradle of a newborn and try to suffocate it. Although there is no evidence that this has happened, the myth persists. However, it is highly unlikely that a cat would sit for long on a squealing, squirming infant.

Another parental fear is that cats may transmit illnesses. It is true that cats and humans suffer from some of the same diseases. But the diseases are treatable—ringworm, for example—or they can be prevented by vaccination and other medical treatments (see Zoonoses, page 186). One health problem is the allergic reaction triggered by the cat's saliva. If this is the only cause of an allergy, you should find another home for the cat. If there are unrelated allergy triggers, it will be more difficult to decide whether the cat should stay or go. A major consideration will be how upset the child might feel if separated from its well-loved companion.

Dogs and cats

'Getting along like cats and dogs' is a popular expression in many countries and cultures. It can denote the close relationship between children or the antagonism between two adults. It can also be used to describe the nature of the ambiguous relationship that exists between our two favourite domestic animals. Generally, cats and dogs get on reasonably well together.

Some breeds—terriers and hunting dogs—remain resolutely hostile towards cats. Fierce hatreds sometimes occur between adult specimens that live outdoors and share the same territory.

First encounters

In urban or domestic settings, cats and dogs meeting for the first time may engage in a game of chase and intimidation. The cat may delight in taunting and teasing the dog. This stimulates a dog's ancestral hunting instinct. The dog pursues the feline intruder. The wily cat may run away or scamper up a tree. Sometimes it threatens its adversary with claws and screams. But, at an opportune moment, the cat dashes away, leaving the dog barking in fury and frustration. Such encounters are usually not serious and rarely

Cats and dogs living in close proximity can often become best of friends

end in a real fight. Because the two creatures do not know one another and do not live together, they revert temporarily to the instinctive reactions of their wild ancestors.

Cats and dogs that share the same household can learn to know and appreciate one another, and often become the best of friends. Many play together free from the fear of attack or retaliation. Female dogs have been known to nurse orphaned kittens. Orphaned cats that were nursed by canine mothers are usually friendly towards all dogs. This attitude may lead to some nasty surprises if the cat encounters dogs unused to its friendly ways.

Introducing new arrivals

Owners need to take special care if they decide to introduce one species into a household where the other already lives. A dog may be willing to accept a defenseless kitten. But a solitary adult cat may be very unhappy if a dog is introduced into its household. It may threaten the newcomer and go off to sulk on its own. The situation is likely to be complicated if the newcomer is an inexperienced puppy that fails to understand the cat's warning signals.

After two or three weeks, the two creatures may come to terms with each other and accept the fact that they are going to be sharing the same household. Unfortunately, their relationship may never achieve the closeness of a dog and cat raised together from an early age.

The cat as companion

The cat became part of the human household about 3500 years ago. Since then, it has learned to please its human owners and to gain their appreciation. The capacity to adapt to different living situations makes the cat an ideal companion. Many apartment dwellers opt for cats as pets because the animals can happily live indoors. Families choose cats because they are less demanding than dogs. For the housebound, the cat can be a comforting and unsweringly devoted presence.

Some cat owners are surprised by the pet's concern if they are ill or depressed. A cat's display of affection is reassuring when things go badly. Just stroking the animal has a relaxing and calming effect that relieves tensions. The cat is wholly dependent on its owners and looks to them for the fulfilment of its needs. Providing for a cat can bolster a sense of responsibility and self-esteem.

The cat is a superb pet for the elderly, particularly the housebound. The two can

Spanish cellist Pablo Casals (1876-1973) with small feline friend.

share common activities, which occur at regular times according to an unchanging schedule. An elderly person and a cat often share mealtimes.

In difficult circumstances, the cat is a model of calm and tranquillity, and a comfort to someone in need. In some instances, the cat provides support for people with physical and mental problems. This may be its finest role and its most significant contribution to the human race.

The cat as healer

During the 1970s therapists first realized that cats have a beneficial effect on the physically or mentally ill. In some cases, children lying in coma recovered after a cat was introduced into their lives.

In 1974, Canada was host to the world's first conference on pets and therapy. One speaker, Dr. Michael Fox, an American veterinarian and animal behaviourist, whose books include *Understanding Cats* (1974) and *Love Is a Happy Cat* (1982), said learning to care for a pet made people more sympathetic to human suffering.

In Texas, a study of 100 men and women who had suffered heart attacks indicated that patients with pets had a better chance of recovery. Cats are used in some hospitals and homes to help people overcome or cope with disorders ranging from heart disease and brain damage to drug addiction and alcoholism. Some psychiatrists believe the animals provide an outlet for feelings that might otherwise remain locked in the subconscious of the emotionally disturbed.

Behavioural disturbances

The domestic cat lives in circumstances far different from its wild ancestors. So it is not entirely surprising that it still has problems adjusting to our society. Life with humans has compelled it to develop a special form of communication. Some of us, unfortunately, do not understand what cats wish to communicate. The cat's failure to adjust and our lack of understanding can trigger serious behavioural problems.

Generally, cats are well balanced. Veterinarians who are specialists in animal behavioural problems report only one case in 10 concerns cats. The most common feline faults are aggression, fear, and dirty or destructive habits. Depression and stress create less obvious behavioural problems. Because the cat is naturally quiet and retiring, and poses no obvious difficulty, owners may decide to leave the animal on its own even when they suspect something is amiss. However, depression and stress require specialist attention.

Aggression

A certain amount of aggression is entirely normal in the life of all animals. It establishes social hierarchies and it also strengthens and protects groups and individuals. It is considered abnormal only when it becomes excessive.

Aggression is a feature of feline sexuality. For example, a female cat threatens and even fights with the male before she permits him to approach her. Males also clash violently when competing for the same female in heat.

In female cats, aggression ensures the survival and well-being of the species. A mother cat retaliates fiercely to protect her kittens and to defend her territory from outside danger.

However, feline aggression may cause problems if it is directed against its owners and other people, or against other pets.

Aggression may take the following forms:
• Territorial aggression is a violent reaction by the cat to an outsider entering its territory or its living space.
• Predatory aggression is rooted in the cat's natural hunting instinct. The cat may play games in which it pursues and ambushes its owner or other individuals. Unfortunately, its overexcitement sometimes transforms a harmless attack into an episode of violence.
• Reactive aggression is displayed when the animal becomes violent due to physical pain, caused by internal diseases such as cancer, joint disorders, or ear diseases, or external injuries such as blows or bites.
• Deliberate aggression occurs when the cat wants something. It deliberately provokes its owner in order to obtain some desired end. For example, it might threaten or scratch, hoping to get a gentle stroke.

The antisocial aggression is closely linked to fear. It is common among cats whose early life was spent outdoors and without human company. Because the cats are unused to people, they remain hostile to them in adulthood. Some of these creatures may learn to accept a particular individual, but their conduct towards other humans is violent and distrustful.

An aggressive cat poses problems for its owners, especially if its violent behaviour becomes established and ritualized. It may even get steadily worse. Any treatment of these problems must be based on

Excessive aggression is a distortion of the cat's natural behaviour.

an analysis of all factors contributing to the outbursts.

Once the cause of the aggression is known, the owners can decide on how best to calm the cat. The owners themselves may occasionally modify their own behaviour. Sometimes the cat may be neutered to reduce any sex-related aggres-

---

STRESS AND DEPRESSION

Cats are sensitive and react as we do to disturbances in their surroundings. This state of tension is marked by symptoms of fear that can lead to aggression, excessive grooming, which can end in self-mutilation, and anorexia or bulimia. A cat may also suddenly become dirty in its habits and may even, in serious cases, abandon its territory to go and live elsewhere.

Depression affects animals that no longer have any defence against the stress to which they are exposed. It may occur, for example, in a cat whose territory has been invaded by another animal and who imagines it has lost the affection of its owners. Or a cat may become depressed if it has been used to living outdoors, and is suddenly moved to a closed apartment. An elderly cat receives less attention from its owners, because it is less lively, and more bad-tempered than it once was, and may pushed into a depressive state.

The main symptoms of depression in cats are prostration, isolation, aggressive behaviour, and anorexia or bulimia. To be effective, treatment must be started early. Behavioural therapy conducted by the owners and appropriate medication if necessary can, however, produce excellent results if the problems are caught in the early stages.

---

sion. The use of tranquillizers, sedatives, or other behaviour-modifying drugs is highly debatable. The results are difficult to control and only temporarily effective.

There is no doubt that an aggressive animal can be a real problem. However, with our increased understanding of feline behaviour, it is possible to improve some aspects of a cat's demeanour and modify adverse reactions. Getting rid of a cat or putting it to death are extreme solutions, which should be considered only as a last resort.

Fear

Initially, the wildcat feared humans. It was a nocturnal animal that lived in deserts or forests, where it could elude people. The process of domestication erased mistrust. The cat has gradually become accustomed to the presence of people. Nevertheless, it retains some of its ancestral fear. If the animal is highly socialized, it hardly shows. The fear is least evident where the relationship between cat and owner is extremely close.

An animal that lives alone with its owners and spends much of its time sitting on their laps loses virtually all inbred suspicion. It feels free to behave towards its human companions exactly as it might towards other cats. It feels at liberty to impose its will, to become head of a household, and to develop the aggressive behaviour typical of a dominant cat. When a cat knows no fear, it may be difficult to live with.

A moderate degree of fear has its advantages. It ensures that the owner has some control. The cat may enjoy helping itself to food on the family table, but it may be wary of doing this if it is afraid of punishment or verbal rebuke. Fear makes the cat less resistant when it takes medicine or gets a brushing. It enables the veterinarian to examine a cat without undue difficulty.

Some cats are fearful of particular situations. In alarm, they adopt a prostrate position: chin tucked in and ears flattened sideways. They are ready to fight or take flight.

The worst kind of fear can lead to panic. The cat becomes uncontrollable, ready to do battle with all its teeth and claws. The terror puts the cat in a really dangerous state. Although its fury usually lasts only a few minutes, it leaves everyone present aghast and at a loss as to what to do.

This panic, entirely unpredictable and uncontrollable, usually has its roots in a fearful event or encounter in early life. The panic may sometimes resurface when the cat is exposed to the original cause of its terror. If its owner cannot protect the cat from the source of its fear, the condition worsens. The animal becomes abnormally aggressive and, ultimately, impossible to be around.

The only solution is to remove the cause of the fear, if possible, and to adopt a calm and understanding attitude. If this can be done, some improvement is possible. But treating a fearful cat is a difficult and lengthy process, one that requires patience and fortitude on the part of the owners.

A detailed analysis of the cat's present situation and its past history often throws light on the source of the problem. It is best to set up a programme that enables the cat to grow accustomed to what it fears and to teach the animal how to live with it or avoid it.

Generally, the cat gradually forgets its fears and can resume a normal life, at

The face of feline fear—dilated pupils, bristling hair, and flattened ears.

least as long as it is protected from confrontations with the original source of its panic.

Behavioural disturbances related to food

The feeding habits of cats living in the wild and of those that live without much contact with humans are often better than those that live with people. For example, neutered animals raised in a pen, and provided with appetizing food that is renewed every two hours, react in the same way: every 24 hours, they eat 20 or so small meals spread throughout the day and the night. Their overall intake stabilizes rapidly after a few days, they remain in good physical condition, and they do not get fat.

Yet in their daily practice veterinarians are constantly encountering household cats that are obese and, conversely, others that refuse to eat. Obviously, the animals' owners and the conditions of their home life play an important role in feeding problems.

Bulimia is the exaggerated consumption of food. Some conditions such as diabetes, and certain drugs such as cortisone and some hormone medications, can cause a cat to develop an abnormally big appetite. As a result, it becomes significantly overweight.

Such digestive disturbances can only be diagnosed and treated after a full biological examination. But if there is no physical disorder, then the disturbance is clearly behavioural.

Bulimia affects two categories of cats: those that are pushed to eat more by their owners, and those that are depressed or suffering from stress.

Feeding one's cat should be a great pleasure. The animal purrs and rubs itself affectionately against its owner's legs. However, some owners offer their cat too much food, and even stroke it while it is eating. For some owners, this ritual is a genuine pleasure, probably a response to their own anxiety. Gradually, the cat reaches the point where it is absorbing two or three times its required food requirements. It is the victim of a bulimia created directly by its unsuspecting owner.

But other cats seem to develop an excessive appetite without the help of human stimulation. They are constantly begging for extra food or attempting to snatch it while the owner is not looking. These animals are emotionally disturbed and are attempting to deal with their stress by overeating, as others do by overgrooming. Cats that display this behaviour frequently live under difficult conditions that aggravate their anxiety and, finding no other outlet for their unhappiness, turn towards food. But an obese animal opens itself to a number of illnesses.

To treat bulimia, veterinarians prescribe diets that are often as ill-received by the owner as by the cat. The animal frequently becomes aggressive during the treatment, which must be implemented gradually over several months and must consist of special food. Sometimes the animal simply refuses the prescribed diet and never gets down to its normal weight. With this disorder, as with any other, prevention is better than the cure; the problem should be treated the minute the first symptoms appear.

Anorexia, the opposite of bulimia, is the refusal to eat. It may be the result of some illness, or be an acquired behaviour. In some cases the cat refuses to eat anything whatsoever. In others, it is selective—the cat appears not to eat, but actually consents to accept certain foods.

A cat may suffer from bulimia, or excessive overeating, due to stress or poor feeding habits created by its owner.

Complete anorexia is usually a side effect of all the more serious illnesses a cat can contract. The affected animal simply stops eating, and will not regain its normal appetite until the underlying condition is treated or cured. Complete anorexia is rare, however, in cases where the cat is not physically ill. A cat may eat significantly less than it does normally if it is nervous, or during a period of sexual activity, but it is unlikely to stop eating altogether.

Partial, or selective, anorexia, on the other hand, is common. Cats are often quite finicky about their food and have well-defined likes and dislikes. Sometimes, a cat may refuse its food for several days, or as long as a week, simply because what is offered is not to its taste or evokes an unpleasant memory. In these cases, anorexia is temporary and disappears as soon as the animal is given different food. However, when an owner reacts by offering an alternative food, this tends to encourage pickiness about the kind or quality of the food. If anorexia recurs, consult a veterinarian and then make every effort not to give in to the cat's every whim. But this is easier said than done.

Dirty and destructive habits

Normal behaviour associated with territorial marking and a certain amount of scratching is to be expected from cats living in apartments or in homes where they do not have access to the outside world. Neutering adults and training kittens can help prevent these problems.

Sometimes, however, more specific measures are necessary. Abnormal urination can be a behavioural problem or the result of an illness. The possibility of an illness can be confirmed or rejected following a veterinary examination and urinanalysis. In the absence of any physical disorders, unruly urination and defecation, or urinating or defecating in inappropriate places, are most likely deliberate soilings. There are a number of possible reasons for such behavioural problems. The first is an absence of proper training. A kitten may never have been long enough in surroundings where it could learn clean habits. For example, it may have been kept too long in a pet shop cage.

Some animals become dirty because the litter they are offered is different from the kind they have used before. Cats raised in the country, for instance, are used to grass and soil and may not take well to a tray or box filled with mineral litter. The cat may also develop an aversion to its usual litter box. This is often the result of putting the box in a place where the cat feels uncomfortable using it. It may be because it is too close to the eating area, for example. Or, it may be because something disturbing or traumatic happened to the cat when it was last in its box.

Finally, stress and emotional upsets can cause soiling. (These negative influences are extremely wide-ranging and are often difficult to identify. It is only by establishing the cause, however, that a cat with dirty habits can be cured.) Get advice from a veterinarian or from an animal behaviour consultant, since professional help in identifying the cause is often necessary before any remedy can be found.

All too frequently, an owner's first reaction is to punish the cat. To avoid such a mistake, keep in mind that there is always an underlying problem directing your cat's behaviour. Rather, you should try indirect punishment like rattling a newspaper in its direction and saying, 'No!' or 'Bad cat!'

Generally, punishment won't work, and the cat will continue its dirty habits until the source of its stress has been removed and it has been calmly taught to behave differently.

Marking territory by scratching furniture is done mostly by young kittens. If your indirect punishment methods are well conducted, this bad habit should disappear. At the same time, train your cat to use a scratching post (see page 205). Wave a toy in front of the post and whisk it out of the way as the cat lunges for it, so that the cat's claws sink into the post. After a few games the cat will get used to the feel of the post. Jiggle the toy in the air to make the cat climb up the post. Play this game two or three times a day.

Some adult apartment cats may become destructive as a result of being lonely and forced to suppress their natural urge to mark their territory. Give them toys, such as objects that roll or that squeak when pressed, and stimulate them to be active by playing hunting games with them whenever you can. If your cat is young, consider getting another cat for it to play with. As a last resort, pet owners occasionally have their cats permanently declawed (see page 203).

Some cats destroy certain houseplants because they like their smell or taste. Spray these plants with a cat-repellent aerosol. If you have no garden, provide your cat with a box planted with herbs, such as catnip (see page 222), thyme, sage and parsley, and grass.

The future

The social status of cats

Feral cats or tame cats that have gone back to the wild have no legal status and are more often than not regarded simply as nuisances. Are they wild animals that deserve protection, or domestic animals that have strayed away from their homes and which may be subject to some urban or rural bylaws?

Unfortunately, the law does not take these animals into account. Some people believe they should be rounded up by the dog-catching authority and sent to the local pound where, if they continue to be unclaimed or adopted, they will be put to death. Animal lovers in some countries, on the other hand, fight for the survival and rights of stray cats.

Domestic cats that have, in effect, a fixed home address are the object of real protection. Once registered and with proof that they have been vaccinated against diseases such as rabies, they become fully recognized entities. For a number of years now, they have been perceived as animals with rights rather than mere chattels. Like all living things, they have the right to live in reasonable conditions, to be treated well, and not to suffer needlessly.

Unfortunately, many unidentified cats end up in laboratories or are released into the wild and left to fend for themselves, once their owners have decided the cats have lost their initial appeal.

Animal protection associations

There are numerous animal protection associations throughout the world, but they vary widely in size and authority. Basically they are formed by groups of volunteers, animal lovers who dedicate themselves to taking in, caring for, and eventually finding homes for the animals they protect.

Some protective groups operate with government funding; others depend on donations raised in various ways. The animal pounds run by municipal governments, humane societies, and cruelty prevention associations like the Society for Prevention of Cruelty to Animals (SPCA) take care of many of these stray or unwanted cats.

There are also thousands of people who make homes—sometimes good, but often unsanitary—for large numbers of unwanted cats until local authorities step in. In the past, many cases like this have ended with the cats being taken to the pound and put to death.

Inevitably, the various animal protection groups are forced to destroy a great many animals, under carefully controlled, strictly legal conditions. It is hardly surprising that many members of these groups find it a difficult job. If they have too many stray cats in their pound they have no alternative but to put them to death, even though their mandate is to keep all cats alive.

With the aim of enlarging their activities and strengthening their financial structure, many of these associations have opened clinics, where people of limited means can take their pets for checkups and treatment. Often local veterinarians volunteer their time at such clinics.

Nearly all animals adopted from SPCA and humane society shelters are already castrated or spayed. The only exception might be kittens too young for this procedure—less than 16 weeks in the case of females, 36 for males. Some shelters refund the adoption fee when an owner later produces proof that the animal has been neutered.

Controlling the cat population

The problem of too many cats has been a matter of concern to animal protection agencies and municipal authorities for decades. The cat population is increasing all over the world, and no more so than in North America. A 1966 survey revealed that there were 35 million cats and 48 million dogs in the United States alone. By 1987 those populations had increased to 56 million cats and 51 million dogs. In that year, cats outnumbered dogs for the first time in North America.

Cat food sales have increased tremendously too. In the United States cat food sales doubled during the 1980s to reach an incredible $2 billion a year—more than the amount paid out for baby food.

The overpopulation of cats is a problem mainly in large cities, where cats can find shelter, food, and care relatively easily, without fear of the larger predators that still roam the countryside.

Tattooing gives a cat a permanent identity that can be easily checked.

Feline overpopulation is a phenomenon of contemporary life.

Two complementary methods have been adopted to control the cat populations of urban centres: the capture and elimination of abandoned cats, and sterilization campaigns conducted with the assistance of veterinarians and animal protection societies. But the results have been disappointing.

The World Health Organization (WHO) recommends vasectomies for males and hysterectomies for females. These interventions have the advantage (for the males) of leaving the cat incapable of reproducing, but not castrated. The animal remains able to prevent strange cats from invading its territory.

Neutering by castration reduces the cat's status in the feline hierarchy (see page 216). When the animal returns to its territory, it is quickly chased away by uncastrated newcomers that continue to reproduce at an alarming rate.

Contraceptives have also been tried. The first contraceptive pill for cats was tested out in the 1980s with great initial success. But this did not last, and the pill was gradually replaced by neutering. This was partly due to the problem owners had making sure that the cat had taken its pill and partly due to the difficulty some owners had administering the pill.

Contraceptive pills for female cats are still available in some places. Different kinds affect the cat's body in different ways. The progestogens, like the human pregnancy hormone progesterone, cause a false pregnancy and increase appetite and weight; these progestogens can be taken as a pill or through injections. A modified version of this pill, proligesterone, is both a safer pill and has fewer side effects.

Another method of contraception inhibits the hormone that triggers the female sexual cycle. This hormone, called gonadotrophin, can be inhibited by means of certain drugs which arrest the oestrus cycle. If you decide your cat should try one of these contraceptives, you must first consult your veterinarian.

Sterilization procedures are the same as for humans: the male can have a vasectomy and the female have her fallopian tubes tied. Neither procedure interferes with the cat's sexual activity and, in effect, prevents it from breeding without desexing. But many owners reject these simpler methods of contraception simply because the sexual caterwauling and other activities associated with reproduction, which they find offensive, continue.

The cat populations of the world's major cities can only be effectively controlled either by the recommendations of such groups as the World Health Organization, or through the use of some form of birth control. Proposals to capture and eliminate abandoned cats are loudly criticized whenever these measures are discussed. Some animal lovers suspect that the fate of animals treated this way would not bear close scrutiny.

The cat protection associations have had good effect in some countries, however. In France, for example, the École du chat has succeeded in giving the stray urban cat a status of its own. This association identifies animals by tattooing them. It also has them vaccinated and sterilized and maintains them within clearly defined areas—the cemeteries of Paris for example. This gives these stray urban cats genuine legal status, and has been a successful and effective experiment in population control.

PROTECTION FOR CATS

The movement to protect domestic animals from overwork and cruelty began in early 19th-century Britain. The wealthy landowner and parliamentarian Richard Martin—who was dubbed 'Humanity Martin' by George IV—led the movement. In 1822, the British Parliament passed the first 'preventive act against the cruel and unjust treatment of animals.' Two years later, the world's first humane society was organized by Martin, William Wilberforce (the anti-slavery leader), and others. In 1840, at Queen Victoria's command, its name became the Royal Society for the Prevention of Cruelty to Animals (RSPCA). Similar organizations were set up in France (1845), the United States (1866), Canada (1869), and elsewhere.

Today, domestic cats receive the same widespread and effective safeguards as other animals. Humane societies, as well as organizations concerned specifically with cats, provide shelters and homes for strays and unwanted cats, veterinary care, legal protection, and funds for research into cats' diseases, behaviour, and genetics.

International cat shows

Cat shows are usually sponsored either by individual cat clubs or by the more formal umbrella associations under which the individual clubs fall.

The shows themselves may last two days, as in North America, or only a day, as they often do in Europe. They usually take place in winter, when the cats' fur, particularly that of long-haired breeds, is thicker. At one extreme these shows may be run on rigidly formal lines; at the other end of the scale, they may be more like social occasions. For many years, and in many countries, informal cat shows have been part of local country fairs.

The one thing the formal shows always have in common is that they strive to exhibit the best cats of various breeds, even non-purebred cats. Their goal is to choose the best of each category as a standard for future specimens of each breed.

New breeds and new colourings are also shown, and advice is exchanged between breeders and competitors.

The first shows

The first cat show predates all the modern organizations and is believed to have been held in England, in 1598, at the St. Giles Fair in Winchester. By today's standards it was quite a different affair, with cats shown in cages and judged according to their looks as hunters. Records of that 400-year-old show have been lost, but the top award may well have gone to the champion mouser. Later shows saw owners parading around the show ring with their cats, but these often ended in a free-for-all.

The first formal cat show was held in London's Crystal Palace exhibition hall in 1871. It was organized by the English artist Harrison Weir, who wrote many of the rules that govern cat shows to this day. In those days, the more common short-haired cats were shown; later, the long-haired Persians bred for show dominated the competitions. Nowadays, the two are often presented in the same exhibition, though some shows are restricted to longhairs, others to shorthairs.

Today, the largest cat show in the world is claimed by Britain. There, the National Cat Club organizes a show each year in which more than 2000 purebred cats and 500 'other' cats take part.

An early U.S. show, held in 1881 at Bunnell's Museum on Broadway, was not a complete success. A reporter from the *New York Times* observed Mr. Bunnell standing in the middle of his museum, fingers bandaged and a deep scratch on his nose. He was surrounded by cats 'half of them yelling, spitting and scratching, as mad as cats can be in uncomfortable quarters and in a strange place.'

Despite Mr. Bunnell's unfortunate experience, the idea of formal cat shows along the British line spread fairly rapidly in the United States and then to Australia, Canada, New Zealand, South Africa, most of Europe, and Japan.

The first major formal U.S. show was held in New York in 1895 at Madison Square Gardens. At that show, a male Maine Coon won top honours out of more than 170 cats on show.

Harrison Weir, who organized that first cat show in 1871, standardized the 'points of excellence' for show cats in 1889. The Persian was required to have a silky, fine coat on both body and tail. The Angora was to be woollier, the tail more like a fox's brush. The Russian was to have a woollier coat still; its tail was to be shorter and fuller than the Angora's, but with a blunt, tassel-like end.

In European cat shows, the judges' remarks and scores are kept secret until the end of the competition.

The North American style of judging is a lively, entertaining affair with comments made public as the cats are being judged.

The colours accepted in the show ring for longhairs were black, white, blue, grey, red, and any other self-colour. Tabby cats could be brown, blue, light grey with white or silver. Weir's idea was to standardize the characteristics around the world, but that has not happened. Instead most of the registration bodies have set their own standards, which vary from group to group.

Cat shows today

Cat shows are essentially beauty contests, in which both males and females are allowed to enter. They are not solely for purebred cats either. They may be organized to exhibit only pedigreed cats, or to exhibit only one breed of cat, or they may be wide open to all breeds, pure and otherwise, including the mongrels of the cat world—Household Pet and Any Other Variety animals. However, the pedigrees usually reign supreme.

Pedigree cats are judged according to a scale of points for their breed. The scale goes up to 100 points. Cats will lose points if some of their characteristics do not come up to the standards set for their breed by the particular club or association holding the show. (See Breeds, pages 66 to 136, for the characteristic standards set by TICA, The International Cat Association).

Unlike most dog shows, cat shows allow cats that have been neutered or 'altered' to compete in their own special class. Most shows present cats in four cat-

egories: Kittens—unaltered cats that are 4 to 8 months old; Championship Class—unaltered cats of 8 months and older; Premier or Peerless Class—altered, or neutered, animals of 8 months or older; Household Pets—cats that do not conform to any standard characteristics. This last category has its own titles and awards.

Most shows then pick the Top 10 or Top 20 cats and, finally, the Best in Show is selected. In Europe, a cat rated a champion by two associations is called a double champion, by three a triple champion and so on, up to four.

Usually, before a cat can compete in a show, it must have a veterinarian's certificate showing it has been vaccinated against major feline infectious diseases and that it is healthy.

Once it has passed that test and been registered with the association running the competition, the cat is eligible for the show. It will be judged on its general appearance, its condition, colouring, fur, and whether it has the breed's standard type of characteristics—head, body, tail, eyes and ears.

If a cat exhibits any signs of being unwell, it may have to leave the show area immediately. This does not happen very often at the major European shows, which are usually vetted shows. This means that a veterinarian will check out each cat and its vaccination certificate before it enters the show hall.

Most British shows are also very cautiously run and participants must always have a veterinary inspection before the show. Checkups are made to ensure that no cats with parasites, fleas, or contagious diseases are allowed to enter the show hall. A sick cat is instantly disqualified.

In North America, however, show organizers feel that incipient illness may not be detected in these pre-show checkups. Also, the cats become upset waiting in the line to see the veterinarian. These shows are self-policing; everyone is responsible for bringing healthy cats to the show and for pointing out any cats that seem ill. If your cat seems to be sick after a show, take it to your veterinarian immediately. If it has a serious disease, it may have contracted the illness at the show, and you should inform show officials as soon as possible so that they can warn other cat owners.

The cat show format runs along the same basic lines wherever it is held, though the rules of entry and judging may vary. In North America, the judging is generally done openly with a running commentary by the judges; in some European shows, the results are kept secret until every cat has been judged.

Shows are usually set up in a fairly large

THESE ITEMS DISQUALIFY ALL BREEDS

Cats entering contests have to be in good health and possess all the characteristics of their breeds. Various health problems or variances from the breed's characteristic standards may disqualify a cat from competition. Some of these are:

- Any intention to cheat by artificial means such as colouring or cutting fur (except in authorized spots) or by cosmetic surgery.
- Any evidence of trickery, any signs of aggression, any refusal to be handled.
- In all European shows and some North American shows, any declawing.
- Any trace of malnutrition, of thinness, or the contrary, obesity.
- Any obvious traces of illness.
- Any signs of pregnancy.
- Any signs of external parasites (fleas), of being dirty, or a lack of grooming.
- Extra toes.
- Protruding or misaligned jaws.
- Misaligned skull bones.
- Monorchidism (only one testicle descended).
- Cryptorchidism (neither testicle descended).
- Deafness, except in white cats.
- Blindness.
- Veiled eyes. Squint.
- Constant cross-eyes.
- Shortened tail (except for the Japanese Bobtail).
- No tail (except for the Manx and Cymric breeds).
- A visible fault in the tail.
- A generally bad condition.

See also detailed disqualifying faults on the standard characteristics set by TICA for each breed (pages 66-136).

hall. In North American shows, there is a space—called the 'benching' cages—where the cats are kept when they are not actually competing. There may be quite a number of show rings, where the actual judging is done, because there may be two or three clubs holding shows in the hall at the same time. Dotted around the hall are booths with the latest cat care products for sale. Often there are places to buy food so that owners do not have to leave the premises.

Professional judges are cat club members and must have experience in breeding and showing cats. They also must undergo a training programme to gain a licence. The judges may face emotional reactions from upset losers, says Richard Gebhardt, former president of the Cat Fanciers' Association of America and a show judge. 'A good judge must be authoritative, fair, quick, and definite in his decisions.'

Between judging sessions, cat owners, breeders, and spectators mingle, usually in the benching area, to look over the competition and to talk about the many aspects of their favourite subject—cats.

Entering a show

To enter a show, order a copy of the show rules and standards from the exhibition organizers or the association running the show, and study them carefully. The rules contain important facts about entry eligibility, entry procedures, and the responsibility of exhibitors. For example, to avoid overtiring your cat, you must wait at least a week before exhibiting it again. The standards for pedigree cats will set out the sponsoring association's guidelines for the ideal cat in each breed, listing colour definitions, and whatever the association considers to be disqualifying features.

Show listings are presented several months in advance in various cat magazines and newsletters. Also listed are show locations, entry fees, and the name, address, and telephone number of the entry clerk.

To select the show you want to attend think about how far you would have to travel for it, and the number of shows you want to attend. If your cat is not yet registered with an association, ask your cat's breeder for some suggestions. You will also need to know where your cat will be most competitive. If you are interested in showing your Household Pet, contact the entry clerk to determine if there will be a Household Pet category. Some shows do not judge this category. Request a show leaflet and entry form. Some clubs offer a low entry fee for early entrants, others may not. All shows have a specified closing date for entries.

Once you have decided which show you want to attend, send in your entry form and entry fee before the closing date. It is best to do this several weeks in advance—at least 16 weeks—to give the entry clerk enough time to respond. You should receive a confirmation that your entry has been received. The cat must have its registration papers, a certificate of current vaccinations, and its confirmation of entry, in order to take part.

Many cat-care items make their debut at cat shows. Manufacturers count on the avid interest of breeders to launch new products.

What you will need

Once your cat is entered for showing, you have to consider how both of you will get to the show. First, you need something to transport your cat. The kind of carrier used to transport animals by air is recommended. Sturdy and easy to clean, these carriers usually have adequate ventilation, and are sold in various sizes. They are available in pet shops or by mail order; most cat magazines advertise them. Cardboard carriers are available, but are dangerous for travelling to shows. Cats have been known to escape from them.

Curtains to line the inside of the cat's cage can be another important purchase. They will prevent the cat from seeing its neighbours in adjoining cages, reducing the risk of any verbal or physical altercations between cats.

The ideal curtains should be one piece of material cut to fit the size of the cage. If you don't want to make your own, a bath towel secured by safety pins will do. Most exhibitors, though, go far beyond this crude approach. They use curtains to show off their cats. For example, darker curtains for a white cat, perhaps to match its eyes, would accentuate the animal's colouring and show it off to great advantage. White curtains, on the other hand, would make a

A well-organized show takes a lot of preparation and planning so that judges, cats, and their owners are comfortable.

white cat look washed out. The material should be strong and easy to clean. You can use silk or velvet curtains, but they are hard to keep clean.

Some cat owners have taken the design of their animals' cages to extremes, installing their cats among linings made of gold lamé, lace, and satin. Even ostrich feathers, which can cost hundreds of dollars, have been used by devoted owners.

Once the show curtains are up, consider what else your cat needs to make it feel at home: a floor covering, a favourite toy, a shelf to lie on, a pillow, or a bed, perhaps. Don't forget a litter box, and the cat's own food and water dishes. Usually the exhibition organizers provide food, water, and litter, but it is wise to bring your own. You know what food your cat likes, and it is better to give the animal the water it is used to. However, your cat may not want to eat because it is nervous.

A comb and brush are essential for grooming. Combs are generally best for long-haired pets, brushes or chamois for shorthairs. A comb is also handy for removing litter or dirt from the cat's breeches. Claw clippers are a good item to have with you, but claws should be clipped before leaving for the show. Show rules demand it, and cats whose claws have not been clipped may be refused entry. Be sure to clip the back claws too, since they are sometimes even more likely to hurt you or the judge.

Some other items you might consider taking along to the show include paper or plastic bags to dispose of litter or garbage, cloth and disinfectant, and a first aid kit. You'll need an inexpensive suitcase, too, to carry everything.

GROOMING

A show cat must look its best. This means its coat must be carefully cleaned with shampoo, brush, and comb. Long-haired cats' coats need the most attention, and the fur should be full and fluffed up.

Be careful how you groom your longhair. Do not use grooming powder just before the show, because any traces will penalize the cat during judging.

The Persian has by far the longest hair. To groom a Persian's fur to perfection will require at least four hours on the evening before a show. But long before the show, its coat must be brushed and untangled daily. Every so often, it should have a bath.

A badly combed Persian is not only ugly, but will suffer from matted hair, which may sometimes leave it unable to move comfortably.

With medium longhairs, grooming is a bit simpler, because the fur, which is flatter and lies nearer the body, gets less tangled, and the undercoat is less abundant.

Shorthairs are much easier to groom, and a good rubdown with a chamois just before the show will give their coat a fine gloss.

Claws must be clipped on both the front and hind legs—but be careful not to cut into the quick of the claw or it will bleed and possibly damage the cat. No judge will handle a cat with long claws, in case the cat decides to use them. In some shows, a cat with long claws will be disqualified. In European and some North American shows a declawed cat will be disqualified.

An essential characteristic for show cats is that they must be amenable to handling by strangers, such as the show veterinarian and the judges. If your cat balks at being handled by strangers, then it will probably be disqualified. You will have to realize that it is just not ready for show business.

Before a British show starts, veterinarians examine the cats and their papers to make sure the animals do not display any signs of illness.

At the show

You can ease the tension slightly by arriving well ahead of time. When you arrive, check in with the entry clerk, who will give you a cage number. The cat retains this number, which keeps it in its appropriate breed and colour class during the whole show. Find your space, set up the cage, and get your cat used to it. Check the judging schedule and, if you're at a North American show, locate each show ring so that you won't miss a judging when it is called.

North American-style judging is different from some European judging methods, and is no doubt more equitable. Certainly it is more entertaining for both the public and the presenters. When the cat's judging time is announced, the owner takes the cat to one of the show rings and hands it to a steward in its cage with its number attached. The steward passes it along to the judge and the owner leaves the ring. The cat is judged in the show ring in full public view. Judges give a running commentary, heard by exhibitors and spectators, on the animal's merits or faults.

In North America, each cat is judged individually in its colour and breed class and the top cats in each class are awarded ribbons. After the class judging is complete, these cats may qualify for the top 10 cats in the show awards. When the judge—and there may be more than one— has seen all the competitors, he or she announces the choice of the 10 best adult cats, 10 best neutered cats, and 10 best kittens.

In some North American shows, the second-best cat in a category is often almost as well featured as the top cat; the judge may select it from among the Top 10 as the Best in Show. This varies between associations. In TICA, Best of Best is determined by points gained in each ring. These are totalled and the cat with the highest point score is the Best of Best in Show, an honourary award that gains the cat no points or title from the association.

In some European and all British shows, the judges go around to the cat cages to look at each cat, which means that not too many spectators can see or hear what is going on. The cat's cage must have no personal identifying marks, because the judges are not supposed to know who owns the cat. It is only at the end of the show, when each exhibitor receives a written report about his or her cat, that the owner and the public know which cat has won.

Titles are awarded as the show proceeds, and as points are accumulated, each 'best' being awarded a certain number of points. Points awarded at each show can be accumulated and a champion of champion named each year.

In Europe, each cat is first judged according to the standards of its breed. If two or more cats are presented in the same class, they are compared and classed successively from first to last. The title will go to the first in the class, but only if the cat merits it. Judges may withhold titles if they feel no cat is worthy.

The cats are then judged to select the best colouring in the show, with all the classes included. When the judging is over, the cats are compared by gender and age. Each judge selects a preferred cat and those cats will then be voted on to find the Best in Show. The same method is followed for all classes, and the top winner of all classes is declared 'the best of best.'

Cat fancy associations

Each country has at least one controlling authority for all its cat clubs and societies. These associations draw up rules and standards for the various breeds of cat. However, each organization has a different way of classifying cats during competitions. To make matters even more confusing, some organizations recognize different breeds as eligible for competition. Take TICA and the Cat Fanciers' Association (CFA), for example: TICA recognizes 40 breeds as eligible, while the CFA recognizes 30.

Most cat associations are supported by cat magazines, newsletters, and periodicals that herald upcoming shows, giving dates and times, and specifying which breeds will be competing.

Many of the associations also provide registration for pedigree and other cats. In addition, they may provide a computerized identification service that records a cat's markings and description, including a freeze-tattooed number on its inner thigh. If your cat is stolen or strays from

Every device conceivable is used to show the animals off to best advantage. Some cages have mirrors, others fancy curtains.

home, it often can be traced and identified. Another, more expensive, tagging system in use is the insertion of a tiny microchip with identifying information under the skin of a cat's ear or cheek.

Although TICA and the CFA are U.S.-based, both have member clubs in other countries. The CFA, the largest and oldest registering association in the United States and the world's oldest club-membership association, held two shows in its founding year—1906—in Detroit and Buffalo. Now it produces more than 350

shows annually, attracting some 83,000 entries each year.

Breeders and exhibitors are members of the local cat clubs that are affiliated with CFA, which has no individual members. Its oldest club member, The Empire Cat Club of New York City, was organized on December 13, 1913. By the early 1990s, the CFA had 605 affiliated clubs worldwide.

The CFA has given awards to the highest-scoring cats (commonly referred to as 'Top Cats'), kittens, and premiership (altered) cats for many years. CFA National Awards are presented to the Top Twenty-Five Cats, the Top Fifteen Kittens and the Top Fifteen Cats in Premiership (alters).

The CFA has registered more than 1 million cats in the United States and Canada and, during 1989 alone, registered 90,000 individual cats.

The other major U.S.-based association, TICA, was founded in Branson, Missouri, in 1979. It is the second-largest U.S. registering association and has a genetic register.

In addition to its U.S. clubs, TICA has clubs in Argentina, Brazil, Canada, France, Japan, the Netherlands, the Philippines, Singapore, and Uruguay. It also holds shows around the world—in North and South America, Europe, and Japan.

Other U.S.-based associations are: the American Cat Association (ACA), which holds shows mainly in southern California and Arizona; the American Cat Fanciers' Association (ACFA), which has shows throughout the United States, Canada, Europe, and Japan; and the Cat Fanciers' Federation (CFF), which exhibits in the northeastern United States.

In Canada, the Canadian Cat Association shows in Ontario and Quebec.

In Britain, the Scottish Cat Club was set up in 1894 and the National Cat Club of London was established in 1898. Today most major British cat shows are run by the Governing Council of the Cat Fancy (GCCF) which was formed in 1910, and the Cat Association (CA) of Britain. The latter, besides offering championship awards for cats, also runs courses to train judges and other exhibition officials.

Many cat clubs around the world belong to the French Fédération Internationale Féline (FIFe), which was founded by the Cat Club de Paris in 1949. New Zealand and Australia are both member countries of FIFe.

Organizing a show

Organizing a formal cat show is an exhausting job. If it is to be done well, it takes a team of experienced coordinators who must handle not only the details of the competition itself, but also all the pre-

Announcing results of the Best in Show competition and presenting the trophies are the high point of a cat show, but perhaps more important than prizes is the shared passion for cats.

show paperwork. After the show's announcement date, registration papers pour into the sponsoring group's office. Each one must be checked to see that it carries the name and address of the exhibitor; the club to which he or she belongs; the name of the cat; its date of birth; its breed; its colouring; the colour of its eyes; its gender; the names of its father and mother; the class in which it is going to compete; proof of titles already won; copies of vaccination certificates and identifying marks; and payment for registration.

The judges then must be chosen and their attendance confirmed according to the type of show, the number of cats, and the breeds to be presented. The administrative office deals with booking hotel rooms for judges and participants, and with drawing up a plan of access to the show hall.

A confirmation slip then must be sent to each exhibitor along with a hall plan, the rule book and various other practical notices. The catalogue is drawn up after the registration is closed. It mentions all the cats in order of breeds and titles, lists exhibitors, judges, and members of the committee. It is a reference for exhibitors and is sold to visitors.

How the hall is organized depends on its shape and size, security problems, the number of cats, judges and stands, and the size of the stage. The cages are usually set up in rows. Exhibitors are usually placed according to their cat's breed and their order of arrival.

The judges' notebooks are prepared last. Each must include the registration number and colouring of each cat, its breed, its age in years and months, and its sex. Judges may be working in more than one class, however, so each book must be customized.

ONE SYSTEM OF JUDGING

As an example of an association's listing, here are TICA's levels of achievement among Championship and Household categories.

CHAMPIONS (pedigreed cats):
Kitten; Novice; Champion; Grand Champion; Double Grand Champion; Triple Grand Champion; Quadruple Grand Champion; Supreme Champion.

HOUSEHOLD
Kitten; Senior; Master; Grand Master; Double Grand Master; Triple Grand Master; Quadruple Grand Master; Supreme Grand Master.

Judges award 100 points, based on the breed's characteristics for head, ears, eyes, body, bone structure, and tail. These points are distributed differently for each breed. (Points for each breed are given in the Catalogue of breeds, pages 66-136).

There are various classes and divisions. The judge selects the three best cats in each division; the best wins 25 points, the second 20 points, and the third 15 points. From among these winners, the judge selects the Best of Breed, the Second-Best of Breed, and the Third-Best of Breed. No points are awarded for these selections, but these cats represent the 'ideal' of their breed. Rosettes are then awarded to the judge's choice of the Top Ten Cats within each major category. These cats are chosen primarily from the Best of Breed winners, although judges may select any cat they have judged during the show provided it does not defeat a cat that has defeated it at a lower level.

Reaching a finals level means that the cat is among the very best in the show. The final awards carry points which are accumulated to attain championship rankings.

Major categories of championship cats and how they may enter: Kitten; Championship Adults; Alters; Household Pet Kittens; Household Pet Adults.

Organizations for cat fanciers

Enthusiasm for their pets has led cat fanciers to form clubs that set breeding standards, register kittens, and regulate competitions that determine the best examples of the various breeds. The following organizations are all concerned with breeding, raising, and showing cats.

AUSTRALIA

AUSTRALIAN CAT FEDERATION INC.
P.O. Box 40752
Casuarina, NT 0811

CO-ORDINATING CAT COUNCIL OF AUSTRALIA
P.O. Box 404
Dickson, ACT 2602

Australian Capital Territory

ROYAL NATIONAL CAPITAL AGRICULTURAL
SOCIETY CAT CONTROL
P.O. Box 404
Dickson, ACT 2602

New South Wales

ROYAL AGRICULTURAL SOCIETY CAT CONTROL OF
NEW SOUTH WALES
G.P.O. Box 4317
Sydney, NSW 2001

Northern Territory

CAT ASSOCIATION OF THE NORTHERN TERRITORY
G.P.O. Box 3870
Darwin, NT 0801

Queensland

COUNCIL OF FEDERATED CAT CLUBS OF QUEENSLAND
19 Clifford Street
Towoomba, Qld. 4350

FELINE CONTROL COUNCIL OF QUEENSLAND
84 Anzac Avenue
Redcliffe, Qld. 4020

QUEENSLAND FELINE ADMINISTRATION
89 Evenwood Street
Coopers Plain, Qld. 4106

QUEENSLAND INDEPENDENT CAT COUNCIL
P.O. Box 41
Esk, Qld. 4312

South Australia

FELINE ASSOCIATION OF SOUTH AUSTRALIA
21 Poole Street
Osborne, SA 5017

GOVERNING COUNCIL OF THE CAT FANCY
OF SOUTH AUSTRALIA
55 Eliza Place
Panorama, SA 5041

Tasmania

CAT CONTROL COUNCIL OF TASMANIA
P.O. Box 116
Glenorchy, Tas. 7010

Victoria

DEMOCRATIC CAT COUNCIL OF VICTORIA
23 Cain Street
West Rosebud, Vic. 3940

FELINE CONTROL COUNCIL OF VICTORIA INC.
Royal Showground
Epsom Road
Ascot Vale, Vic. 3032

THE GOVERNING COUNCIL OF THE
CAT FANCY IN VICTORIA
P.O. Box 318
Belgrave, Vic. 3160

MURRAY VALLEY CAT AUTHORITY
P.O. Box 406
Mildura, Vic. 3500

Western Australia

CAT OWNERS ASSOCIATION OF WESTERN AUSTRALIA
P.O. Box 711
Applecross, WA 6153

FELINE CONTROL OF WESTERN AUSTRALIA
G.P.O. Box 232
Gosnells, WA 6110

CANADA

CANADIAN CAT ASSOCIATION
83 Kennedy Road South, Unit 1805
Brampton, Ont.
L6W 3P3

EUROPE

FÉDÉRATION INTERNATIONALE FÉLINE (FIFE)
Boerhaavelaan 23
NL - 5644 BB
Eindhoven, The Netherlands

NEW ZEALAND

NEW ZEALAND CAT FANCY INC.
P.O. Box 3167
Richmond, Nelson

NEW ZEALAND CAT FEDERATION
20 Warren Kelly Street
Richmond, Nelson

SOUTH AFRICA

GOVERNING COUNCIL OF ASSOCIATED
CAT CLUBS OF SOUTH AFRICA (GCACC)
P.O. Box 532
Florida
Transvaal 1710

SOUTH AFRICAN CAT REGISTER
P.O. Box 4382
Randburg
Transvaal 2125

***Member clubs of the GCACC
of South Africa:***

ALL BREEDS CAT CLUB
P.O. Box 1078
Cape Town 8000

CAPITAL CAT CLUB
P.O. Box 100311
Morreletta Park
Transvaal 0044

CAT FANCIERS CLUB
P.O. Box 5509
Weltevreden Park
Transvaal 1715

EASTERN PROVINCE CAT CLUB
P.O. Box 5166
Walmer, Port Elizabeth 6065

FREE STATE CAT CLUB
P.O. Box 165
Kroonstad, Orange Free State 9500

NATAL CAT CLUB
36 Marion Road
Westriding, Hillcrest
Natal 3610

RAND CAT CLUB
P.O. Box 5836
Bracken Gardens
Transvaal 1452

TRANSVAAL CAT SOCIETY
P.O. Box 3449
Randburg 2125

WESTERN PROVINCE CAT CLUB
P.O. Box 3600
Cape Town 8000

UNITED KINGDOM

THE CAT ASSOCIATION OF BRITAIN
Mill House
Letcombe Regis
Oxfordshire, OX12 9JD

THE GOVERNING COUNCIL OF THE CAT FANCY
4-6 Penel Orlieu
Bridgwater
Somerset TA6 3PG

UNITED STATES

AMERICAN CAT ASSOCIATION
8101 Katherine Avenue
Panorama City, CA 91402

AMERICAN CAT FANCIERS' ASSOCIATION
P.O. Box 203
Point Lookout, MO 65726

CAT FANCIERS' ASSOCIATION
P.O. Box 1005
Manasquan, NJ 08738-1005

CAT FANCIERS' FEDERATION
9509 Montgomery Road
Cincinnati, OH 45242

THE INTERNATIONAL CAT ASSOCIATION
P.O. Box 2684
Harlingen, TX 78551

Care and protection agencies

These organizations are leaders in animal welfare. Their national headquarters (see addresses below) can refer you to local agencies concerned with cat welfare.

AUSTRALIA

Royal Society for the Prevention of Cruelty to Animals Inc.
4 Hotham Crescent
Deakin, ACT 2600

Australian and New Zealand Federation of Animal Societies
P.O. Box 1023
Collingwood, Vic.

CANADA

Canadian Federation of Humane Societies
30 Concourse Gate, Suite 102
Nepean, Ontario
K2E 7V7

NEW ZEALAND

Society for the Prevention of Cruelty to Animals, Royal New Zealand
National Office
3 Totara Avenue
New Lynn, Auckland

SOUTH AFRICA

Animal Anti-Cruelty League
P.O. Box 7
66 Marjorie Street
Rosettenville 2130

Friends of the Cat
P.O. Box 52429
Saxonwold 2132

Society for the Prevention of Cruelty to Animals, National Council of South Africa
P.O. Box 82831
Southdale 2135

UNITED KINGDOM

Cats Protection League
17 Kings Road
Horsham, West Sussex
RH13 5PP

Royal Society for the Prevention of Cruelty to Animals
The Causeway
Horsham, West Sussex
RH12 1HG

UNITED STATES

American Humane Association
63 Inverness Drive East
Englewood, CO 80112

American Society for the Prevention of Cruelty to Animals
424 East 92nd Street
New York, NY 10128-6899

The Humane Society of the United States
2100 L Street Northwest
Washington D.C. 20037

INDEX

Credits and Acknowledgements

To identify a photograph or illustration on its page, the following referencing has been used: *r*, right-hand column; *l*, left-hand column; *t*, top of the page; *b*, bottom of the page; *c*, centre.

PHOTOS

Cover: PICTOR/UNIPHOTO

8t: MUSEUM NATIONAL D'HISTOIRE NATURELLE/D. Serrette. **8c:** JACANA/Danegger. **8b:** SUNSET/Animals Animals. **9:** Ed. La Farandole, 1978. D.R. **10t:** MINDEN picture. **10b:** Excerpt from *Les Mammifères* de Carl VOGT, 1884, MASSON S.A, Paris. **11t:** Excerpt from *Précis de paléontologie des vertébrés* de J . P. VETEAU, 1978, MASSON S.A., Paris. **11b:** MUSEUM NATIONAL D'HISTOIRE NATURELLE/D. Serrette. **14t:** SUNSET/G. Lacz. **14c:** COGIS/R. Seitre. **15t:** SUNSET/G. Lacz. **15c:** G. DAGLI ORTI. **16t:** SUNSET/Photo S.T.F. **16b:** PHOTOTHÈQUE DU MUSÉE DE L'HOMME. **17t:** COGIS/R. Seitre. **17c:** JACANA/Ziesler. **17b:** JACANA/McHugh. **18, 19:** SUNSET/Animals Animals. **20t:** JACANA/Devez, CNRS. **20b:** GIRAUDON. **21t:** JACANA/McHugh. **21c:** JACANA/J.M. Labat. **21b:** JACANA/Frédéric. **22c:** COGIS/R. Seitre. **23b:** COGIS/Lanceau. **24b:** COGIS/J.M. Labat. **25c:** drawing by W. Kuhnert, excerpt by A. Ménégaux: *La vie des animaux illustrée*, 1903. **25r:** Excerpt from *A Cat Is Watching* by Roger A. Caras, reprinted by permission of Simon & Shuster. **26t:** G. DAGLI ORTI. **26b:** ÉDIMÉDIA. **27t:** M. HOLFORD. **27b:** R.M.N./Chuzeville. **28:** R.M.N. **29, 30c:** GIRAUDON. **30b:** ÉDIMÉDIA. **31b:** ARTÉPHOT/Nimataliah. **32b:** BRITISH MUSEUM. **32tr, 33b:** G. DAGLI ORTI. **34l:** BIBLIOTHÈQUE NATIONALE, Paris. **34r:** ÉDIMÉDIA. **35:** EXPLORER archives/J.L. Charmet. **36t:** BULLOZ. **37t:** GIRAUDON. **37b:** LAUROS-GIRAUDON. **38t:** GIRAUDON. **38b:** ÉDIMÉDIA. **39:** H. JOSSE. **40:** EXPLORER archives/J.L. Charmet. **42t:** LAUROS-GIRAUDON. **42b:** EXPLORER archives/J.M. Labat. **43t:** COGIS/Lanceau. **44, 45t:** ÉDIMÉDIA. **45b:** H. JOSSE. **46:** ÉDIMÉDIA. **47t:** H. JOSSE/ADAGP/SPADEM, Paris, 1992. **47cl:** Coll. VIOLLET. **47cr:** RAPHO/H. Gloaguen. **47b:** TAPABOR/Kharbine. **48t:** GIRAUDON. **48b:** COGIS/Fr. Varin. **50:** SUNSET/G. Lacz. **50l:** Morris, Courtesy of Heinz Pet Products. **156tl:** COGIS/Fr. Varin. **156bl:** COGIS/Hutin. **156r:** COGIS/Gauthier. **158:** JACANA/J .M. Labat. **159:** COGIS/Amblin. **162l :** COGIS/Fr. Varin. **160r:** COGIS/Remy. **161:** JACANA/M. Viard. **163:** A. GANIVET. **165:** JANSSEN. **167t:** A. GANIVET. **167b:** Cliché Imagerie Médicale ENV of Lyon. **169:** FOTOGRAM/E. Berne. **170, 171, 172:** ENV d'Alfort, Service de parasitologie. **174:** ENV of Lyon, Service de médecine. **179t:** COGIS/Amblin. **179b:** COGIS/Dillschnieder. **180, 181, 182:** A. GANIVET. **183:** COGIS/Lanceau. **184:** A. RULLIER. **185:** ENV of Nantes/Service de médecine. **187:** CÉDRI/S. Marmounier. **190:** DISNEY, with special permission from The Walt Disney Company, France; photo coll. CHRISTOPHE L. **191:** A. GANIVET. **193:** COGIS/Lanceau. **195:** JACANA/Méro. **196:** FOTOGRAM/E. Berne. **199:** COGIS/Lanceau/Labat. **200:** A. RULLIER. **201t:** A. GANIVET. **201b:** ST. REMY PRESS. **202, 203:** A. GANIVET. **204:** JACANA/G. Thouvenin. **206:** SUNSET/Lacz. **207l:** COGIS/Amblin. **207r:** SLIDE/Mauritius/Reinhard. **209, 210tl, 210bl:** A. GANIVET. **210r:** COGIS/Lanceau. **211l:** A. GANIVET. **211r:** SUNSET/G. Lacz. **214:** J.M. LABAT. **215:** COGIS/J.M. Labat. **216:** JACANA/Méro. **217:** FOVÉA/Ch. Lepetit. **218t:** RAPHO/ Le Guillou. **218b:** SUNSET/G. Lacz. **219:** JACANA/Danegger. **220:** COGIS/Fr. Varin. **222t:** COGIS/J.M. Labat. **222b:** COGIS/Excalibur. **223:** COGIS/Gissey. **224t:** COGIS/Fr. Varin. **224b:** SUNSET/S.T.F. **226l:** JACANA/J.P. Thomas. **226r:** COGIS/Fr. Varin. **227:** SUNSET/G. Lacz. **228:** COGIS/Amblin. **229:** FOVÉA/Bacchela. **230:** COGIS/Lepage. **231:** SUNSET/G. Lacz. **232:** JACANA/Axel. **233:** EXPLORER/D. Clément. **234:** COGIS/Fr. Varin. **235t:** COGIS/Remy. **235b:** COGIS/Vidal. **236:** JACANA/B. Rebouleau. **237:** Arch. S.R.D./R. Hauert. **238:** SUNSET/G. Lacz. **240t:** COGIS/Fr. Varin. **242:** FOTOGRAM/E. Berne. **243:** COGIS/J.M. Labat. **242 to 250:** É. BROCHARD.

ILLUSTRATIONS

Excerpt from *Steinlen, chats et autres bêtes,* édition Eugène Rey, 1933: 9, 11, 14, 19, 23, 24, 30, 31, 32, 33, 34, 36, 37,41, 42, 48, 49, 50.

Sibylle de Fischer: 7, 51, 61, 189, 213.

William Fraschini: 52, 53, 54, 55, 56, 57, 58, 59, 60, 70, 71, 77, 82, 83, 84, 89, 90, 93, 96, 100, 104, 105, 106, 107, 108, 109, 111, 112, 114, 115tr, 116c, 118, 120, 121, 123, 124, 126, 128, 131, 132, 133, 135, 136, 137, 141, 160t, 181t, 186, 203, 205, 212, 242.

Patrick Morin: 66, 68, 72, 74, 75, 79, 81, 86, 88, 92, 94, 98, 99, 101, 103, 110, 113, 115tl, 115c, 115b, 116t, 116b, 117, 119, 122, 129, 130, 138.

Olena Kassian: 101,146, 147, 149, 150.

Reader's Digest acknowledges with thanks the assistance of the following: Dr. Stuart Halperin, D.V.M., Small Animal Clinic, Veterinary Teaching Hospital, University of Guelph, Guelph, Ont.; Dr. Susan Cochran, University of Guelph, Guelph, Ont.; Dr. Maurice Barrette, Hôpital vétérinaire du Nord, Montreal, Que.; The Canadian Veterinary Medical Association; Canadian Federation of Humane Societies.

St. Remy Press would also like to thank the following persons who assisted in the preparation of this book: April Bac, Hazel Blanford, Elizabeth Cameron, Hélène Dion, Vere Dodds, Rory Gilsenan, Sara Grynspan, Marianne Hamilton, Mrs. M. Jones, Robert Lutes, Mrs. L. K. Pring, Doug Smith.